Contents

D1425815

Chapter 36:
Survival and outsourcing in the South African clothing and textiles industry:
The case of ClothTran

About the editors

Tony Dundon is Senior Lecturer at the J.E. Cairnes School of Business and Economics, National University of Ireland, Galway. His research interests include international and comparative systems of employee voice, representation, and trade union organisation. Tony is co-author of *Employment Relations in Non-Union Firms* and *Understanding Employment Relations*. He is also co-Editor-in-Chief of the *Human Resource Management Journal* (HRMJ) and a Fellow of the Chartered Institute of Personnel and Development (CIPD).

Adrian Wilkinson is Professor of Employment Relations and Director of the Centre for Work, Organisation and Wellbeing, Griffith University. His research interests include the changing nature of employee participation and voice and international and comparative employment. Adrian is Associate Editor for the *Human Resource Management Journal*. His latest books include *The Oxford Handbook of Participation in Organizations, New Directions in Employment Relations* and *The Handbook of Comparative Employment Relations*. He is a Fellow and Accredited Examiner of the Chartered Institute of Personnel and Development (CIPD) in the UK, and a Fellow of the Australian Human Resource Institute.

About the contributors

Hani G Abdalla is the Assistant Manager for Assessment of Development and Infrastructure Projects, Research Triangle Institute, Abu Dhabi. Hani graduated from the University of British Columbia, Canada, with a Bachelor degree in Chemical Engineering and a Bachelor Degree in Biochemistry. He obtained his Masters degree in Project Management from the British University in Dubai, where his dissertation research studied the application of leadership theories to private and public sector environments in non-western countries. His most recent work concentrates on training programs for transformational leadership in the public sector.

Rowena Barrett is Professor and Head of the School of Management at Edith Cowan University, Perth. Her research focuses on work and employment in small firms. With a background in Industrial Relations, Rowena's research interests have generally considered how people are managed in smaller firms, particularly given that many small firms operate without formalised management systems. Her most recent co-edited book is the *International Handbook of HRM and Entrepreneurship*, published by Edward Elgar.

Vikram Bhakoo is a Lecturer within the Operations Management discipline at the Department of Management and Marketing at the University of Melbourne. His current stream of research focuses on technology adoption issues, strategic supply chain management and use of qualitative techniques within the Operations Management discipline. He has published his work in leading international journals such as *Supply Chain Management* and *Production Planning & Control*. Prior to embarking on an academic career Vikram worked in the textile manufacturing, financial services and Information Technology sectors.

Christine Bischoff (Psoulis) is a PhD candidate in the Department of Sociology, University of the Witwatersrand, South Africa. She is an experienced social statistician. She has worked on a number of surveys of union membership in South Africa. Her current research is on the unemployed youth of South Africa.

Paul Boselie is a full Professor in the Utrecht University School of Governance at Utrecht University, the Netherlands. His research traverses human resource management, institutionalism, strategic management and industrial relations. His research is published in many international academic journals including the *Journal of Management Studies*, *Human Relations*, *Human Resource Management* and *Applied Psychology*. Paul's teaching involves executive training in strategic HRM for HR and non-HR professionals, a master course in HR Studies and a bachelor course in Strategic HRM. He is the European Editor of *Personnel Review* and a member of the Editorial Board of the *Journal of Management Studies*. In 2010 his text book on *Strategic HRM* was published by McGraw-Hill (London) and is now widely used at universities and in executive training.

Chris Brewster is Professor of International Human Resource Management at Henley Business School, University of Reading, UK. He researches comparative and international HRM.

Georgina Caillard is a PhD candidate, researcher and tutor in the Department of Management and Marketing at Deakin University and has previously lectured at RMIT University. She recently received a teaching award for outstanding contribution to Deakin's Faculty of Business and Law in 2010. Georgina was once a lawyer and is studying legal practice for her PhD thesis.

Lisa Callagher is a PhD candidate in the Management and International Business Department, University of Auckland Business School, New Zealand.

Craig Cardinal has been associated with Defence Signals Directorate (DSD) for 25 years through service with two different arms of the Australian Defence Forces and as a civilian public servant. Craig has held various roles within DSD including operational and strategic intelligence collection and analysis positions.

Amy L Collins is a research assistant and PhD student at the Griffith Business School, Griffith University. Amy has completed a degree in Psychology with Honours at the University of Queensland, and is currently researching emotions in organisations.

Niall Cullinane is a lecturer at the Queen's University Management School, Belfast. His research interests fall within the broad areas of employee voice and the application of political-sociological understandings to the employment relationship.

Jimmy Donaghey is Associate Professor of International Comparative Industrial Relations at the Industrial Relations Research Unit, University of Warwick, UK. His research focuses on employee voice, Irish social partnership in comparative context and the consequences of European integration on employment relations. Recent publications have featured in journals such as the *British Journal of Industrial Relations*, *Economic and Industrial Democracy* and the *Industrial Relations Journal*.

Rory Donnelly is a Lecturer in Human Resource Management and Organisational Behaviour at Birmingham Business School, UK. He is the Director of the HRM MSc at the Business School and his research interests include managing the employment relationship, careers, and flexibility. He is the author of numerous refereed journal articles on human resource management.

Ben French is a Lecturer of Employment Relations & Equal Employment Opportunity Law & Practice, Griffith University Business School, and an affiliate member of the Griffith University Centre for Work, Organisation and Wellbeing. Ben lectures in Employment Relations Law, Discrimination Law and Introductory Business Law for the Griffith Business School. He is an admitted Legal

Practitioner in the State of Queensland, Australia and practices workplace law at an independent, non for profit voluntary law association.

Roy Green is Dean of the University of Technology (UTS) Business School. He is a graduate of the University of Adelaide with a PhD in economics from the University of Cambridge. He has published widely on innovation policy and management and has worked with universities, business and government in Australia and overseas, including the OECD, European Commission and Enterprise Ireland. He is chair of the Australian Government's Innovative Regions Centre, CSIRO Manufacturing Sector Advisory Council and NSW Manufacturing Council and a member of the Enterprise Connect Advisory Council. With Dr Renu Agarwal, he led Australian participation in the global study of management practice and productivity for the Department of Innovation, Industry, Science and Research.

Irena Grugulis is the Professor of Employment Studies, Durham Business School, UK an AIM/ESRC Services Fellow and an Associate Fellow of SKOPE. Her research focuses on all areas of skills and training and has been funded by the ESRC, EPSRC and EU. She is currently Joint Editor in Chief of *Work, Employment and Society*.

Rachel Hilliard is a Lecturer in Management at J.E. Cairnes School of Business and Economics, NUI Galway. Her research interests include dynamic capability theory, environmental innovation, innovation management and innovation policy. She has published in journals such as the *Journal of Economic Issues*, *European Environment*, the *Journal of Cleaner Production and Regional Studies*.

Kate Hutchings is Professor of HRM in the Department of Employment Relations and Human Resources, Griffith University. In addition to appointments at Monash University, Queensland University of Technology, and the University of Queensland, Kate has held visiting research positions at Copenhagen Business School, Denmark; Rutgers University, USA; and Ceram Graduate School of Management, France, and has taught short courses in China, Malaysia and Sri Lanka. Kate is a research specialist in International Human Resource Management and has co-authored/edited three books and published over 60 book chapters and journal articles. Amongst others, her research has appeared in prestigious international journals including *Human Resource Management*, *Human Resource Management Journal*, *International Business Review*, *International Journal of Human Resource Management*, and the *Journal of Management Studies*. Her current research interests include: expatriate management; human resource management in developing economies; training and development; and women in international management.

Kenneth Husted is a Professor of Innovation and Research Management in the Management and International Business Department, University of Auckland Business School, New Zealand.

Glen Jenkins is a Principal Lecturer in Management at Swansea Business School, Swansea Metropolitan University, UK. He is Head of Postgraduate Research at

Swansea Business School and CIPD Chief Examiner for Employee Reward and member of the British Academy of Management and the British Universities Industrial Relations Association. His research interests cover reward management, employee participation, management of information in organisations, unemployment and managerial attitudes to human resource management. He has published in the *Journal of General Management*, *Public Administration*, *Personnel Review Select*, the *British Journal of Industrial Relations*, the *International Journal of Human Resource Management* and the *International Journal of Information Resource Management*. He is author (with Michael Poole) of *The Impact of Industrial Democracy* (1990); *New Forms of Ownership* (1990) and *Back to the Line?* (1996).

Peter J Jordan is a Professor of Organisational Behaviour at the Griffith Business School, Griffith University. Peter's current research interests include emotional intelligence, emotions in organisations, team performance and toxic emotions in organisations.

Ashlea Kellner is studying for a PhD at Griffith University. Her PhD thesis is examining the approach adopted by four franchise firms in the food industry to developing, managing and assessing HR strategy.

Linzi Kemp is Assistant Professor, School of Business and Management, The American University of Sharjah, United Arab Emirates.

Eva Knies is a PhD candidate in the Utrecht University School of Governance, the Netherlands. Her research focuses on the way in which organisations deal with social transformations (such as an ageing population and an increasing diversity of the labour force) in their human resource management. Her research is accepted to be published in the *International Journal of Human Resource Management* and *Labour & Industry*. Eva is a member of the study group on public personnel policies of the European Group for Public Administration and the HR division of the Academy of Management.

Anastasia Kynighou is a Visiting Lecturer at the University of Cyprus and External Research Associate at the European Work and Employment Research Centre, Manchester Business School, UK, where she received her PhD. She has previously held the position of Lecturer in Human Resource Management at the University of Central Lancashire and she is a Chartered Member of the CIPD.

Jonathan Lazarus is in the Management and International Business Department, University of Auckland Business School, New Zealand.

Fang Lee Cooke is Professor of Human Resource Management and Chinese Studies at the Department of Management, Monash University. Previously, she was a chaired professor at Manchester Business School, University of Manchester, UK. Her research interests are in the areas of employment relations, gender studies, strategic HRM, knowledge management and innovation, outsourcing, Chinese outward FDI, and employment of Chinese migrants.

Peter Leisink is Professor of Public Administration and Organisational Science in the Utrecht University School of Governance, the Netherlands. His research interests are in the areas of strategic human resource management and the study of social issues from a governance and corporate social responsibility perspective. His research is published in international journals such as *the European Journal of Industrial Relations*, the *International Review of Administrative Sciences* and the *Review of Public Personnel Administration*. He is co-chairing the study group on public personnel policies of the European Group for Public Administration.

Alma McCarthy is Director of the Executive MBA Programme and lecturer in Management at J.E. Cairnes School of Business and Economics, NUI Galway. Her research interests include performance management, human resource development, work-life balance, and multi-rater (360°) feedback systems. She has published in outlets such as the *Human Resource Management Review*, *Personnel Review*, the *International Journal of Manpower Studies*, and the *Journal of Vocational Educational Training*.

Anthony McDonnell is Lecturer at the School of Management, University of South Australia. His research interests lie in the areas of international human resource management and global talent management.

Ruth McPhail has wide experience in management consulting, human resource management and leadership, having trained management teams in Australia, China, Malaysia, Thailand, the USA and India. She advises and trains with major multi-national corporations, as well as Australian chains, especially hotel groups. Ruth was previously a Director of Human Resources in industry before joining Griffith University. Her research interests include cross- cultural management and international human resource management.

Teresa Marchant is at Griffith University Business School and has previously worked at Southern Cross University, Queensland University of Technology, the University of Southern Queensland, and London University. She was involved in developing the 'blue ribbon' Public Sector Management Program for the Australian Public Service Commission.

Mick Marchington is Professor of Human Resource Management at Manchester Business School, University of Manchester, UK. He has also held visiting posts at the Universities of Sydney, Auckland and Paris. He has published widely on HRM, both in books and in refereed journals. He is best known for his work on employee involvement and participation and on HRM across organisational boundaries. He is Co-Editor of the *Human Resource Management Journal* (HRMJ) and is Joint Chair of the HRM Study Group of the IIRA. He is a Chartered Companion of the CIPD.

Jane P Murray currently teaches Organisational Behaviour, Human Resource Management and Negotiation in the Faculty of Business at Bond University, Queensland. Prior to entering academia Jane worked for one of the UK's leading retailers and as a trainer for one of Australia's largest banks. Jane's current research interests include the training of emotional intelligence and examining the causes and consequences of workplace bullying in organisations.

Olav Muurlink is a research fellow at Griffith University's Centre for Work, Organisation and Wellbeing. He has degrees in psychology and communications from Charles Sturt University, the University of Queensland and the University of St Andrews, and completed doctoral studies examining the differential between real and laboratory environments in producing attitude change, and the nature of genuine, as opposed to strategic, attitude change. During the period 1999-2009 he was managing director of a media company, with primarily community newspaper interests, and also owned a SME involved in printing newspapers and magazines. His current research work centres on the notion of constraints and impacts of change, as well as innovation in employment relations in new workplaces and the wellbeing of coal miners, their families and communities.

David O'Sullivan is Lecturer, Research Director and Director of Quality, NUI Galway. In addition to academic roles, David advises industry on innovation and project management processes. He has also worked with a large number of small to medium sized industries and service organisations on innovation management including hospitals, local government and public services. His current research interests are in distributed innovation management across extended enterprises. David has over 100 publications including books – *Applying Innovation* (Sage); *Manufacturing Systems Redesign* (Prentice-Hall); *Reengineering the Enterprise* (Chapman & Hall) and; *The Handbook of IS Management* (Auerbach).

Ashly H Pinnington is Professor of Human Resource Management and Dean of the Faculty of Business, The British University in Dubai, United Arab Emirates. He has published extensively on the management of professionals, in journals such as *Human Relations*, the *Journal of Management Studies and Organization Studies*, chiefly addressing institutionalist perspectives in HRM, IHRM and organisational change. He has recently published co-edited books on *International Human Resource Management* (Sage 3rd Edition 2011) with Anne-Wil Harzing, and *HRM: Ethics and Employment* (Oxford University Press 2007) with Macklin and Campbell. His most recent work concentrates on careers, ethics and social responsibility.

Paul Ryan is College Lecturer at the J.E. Cairnes School of Business and Economics, NUI Galway. He teaches and researches in the areas of international business and strategic management. He earned his PhD from the University of Cambridge, UK.

Hugh Scullion is Professor of International Management at the J.E. Cairnes School of Business and Economics, NUI Galway. He has published in the *Academy of Management Journal,* the *Journal of World Business,* the *Human Resource Management Journal,* and the *International Journal of Human Resource Management.* His research interests include global talent management, global staffing and the role of the corporate HR function in MNCs.

Don Scott-Kemmis, Senior Fellow, Australian Centre for Innovation, University of Sydney is a researcher, consultant and lecturer in innovation management and policy. He has extensive experience of policy-related research in several countries. He was a Research Fellow of the Science Policy Research Unit, University of Sussex from the late 1970s to the early 1980s, and then led the Innovation Program, at the Centre for Technology and Social Change, University of Wollongong. Over much of the 1990s he worked within the public sector, managing policy development, review and implementation. He also served as the Science & Technology Adviser to the Minister for Industry, Science and Resources. From 2001 to 2008 he was an Associate Professor at the Australian National University.

Tristan Smith is a recent graduate of a Bachelor of Business at Griffith University. Majoring in Human Resource Management and Employment Relations he has, throughout his education and beyond, researched different organisational approaches to workplace wellness and been a champion for change within his university.

Ebrahim Soltani is Senior Lecturer at the University of Kent Business School, UK. He gained degrees in accounting & finance, MBA and management science. After gaining his doctorate from Strathclyde (UK), he was awarded a postdoctoral fellowship by the ESRC. Ebrahim's research interests focus on managing operations and HR improvement practices and more specifically, HR issues that are relevant to operations improvement initiatives. Ebrahim is now working on an ESRC-funded research project to investigate the role of senior management as a mediating factor linking management practices to the organisational performance. Ebrahim has published papers in peer-referred journals such as the *British Journal of Management*, the *International Journal of Human Resource Management*, the *International Journal of Operations and Production Management*, and the *Journal of World Business*.

Paul Sparrow is Professor of International Human Resource Management at Lancaster University Management School, UK and Director of the Centre for Performance-led HR. He researches international HRM and HR strategy.

Dimitrinka Stoaynova is a Lecturer in Management at St Andrews School of Management, UK, Researcher at the Institute for Capitalising on Creativity at St Andrews University and an AIM Associate. Her research interests are in the area of learning and skills development, employment in the creative industries, creative careers and freelance work.

Jane Suter is a Lecturer in Human Resource Management at York Management School, University of York, UK. She studied psychology at the University of Liverpool and completed her Masters and PhD in HRM and Industrial relations at the Manchester Business School, University of Manchester. Her research interests include employee involvement and participation, employee commitment, and front line manager styles and behaviours.

Margaret Tallott is a Doctoral Fellow at the Centre for Innovation and Structural Change (CISC), NUI Galway. Her research interests include organisational learning, environmentally sustainable management strategies, environmental policy and action research. Her practice career spans over twenty years and includes research in a diverse range of industries including electronics manufacturing, electricity networks, construction, arts and sustainable energy.

Stephen Taylor is a Senior Lecturer in Human Resource Management at the Manchester Metropolitan University Business School, UK and a national examiner for the Chartered Institute of Personnel and Development (CIPD). Research interests include employee retention, occupational pensions and regulatory issues. He is the author/co-author of several books including *People Resourcing; Employment Law: An Introduction* (with Astra Emir), *The Employee Retention Handbook* and four editions of *Human Resource Management* (with Derek Torrington and Laura Hall). His latest book is *HRM: Contemporary Trends and Future Agendas* (2011). He also regularly represents parties in employment tribunals.

Keith Townsend is a Senior Research Fellow in the Centre for Work, Organisation and Wellbeing at Griffith University. In addition, he holds a post as Senior Lecturer in the Department of Employment Relations and Human Resources in the Griffith Business School.

Herman Tse is a Senior Lecturer in the Department of Employment Relations and Human Resources at the Griffith Business School, Griffith University. His research interests include transformational leadership, relational leadership, emotions in teams and multi-level leadership in organisations. Dr Tse has published several articles in internationally respected journals such as the *Leadership Quarterly*, the *Journal of Occupational and Organizational Psychology*.

Julie Wolfram Cox is Professor of Management (Organisation Studies) and Discipline Group Leader (Governance, Leadership and Organisation) in the Department of Management at Monash University. Julie holds an Australian Research Council Linkage Project Grant with Victoria Police and with Owen Hughes, also at Monash University, and developed this project while at RMIT and Deakin Universities.

Geoffrey Wood is Professor of HRM, School of Management, University of Sheffield, UK. He is also Visiting Professor, Nelson Mandela University and Honorary Professor, University of Witwatersrand, South Africa. Geoff has authored over one hundred peer reviewed articles (including journals such as *Economy and Society*, *Human Relations*, *Human Resource Management* (US), and the *British Journal of Industrial Relations*), and edited/co-edited thirteen books (Oxford University Press, Palgrave, Routledge, etc.). His current research interests revolve around the relationship between institutional setting, firm finance, and work and employment relations outcomes.

Les Worrall is Professor of Strategic Analysis at Coventry University Business School, UK His research interests include organisational analysis, changing patterns of work and organisational behaviour. He has conducted extensive research on the changing nature of managerial work for the Chartered Management Institute in the UK and for the Australian Institute of Management. He has undertaken research and consultancy for PricewaterhouseCoopers, Aviva, Adecco, the Health and Safety Executive, Simplyhealth, the Post Office and a large number of UK public bodies and local authorities.

Rachid Zeffane is Associate Professor in Management (Organisational Behaviour & Human Resource Management), Department of Business and Public Administration, College of Business Administration, the University of Sharjah, United Arab Emirates.

Chapter 1

Integrating innovation, strategy and people management: Introduction and overview

TONY DUNDON AND ADRIAN WILKINSON

Many textbooks on business and management combine a discursive, prescriptive and theoretical or critical dimension covering the defined topics of a particular field or discipline: strategy, HRM, quality or marketing for instance. Most have the admirable aim of synthesising information and concepts to impart a degree of knowledge. Some even seek to contrast alternative or differing interpretations of such knowledge with demonstration through models and case descriptions. However, because of the nature of much college and university learning, many texts have one major drawback – with the *application* of knowledge afforded a low priority. At best, many texts present very brief scenarios and/or hypothetical situations for students to consider with the concepts and theories they are studying. These scenarios hardly emulate the complex and often contradictory ideas and theories of the real world.

This book provides a bank of evidence-based case studies. The materials developed offer students and educators a means of extending knowledge generation through application and critical analysis, reflection and synthesis. The cases were derived from scholarly research into one or more specific management or organisational problems that the chapter authors were pursuing. The cases were not written as teaching aids *per se* but derived for the most part from ongoing research pursuits. Thus the case studies are first and foremost real world situations, written by leading scholars from the fields of people management, corporate strategy, innovation studies, organisational analysis and human resource management. The intended audience is students and educators seeking study materials for critical analysis and reflection at higher or advanced levels of business and management learning, such as:

- bespoke masters programs in innovation

- human resource management
- operations management
- strategy-type degree programs
- the broad MBA syllabus found at many educational institutions across the globe.

Structure of book and cases

The cases vary considerably and are grouped in the book with related thematic content. In Part I, five case studies cover in some detail issues concerned with 'strategy and strategic management'. Several debatable issues surrounding the strategic imperatives of image and (re)positioning of a brand are shown to be far from straightforward in Chapter 2 when assessing Bulmers Cider. Chapter 3 gives other related aspects of working with consultants and the approaches to analysing organisational issues, showing that organisational complexities mean issues cannot be easily read-off from some management guru checklist. In Chapters 4, 5 and 6 issues of strategy, franchising, supply chain networks and business failure are covered.

Part II picks-up issues raised in the previous cases by looking at 'corporate innovation', a concept that is difficult to define as a management system let alone operationalise in practice. The five cases here look at ideas about innovativeness from various perspectives, ranging from macro policy objectives of government to micro organisational dynamics and learning capacities at enterprise levels. A strong message in Part II is the importance of understanding the process or system of innovation as a journey, which leads to variable and uneven outcomes.

Part III includes five cases concerned with 'change and culture', including issues resulting from changes in familial ownership and integration across organisational boundaries and hierarchies. The transfer and acquisition of knowledge is crucial in these cases, with highly significant practice outcomes reported through cultural adaptation, redundancy and workforce dissatisfaction. Some instances show that knowledge transfer can carve out new career paths within and between organisations. The issues covered in Part III also point to the contradictory patterns of flexible specialisation, resistance to change and patterns of workforce conflict and misbehaviour.

Part IV groups together five cases that bridge variable aspects of 'management leadership'. How leaders can motivate and transform are covered in both private and public sector organisations. Issues to do with work-life balance, front line managers, variation in leadership styles and the roles of senior executives are shown to be crucial elements in leading and managing others for organisational success.

Part V is much connected to the previous chapters, with seven cases each reporting on the use and application of different 'human resource management' practices and strategies. These cases cover brand management as a source of strategic resourcing; pay systems; learning and skill development; employee voice; and high performance work system.

Part VI includes eight cases that are dedicated to specific 'global aspects of innovation and people management'. These cases cover topics surrounding talent management, international business strategy, subsidiarity and cross cultural change management. There is a focus among these cases on the application of issues and practice in multinational corporate settings, across global boundaries and within national borders. As a group of cases, the material stretches from the national to the global, including how corporate and government objectives are applied in the areas of management and business.

Content and themes

The cases described for each part of the book are not necessarily exclusive to a given theme or issue. Many overlap and show how the intricacies of one issue or problem can dovetail and affect other ideas and concepts, some of which may not have been initially perceived in such a multi-level approach. Problems of employee voice, for instance, are affected by line management as much as by higher order corporate strategies in the areas of company restructuring, employer branding or supply chain options. Likewise, discrimination and diversity issues are not confined to matters in any single location or the preserve of one subject domain, but reach across international boundaries and scholarly areas of enquiry.

All the cases are contemporary, relevant and cover different sectors, countries, occupations and experiences. As a bank of evidence-based cases the collection is significant in its own right and unique for its global and sector variability. The cases are also important given the timing of many of the research enquiries from which they have been drawn, including the synthesis of business and management concerns before, during and after the global financial recession. While the cases do not report specifically on responses to the global economic crisis, they do allude to the vast ingenuity of employers, workers, unions and other stakeholders in seeking solutions to huge problems encountered in their business and workplace situations. Above all, the *capacity-building power* and *role of agency* is testimony to the ingenuity and creativity of people as a collective dynamic for change and improvement.

Structures of accumulation matter. How corporate enterprises respond to and are shaped by global neo-liberal forces amplifies the political tensions that shape management and policy decision-makers. Importantly, the interplay between structure and agency is not confined to a single space or time and enduring legacies exist across cultures and international boundaries.

Finally, the collection of case studies shows how an engaged pluralist *multi-disciplinary perspective* can shed insights into the problems of management. It is the case study methodology and its associated pedagogical application of learning that offers a particularly unique and deep insight into the real experiences of organisational members.

The sequences of cases, themes, sector/industry and location is summarised in Table 1.1.

Table 1.1 Sequence of cases

Case / Chapter Number	Summary of Title	Author(s)	Themes / Questions Covered	Sector and Country
1	Integrating innovation, strategy and people management: An overview	Tony Dundon and Adrian Wilkinson	• Interconnections between parts and structure of the book	
Part I: Strategy and Strategic Management				
2	Strategic positioning at Bulmers Cider	Paul Ryan	• Strategic positioning and re-positioning • Image and brand management • Market development and diversification	Food and drinks; Ireland (and global)
3	Organisational analysis	Les Worrell	• Organisational analysis in developing strategy • Working with outside consultants	Public sector local authority; UK
4	HR strategy at the Coffee Club	Ashlea Kellner	• Business life cycle stages • Strategy adaptation: growth to maturity • Franchising	Retail/ servicing: Australia, New Zealand and Thailand
5	Technology adoption and supply chain networks	Vikram Bhakoo	• Complex business systems and supply chains • Factors affecting technological adaptation • Coercive, normative and mimetic supply chain network pressures	Pharmaceutical hospital supply chain networks; Australia
6	Business failure	Olav Muurlink	• Rigidity theory • Company merger/buy-out • Micro- and macro-economic crisis threats	Small firm manufacturing; Australia

Part II: Corporate Innovation				
7	Dynamic capability in action	Rachel Hilliard	• Environmental management • Capability formation • Clean technologies • Path perception capability	Pharmaceutical industry; Ireland
8	Innovation and public policy for SMEs	Don Scott-Kemmis and Roy Green	• Public policy towards SME innovation and capability knowledge • Transformational capability • Role of the State	Public policy and SMEs; Australia
9	Empowerment for innovation	Jonathon Lazarus, Lisa Callagher and Kenneth Husted	• Collaborative knowledge production • Transdisciplinary research; • Effectiveness of innovation and transdisciplinary research approaches	Medical Health; New Zealand
10	Applying innovation in information systems at Ingersoll-Rand	David O'Sullivan	• Innovation planning and goals • Innovation and role of stakeholders • Innovation as a system process	Multinational manufacturer; Ireland (and global sites)
11	Becoming an innovative learning organisation	Margaret Tallott, Alma McCarthy, Rachel Hilliard	• Principles of learning and innovation • Innovation and system thinking • Evaluating learning organisation principles	Forestry; power lines service provider; Ireland
Part III: Integration, Culture and Change Management				
12	Changing organisational hierarchies	Rory Donnelly	• Knowledge-intensive industries • Changing organisational hierarchies and flexibility	Professional services, HQ in UK (also global across 151 countries)

13	Family business: Succession and change	Rowena Barrett	• Next generation family business • Succession planning and ownership change • Management control	Road Haulage; Australia
14	Embedding a culture of workplace wellness	Ruth McPhail	• Employee and management attitudes towards wellness • Planning and integrating wellness	Public/university sector
15	Age discrimination at Virgin Blue	Ben French	• Legal processes and cultural factors • Selection decisions and tribunal procedures • Equity and fairness	Airline industry; Australia
16	Understanding change: Conflict and resistance in the workplace	Keith Townsend	• Change using new work technologies, just-in-time, teams, etc. • Employee behaviours, including resistance to change	Food processing/ supply chain; Australia
Part IV: Management Leadership				
17	Leadership at Qantas	Amy Collins and Peter Jordan	• Industry regulation; privatisation; transformational leadership • Change agents	Airline industry; Australia
18	Managing leadership talent in multi-media	Herman Tse	• Developing and nurturing human capital • Leadership vision • Leadership effectiveness	Creative industries; Australia
19	Leading change at the Defence Signals Directorate	Teresa Marchant and Craig Cardinal	• Public sector management change • Cultural change • Change agents	Public department/agency; Australia

20	Leadership and motivation in the IT sector	Jane Murray	• Founders as leaders • Dynamic flexibility and process-driven consistency • Motivating and managing expectations • Motivational theories	Software and IT sector; Australia
21	Transformational leadership in the public sector	Hani Abdalla and Ashly Pinnington	• Macro and micro relationships affecting leadership • Transformational, transactional, and avoidant leadership approaches • Long-term change and innovation	Public sector agency; Dubai, United Arab Emirates
Part V: People Management and HRM				
22	Resourcing: Enhancing the corporate brand at McDonalds	Stephen Taylor	• Changing employer brand and reputation • Employee resourcing initiatives	Food restaurant outlets, corporate HQ; UK (and global)
23	Reward: Job family remuneration strategies	Glen Jenkins	• Re-structuring pay through job family reward systems • Flexibility and performance-related pay initiatives • Reward and role of front line managers	Public sector/university, UK
24	Relations: Line managers and employee voice	Jane Suter and Mick Marchington	• Line managers and capability frameworks • Recruiting line managers as leaders • Line management leadership via formal and informal voice	Restaurants; Franchise business outlets; UK
25	Voice: Union and non-union employee representation	Niall Cullinane and Jimmy Donaghey	• Union and non-union channels of voice • Systematic double-breasting voice arrangements • Management motives for different voice arrangements	Privatised former public utility; Northern Ireland and Republic of Ireland

26	Development: Learning on the job in TV production	Irena Grugulis and Dimitrinka Stoyanova	• Comparing 'in-house' and 'freelance' on the job learning • Fragmented labour markers and learning on the job • Learning beyond organisational boundaries	TV freelance professionals, UK
27	Diversity: Gender management at Victoria Police	Julie Wolfram-Cox and Georgina Caillard	• Assessment of diversity management initiatives in practice • Gendered work and gendered talk	Public sector/police force; Victoria; Australia
28	High performance work systems	Eva Knies, Peter Leisink and Paul Boselie	• HR, performance and multi-stakeholder contexts • Employee representation in HPWS initiative design • Barriers to HPWS • Line managers and HPWS	Insurance sector; multinational organisation; Netherlands
Part VI: Global Innovation, Strategy and People Management				
29	HRM in global perspective: Reuters	Paul Sparrow and Chris Brewster	• Globalisation and pragmatic strategising • Aligning the global and regional • Global sourcing and shoring options	Reuters, high technology information and news service; global.
30	HRM in multinational corporations: Local or global standardisation	Anastasia Kynighou	• Cultural, institutional and organisation factor effects • Competing global and local objectives and practices • Role of expatriate managers	Banking and global investment; Cyprus
31	Managing international talent	Anthony McDonnell and Hugh Scullion	• International business growth strategy • Parent and host country management options	Building materials and conglomerates multinational; Eastern European operations

			• Challenges to talent management in global context	
32	From local to global: Cross-cultural adaptation	Kate Hutchings	• Establishing international operations in China • Cross-culture tensions	Fashion, high-end boutiques; Australia and China
33	Managing diverse workgroups in Islamic cultures	Ebrahim Soltani	• Different global diversity and equality approaches • Managing diversity in non-western contexts • Analysing equality and inequality in practice	Brick manufacturing; Tehran
34	Strategy and people management in China	Fang Lee Cooke	• Front line management behaviours • Shopfloor sabotage • Globalisation of Chinese firms	Auto parts manufacturer; family-owned; China
35	Strategy, change and Emiratization in the United Arab Emirates	Rachid Zeffane and Linzi Kemp	• Emiratization strategy • Retention on national workforce • Generational barriers and perceptions	State modernisation and employability policy; employability; United Arab Emirates
36	Strategy, survival and outsourcing in South Africa	Christine Bischoff and Geoffrey Wood	• Union-management tensions and employment antagonism • Outsourcing as a HR strategy • Debates about government protection of indigenous markets	Clothing and textile industry; South Africa

Part I
Strategy and Strategic Management

Chapter 2

Bulmers original cider: A case of strategic positioning for market expansion

Paul Ryan

Background and introduction

The management at Bulmers, producers of original cider in Clonmel County Tipperary since 1935, were, as every year, hoping for a warm summer. Consumer demand for cider increases greatly on hot summer days as drinkers deem it refreshing, particularly with ice. The company was therefore subject to the vagaries of the unpredictable Irish weather. However, other determinants of consumer demand such as product image, crisp taste and brand loyalty were within the control of Bulmers' strategic management team. Also, the opportunity to minimise exposure to Irish climatic uncertainty and expand sales arose from overseas market potential. Given cider's history of poor image, management appreciated the need to reposition the drink in the mindset of consumers prior to entering foreign markets.

The legacy of cider's abysmal image

Bulmers Co. is Ireland's leading manufacturer of cider. Its activities began in 1935, when local William Magner decided to produce the drink commercially in Dowds Lane, Clonmel. In 1937 he joined forces with the established English cider maker H.P. Bulmer and Co. In 1949 Magner retired from the firm and the name Bulmers came to the fore. The company changed its name to Showerings (Ireland) Ltd in 1964 and moved its operations to Annerville, which is located about 3 miles from the centre of Clonmel town. The historical image of cider in Ireland (as elsewhere) was appalling. It had a reputation of being cheap and high in alcohol content, and it was thought to be associated with binge drinking – often out of doors. It further served as a convenient scapegoat for many of the alcohol abuse problems of the time in Ireland. This negative perception also existed amongst the licensed trade, and many publicans refused to stock the drink because of its image problem. In addition to this, cider had low margins and showed little promise of future growth. Furthermore, Bulmers cider had a somewhat shoddy reputation as the alcoholic beverage of choice for teenagers, including those under age. The product was sold in brown, two litre plastic 'flagons', and it was not unusual to find empty Bulmers' bottles strewn all over public parks, the residue of a night's 'bush drinking'.

Bulmers was seen as a company in disarray. As John Keogh (Marketing Director, Bulmers Ltd) stressed,

> The brand had a low price point with a very poor image going nowhere. It was decision time – what to do. What would you do about it?

The product had a very poor consumer image, allied to the devastating media coverage, and as a result, most publicans refused to stock it. It was clear that something had to be done. One way or another, the management team could not keep producing and selling the product the way that it was.

Bulmers' management decided to start their turnaround repositioning strategy with a marketing campaign aimed at drawing parallels with the beer industry. The company initially tried to position the Bulmers cider product as a beer, using somewhat tacky advertising with the aid of ZZ Top-type advertisements, reinforced with rather coarse posters saying, 'everything else tastes like pils'. Using a variety of shock tactics, this initiative was aimed at showing the public that cider was superior to beer (cider is basically fermented apple juice). Although it had a high recall factor, the campaign did nothing for the brand or to correct the image problems that it was suffering from.

Following this campaign, Bulmers' management took stock of their situation. Key research carried out by Bulmers' marketing department confirmed that people were concerned with the product's negative image and its adverse effects. Bulmers at this time had colloquial labels such as 'lunatic juice' and 'electric lemonade', partly due to the high alcohol content of the drink. Nevertheless, the company discovered that the public didn't want to see the drink removed from the marketplace. Essentially, people had a certain regard for the product but abhorred the image and baggage that came with it. Bulmers cider did have redeemable features that no one could quite put their finger on at the time. The problems and potential of the brand were highlighted by Brian Hayes (Bulmers Account Executive, Young Advertising):

> The research showed it was an image problem, but what specifically about the product? Was there anything wrong with the product? And most people would tell you in response 'no, but my perceived idea is that it is jungle juice'.

This research also allowed Bulmers' management to identify the faults in their previous strategy of positioning the product head to head with beer. It was apparent that it was too big a challenge to try to convert all lager drinkers to cider drinkers. Thus they began to look at their own drinkers.

Three varieties of Bulmers' drinker were identified:

- the regular core drinker
- the regular repertoire drinker
- the occasional repertoire drinker.

The regular core drinker drank cider the majority of the time due to its taste and alcohol strength. The regular repertoire drinker might play a football match on a Wednesday night and start with Bulmers before moving on to Guinness after two or three pints, simply using Bulmers for the refreshment value. The occasional repertoire drinker only drank Bulmers when he was in the countryside or when the sun shone on a Sunday afternoon.

While Bulmers would never be perceived as another beer, there were lessons to be learned from the beer market in Ireland and its main participants. Brendan McGuinness (former Managing Director, Bulmers Ltd) was firmly of the opinion that the market was characterised by rapidly changing preferences, and that one product's decline meant another product's gain:

> Well there's no clearly defined sort of population the consumer is in. If you look back in the history, you know stout was a dominant category and stout has declined. You know, there was a time when stout was I think sixty per cent of beer consumed in Ireland, so clearly if categories are in decline there's opportunities for other brands.

Once the groundwork was done, Bulmers' repositioning strategy began to fall into place. There was broadly positive customer response to the product – but not in the form it had been conceived and marketed. There was an apparent significant opportunity to take market share from major competitors in the Irish beer market. The company began to develop a distinct product profile for Bulmers cider that reflected customer preferences; this helped to differentiate it from stout, ale and lager beers. Bulmers' management had already developed a market segmentation plan based on ideal cider consumption patterns. Nonetheless, the problems of negative consumer and trade perceptions of Bulmers, and cider in general, remained. Creative and bold action was clearly required in relation to the product's image, and the answer lay in a return to the roots of the company and the cider-making business. Brendan McGuinness recalled:

> Clearly the first attempt to reposition cider as beer failed, and it was out of that we said let's get back to basics, and the basics were telling us that it was all about tradition, naturalness and heritage. Those are our properties.

The catalyst for this fundamental change was external cues from the company's competitive environment, allied to management insight and experience. Brendan McGuinness explained:

> For example, Guinness departed from their traditional strategy ten to fifteen years ago and started appealing very clearly to young people, and they chopped and changed their advertising, and I suppose we moved in and took part of their territory which was the whole naturalness and heritage and

tradition area and product qualities and craft of making it. Guinness went modern and alienated all its older consumers and didn't recruit new consumers because they didn't believe it. They said Guinness is what my grandfather drank and it's thick and it's heavy and don't tell me it's now light.

Similarly, Maurice Breen (Marketing Director, Bulmers Ltd) commented:

The product had a lot of good things going for it, in terms of its naturalness and how it's produced.

Bulmers then embarked upon a marketing and advertising strategy to change consumer prejudice about their cider brand. Colin Gordon (former Marketing Director, Bulmers Ltd) stressed that,

Everything we did was fundamentally around how to continuously improve the image.

Colin Gordon also elaborated upon the need to be ahead of the consumer, providing guidance and direction that would portray Bulmers cider in a more favourable light:

Everything we did in advertising in the early days, and I guess right up to the present, was based on the image being ahead of the consumer... because there was such a negative perception of the product. Everything we did was literally super premium, it was always ahead of the consumer, the opinion leaders generally and the trade.

Management decided to use a theme based on 'time' throughout all the company's advertising. Colin Gordon reflected on the inception of the idea and the snowballing consequences:

Once you had the copy line, it actually became unstoppable what you could put in against it. So, 'nothing added but time' allowed you to be natural. What is natural? Well, standing in the middle of a river, fishing on your own, is as natural as you can think of. You have time; you have all day to fish. You can pick on the tradition, the craft, heritage, all to do with time. You could pick on the absence of things because of the 'nothing added' part of the by-line. It really became a way of having one central ad, and then having loads of different themes to address different consumers in different ways to try and tweak people's emotional response to the image by using image, giving it something unique within the beer world or the long alcohol business.

This consistency of message was achieved through several communication media, all portraying the same meanings: those of naturalness, tradition and heritage. Bulmers has maintained the 'time' theme in all advertisements. It initially began as 'Nothing added but time', but although this proved to be very successful, the company was forced to change the slogan due to a European Union ruling on misleading advertising (a colorant is added to the cider). The next campaign focused on 'All in its own good time'. This, in turn, was superseded by 'Time dedicated to you'.

The dedication aspect (as in 'Time dedicated to you') highlighted that single-minded devotion to success is paramount to being first in a particular field. Bulmers used many symbols and legends in different areas to draw a parallel between themselves and the person who puts in everything to succeed. For example, 'Jules Leotard', the world's first flying trapeze artist, is depicted in one of their advertisements. Another advertisement focused on the 'Ski jump' – featuring Sondre Nordheim, the first person to 'fly' through the air.

The second creative platform added was 'craft'. The advertising reflected the brand's mood and style while successfully adding another aspect to the brand's character – the time and craft necessary to produce the product. The aim of this constant brand building and learning was to allow the Bulmers brand to evolve while at the same time retaining the initial focus and qualities identified at the outset of the strategy. Therefore, although the message was changing in being responsive to the consumer, market and product, it still retained its core meaning. Brian Hayes summarised the process:

> We added another layer, which was craft, with ads showing fly-fishing. These ads showed craftsmen at work and implied the same for Bulmers with the line, 'True Craft implies time'. Again, these ads had a slow pace, melodic mood and the rich palette of colours established with the previous ad. These ads researched very well and were further developed with mosaic making and press ads showing golf. These ads related interacting snippets around dedication to being the best.

Industry measures

The bad public image of cider, nevertheless, remained a critical issue that Bulmers' management seriously needed to address. Colm Carey (Managing Director, the Research Centre Qualitative Research Company) recalls that:

> The image was the tail on the kite that was pulling the kite down, so you had to cut that free so that it could soar.

The first element addressed was that cider has a very high alcoholic strength. Historically, the alcoholic content of Bulmers was 5.0% by volume for draught, and 4.5% for bottles. This compared with levels of 4.2% or 4.3% for beer. The reasons the higher alcoholic content were historical: when UK cider brands had first entered the Irish market, they had a high alcohol content and Bulmers matched it. And reflecting insufficient controls, the alcohol content of flagons sold through the retail trade varied between 4.0% and 8.5%. As a result, Bulmers was suffering from an unnecessarily high cost of production as well as an image associated with drunkenness – partly caused by the high and inconsistent alcoholic strength of its cider. Thus, Bulmers' management took action to reduce and standardise alcohol levels.

The image problem was compounded by adverse press coverage. Newspaper headlines such as, 'Cider crazed youths', 'Residents at war on cider parties and vandals', 'Cider thugs started library blaze', and 'Cider party turned nasty, court told' were commonplace. Needless to say, this did little for the Bulmers' image in the mindset of the general public.

Brendan McGuinness identified the problem thus:

> There is a whole history of it (cider) being a cottage industry, which wasn't very well controlled; therefore it got its image of being cheap. The only way to resolve that was to go through what we call a total repositioning exercise and that involved a whole range of initiatives. Obviously we had problems with consumer attitudes to cider; we had huge problems with trade attitudes to cider as well in those days with Bulmers. They wouldn't stock it or were reluctant to stock it because of the type of consumers it attracted. We also had a problem with the media in that any form of alcohol abuse by the young was attributed to cider, so we addressed these three areas.

The Cider Industry Council (CIC) was set up with a substantial initial fund of £100,000. Its stated aims were:

- to encourage an appreciation of cider amongst responsible and mature drinkers

- to encourage the use of cider in cooking as an accompaniment to food

- to help combat underage drinking.

Its real aim was to counteract the negative media reports that could be seen to lead to the negative consumer and trade attitudes. As John Keogh pointed out:

> We formed a council with the objectives to address the question of underage drinking, encourage responsible attitudes and to encourage increased appreciation to ensure that members' advertising did not denigrate the category. This was good work, needs to be done and positioned cider very positively as taking a responsible attitude. We were seen as the irresponsible ones of the past acting responsibly.

Although claiming to represent the major companies engaged in the production, distribution and marketing of cider in Ireland, Bulmers provided CIC with 95 per cent of its funding. Bulmers moved to get all of the other industry players involved in an effort to camouflage the fact that it was the principal driver behind the scheme. The CIC played a very important role for all industry members in changing media and consumer attitudes to the product. The Marketing Director of Bulmers at the time, Colin Gordon, reflected on the deeper motives for the creation of the Cider Industry Council:

> We were always scared that a misreported accident, attributed to cider, would have a seriously detrimental impact on the whole business. Trade could have delisted us and whatever ... So everything we did was fundamentally around how to continually improve the image, where we could bring truth into the public domain.

At the same time, some of the marketing employees were given the task of counteracting the negative media image of cider by contacting any journalist who reported on 'cider parties'. When contacted, these journalists were asked to verify the amount of cider involved. If it could not be verified that a substantial amount of cider had been consumed, the journalist was then asked to retract the article or print an apology. Bulmers also funded various initiatives that were supported by the police, such as alcohol awareness schemes, which helped to raise awareness that the cider industry was becoming more socially responsible. Over time, the establishment of the CIC and company measures to counteract inaccurate reporting proved very effective in reducing negative media coverage of cider from over 120 stories to less than 20 in the space of five years.

Further repositioning tactics

Aside from advertising, Bulmers' management addressed other elements of the repositioning plan. A long-standing issue had been the relatively low price of Bulmers cider in relation to major selling beers. This potentially undermined the high quality product image engendered by the company's advertising. Over a number of years, the price of Bulmers cider was increased to reflect its new 'premium product' positioning. In the 1990s and early 2000s, Ireland's economy experienced robust recovery from the previous period of stagnation, and this was accompanied by higher consumer price inflation. These circumstances facilitated a phased increase in the price of Bulmers cider over an eight-year period. Initially, it was brought up to the level of stout prices charged by Guinness and others. The next step was to match the price of Bulmers cider to that of ale and then to the same level as lager. The Irish Government introduced two selective excise duty increases, which meant that cider prices went up but beer was exempt. This allowed Bulmers to pass on these duties to the consumer and again increase the price of the product. As a result, Bulmers cider sold at a premium to lager.

In addition, the company learned from past failures to stop the previous in-pub promotion policy, which was judged by management to show Bulmers in a bad light. It was concluded that, by giving Bulmers cider free to customers in pubs and bars, the company was actually increasing the negative image of the product through encouraging drunkenness. This was stopped completely and the money was utilised elsewhere in the marketing budget. The focus of the company's promotion shifted to public relations and sponsorship in areas more in keeping with Bulmers' repositioned product image, such as golf and other sports events. Colin Gordon commented:

> I was very conscious that you went into the trade and regularly the bar owner would tell you that, 'I'm not going to have that in here because I've heard a bad story', or 'I've had a bad experience'. A lot of it was driven because of the promotions that were run. The promotions on cider tended to be volume driven activity rather than image building activity, and therefore a lot of publicans, as indeed consumers, their only real experience of cider was people drinking it and getting too much of it and becoming slightly negative, image wise, because of it. The trade were afraid, therefore, and that was the only trick that we had to play. So convincing them, in fact it wasn't even a matter of any sort of democracy, we withdrew all promotions to the trade, every single thing and we put all the money into image correction.

Bulmers also adopted several innovative approaches to product packaging, which further served to reinforce the changed image of the product. The company introduced the pint bottle of cider served with ice, which over time became a trademark of the Bulmers' brand in Ireland. This arose from management spotting a consumer usage pattern and developing it. In addition, a long neck bottle of Bulmers cider was introduced, arising from a suggestion by a lower level employee.

Success in the end?

The deliberate repositioning strategy, and the set of industry, marketing and other initiatives, proved to be hugely successful in enhancing the image of Bulmers cider. They significantly changed the mindset of consumers in relation to a product that looked to be in decline. The result was a huge increase in the sales of cider with a 900 per cent increase in a decade, of which Bulmers Ltd, as the dominant market leader, was the chief beneficiary.

Following major adjustments in consumer attitudes to the product, the volume and market share gains for Bulmers after just a few years were astonishing. Brendan McGuinness commented:

> They (the consumers) think of Bulmers in the same breath as Guinness, Bud and Heineken. So that is the scale of the transition that we have managed to make over the twelve year period and that has resulted in Bulmers moving from about two per cent of the beer/cider market to about twelve per cent of the beer/cider market over that period.

Ultimately, Bulmers cider was on sale in virtually every pub in the country compared to only 40 per cent of pubs ten years previously. Over the same period, annual consumption of cider rose ten-fold from just over seven million litres to more than 70 million litres. Now the strategic management team at Bulmers were faced with the task of deciding how to avail of their successful product repositioning in existing and new markets.

Discussion questions

1) Explain the rationale for the strategic repositioning of Bulmers cider.

2) Describe the elements of the repositioning strategy.

3) Outline and explain the product-market strategic options open to Bulmers.

Chapter 3

A case study in organisational analysis and organisational development

LES WORRALL

The context

This case study describes an eight year program of organisational development in a UK local authority. It describes how organisational analysis – primarily using an employee attitudes survey – was used to develop strategic human resource management and organisational development policies, practices and initiatives, and how the implementation of these policies, practices and initiatives was monitored and reviewed over time.

The organisation that is the subject of this case study is a UK local authority that became a unitary authority in late 1998. Before the authority was upgraded to a unitary council, the organisation had been a second tier authority (a shire district) onto which several functions from a county council were then grafted. The services that were grafted onto the shire district included social services, education and a range of community-based services and facilities. In one stroke, the size of the organisation – as measured by headcount – trebled. The new council faced a wide range of organisational issues. For example, at the time of merger, the previous second tier authority was effectively wound up and a new corporate entity (a unitary council) created.

At this time the council resolved to create an entirely new set of employment terms and conditions for the new council. However, due to staff resistance, the employees of the old shire district were allowed to maintain their old terms and conditions and so were the former employees of the county council who moved across. Any new employees to the unitary council who were neither former employees of the shire district nor the county council were employed on the new set of terms and conditions. The key problem facing the new council was how to build a new organisation out of three distinct sets of employees: the former employees of the shire district; the former employees of the county council and the newly recruited employees of the new unitary council (each of which were working with different sets of terms and conditions).

The need for information and intelligence to inform the organisational development process

The then chief executive and the newly created board of directors decided that they needed information on the newly created unitary council. In particular, they determined a need for a baseline view of employees' perceptions of the organisation as a place to work. This could also be used to identify the issues that a sustained program of organisation building and organisational development would address. The senior management realised that, while a one off survey would be useful, they needed to take a longer-term view if they were to effectively monitor the organisation's development path as it (hopefully) became transformed into a more unified and cohesive organisation over time.

The senior management team were strongly of the view that the research aspect of this long-term organisational development program needed to be conducted independently of the council. Thus in early 1999, the Management Research Centre at the University of Wolverhampton Business School was contracted to work with the team as a long-term partner on the research aspect of the project. The council appointed a head of organisational development, one of whose roles was to work closely with the university to: first, design an employee attitude survey; second, implement the research process; and third, design and implement a communications process through which the results of the research would be fed back to the entire organisation. At the outside, a transparent communications strategy and an open and honest approach to dealing with the results of the survey were seen as paramount.

The design of the questionnaire and the wider research process

Organisations who are considering putting in place a large-scale employee attitudes survey should do so with care as the potential for large-scale organisational damage is considerable. A parallel study of another organisation conducted by the Management Research Centre at the University of Wolverhampton Business School resulted in the replacement of the organisation's entire senior management team after the survey results exposed severe levels of organisational and managerial dysfunction.

The first phase of the research design process was to negotiate the terms of engagement under which the university-based researchers would operate. To its credit, the council, from the beginning, encouraged a high level of transparency and openness in the conduct of the survey. In particular, a dissemination and communications strategy was agreed very early in the process. The university team were assured that as long as they could justify and support any points they wanted to make, they would be able make these points publicly. Throughout the entire process all key stakeholders (e.g. councillors, trade unions and specific groups of employees such as a group that represented Black and Asian employees and another that represented disabled employees) were kept fully informed of the development of the research process. As an input to questionnaire design, the head of organisational development in the council facilitated a number of employee workshops in all the council's departments to give all employee groups the opportunity to raise any issues, themes and topics that they wanted the questionnaire to cover. A number of employees from these groups were involved in subsequent phases of the research process as the questionnaire was piloted and further refined. The process phases ensured that the questionnaire dealt with the areas that both the council and the employees wanted covered.

At the time of the first survey, the newly created council employed almost 6,000 people in six directorates. A key issue to resolve in the design of organisation-wide surveys of this type is how finely to disaggregate the organisation into groups of employees. Initially, the council was 'salami sliced' in rather a coarsely grained way. The decision was made that data would be collected at what was known as 'service group' level within the council. A service group was a bundle of business units that reported to a specific service group head with service group heads reporting directly to a departmental director. There is always a compromise to be struck in how organisations are disaggregated in employee surveys: managerially, there is usually a demand for fine grained information which requires the definition of a large number of relatively small units of analysis; but employees are often concerned about the possibility of their individual views being identifiable as the size of the data collection unit (i.e. a group of employees) gets smaller. In later surveys, the demand for finer and finer grained information increased, with a decision being made to collect data at the 'business unit' level – each of which was headed by a business unit manager who reported directly to a service head.

The number of units on which data was collected increased over time from 20 to 80 as the size of the council declined from 6,000 in 1999 to 3,500 in 2007. The structuring of the data ultimately allowed analysis to take place at four distinct levels in the organisational hierarchy: the whole organisation level; the directorate level; the service group level; and, the business unit level. In addition to location within the council's structure, data were also collected on

- an employee's level in the organisation, categorised as:
    - chief executive or director
    - head of service group
    - business unit manager
    - professional and technical
    - administrative and clerical
    - operational

- gender

- ethnicity

- disability

- union membership

- employment history – whether the respondent had been:

  - employed by the previous shire district council

  - employed by the county council

  - recruited directly to the unitary council.

The inclusion of the variables listed above allowed the data to be cut in many ways, and this created the danger that the council would become overwhelmed with information leading to 'paralysis by analysis'. A prime role of the academic research team was to assist the council in making sense of the data by structuring the analysis to focus on the issues most relevant to the organisational development process.

The key themes for analysis

The design of the questionnaire involved a multistage process. The council had done an initial requirements analysis, but this had been done primarily from a managerial perspective and it focused essentially on what the senior management team wanted to know. The council had decided to look on the questionnaire study as a major and longitudinal element and as an initiative to encourage employee involvement in a wider organisational development and organisation building strategy. This meant that other stakeholders' views needed to be built into the process if the outcomes were to be seen as legitimate and valid by all employees. In addition to this, a transparent, open and honest communications strategy was seen as essential.

After a long process of discussion and questionnaire piloting, a final version of the questionnaire was developed; it focused on a number of key issues, themes and topics. The questionnaire was built around gathering evidence on the following issues:

- To what extent do employees identify with the council's aims and with the council as a whole?

- How does the council treat you as an individual?

- How are senior managers (chief executive and directors) perceived within the organisation?

- How do employees perceive the prevailing management and leadership styles in the organisation?

- How good are employees' relationships with their immediate line managers?

- How do employees feel about the work they do, the design of their jobs and the council as a place to work?

- What are co-worker relationships like in business units/teams?

- How satisfied are employees with their jobs overall and various aspects/facets of their job?

- How effective is training and how well is the personal and performance development process working?

- How are employees treated at work and is there any bullying, harassment or inappropriate management behaviour?

The academic input to the research process was geared mainly towards enabling the council to get clarity about the questions it wanted answered and to advise on the best ways to ask specific questions to enable benchmarking of the council against external data sets. While the ability to conduct external benchmarking was limited, the academic research team did have access to longitudinal data from another data set which had several key questions in common with the council questionnaire (see, for example, Worrall & Cooper 2007; Worrall, Lindorff & Cooper 2008). Over the period from 1999 to 2007, variants of the questionnaire were circulated to all council employees with overall response rates in each case being around 50% – but varying considerably by business unit from around 15% to 100%.

Communicating the results

A transparent communications strategy had been agreed at the inception of the research process in 1997. At the launch of each biennial iteration of the survey, the dates for a series of departmental feedback sessions were announced. The council visibly committed itself to a program of feedback sessions to help assure employees that 'something would be done' as a result of the survey. After each survey, the university team produced a full feedback report that was made available to every council employee, either in hard copy or on the council's intranet. The university team was given relatively free rein to write the report, but the draft versions were discussed with the chief executive, the head of personnel and the head of organisational development (not directors) before the final report was agreed upon and released into the organisation.

Feedback sessions were held for each department and in many cases over 100 departmental staff attended. Again, the university team was given relatively free rein to construct and deliver the presentations. Occasionally, there were difficult messages to be communicated, and on more than one occasion the chief executive indicated that the research team should 'tell it like it is'. In one instance, the chief executive stated that he felt that the research was holding up a mirror to the organisation and that the organisation should be big enough to look into the mirror. In many cases, directors and other senior managers, including the chief executive, had to listen to feedback that was not flattering to them or their management styles, but they did listen. On only one occasion did a director make a concerted attempt to censor the research team by telling them what they could or could not say at a departmental meeting – he was overruled by the chief executive.

There are clear messages to be learnt here: a transparent communications strategy is imperative if you are going to ensure that employees see surveys of this type as worthwhile and honest. Employees are not stupid, they experience organisational life on a daily basis and they know when they are being lied to and when difficult issues are being glossed over or downplayed. It was very clear from the way the survey was conducted, that the managers who were most resistant to the survey or who most tried to censor the results were regarded by their staff as having the worst leadership and management styles. It was these managers who led the departments that were characterised by low reciprocal trust, a climate of secrecy, managerial invisibility and inaccessibility and poor upward and downward communications. The survey proved very effective in identifying poor management behaviours and indifferent leadership styles not only at departmental and service group level but also at the business unit level. It was also very noticeable how poor management behaviours tended to cascade down specific lines of the management hierarchy. Analysis of the survey data revealed that the most potent driver of job satisfaction in the organisation was the quality of the working relationship that employees had with their immediate line manager – this finding encouraged the council to look hard at the management behaviours and leadership styles that it wanted to develop in the 125 people that had significant managerial and leadership responsibilities in the council.

What were the key issues that the surveys exposed and how did the council react to them?

Over the five iterations of the survey, the research exposed a number of important issues, problems and tensions. It also revealed that the council had much to be proud about as an employer and that it displayed many positive attributes which it needed to build on. During the time in which the surveys were being conducted, the council was assessed to be an 'excellent' council by the Audit Commission in the UK. Perhaps one of the key issues to emerge was that while the council overall tended to achieve very high scores on 'bell weather' measures such as job satisfaction and organisational identification, scores on these measures were very variable within the organisation. For example, in one survey, while several parts of the organisation reported that there was no bullying by management at all, in some parts of the council over 30% of employees reported that they had experienced bullying by management – and in one particular business unit this peaked at over 50%. Job satisfaction also showed wide variation: in one survey job satisfaction across business units ranged from 20% to 100%. Interestingly, job satisfaction and a range of other measures were systematically lower for respondents who saw themselves as professionals (e.g. social service case workers and education officers) compared to those who saw themselves as managers.

One of the key outputs of the survey was a realisation that, across the organisation, employees' experiences varied considerably. When this was pointed out, one chief executive remarked that all employees had the right to a high quality employment experience within the organisation irrespective of where they worked or their level within the organisation. He also stated that a priority for organisational development was to level-up the employment experience across the council.

While there was considerable transparency in what information was made available from the surveys, there were some outputs that had limited circulation because of their sensitivity. One output that was restricted to the chief executive, the head of personnel and the head of organisational development was a chart which was labelled the organisational 'heat map' (see Figure 3.1).

Figure 3.1 The organisational heat map

(Note: the Heat Map presented to the organisation was in four colours and at a much larger scale to enhance its readability.)

The organisational heat map is in effect a data matrix portrayed graphically. The rows of the matrix refer to each business unit in the council. The business units are grouped together in rows that together comprise service areas (accountable to one service group manager) which are in turn grouped into departments (accountable to a single director). Consequently, it is possible to pick out the groups of business units that report to a particular service head and to compare responses in these business units to those achieved by business units that report to another service group head. The rows of the matrix comprise the questions asked in the survey. The questions are grouped by theme and so it is possible to look, for example, at the bundle of questions that ask employees about their perceptions of senior management leadership styles or job facet satisfaction or their views about how well their line manager is managing their business unit. Cells painted white are the best performing business units on given questions while cells painted black are the worst performing business units on these questions.

The heat map enabled an immediate visual impression of where things were at their best and also where the employee experience of working for the council was at its worst. The fact that areas of black often appeared in horizontal lines and in vertical blocks enabled the council to identify that those people working in some business units were either unhappy across the board or unhappy with specific aspects of organisational life given that the questions had been thematically grouped.

The survey proved to be very valuable in bringing issues to the surface within the organisation. For example, it identified those businesses in which most staff had bad perceptions of working for the council generally. The data for these particular business units could then be analysed in more detail to try to develop an understanding of what was driving employees' dissatisfaction and negative attitudes. Additionally, it was possible to identify those business units that were generally performing well but had problems in specific areas – perhaps in relation to how well a particular business unit manager was performing or certain aspects of job design. It was also possible to isolate those service groups (i.e. bundles of business units) where dissatisfaction and negative attitudes were most prevalent, and to link attitudes in these bundles to responses about the management and leadership styles of more senior council managers. The heat map proved to have considerable value in helping the council develop actions targeted either on specific business units, service areas or departments or on specific issues within specific business units, service areas or departments. As a related exercise, the chief executive asked the academic research team to suggest measures and actions that should be included within the annual performance objectives of directors and service heads based on the analysis of the data that informed the heat map.

Having brought these issues to the surface, the council had to develop responses to address the problems and tensions if it was to retain any credibility and convince employees that the survey was worthwhile. Over the eight year period, various top level approaches were used to address the issues that the survey had raised. After one survey, a departmentally focused approach was adopted: directors would agree with the chief executive on the key issues that were affecting their department; they would then be left to address the issues within their departments. This was a conspicuous failure, with some directorates responding and others not. Responses to issues affecting the whole council were patchy – this led to increased employee frustration because by conducting surveys of this type increases employees' expectations that something will be done about issues that strongly affect the quality of their organisational lives. After the next survey, a more corporate approach was taken where specific cross-departmental working groups were set up to address wider organisational issues and problems such as bullying by management and poor management behaviours. In the surveys following the establishment of this group, the level of bullying across the council declined consistently and became much less variable across the council. In some instances, managers were given leadership skills development training and in other more extreme cases they were replaced.

A more detailed analysis of the data revealed that many of the problems raised in the surveys could be traced back to specific managerial behaviours and other leadership issues. The analysis of the performance of departments, service groups and business units, using tools and techniques such the organisational heat map, allowed the council to identify those areas of the council that were being well led and competently managed, and those that were not. This stimulated the council to embark on a council-wide management and leadership development program which was again strongly grounded analytically. Each manager was subjected to a full 360 degree assessment, and development plans were put in place for each manager. This process was overseen by the heads of personnel and organisational development, both of whom commented that the analysis emerging from the 360 degree appraisals was 'uncannily' similar to the analysis that emerged from the employee survey.

Implications for organisational development

While many organisations have conducted employee attitude surveys, few will have so systematically embedded their surveys into their organisation's wider organisational development process. The surveys were used to identify those parts of the council that were performing well and badly to identify where and how interventions could have the greatest effect. They tested how well corporate initiatives on personal development and training were working and exposed patchiness in the take-up of development and the areas where some managers were being less than assiduous in responding to corporate drives to enhance the quality of all employees' working lives. The surveys allowed to the council to identify hot spots within the council where employees were overloaded, where jobs were badly designed, where teams were not functioning well, and where managers were displaying leadership styles and management behaviours that did not conform to council expectations. Finally, they allowed the council to see which factors were reducing individual and collective job satisfaction.

As the council got used to running these surveys, it got far more adept at learning how to use the information the surveys provided. Initially, many managers at all levels were fearful about just what the surveys would reveal. The more effective managers used the information analytically and diagnostically to develop insights about how particular issues could be addressed and to learn about how they were being perceived as leaders and managers. The less effective managers became defensive, attempted to undermine the survey and in one case called the department together to tell them all that 'they had got it all wrong'. As a result of the surveys, the council developed a clearer view of the management and leadership behaviours that they wanted all their managers to display. Over a period of time, all council managers were put through extensive leadership development training to embed these values into management practices across the council. Over the eight year period, the council made a significant investment not only in researching the organisation but in developing organisational responses to the problems and tensions identified. As with any investment, the issue is to achieve a good rate of return.

Discussion questions

1) How can organisational development and strategic human resource management be effectively underpinned by research?

2) What lessons can be learnt from how organisational development was undertaken in the case organisation?

3) How can HR managers based within organisations most effectively work with outside consultants to ensure that the consultants deliver added value?

4) How would you have gone about developing and monitoring organisational development policy and practices in the case organisation?

References

Worrall, L & CL Cooper 2007, 'The quality of working life: a survey of managers' experiences of organisation', Chartered Management Institute Research Report CMI: London.

Worrall, L, Lindorff, M & Cooper, CL 2008, 'A comparison of the perceptions of UK managers and managers in Victoria, Australia', Victoria: Australian Institute of Management, http://www.aimvic.com.au/QualityofWorkingLife2008.pdf.

Chapter 4

Human resource strategy at The Coffee Club Group

ASHLEA KELLNER

Introduction

The Coffee Club Group is one of the largest Australian-based café groups, operating almost 300 stores across Australia, New Zealand and Thailand. The Coffee Club Group is a franchise organisation (also referred to as a 'franchisor'), in which most of the business units are owned and managed by 'master franchisees' and/or 'franchisees'. A master franchisee is the entity that is given rights by the franchisor to develop franchise units within a country or territory by appointing sub-franchisees. Franchisees are the individuals or entities that purchase the rights to use a franchisor's trademarked name and business model to sell a product or service. The parties enter into agreements where they are granted certain rights to use The Coffee Club brand, intellectual property and systems. There are number of store variations, from counter service kiosks to fully licensed, table service restaurants serving chef prepared meals. Since its inception in Brisbane in 1989, The Coffee Club Group has experienced significant expansion, particularly in recent years, and plans for this trend to continue. The following case explores the Human Resource Management (HRM) strategy adopted by The Coffee Club Group as it moves between stages of the organisational life cycle. This case also highlights the complexities faced by franchise organisations in developing and implementing Human Resource (HR) systems, which are not as easily explained by classical management theory.

Business overview

The Corporate (Head) Support Office for The Coffee Club Group is based in Brisbane, and different entities within the group represent the master franchisor, franchisor, licensor, developer and/or owner of The Coffee Club brand, system and operations. The Corporate Office maintains a number of functions, including marketing, finance, operations and site development, and exists to support the master franchisor and/or franchisees (the business unit owner-managers) and employees of a small number of corporate-run stores within Australia. The Coffee Club Group has long considered itself to be a young, small, family-style business; however, recent expansion has forced the company to reconsider this image. Already employing over 6000 staff via The Coffee Club Group, its licensees and franchisees, The Coffee Club Group plans to move into markets as diverse as China, Hong Kong, New Caledonia and the United Arab Emirates in the near future. The organisation is shifting into a new stage of the business life cycle, which is often described as comprising four stages: start-up, growth, maturity and decline (Sisson & Storey 2000). The Coffee Club Group has recently transitioned from the start-up stage to a phase of growth that has seen corresponding changes in the business and HR strategies.

Management literature suggests that each stage in the business life cycle is associated with a corresponding approach to HRM. During the early stages of business growth, small start-up organisations are far less likely to have an HR department, employ specialists or have a dedicated HR strategy compared to large organisations (Edwards & Ram 2009; Forth, Bewley, & Bryson 2006). Such firms are also typified by a high level of informality and an ad hoc approach to HR activities, including recruitment, selection, career advancement and training (Cardon & Stevens 2004; Dundon & Wilkinson 2009). During the start-up phase, HRM at The Coffee Club Group exhibited the typical characteristics attributed to businesses in this stage. The company did not operate an HR department, and HR support provided to its Australian franchisees was ad hoc and minimal. As they grew in size, a need arose for someone to manage the initial and ongoing franchisee training more formally – at least in respect to its Australian franchise operation. In 2007, the Corporate Office recruited a Learning and Development (L&D) Manager, with an established HR background in non-franchised organisations. The L&D Manager recognised an opportunity to provide a higher level of support to the Australian franchisees in the broader area of HRM, while raising general matters of consideration for its master franchisees.

> *I came into this organisation with a corporate background, including a number of years in the most risk adverse industry you can get – insurance! Because my experience was providing information and advice to line managers, when I came here I saw a gap and corresponding potential risk - we're not providing information nor supporting our franchisees in this area. My philosophy, stemming from an L&D background, is that 'people can only do what they know'. If our franchisees don't know, they can't act accordingly. I could see a possible risk to The Coffee Club brand. The more I think about it retrospectively, the more I realise it's my corporate background that has influenced my actions. Having not come from the franchising sector, I had no preconceived ideas nor paradigms about what the franchisor should or should not be doing.*

The Coffee Club is a brand which employs thousands of full and part-time employees and is in a phase of rapid growth. Characteristically, organisations of this size and life cycle stage would have established an HR department earlier, but because of the franchise model, such infrastructure is frequently absent. In some franchise organisations, franchisees are directed to consult an external agency or association at their own expense for support in employment related matters. Although the franchise Corporate Office generally provides support in operational aspects of store management, when it comes to advising franchisees on issues such as recruitment, performance management or industrial relations (IR) there is much variation in the support provided between franchise firms. When the L&D Manager at The Coffee Club convinced the CEO that the Australian franchise would benefit from providing Corporate Office funded HR support to franchisees, there were two key issues that had to be considered before a strategy could be formulated: the risks of liability and brand damage.

The risk of Corporate Office liability

During this time, Australia was experiencing a prolonged period of labour market reform, which had seen significant changes to employment conditions. In the 2007 federal election, the Australian Labour Party came into power and the existing legislation governing IR (the *Workplace Relations Act* 1996 and subsequent amendment) was soon repealed. As the government began designing a new workplace relations system (that would later be governed by the *Fair Work Act* 2009) it appeared that the IR environment in Australia was going to become even more complex and difficult for franchisees to interpret. The Coffee Club Group realised that they would need to consider providing a high level of support in all areas of people management, including IR. The L&D Manager came from a strong HR background but was less comfortable advising franchisees in complex employment matters such as unfair dismissal claims or determining the correct Awards[1]. Any advice given could thus potentially place the Corporate Office at risk of liability for providing misinformation. For example, if the L&D Manager advised franchisees to use an Award that turned out to be incorrect, staff could be underpaid, and the Corporate Office – rather than the franchisee – may be legally responsible. So the first problem faced by The Coffee Club Group was how to avoid the risk of liability posed by providing advice to franchisees.

The risk of franchisees damaging the brand

The risk of liability is a sufficient deterrent for many franchisors to refrain from providing advice to franchisees on employment relations issues. As mentioned earlier, many franchise firms choose to negate this risk by directing franchisees to seek their own advice from external agencies. However, if the franchisor does not support franchisees, they face another risk – the risk of franchisees damaging the brand through non-compliance with ER laws. Franchisees may become involved

---

[1] Legal instruments that determine minimum wages and conditions in an industry.

in misconduct relating to the way they manage employment due to a poor understanding of their responsibilities. This could range from inconsistent staff training to more serious offences such discrimination or unlawful termination. The Coffee Club Group was aware of a number of other Australian operated franchise groups that had recently received negative media attention in relation to handling employment issues. The organisation found itself in a no-win situation – if they provided support they risked liability; if they did not provide support they risked damage to the brand. Eventually, it was agreed that protection of the brand was paramount, and that all steps would be taken to minimise the risk of liability.

Determining the best approach to HRM

A number of changes took place to establish an HR support service at The Coffee Club Group. The L&D Manager's role was renamed 'People Manager' in recognition of its broadening beyond the scope of training only. The manager recruited a 'People Advisor' who specialised in IR and could provide advice on the technical issues which posed the greatest challenge to the company. Work began on establishing core policies, procedures and support systems to guide franchisees in HRM. However, this action was only taken with respect to the Australian franchisees, with some assistance and direction given to master franchisees who would take on a more proactive role with their franchisees overseas.

The small team of two took steps to protect the franchisor from liability. Legal notices, including disclaimers, were included in all materials provided to franchisees, and included in any presentations and emails sent out by these people. This reconfirmed amongst other points that information provided by the team was of a general nature and that franchisees should seek specialist advice. Notes of all verbal conversations with franchisees and corporate office staff were documented. Written communications and policies were regularly passed through the legal department (internal and/or external for further added protection) to ensure the company was not putting themselves at risk – or at least reducing the risk as much as possible. Even the basic methods of communicating and phrasing of advice had to be considered, as the People Advisor explained:

> You have to be so careful with what you tell franchisees. I structure all of my emails as employer-employee… So I say, 'if the employer has a situation like this then the employer must do this'. I'm not telling them what they should be doing… They take that information away and think – is that my situation? Should I do that? So I'm not giving specific advice. I am very, very careful.

Despite all of these precautions, senior management was still concerned about providing advice to franchisees in very complex employment matters. In 2009, with the upcoming introduction of a new workplace relations system (Fair Work), the team wanted to run some information sessions to assist franchisees in understanding their new responsibilities. However, senior management was hesitant to support the move, as the People Manager explained:

The organisation at that time was not supportive of the workshops... it was an area in which it had not operated in before and it was an area other franchisors were not addressing in any form. So we actually put together a program which we ran as a trial. I knew that after we had run the first few workshops, we would be able to demonstrate their value to franchisees and the brand. After the first two workshops, positive feedback started to come in – much of it going straight to our directors. They were receiving feedback from franchisees like, 'we went to the workshop and it was great to see that The Coffee Club is being proactive and trying to help our business'. Consequently, our senior management are now supportive of our initiatives and the value it adds to our franchisees and our brand. A recent Franchisee Survey conducted by Franchise Relationship Institute showed that this ER support and service is highly valued by franchisees. We now see our strategy as a point of difference in the market, helping us to achieve our vision of being a global leader in retail food, coffee and franchising.

The chosen strategy for support at The Coffee Club Group

Following the positive feedback from the initial information seminars, managers at The Coffee Club Group felt confident in expanding the HR advisory service provided to its Australian franchisees. The team began developing a formal HR strategy to guide the development of new systems of support. An overview of the support the company offers to franchisees in key areas of HRM is provided below.

Franchisee induction

The induction program consists of one week of classroom-based theory and four weeks of in-store training. Of the five days of formal training, around one full day is focussed on learning about people management. This includes sessions on OH&S, Equal Opportunity Employment and responsibilities around the payment of superannuation.

Ongoing skill development

After the induction program, ongoing workshops and information sessions are held on an ad hoc basis. However, the team are developing a more formalised approach to franchisee training. A franchisee leadership program will soon be rolled out and there are plans for a workshop catering to franchisees who own multiple stores. Such training is also provided to the Business Development Managers (company employees who act as management coaches to franchisees) in order to build their capacity in supporting and advising franchisees.

Recruitment and training of store employees

The company offers a full recruitment and selection service to Australian franchisees opening a new store. For ongoing recruitment support, franchise consultants (employed by the company) who visit franchisees regularly are able to offer certain guidance. To assist franchisees with the induction and training of new employees, the team have produced a comprehensive staff manual covering all aspects of working for the company. At the time of writing, the team were working on the development of an online training platform, where employees will be able to complete induction modules prior to even starting their first shift.

Workplace relations

The company provides its Australian franchisees with an overview of basic employment conditions in their induction, and runs ongoing workshops to teach franchisees about their responsibilities. Although this area is most complex and open to legal risk, the support mechanisms relating to IR are quite developed. The company prefer to provide the franchisees with the tools they need to manage IR themselves, but occasionally where an issue occurs that poses a threat to the brand, the People Manager or Advisor may step in to defuse the issue. As summarised by the People Manager:

> In the majority of cases we leave it up to the franchisee to address specific issues and take the appropriate action. However, there are a few occasions when we do get actively involved in a situation. This might take the form of a facilitated discussion between a franchisee and an employee, making them both aware of their respective obligations.

Summary

The Coffee Club Group franchise has evolved in the business life cycle from start up to growth and their HR strategy and systems have progressed alongside. The developments described in this case fit neatly with the theory on business life cycles and HRM; however it is clear that other factors have also influenced this change. Ultimately, any analysis of HRM needs to take other theoretical models and contextual factors into account, such as the influence of senior management philosophy and internal politics, or the impact of resource constraints and the competitive strategy of the firm.

In the case of franchise organisations such as The Coffee Club Group, there are additional factors to be considered prior to determining the appropriate HR strategy. Franchisors should be aware that their chosen advisory approach may expose them to risks relating to potential liability and damage to the brand. The Coffee Club Group provides an example of how these risks can be effectively managed while providing a high level of support that benefits both the franchisor and franchisees.

Discussion questions

1) Referring to theory on the relationship between HR strategy and the business life cycle, describe how a firm's approach to HRM may change in the stages of maturity and decline.

2) In regard to Porter's (1985) strategies for competitive advantage, The Coffee Club could be classified as pursuing a 'quality enhancement strategy'. How might this competitive strategy influence the HR approach of the firm?

3) If The Coffee Club were pursuing a 'cost reduction strategy', how might the HR approach be different?

Further reading

Cardon, M, & Stevens, CE 2004, 'Managing human resources in small organizations: What do we know?', *Human Resource Management Review*, 14(3): 295-323.

Dundon, T & Wilkinson, A 200, 'HRM in small and medium sized enterprises', in G Wood, & D Collings (Eds.), *Human Resource Management: A Critical Introduction*, London: Routledge.

Edwards, P & Ram, M 2009, 'HRM in Small Firms: Respecting and Regulating Informality', in A Wilkinson, N Bacon, T Redman, & S Snell (Eds.), *The Sage Handbook of Human Resource Management*, 524-540, London: Sage Publications.

Forth, J, Bewley, H & Bryson, A 2006, *Small and Medium Sized Enterprises: Findings from the 2004 Workplace Employment Relations Survey*, London: Routledge.

Marchington, M & Wilkinson, A (Eds.) 2008, *Human Resource Management at Work*, London: Chartered Institute of Personnel and Development.

Porter, M 1985, *Competitive Advantage*, New York: Free Press.

Sisson, K & Storey, J 2000, *The Realities of Human Resource Management*, Milton Keynes: Open University Press.

Chapter 5

Drivers of technology adoption within health care supply chain networks

VIKRAM BHAKOO

Background and context of the study

This case study is set within the Australian pharmaceutical hospital supply chain. Figure 5.1 provides a simplified version of the structure of the supply chain and the key business entities participating in the chain. The scope of the supply chain begins with the pharmaceutical manufacturers (designated as 'manufacturers' in Figure 5.1) and ends when the products reach the pharmacy or materials management department (MMD) within public hospitals (designated as 'hospitals: pharmacy and MMD' in Figure 5.1). The manufacturers could be (i) large multinational organisations involved in research and development and producing branded products, (ii) local manufacturers producing generic medication suitable for sale over the counter, or (iii) Biotechnology or drug discovery companies that are start-ups with minimal manufacturing capability.

The Australian pharmaceutical industry is highly regulated. Figure 5.1 therefore includes 'government regulatory agencies' – such as the Therapeutic Goods Administration (TGA), Health Purchasing Victoria (HPV) and other organisations including the National e-health Transition Authority (NEHTA). The TGA carries out a range of assessment and monitoring activities to ensure that manufacturing practices for therapeutic goods such as medicines and medical devices are of an acceptable standard. State contracting bodies such as HPV play a significant role in developing policies, standards and regulations that affect all entities in the supply chain. Thus, policies, procedures and standards developed by the TGA and other regulatory agencies such as HPV impact manufacturing and procurement practices in the supply chain. These agencies are also instrumental in building relationships and establishing partnerships with product manufacturers, suppliers and clinicians. The technology providers play a significant role in administering bar coding standards and providing the necessary software infrastructure to entities such as manufacturers, wholesalers/distributors and hospitals in the supply chain. Prominent amongst these organisations is GS1, a not-for-profit organisation responsible for administering bar codes and facilitating electronic messaging based on internationally accepted standards referred to as the GS1 system. Organisations such as GS1 play a crucial role by influencing regulatory and technology standards within the pharmaceutical sphere. The role of the 'third-party logistics providers' (at the bottom of Figure 5.1) is to distribute the products from the manufacturers to the wholesalers/distributors or from the wholesalers/distributors to the hospital pharmacy, depending on the supply chain of the individual organisation.

Most public hospitals in Australia have two different departments that handle procurement: a Pharmacy department and an MMD. Pharmacy departments usually carry pharmaceutical products, drugs, intravenous fluids etc., whereas the MMD handles medical consumables, furniture, stationery etc. The delivery of the products to the end patient either in wards or emergency theatres is conducted through either the pharmacy or the MMD. The focus of the current study is not the end patient; rather it is to study the drivers for the adoption of e-business technologies across three key business entities (pharmaceutical manufacturers, wholesalers/distributors and hospitals). Each of these entities in the current case had implemented an e-business solution to facilitate information exchange with their trading partners. These e-business solutions could range from bar coding, electronic data interchange and internet, to enterprise resource planning systems or radio frequency identification technology. Pseudonyms have been used for each of the following three organisations representing different trading partners in the supply chain.

Figure 5.1 Structure of the Australian Health Care supply chain

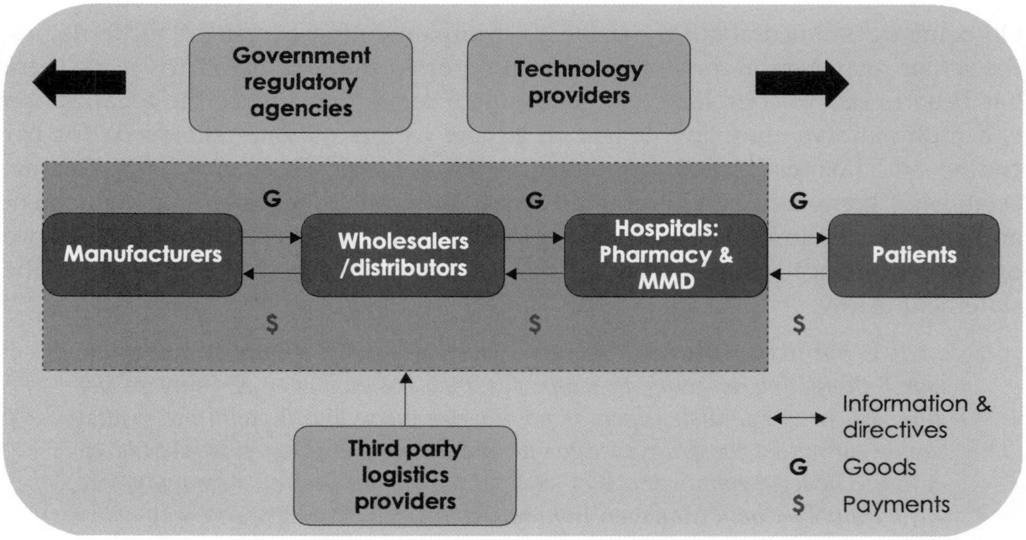

Bonton Group

Bonton Group is an Australian-based pharmaceutical organisation that focuses on the development, manufacture, sale and distribution of drugs used by oncologists. Bonton Group employs 1600 employees worldwide and distributes products to over 65 countries across the world. It is also listed on the Australian Stock Exchange. The organisation manufactures over 1200 stock keeping units (SKUs), and these products vary from a very heavy focus on chemotherapy through to antibiotics and pain killers. Recently, the organisation has also expanded from its origins in generic chemotherapy medicines to other related therapeutic drugs used by oncologists in the treatment of cancer such as antibiotics and pain management. Bonton Group reported gross sales of $687 million in the financial year 2008–2009. Although it is an Australian-based company, 70 per cent of its sales revenue in 2005 was derived from the northern hemisphere.

The supply-chain manager highlighted that the organisation was in the process of implementing a supply-chain management system (Oracle) with the aim of streamlining its supply chain. The focus of this implementation seemed to be primarily driven by the objective to integrate the upstream segment of its supply chain. Due to the inherent complexity in manufacturing Oncology products, this organisation has a vertically integrated supply chain for some of its products, but for others, the Bonton Group also has huge farmlands in the USA to cultivate specific plants and trees. After the completion of the manufacturing process (in Australia), a third party logistics provider (3PL) is used, with the choice of provider dependent on the required method of shipment either by air, rail or road transport. The most effective method for transportation for overseas destinations is through Fed Ex whereas a local 3PL company is employed to supply the products to the distributor who further delivered to the end customer – the hospital.

On being questioned about the drivers for implementing e-business technologies, the senior managers in the Bonton Group reported that the major driver for them has been to secure compliance to government regulations. Since the organisation is a multinational company, it had to adhere to international standards for bar coding and financial accounting such as the *Sarbanes–Oxley Act* 2002. This act establishes compliance requirements across different functions for management and public accounting firms operating in the USA. The intensity and importance of the compliance pressures within the pharmaceutical sector is evident in the statement below:

> … *It is not like in the retail sector – if you got the fax number wrong the worst thing that is going to happen is that the customer is going to get annoyed. In our industry there is no other recourse and it could prove fatal so you cannot let the drug 'just go out into the market place' it is just not an option. The legal ramifications of such an action can destroy a company like ours. (Supply-Chain Manager, Bonton Group)*

Besides the potent issue surrounding regulation, the other issues stimulating the adoption of e-business technologies was the desire to have a faster cash flow and hence a higher working capital, which is so vital for this sector. This was essentially because for most of the drugs produced by the organisation, the raw material costs constitute around 65% of pharmaceutical drug costs, and since these inputs are generally imported, the pharmaceutical manufacturers were interested in a faster inventory turnaround.

The other salient issue that surfaced in the course of the discussions was that several key drugs launched by the Bonton Group a few years back were coming to an end through their patent protection tenure. Once a drug was not protected through patents, the organisation would cease to make the windfall gain on these drugs and would have to compete with generics that would enter the market place. This was putting tremendous pressure on senior management who were seeking alternative means of achieving savings through their supply chain. This issue with patent expiry was also causing complications with its relationship with the wholesalers/distributors in the supply chain. This was essentially because when a newly launched drug enters the market and is protected by patents, the marketing representatives sell the benefits of the drug to the physicians since they are decision makers for the patient prescriptions. The marketing representatives do not, however, keep the wholesaler/distributor in the loop while they 'encourage' the physicians to make the switch. This leads to a build of obsolete inventory in the supply chain particularly with the wholesaler/distributor.

On the other hand, the Bonton Group was achieving a competitive edge by being extremely responsive to the needs and requirements of the hospitals. The decision to link its e-business systems with the health care provider comes with this objective as is evidenced in the statement below:

> If the healthcare provider wasn't asking for it, we wouldn't even be looking at it. Absolutely, the push is 100% driven from the health care provider (Supply-Chain Manager, Bonton Group)

Amongst the other issues discussed, the senior IT Manager also highlighted a key concern that had confronted the Bonton Group two years ago: unsatisfactory stock recall times. An effective technology implementation would facilitate a faster response to stock recall. The senior IT Manager was also interested in implementing e-business solutions that interfaced directly with the hospitals and their upstream suppliers and was inclined towards using radio frequency identification technology (RFID) within the internal operations. The application of this technology could then be extended within an SCM context.

Snapx Inc.

Snapx Inc. is one of Australia's largest wholesaler/distributors supplying pharmaceutical and other product lines to public and private hospitals and retail pharmacies. This organisation has a turnover of A$3.4 billion, around 6000 employees, and deals with 17,000 SKUs. The SKUs are fairly diverse, including pharmaceuticals, surgical instruments and other consumable products used in health care such as gloves and syringes. There has been a series of mergers and acquisitions in the Australian sector within this space, with each organisation operating in the wholesaler/distributor segment seeking alternative paths to differentiate their value offering. The merger and acquisition activity was driven primarily by the fact that distribution margins were declining. In terms of its IT capability, Snapx Inc. had implemented an ERP (Enterprise Resource Planning) system internally and was using a web-based EDI (Electronic Data Interchange) system to interface with the hospitals. The systems being developed were also being given the necessary functionality to interface with the manufacturers.

In providing a historical snapshot, the CIO (Chief Information Officer) explained that the Australian Defence Force (ADF) was the catalyst in the initiation of using technology standards in the supply chain due to a contract condition that a supplier to the ADF had to comply with GS1 messaging standards. Since this entity was strategically positioned within the supply chain, performing the vital function of delivering the products to the end customer (hospital), the drive for the adoption of technology stemmed from the external environment. This statement sums up the sentiment of the wholesaler/distributor segment:

> The pressure (for e-business adoption) is a lot from the customer side (hospital), the supplier side and the competitor side what they are doing and what we need to do. We also have to conform to industry norms and the technology providers, government regulatory agencies and because we are supplying to retail pharmacies we are being pushed from all sides. (Customer Relationship Manager, Snapx Inc.)

Although the drive seemed to be coming from all trading partners in the supply chain, the intensity of the pressures were quite intense from the customer end (hospitals) and milder from their suppliers (manufacturers).

Drilling down into the internal operational drivers, the Operations Manager complained that there was a colossal wastage of time in invoice matching. He explained that

> Last month, there was a minor error of $2 in an invoice, which caused payments over $20,000 to be blocked. Therefore it becomes really critical to streamline the procurement function for our perspective. Further, since our survival in the business depends on customer service, implementation of technology that is responsive to our customers' needs and enables following up on back orders – and with minimal problems with stock-outs – would mean that they are able to decrease the number of operators in the call centres as well.

These seem to be the key issues from his perspective.

Interviews with the CIO also highlighted that there were a series of strategic initiatives that the organisation was embarking upon where e-business technologies would play a crucial role. There was an outsourcing arrangement with a small specialist hospital in Metropolitan Melbourne where Snapx Inc.

would be responsible for the materials management department (MMD). The responsibilities would include setting the procurement contract and handling the appropriate negotiations, seeking regulatory compliance and reporting to the executive management in the hospital. These services were being provided for a contract fee and Snapx Inc. was looking at implementing this arrangement at other hospitals. A key factor for the success of the arrangement was that the information systems used at the MMD at the hospital connected in real time with the wholesaler/distributor. Further interviews with the senior management revealed that there was a tension in the relationship that Snapx had with the manufacturers upstream in the supply chain, and the manufacturers were not interested in sharing forecast and capacity planning downstream in the supply chain. This is something that Snapx identified as a bottleneck within its supply chain.

Melbourne Metropolitan Hospital

Melbourne Metropolitan Hospital is the largest public hospital within the network of hospitals providing health care services to east and outer east areas of metropolitan Melbourne. It provides a range of acute, sub-acute, mental health and community health services for over 50 sites. Supporting the health care needs of a geographical catchment covering approximately 2,800 square kilometres, Melbourne Metropolitan Hospital (the largest hospital in the network) and its satellite hospitals provide inpatient services to over 100,000 patients and ambulatory services to close to 600,000 patients/clients annually. The entire network's budget is approximately $450 million and 4,200 full-time employees are on the hospital network's payroll. The hospital also provides a complex range of high-level clinical services to 45,000 in-patients annually – which were feasible through 365 in-patient beds, six operating theatres and an emergency department with 40,000 emergency presentations per annum. Since the hospital had a separate pharmacy and MMD, interviews were conducted with senior managers in both these departments as well as the senior manager responsible for IT applications. The interviews highlighted that the MMD was more progressive, compared to its pharmacy counterparts, in the application of IT and both the departments operated in silos without any information sharing or a consistent approach towards the implementation of IT.

A key problem being faced with the pharmacy department was stock-outs of important drugs. Key senior personnel acknowledged that the hospital was a laggard within the sphere of IT applications within the supply chain. They were looking for a progressive hospital with a view to using it to accelerate e-business adoption within their organisations, and/or looking to reap the benefits from the experience of the retail sector. The comment below testifies to this fact:

> The other path that interests me is how can we learn from and adapt out of the supermarket chains and others. Well Safeway (a large supermarket chain) has got pretty good relationships with their suppliers and we know they are the most successful company in its field, so how can we learn from perhaps those models and they've done the research. The have approached them and

since we are not competing in the same space they are willing to share their experiences with us and maybe if we get it right then we might even leap frog the grocery supply chain (Deputy Director Pharmacy, Melbourne Metropolitan Hospital)

In terms of the internal drivers for e-business adoption, a focus on error reduction seemed to be a consistent theme with the interviewees in the hospital. A salient concern specifically for pharmacy departments within the hospitals was improving patient safety. The comment below appropriately captures the spirit of the hospital for undertaking error reduction:

Pharmacy is different to a retailing environment or to a supply type environment. We don't just facilitate the movement of goods from one place through ourselves to another place. We act as gatekeepers to a large degree. We influence the demand kind of things as well as the supply and we take very seriously our safety responsibility. We have to assess everything that passes through us to see that it actually should end up in the interests of the patient; sort of foremost in our mind is the issue of patient safety. (Director Pharmacy, Melbourne Metropolitan Hospital)

The other concern that dominated the pharmacy departments was the issue of inventory management. Several reasons motivated the pharmacy departments in the hospitals to focus on inventory management. First, shrinking floor space for pharmacies in hospitals due to the increase in the number of SKUs, and escalating prices of pharmaceutical products, was exerting considerable pressure on the finite budgets of pharmacy departments. Further, application of inventory management technologies facilitated maintenance of accurate usage patterns, calculation of stock turns and adoption of progressive stock rotation practices. The importance of e-business technologies for inventory management purposes was explained in the following quote by the Deputy Director of Pharmacy at the Hospital.

...one of the big issues is cost within health. Now, one way that we can reduce costs within pharmaceuticals is by having a small inventory, which means if we have a smaller inventory, we have to turn the stock over more often, which means we have to place more orders. Now, one of the problems with placing more orders is the increased amount of invoicing. There is more invoicing, with more order placements. There are bits of paper floating around, but with the introduction of e-commerce with the development of paperless systems using things like GTIN and the bar-codes, we should be able to place more orders more frequently for smaller amounts of stock. Subsequently we'll have smaller amounts of stock on the shelf, and therefore be able to keep the amount of money tied up in inventory by the Hospital – be able to reduce that – and that is one of the demands being placed on us from the executive of the hospital to reduce our inventory as much as possible. So, e-commerce will provide us with a way of improving our inventory management. (Deputy Director Pharmacy, Melbourne Metropolitan Hospital)

Since the public hospitals were not competitive in nature, they were seeking to employ IT so that they could share information regarding medication usage and create a virtual database of pharmaceutical products. The database could be used in the case of an emergency, where critical drugs could be transferred between public hospitals, and doing so would also decrease the safety stock of key drugs maintained by each hospital. As explained by the IT manager, this kind of arrangement was possible because the public hospitals were non-competitive in nature. Despite this it was important to pilot this solution with the other sites of the hospitals before implementing it across all other public hospitals in Victoria.

Discussion questions

1) How is the health care supply chain more complex compared to typical retail and manufacturing supply chains?

2) What are the key motivational factors for implementing technology for each trading partner in the supply chain?

3) What is the implication of having coercive, normative and mimetic pressures in the supply chain?

4) What recommendations do you have for the entire supply chain for the effective implementation of technology?

Chapter 6

Rigidity as a cause and effect in SME business failure

Olav Muurlink

Introduction

Wyoming Production Company was a manufacturing firm in a very traditional mould. A family firm established in Brisbane, Australia, in the 1950s, it engaged in producing – largely by non-automated processes – specialist tools for the shipping industry. These tools, heavy-duty metal paint buckets and sheepskin paint rollers built on heavy wooden cores mounted in metal frames, were sold direct to shipping lines and ship chandlers. The Grange family purchased the business in the 1970s, at which stage Wyoming was still, literally, a garage-based operation. The new manager, Rhett Grange, was a professional engineer with minimal business experience, but he was supported by an enthusiastic spouse and three young children. The company moved to a much larger garage, with a dedicated office. After school, the children would help in manufacturing and assembling the paint rollers for piecework rates, to supplement their pocket money.

This is an outline of the last days of Wyoming, which formally ended with the purchase of the business by the Oldfields Holdings Limited, an Australian public company, itself listed on the ASX since 1960. Oldfields would, in the months following, mothball the brand, the plant and equipment, and largely discontinue producing the products for which Wyoming had been well known in specialist painting circles for close to 50 years. This story is in many senses the story of the author's own business history. Key elements of the story have been changed to protect identities, by incorporating elements of other businesses the author was involved with, either as a consultant or director, in the period 1980–2009.

Threat rigidity and crisis response

Threat rigidity theory suggests that in times of crisis, we often react non-creatively, focusing on the immediate tasks at hand and familiar ways of doing things (Chapman, Lahav *et al.* 2009; Staw, Sandelands *et al.* 1981). Threat rigidity theory has its roots in the work of Canadian psychiatrist J.A. Easterbrook in the 1950s (Easterbrook 1959). Easterbrook's work suggests there is a 'U-shaped' relationship between threat and cognitive processing (Anderson & Revelle 1982), also known as the Yerkes Dodson law. In other words, at low levels of stress, people tend to be insufficiently motivated to respond optimally, with their responses improving as stress increases, to the point where stress begins to hamper response. Threat rigidity clocks in at the high end of the inverted U curve. The Yerkes Dodson law has wide application, a recent study for example replicating the effect with rats, using temperature as a stressor (Salehi, Cordero *et al.* 2010).

Threat rigidity responses are in a sense a negative form of what has been identified as one of the keys to success for small and medium sized industries (SMEs) –'sticking to the knitting'. For example, Oke, Burke and Myers (2007) found, in a study of British SMES, that successful SMEs were more likely to focus on incremental innovation than bold, broad innovation. These findings ran counter to previous theory, which suggested that smaller firms were incubators of innovation. Barker and Barr (2002) directly examined threat rigidity relationships in SMEs faced with shifting market conditions, and found that smaller firms were indeed more prone to 'freezing' in a crisis. In summary, it seems that some conservatism –'sticking to the knitting' – is a good thing in managing SMEs, but at times of crisis, rigidity in response can be a counterproductive for management.

The crisis

To return to Wyoming Production Company, in 1978 the business entered a significant transition period, and in the following decade changes were implemented that saw the company's main brand, Wyper, become nationally recognised in a market outside its original core. The company moved to a location in rural Queensland. It introduced key innovations in both product and process. Notably, instead of making sheepskin paint rollers by sewing inside-out sleeves of sheepskin, and then inverting these sleeves, which were in turn pulled over the paint roller cores and glued, sheepskin was cut into strips, and rolled onto pre-glued pipes. The process expedited the manufacture of sheepskin paint rollers, was conducive to automation, and allowed the creation of a huge range of new products, including corrugated rollers (for roofs), pipe rollers (for painting curved surfaces such as pipes) and micro and macro rollers of varying diameters. The company also expanded into the domestic painting market, ceased selling direct to painters, and instead operated its own warehouse supplying trade retailers such as Bristol, Taubmans and Dulux Trade Centres. It won a series of government grants that enabled it to begin export of its products to Scandinavia and move to a yet larger location on the Warwick Crown Industrial Estate.

Expanding its horizon beyond family members, the company began to recruit staff for the factory floor and administrative positions. However, the company continued its policy, unusual for a nationally-distributed product, of having no agents and no sales people. Instead, the product relied on word of mouth high production standards and innovation to gain a foothold in new stores.

The company grew rapidly through the 90s, but the seeds of its destruction were being sewn. It employed an accountant who had impressive European qualifications as a tax accountant and auditor. This recent immigrant, Kees Vaneck, became a trusted confidant of the managing director, and was given a loosely-defined roving role in terms of office administration. A second key player was a fitter and turner, Ivor Javier, who developed into a leading hand on the factory floor.

The macro-economic environment was changing. Formerly protected by substantial tariffs, the footwear and clothing industry in Australia, which included a large domestic manufacturing industry centred around sheepskin seat covers, was undergoing reform driven by the Hawke Labor government. A program of dramatic tariff reductions in this labour-intensive industry were announced under the 1987 Textile, Clothing and Footwear (TCF) Industry Plan, an element of a more general trade liberalisation policy. The 1991 Industry Statement set out a tariff phase-out calendar, which envisaged a maximum tariff rate on TCF items of 25 per cent by the year 2000. Wyoming management did not react by diversifying its product line, instead focusing on improving efficiency in the factory, with Javier introducing time and motion studies as part of the company's attempt to expand into a highly competitive export market in the US. Unlike the company that would eventually absorb its operations, Oldfields, Wyoming also made no moves to set up an off-shore plant to handle labour-intensive aspects of its production. It only began moves to explore offshore manufacturing in Malaysia in 2004. At this stage, the company had less than two years left to live.

On the sales front, Wyoming was facing a consolidation in its customer base. Taubmans and Bristol (two of its main customers) merged, and Dulux similarly entered a period of acquisitions that shored-up its position as market leader. Close to 70 per cent of Wyoming's customer list was suddenly consolidated into just two entities. The Taubmans-Bristol conglomerate gave Wyoming preferred supplier status for its sheepskin rollers, a move not matched by Dulux, and repeatedly ran national catalogue promotions. A larger and larger percentage of its sales became concentrated on a single line item. These promotions were backed by supplier rebates to the Taubmans-Bristol head office that further bit into tight margins. Furthermore, crucially, Bristol had managed to secure a contract with Wyoming that required Wyoming to supply Bristol-branded (not Wyoming-branded) paint rollers to its stores. Wyoming management became aware that one of its new competitors was an importer of Chinese-manufactured sheepskin rollers. The Chinese product was made using Australian sheepskin, with significantly lower quality control, and in order to facilitate the import of container quantities of product, the competitor offered a much smaller product range. The Chinese product offered solely a price advantage, and that advantage was not sufficient to dislodge Wyoming's relationship with the major chains. Nevertheless, Wyoming was offering prices to Taubmans-Bristol and Dulux that, after rebates, were no higher than their sale price 15 years before. Margins were under pressure. Management was under pressure. Unbeknownst to the major players, the managing director, Mr Grange, had contracted bowel cancer. The symptoms started to emerge during a trip to Malaysia to explore overseas manufacturing options in 2005.

In an attempt to cut one of its most significant input costs, the Grange family had also begun to source their own sheep skins from abattoirs across Queensland for processing either in Australian tanneries on a contract basis, or at Turkish and Chinese tanneries. The process achieved its goal in delivering cheaper, and in many cases better quality skins, but it exposed the company to currency risk, significant financial costs (due to long lead times between the purchase of raw salted skins and the delivery of tanned skins to the factory floor), and risks associated with an overwhelmingly corrupt industry.

The end game

The elements were now all in place. Suddenly, in July 2005, a sequence of events that ultimately determined the fate of Wyoming commenced in rapid succession. Javier left the company, and shortly after, established a small manufacturing plant selling sheepskin paint rollers direct to painters. In the subsequent stocktake, large discrepancies between expected and actual values emerged. Upon being questioned, factory floor staff revealed that they had seen Javier, who had a factory key, parked with his utility at the rear of the factory on weekends. Police were called, and following investigations, arrested Javier in 2006 – but a stock shortfall of some $150,000 was not recovered.

Bristol-Taubmans' tendering process in 2005 was more protracted than normal, and much of the costing and pitching process was delegated to the youngest son of Mr Grange, Bryce. It took place in Sydney in front of a panel, the members of which appeared to be signally unimpressed with the presentation. By November, the decision was revealed. Wyoming had been supplanted as supplier of Bristol-home branded product to the national network of Bristol-Taubmans stores. Instead, Chinese rollers using identical Bristol-branded packaging were smoothly introduced in to the stores in January 2005. In one fell swoop, Wyoming appeared to have lost close to 40 per cent of its sales. While some stores continued to buy Wyoming rollers under-the-counter, turnover fell immediately and dramatically.

Wyoming was also badly damaged by two events on the supply side. Relations with a Turkish tannery had begun to deteriorate when a full container of supposedly paint-roller-quality skins arrived at the factory floor. The container was opened, to reveal small, discoloured, misshaped and knife-damaged skins that were unusable for production. The company was forced to buy skins on the costly Australian spot market to meet commitments. Coincidentally, one of the company's arm's length skin agents, who bought skins from Wyoming that were unsuitable for paint roller production, presented a cheque for $60,000 that was subsequently dishonoured. He disappeared, with police unable to subsequently locate him.

On Boxing Day 2005, the day of the Indonesian tsunami, Mr Grange was diagnosed with cancer, and he passed away four weeks later. Immediate management of the business passed to his youngest son, for whom management of the manufacturer was of necessity a part-time pursuit, having substantial other business interests. The new manager had a stronger marketing background, but relatively little administrative experience, and he leaned heavily on Kees Vaneek, the trusted in-house accountant, for support. Cash flow management became crucial, with payments from the old Bristol-Taubmans accounts rapidly drying up and a slow-down in the economy seeing more accounts stretch beyond 90 days. Faced with the prospect of either having to find replacement customers rapidly, or retrench experienced skilled staff, the new manager took on a new account of small stores despite hearing industry whispers that this new group had a history of buying up big before defaulting on payment responsibilities. The new manager's worse fears came to pass. At first the new customer's payments were merely slow. Then they stopped altogether.

Focusing on sales in a market where sales at satisfactory margins were increasingly hard to find, the Chinese had emerged as full-blown competitors by now – and Bryce Grange was paying less attention than ever to administrative issues. As public officer for Wyoming, he was contacted in early 2006 by the Australian Tax Office (ATO) regarding late payment of the company's Quarterly Business Activity Statement (BAS) tax instalments. The company had earlier entered a repayment plan agreement with the ATO. This phone call was in fact the first solid inkling Mr Grange had that the company's cash flow was in crisis, but he was repeatedly given assurances by Mr Vaneek that 'everything's fine', and that 'we'll muddle through'. On one occasion, Mr Vaneek assured Mr Grange that, should the company face temporary cash flow problems, he would simply transfer money from his own personal cash account into the company's accounts to tide the company over. He was told by the manager on no account to do so.

The two sat together and prepared cash flow charts, with Mr Vaneek urged to give the manager as much notice of possible at the first sign that payments would have to be delayed due to cash shortages. In the end, no such warning came. A second phone call from the ATO, followed at the next instalment period by a third, meant that the company was hanging by a thread with the tax office. His confidence in Mr Vaneek damaged, but still unwilling to fire his father's trusted aide, Mr Grange urged the accountant, who was showing physical signs of severe stress, to take some of his two months accumulated holidays. This allowed Wyoming to install a temporary accountant to deal with what was gradually revealed as a highly disorganised state of finances. At first passively, and then actively, Mr Vaneek resisted taking his leave, finally agreeing to take leave, but nevertheless turning up for work the following Monday as if no such agreement had been reached. In an atmosphere of strain, the accountant was ordered home, and did not return to work after his holiday pay expired.

In the days that followed it emerged that Mr Vaneek had been withholding payments to super funds in order to make ATO payments, and had indeed used his own personal funds to supplement company funds in a desperate effort to meet the shortfall. The company entered immediate negotiations for sale with a number of parties, with Oldfields emerging as the successful bidder. Despite purchasing equipment and know-how capable of manufacturing paint rollers locally, Oldfields chose to source its 'Wyper' rollers from China. Shortly afterwards, the 50-year-old brand itself was withdrawn from the market.

Discussion questions

1) Wyoming management faced both macro-economic and micro-economic threats. Give an example from the case of each, and how management might have responded differently to the threats.

2) From the perspective of threat rigidity theory, what aspects of the response to crisis by Wyoming management were not typical?

3) Threat rigidity theory suggests that rigidity in response to a crisis is often maladaptive. What is it about crises, as opposed to the day-to-day challenges of managing a business, which requires a novel response?

4) For a company like Wyoming, what are the risks in taking a more bold approach to threats? Refer to evidence from the case study.

References

Anderson, KJ & Revelle, W 1982, 'Impulsivity, caffeine, and proofreading: A test of the Easterbrook hypothesis', *Journal of Experimental Psychology: Human Perception and Performance*, 8(4): 614-624.

Barker, VL & Barr, PS 2002, 'Linking top manager attributions to strategic reorientation in declining firms attempting turnarounds', *Journal of Business Research*, 55, 963–979.

Chapman, CN, Lahav, M & Burgess, S 2009, 'Reexamining Threat Rigidity: Implications for Design', proceedings of the 42nd Hawaii International Conference on System Sciences, IEEE Computer Society: 1-10.

Easterbrook, J 1959, 'The effect of emotion on cue utilization and the organization of behavior', *Psychological review*, 66(3): 183-201.

Oke, A, Burke, G & Myers, A 2007, 'Innovation types and performance in growing UK SMEs', *International Journal of Operations & Production Management*, 27(7), 735-753.

Staw, BM, Sandelands, LE & Sutton, JE 1981, 'Threat Rigidity Effects in Organizational Behavior: A Multilevel Analysis', *Administrative Science Quarterly*, 26(4): 501-524.

Salehi, B, Cordero, M & Sandi, C 2010, 'Learning under stress: The inverted-U-shape function revisited', *Learning & Memory*, 17(10): 522.

Part II
Corporate Innovation

Chapter 7

Dynamic capability in action at PharmaCorp

RACHEL HILLIARD

Background and context

PharmaCorp is a subsidiary of one of Japan's largest pharmaceutical companies, employing 60 people in its Dublin bulk pharmaceutical manufacturing plant. The plant makes the active ingredients for four products, supplying them for conversion to other, larger pharmaceutical companies that are licensed to sell the drugs. It is common practice for Japanese firms to licence sales of their products outside Japan to companies who have stronger brand image and marketing capability in these markets.

Because of the nature of its production, PharmaCorp is licensed by the Irish Environmental Protection Agency (EPA). PharmaCorp's integrated pollution prevention control (IPPC) licence requires, amongst other obligations, the company to maintain an environmental management system and to demonstrate continuous improvement of its environmental impact. Companies are expected to pursue environmental change through the adoption of 'cleaner technology': cleaner technology is when production process produces less waste, use fewer resources and consumes less energy. This can be achieved by changing the raw materials used to less toxic alternatives, improving the efficiency of processes and equipment, and increasing the use of recycling etc. Adopting cleaner technology requires companies to change their production technology radically and can be very challenging; companies in Ireland have struggled with the demands of IPPC licensing.

Early influences on capability formation

The plant has taken an integrated approach to environmental management from the beginning, with the design of the physical plant incorporating a high level of environmental protection. This is a reflection of the vision of the CEO who has been responsible for PharmaCorp from its conception and was given free reign in the physical plant design and management structures.

> *When I joined ... I spent four months living in Japan on my own. The mandate I had was 'look, come over, have a look at what we are doing, see what we are doing, and put together an organisation'. And what I did was in the last month really sat down and put the structures together and incorporated within that would have been the environmental aspect of the business.*

The management approach at PharmaCorp is characterised by a strong sense of ownership and responsibility for its own future. This is a reflection of Japanese practice in the management of subsidiaries.

> *In [PharmaCorp] it is not like a big American multinational, they will support you but you do it; that is the difference. Direction is ... very much left to the team that is working on it. There is a clear policy on what you do; how you do it is your responsibility.*

Environmental responsibility was integrated into the management structure of the new operation.

> *What I was able to do was to put together a management structure and incorporated within that would have been the environmental aspect of the business ... By actually incorporating it in there and putting it in each department rather than saying 'I am responsible for the environment and you will help me to do it.' We don't actually have that; every department has its own environmental side to it.*

The original organisational design aimed to diffuse environmental responsibility throughout all departments and represented an early commitment to the development of learning. Practices to support integrated responsibility and environmental learning opportunities included removing the distinction between environmental and production operators, and making sure that all operators have some experience of the environmental processes.

> *People come in here one thing, and they change completely over the years, because it is a small team and they want to learn. Even with our operators, we move them around quite a lot and some companies would give their right arm for that, in other companies the operators would say, well we want more money for doing that. Here if you tried to stop it you would have a problem on your hands.*

The plant's early and proactive involvement in environmental management has been recognised with national and international awards, including in 1990 the European Community and United Nations Award for Good Environmental Management. This led to an invitation to become part of the pilot study for the EU Eco Management and Audit Scheme (EMAS). The company was the first pharmaceutical company in Ireland and the UK to be accredited to the BS7750 environmental management standard. The company was accredited to further environmental management standards, the international standard ISO14001 and the European standard EMAS. The early recognition of their environmental management was a significant encouragement and validation of their approach:

> *A good thing happened to us, back in 1989 we won the good environmental management award, in Ireland, and … we went on the next year to win the European award, and that was a very good thing for the factory here. People knew that they were the best, and when you are the best what do you do? You try and hold onto it, and you don't hold on to draw, you hold on to excel. That has stood us in very good stead.*

Implementation of cleaner technology

The plant is rare in its use of a systematic approach not just for management of treatment and monitoring but also for planning and implementing waste reduction. The plant was able to use the involvement in the EMAS scheme, and the external expertise provided to develop a strong EMS – and most significantly a thorough understanding of the plant's environmental impacts through the development of the EMAS site profile. As part of the EMAS pilot, the company prepared a site profile that identifies and quantifies 'how does [PharmaCorp] interact with the environment'[2]. The understanding gained from the site profile has been crucial in driving the plant's program of cleaner technology projects. By identifying and prioritising impacts it has encouraged the plant to explore projects in areas outside its past experience, developing new technical skills and wider future options. The CEO identifies 'routine setting of new environmental targets and objectives with subsequent evaluation of performance' (Sheerin 1997, p. 7) as one of the core elements of the plant's EMS.

> *We would set ourselves objectives every year, the whole group would be involved in that, myself included. We would go through what we did in the last year. Unfortunately management sometimes concentrates on what is ahead and forgets to look back and see what did we do. We will have set ourselves pretty reasonable but demanding challenges for the next year … and sometimes we fail, but we record that as a deviation, that's life.*

The systematic use of the site profile to plan future work, but also to review and consolidate past achievement has encouraged PharmaCorp to explore environmental improvement in many directions, not just in the area it was traditionally strongest in, environmental technology for containment. The plant has accumulated problem-solving knowledge capital, built on routines for problem identification, information gathering and solution generation. Using this capability the plant has undertaken projects in a broad range of areas: clean technology, solvent recovery, solvent recycling, resource use reduction and material substitution. The current projects being driven by the site profile are utilities reduction projects and waste minimisation in production.

---

[2] PhamaCorp's EMAS Statement, 1997

An energy profile carried out by the Clean Technology Centre (CTC) at the Cork Institute of Technology has set the priorities for utilities reduction work. The plant has put in place cross-functional routines for developing a thorough understanding of site energy use and generating a broad range of solutions. A site Energy Group has been formed, with members from engineering, environmental management, environmental systems operators and R&D. Overall energy consumption (gas and electricity) per tonne of product was reduced by 33 per cent in one year.

Projects included:

- a boiler plant and control system

- a condensate recovery project; waste heat recovery from the incinerator

- improved efficiency of refrigeration plant.

Water meters were installed and a water mass balance calculated, in conjunction with advice from the CTC. This revealed that the site was a very high user of mains water. PharmaCorp has made changes to substitute well and rainwater for mains water use, where possible. The introduction of condensate recovery and a new cooling tower achieved a reduction in mains water use of 7.2 per cent, as well as improved energy efficiency gains. Further water reductions of 20 per cent are being pursued through a project to recycle extra cooling water through the new cooling-tower system; this project has experienced some difficulties.

Developing capability in process development

In the area of waste minimisation, in 1994 PharmaCorp undertook its first solvent elimination project, to explore the removal of very toxic solvents, toluene and methylene dichloride, from the production of nicardipine. This project is a good example of how management at PharmaCorp are prepared to undertake projects in areas outside its familiar activity and competences. Historically PharmaCorp has had limited opportunities to undertake process development projects. The company is not typically a start-up plant for the production of new products, but receives established products and technology from the parent company. The work of R&D has been confined to process optimisation (minor adjustments to process conditions) and exploration of recovery, and as the plant produces only four products, there are limited opportunities even for this type of work. The solvent elimination project involved collaboration between PharmaCorp, the parent company and the CTC in Cork. PharmaCorp carried out the lab work, and successfully demonstrated solvent elimination in the pilot plant.

PharmaCorp sees the real achievement of the solvent elimination project as being in building capability and experience. This contributes to the plant's strategic commitment to create a process development capability at PharmaCorp. The plant has a direct relationship with its commercial customers (licensees) and works hard to maximise the value and therefore profitability of these relationships to the company. Although typically PharmaCorp has not been involved in process development, the CEO took the decision that expertise in this area was important

– to maximise efficiency of production but also as part of the CEO's overall strategy for the evolution of the plant. To this end, PharmaCorp opened its new Manufacturing Technology Building. It is intended that this will increase the involvement PharmaCorp have in R&D and process development:

> That is something which we are now facing up to … where we are heading at the moment is to lift the intellectual capacity of our organisation, and that is process development.

PharmaCorp is heading into a period of expansion, with a number of new products being introduced to the plant. The new group's function will include the improvement of existing products, including environmental impacts. Process development work pursued for environmental goals, using external and corporate expertise, is cited by the CEO as having had a role in building the skills and experience within the plant that will now support a Process Development function. In the development of this facility the plant's capability for maximum learning is again expressed:

> What I have tried to do in this building is I have put a load of chemical engineers and a load of chemists in, in the belief that they can talk to one another, work together.

A waste minimisation group was formed to identify waste minimisation opportunities through process development, based on priorities identified in the site profile. The company feels that it has learning, experience and physical resources to make this initiative feasible. This is an area in which the plant will again be ahead of practice in the parent company, and PharmaCorp anticipates that this group will act as a corporate resource so that the benefits of their learning can be shared within the company. The change is driven by commercial factors, to offer a better service to commercial customers:

> It is extremely important for us at each and every opportunity, and with my own staff I emphasise that point, for us to be more efficient.

PharmaCorp's strategy is to develop the plant's importance and competitiveness by developing its relationship with its commercial customers and upgrading the quality of the service they offer:

> If you take the evolution of a plant like ours: you are kind of a local manufacturer supplier; then you become a contact point for your customers and you add value to the system; then you start developing the directed approach of supporting your customers.

Role of external help

Maximising the learning capability of the plant is central to the CEO's management strategy. Another commitment that the firm has made is to avoid the use of external consultancy.

> We try and avoid consultants …, we try and do as much as possible ourselves.

For example, the company did not use any external consultants in their preparation for ISO9000 or ISO14001 accreditation. The company draws a distinction between consultancy advice and accessing and internalising external knowledge. If they need external expertise, they ensure that it is used as an opportunity for learning within the company.

> *Where there are areas, what we do there is rather than sending out people to do these courses we would bring in the leaders, wherever they may come from, here. We will put in a bunch of maybe 10 people, people that may not have any great bearing on that but who would like to learn ... So our competency is increasing all the time.*

PharmaCorp is committed to accessing fundamental research in order to increase its environmental capability and has a policy of working with research institutes to increase knowledge of environmental technology. It is a founding member of The Clean Technology Centre at the Department of Chemical Engineering in Cork Institute of Technology. It is also a founding member of Questor, a research centre based at the School of Chemistry, The Queen's University of Belfast. PharmaCorp has worked with these and other institutes to develop understanding and solutions to particular environmental problems.

Summary

A strong sense of ownership can be seen in both commercial and environmental management decisions that, while challenging in the short term, are important for the plant's long-term development. The plant has a high awareness of its external (commercial and regulatory) environment and puts effort into planning. This has allowed it to anticipate changes such as new stringent environmental legislation. Importantly for a small company, it is then able to absorb new requirements at its own pace and according to a planned program that allows it to maximise the learning opportunities associated with new developments. This attitude is partly a reflection of the self-directed management style, and the management style of the parent company.

> *If you are working in the likes of [a US pharmaceutical multinational company] and you are going to build a new plant, well before you know where you are you will have whole team of experts out there. We don't have that. But what is has allowed us to do, we have had to work harder, we have had to build up our own expertise in many areas that people would not have been qualified or trained on. That's actually good, it has added a little bit of excitement, and the knowledge base.*

The company has a very good record of compliance. In 10 years of operation it has never received a complaint from the public. In records kept for the FDA it has recorded only one quality non-conformance. The plant has 100 per cent compliance with the emission standards in their environmental licence. A benefit and reinforcement of their environmental strategy has been the increased standing that it gives them within the corporation.

> *The Japanese would not have had a very clear view on environmental issues ... They had on certain areas but not to the extent that we have now here. And in fact a lot of them now would be copying our systems. As well as the technology coming in we are actually exporting it out... For instance we didn't use any consultation on the ISO1400, or ISO9000, we did it all in-house. We are now actually giving these data to some of our sister plants around the world. And we would be seen by the parent company as being leaders in that area.*

As well as having a commercial importance, competitiveness is important to maintain the plant's standing within the corporation and to ensure that the plant is selected to produce future products. The integrated nature of the plant's environmental capabilities is reflected in how they support and are supported by more general competitive capabilities.

> *Don't worry about the competition outside ... Worry about your own internal competition ... We are here to try and bring them [the parent company] more business, more added value business, and that is what it is all about. Why should they give us something if we are not competitive?*

PharmaCorp has a strong, integrated and broad-based array of environmental management capabilities founded on the strong dynamic capabilities for learning and planning that underpin all of the firm's activities. Common to all decisions about future activity is the plant's concern to anticipate and plan change in a way that ensures that the change can be absorbed at a pace that allows for the maximum leverage of learning and experience within the firm. These deliberate efforts to 'lift the intellectual capacity of the organisation' result in a wider array of strategic options in the future. Environmental management at PharmaCorp is not characterised by the development of any particular technical capability, but by the importance placed on integrative organisational processes for generating learning and deep understanding throughout the facility. This can be seen in the most recent plans for future expansion, and in the CEO's description of the development of environmental management at the plant.

Discussion questions

1) Dynamic capability is the capability to identify and acquire new capabilities. Dynamic capability is underpinned by 'search routines' – routinised processes within companies that are aimed at changing other processes. What are the search routines that you can identify at PharmaCorp?

2) An early contributor to capability theory, Edith Penrose (Penrose 1959) developed the concept of 'image' – she believed that the management's perception of future paths open to the company is a reflection of the plant's current capability set and past history. Do you think PharmaCorp has a perception that affects its dynamic capability?

3) What would you say are the broad categories of dynamic capability as seen at PharmaCorp?

4) How has dynamic capability in environmental management benefited PharmaCorp overall?

References:

Penrose, E 1959, *The Theory of Growth of the Firm*, Oxford: Basil Blackwell.

Sheerin, J 1997, *Successful Environmental Management*, Sligo: Enviro Éire.

Chapter 8

Innovation and public policy: Building management capability in Australian SMEs

DON SCOTT-KEMMIS AND ROY GREEN

Background

The opening-up of the Australian economy, with the progressive reduction of tariffs from the early 1970s, increased competitive pressure. Responding to this pressure, and the challenge of continuous technological and market change, requires new workforce skills and enterprise leadership competence – including the ability to formulate strategies to succeed in a more complex environment.

Despite the vital importance of continuous upgrading, many SMEs do not use the support services available from market-based service providers. There appear to be four major reasons for this 'market failure' (Scott-Kemmis *et al.* 2007):

1. Many SMEs have trouble identifying and prioritising their specific needs in a way that can easily form a clear demand for service providers.

2. Most SMEs do not know how to identify and evaluate experts, whether to trust their advice, and how to assess the costs and benefits of interaction with an expert. Typically short of cash, SMEs have to put this scarce resource at risk before they are able to assess whether the outlay has been worthwhile.

3. The senior managers of the firm may lack the knowledge required to grasp the relevance of particular areas of new knowledge.

4. Firms may lack the complementary assets that will have a major role in shaping the 'level of return' to 'investment in knowledge acquisition'. For example, a firm may have difficulty raising capital on reasonable terms, accessing skilled labour, or entering new markets.

Governments around the world have introduced various policies and programs to address this market failure. A recent review concluded that policy interventions to support knowledge development in SMEs face particular design challenges:

- Entrepreneurs and SME managers tend not to see government agencies as credible or relevant sources of advice.

- Generic programs are generally far less successful than programs that are locally focused and designed to fit the regional and/or sectoral context. (Thorpe *et al.* 2005)

Hence, the challenges that firms face in upgrading performance and capability are a significant policy issue in all countries. A large international comparative study of management capability and performance concluded that: 'Governments can play their part in encouraging the take-up of good management behaviour', and went on to suggest that , 'doing so may be the single most cost-effective way of improving the performance of their economies' (Bloom *et al.* 2007, p.10).

The policy context - legitimising frameworks

Programs designed to support management development in SMEs face an initial problem – they lack legitimacy in orthodox economic policy frameworks (Dodgson *et al.* 2010). The legacy framework of industry policy stresses the requirement to identify a 'market failure' as a first requirement for justifying policy action. The second test, the 'double market failure test', involves ensuring that such intervention generates net benefits.

The relevance of the market failure approach to industry policy is, however, now widely questioned, in large part because

> [a] fundamental problem with the concept of market failure…is that it describes a situation that exists everywhere…an analyst in search of externalities and market failures can find them anywhere he or she looks, providing a universal justification for any sort of government intervention that one might want to undertake. (Zerbe & McCurdy 1999, p. 564)

The limitations of the market failure approach to industry policy have long been recognised. Nelson commented: 'there is no satisfactory normative theory regarding the appropriate roles of government in a mixed economy' (Nelson 1987, p. 542). Norgren and Hauknes (1999) argue that the market failure rationale does not provide an adequate basis for innovation policy because its fundamental assumptions about the dynamics of innovation and economic growth are unrealistic.

Zerbe and McCurdy point out that both the appeal and the limitations of the market failure approach arise from its origins in idealised models of the economy:

> The market failure concept is not inherently empirical and as such cannot provide answers to empirical questions…The market failure model ultimately fails, like other deductive models, because it is not sufficiently derived from an empirical base. (1999, p. 571)

Many policy analysts now focus more on the 'system failures' that impede the ongoing development of capabilities in firms and other actors in an innovation system. In relation to SMEs, two types of 'systems failure' are most common:

1. **Capabilities failures** – Inadequacies in SMEs' ability to act in their own best interests arise due to, for example, lack of management capacities, lack of understanding of technology or markets, or inadequate capacity to absorb new technology. Gaps in capabilities impede the adaptation to new technologies and the response to new opportunity, leading to transition failures or learning failures.

2. **Interaction failures** – Collaborations among firms, and with support organisations, are increasingly vital for learning and innovation. SMEs in particular can become 'locked in' to a narrow an inward looking set of linkages that make them vulnerable to change. (Carlsson & Jacobsson 1997; Woolthuis, Lankhuizen & Gilsing 2005)

Behind the current debates about the appropriate rationale for intervention in the market-based economy are three issues (Chaminade & Edquist 2006; Rodrik 2004):

1. While the market failure theory is the generally accepted basis for intervention, it provides little guidance to policy makers in determining the level or focus of intervention. The foundations of the theory assume that knowledge is information and that all economic agents have perfect information. Yet competence in all of its forms is clearly unevenly distributed among firms. Where knowledge is the most important resource and learning the most important process, a theory that assumes away such resources and processes is an inappropriate base for policy.

2. The 'systems of innovation' approach recognises the uneven distribution of knowledge and capability. It also emphasises that firms do not produce, change and innovate in isolation, but interact through market-based and non-market relationships. However, it does not necessarily provide guidance on how to select areas for intervention.

3. The historical evidence shows that government intervention has played a fundamental role in shaping the path of the development of industries in industrialising economies and in the emergence of major new technologies and sectors.

A framework for program design parameters

The systems failure approach has four major implications for the design of SME capability development programs:

1. Intervention should focus on specific problems that impede change.

2. Alignment across areas of government will often be essential for effectiveness.

3. Policy-making organisations should have significant degrees of freedom in policy design and implementation, within frameworks set at a higher level in government.

4. Due to the need for policy learning and program evolution, rather than simply implementation of 'ideal' policies, a close connection between policy making and policy delivery will be essential – and program evaluation will be as much a learning mechanism as an accountability measure.

Promoting ongoing learning, coordination and evolution within the program delivery and governance system will involve a capacity for distributed decision-making and self-organisation (Anderson 1998). Policy learning, building on effective feedback, will be essential in a robust program evolution cycle, as shown in Figure 8.1.

Figure 8.1 Program evolution cycle

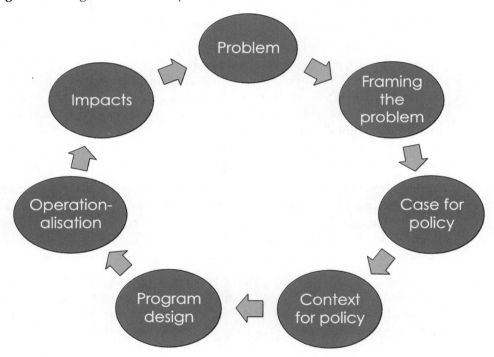

Source: Authors

Beyond these, dynamic program development challenges are a set of specific design dimensions, as shown in Table 8.1.

Table 8.1 Designing an SME capability development program

Dimension	Components and Options
What goal?	Awareness; specific capability development; decision support; implementation of systems (e.g. TQC, ISO9000, IT); relationship building (e.g. networks, research-industry links)
What services?	Benchmarking; diagnostic; advice; mentoring; information; training; knowledge transfer / standardised v customised
To whom/ target users?	Type of firm (e.g. SME, sectoral, high tech) / selective v entitlement
How and by whom are services delivered?	Government agency; existing non-government service providers; new infrastructure; new channels
What level of subsidy?	Free; cost recovery; loan; grant / single interaction; sustained relationship

Source: Authors

An SME capability development program aims to stimulate and support a transition to self-directed firm-level learning. The choices among the wide range of options will depend largely on the policy and organisational context, as indicated in Figure 8.2. Ongoing, self-directed upgrading requires the integration of capabilities and management processes in the context of strategies setting development goals, as indicated in Figure 8.3. Hence, a support program must aim to develop all three of these dimensions in SMEs.

Figure 8.2 Aligning learning

Source: Authors

The international experience of SME capability development programs suggests that the key criteria for the design of effective programs are:

- having a focus on SMEs committed to change and growth

- being located near to firms and being linked into local networks, but being integrated into national information and support networks

- the client firm contributing a significant share of overall costs

- having access to a broad spectrum of credible and experienced professional advisory services

- facilitating linkages to local, national, and international information sources, service providers, potential business partners and research organisations

- having a broad portfolio of services (for example, advice, finance, networking) but a flexible delivery customised to the needs of the individual SME

- delivering services through capable experts who work with firms to develop a combination of objective performance assessment and flexible service delivery

- having low transactions costs with a high level of payoff for the time involved in the application process.

Figure 8.3 Foundation for SME improvement

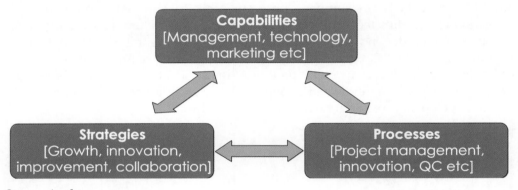

Source: Authors

The policy context - evolution of SME capability policy in Australia

An influential report of 1995, 'Enterprising Nation', identified a need for management education and for stronger leadership skills in Australian business (Karpin 1995). It emphasised five challenges:

1. to develop a positive enterprise culture through education

2. to upgrade the capabilities of the vocational training and education sector

3. to capitalise on the talents of diversity

4. to achieve best practice management development

5. to reform management education.

A further more recent assessment of management development needs in Australia concluded that the issues raised in the 1995 report had become of even greater importance (Nicholson & Nairn 2006). In addition, there has been an ongoing debate about the role and mechanisms of industry policy in raising firm-level capabilities in Australia (Jones 2005), as well as new insights into the relevance of formal structure and strategy for innovation in SMEs (Terziovski 2010).

In 2008, the government initiated the Review of the Australian Innovation System. The report of this review recognised that: 'Innovation is fundamentally a people-driven exercise and a nation's capacity to innovate is inextricably linked to the breadth and quality and focus of its education and training systems' (Cutler 2008, p. 45). Many of the submissions to the review emphasised the importance of better equipping people, through all levels of education, with the skills to be able to innovate successfully. The review recognised that the firm is at the core of much innovation and learning. It concluded that the tendency for firms, particularly SMEs, to invest little in employee training represents a 'market failure'.

The review concluded that there is a strong case for greater effort to build innovation capacity in firms. The review saw management capability as the essential foundation for innovation – '…the capability to manage and lead organisations that invest in human resource development, and that develop cultures and systems that mobilise those capacities for innovation' (Cutler 2008, p.55). It recommended that the government's new Enterprise Connect program (see below) be expanded to include assistance to build innovation performance and capability in firms and to ensure that the needs of service sector firms are addressed.

Reviews of the Automotive and of the Textiles, Clothing and Footwear sectors were also carried out in 2008. These two reviews also concluded that lifting management capability was a prerequisite to raising productivity and innovation performance.

The Review of Australia's Automotive Industry argued that:

> [G]iven the competitive pressures the industry is experiencing, a greater emphasis on improving productivity, reforming work and management practices, and promoting a productive workplace culture will be required if the Australian industry is to remain competitive in the longer term. (Bracks 2008)

The Review of the Australian Textiles, Clothing and Footwear Industries noted that all industries in high-wage, globalised economies like Australia's depend for their success on:

> the development of innovative capability at the level of the enterprise and workplace. This is driven not only by research and technology development but also by the increasing emphasis on business model transformation, market-led organisational change and the integration of firms into external collaborative networks and supply chains. (Green 2008, p. 100)

The 2009 innovation white paper, 'Powering Ideas: An Innovation Agenda for the 21st Century', summarised the government's response to the reviews. The white paper set out a target of raising the proportion of businesses innovating by 25 per cent. But it recognised that many firms lack the capacity to respond to innovation opportunities and incentives. It concluded that, 'One future focus of the Australian Government's industry and innovation policies will be on building innovation capacity and performance at the enterprise level' (Australian Government 2009).

With this focus in mind, the Department of Innovation, Industry, Science and Research also commissioned a survey of Australian management practices and productivity as part of a global comparative study (Green *et al*. 2009). This survey of 439 manufacturing firms, 'Management Matters in Australia', found a strong positive relationship between specific management practices and both firm productivity and a range of measures of success including, sales, employee numbers and market valuation. Investing in implementing management practices is usually a much more cost effective way for firms to boost productivity, relative to hiring additional employees or direct investment in fixed capital.

The survey found that relative to 16 other countries participating in the overall international study, Australian firms were good at performance and operations management, but less effective at people management, particularly 'instilling a talent mindset'. Australia ranked sixth overall among the 16 countries in the study in terms of 'good management practice'. The top 27 per cent of Indian and Chinese manufacturers are already 'better managed' than the bottom half of Australian manufacturers. The study found that smaller firms, and those where managers had relatively low education, had comparatively low levels of implementation of good management practices.

Building capability in SMEs – the Enterprise Connect program

Over the years there had been a considerable effort to produce programs to support improvement and innovation in SMEs in Australia. In the 1980s and 90s, the National Industry Extension Service, a collaboration between the federal and state administrations, was charged with disseminating 'best practice' approaches to firms. It generated a series of standard product offerings, most importantly the World Class Manufacturing (WCM) program, delivering them through consultants accredited to the program. The Business Networks Program, initiated in 1994, was designed to link firms with complementary capabilities to help them innovate collectively. Governments have also sought to assist exporters through Trade Start (and its predecessor, Export Access) by funding placements of export advisers in industry associations.

Advocacy for a new national approach to supporting SME development was active before 2007. A manufacturing industry summit in 2006 had proposed the establishment of a national manufacturing advisory service as well as the replication in all states of the model of the Queensland Manufacturing Institute.

Likewise, the Business Council of Australia called for programs to 'support the development of innovative capabilities within organisations' (BCA 2006, p. 27). In mid-2007, the then Coalition Government announced support for an Australian Industry Productivity Centres program, with funding of A$350 million over ten years. The program design incorporated features from overseas programs (including the UK Manufacturing Advisory Service), provided a free business diagnostic service and then matched funding for advisory services to follow up the specific recommendations. The centres were to operate in partnership with industry associations and centres and were to target manufacturing and 'trade exposed' service sector firms.

In 2008, implementing an election commitment, the incoming Labor Government announced the formation of Enterprise Connect (EC). Funded at approximately A$50 million per year, EC was to be the Commonwealth's primary vehicle for delivering enterprise-level support. It replaced the Australian Industry Productivity Centres introduced by the previous government.

In developing the EC program, the basic design assumptions were:

- The problem is primarily demand-side – there are capable business advisors and other resources in the innovation system – and the program would need to actively market to SMEs to secure engagement.

- The basic diagnostic services should aim to enable firms to develop a strategic framework for improvement within which the need for, and value of, specific support services becomes clear.

- The quality and independence of the advisors is critical for their acceptance by SMEs.

- The services will be aimed at existing firms of some substance (rather than micro and start-up firms) – so influencing the type and extent of service provision.

Hence, the foundation design parameters were:

- It should be an entitlement program where the basic services are available to all eligible firms; this allows for a very simple entry process. Once a program is competitive, merit criteria come into play with consequent paperwork implications. An application needs to be considered relative to others, which means approval processes are batched, with consequent delays.

- The business advisors should be highly competent and able to exercise professional judgement free from bureaucratic considerations. They should be full time, overseen by capable and experienced directors with senior private sector backgrounds in each centre, but should have significant freedom to operate within an overall performance contract.

The level of support available to each SME – in effect the level of subsidy – should enable them to become competent users of commercial advisory services and be sufficient to have embedded, ongoing, self-directed change. Hence, EC promotes enterprise improvement and innovation in SMEs through a national network of centres. It includes six Manufacturing Centres which also function as the main office of EC in each state, and several largely sectoral and cross-cutting Innovation Centres (for example, Resources Technology Innovation Centre - Mackay, QLD; Innovative Regions Innovation Centre - Geelong, VIC; and Creative Industries Innovation Centre – Sydney, NSW). All the centres are staffed by teams of business advisers who deliver business review services to SMEs. Each centre has an advisory board that includes industry and research-sector representatives, and the chairs of the boards comprise the Advisory Council for the EC network as a whole.

For example, the Clean Energy Innovation Centre (CEIC) provides a range of services designed to link businesses in the clean energy sector to new ideas, technologies and markets. Its business advisers aim to help firms improve productivity and build internal capacity. The Innovative Regions Centre operates in a different way to the other centres. Rather than working with individual business, facilitators attached to the Innovative Regions Centre work closely with local governments, businesses, researchers, and communities in ten specific regions across Australia. The core services of EC are:)

- a business review conducted by a skilled business adviser at no cost to the firm (and hence involving an effective subsidy of about A$20,000 per firm) which includes an assessment of:
  - the strengths and weaknesses of the firm
  - strategic business issues
  - potential areas for business improvement
  - potential areas for growth.
- the Tailored Advisory Service (TAS), which provides matching funding of up to $20,000 to implement actions identified in the business review
- Client Management, which is an ongoing advisory service for all client firms for up to twelve months following a business review.

In addition, EC aims to develop linkages to promote knowledge flows and collaboration with research groups and other knowledge providers through a number of specific programs within EC, such as Researchers in Business.

From its formation to its end of 2009, EC had approved over 2000 applications for business reviews and had completed the majority of these. Over 85 per cent of firms undertaking the business diagnostic services had implemented two or more of the recommendations. About a half of the firms implementing the recommendations had gone on to seek subsidised services for that implementation under the TAS. Relatively small numbers of firms had used EC for accessing technology or researcher involvement. Under the program guidelines, an individual SME can remain a client, receiving subsidised support, for up to three years.

Learning and program evolution

An important lesson from the experience of the program has been the recognition that embedding a self-driven improvement strategy in many SMEs requires a sustained engagement by external advisers. The work of the Business Advisors in almost 2000 SMEs also provides insight into the issues that limit performance in these firms. The great majority of issues in the type of firms which EC has attracted as clients are at the more basic management level involving human resource management and developing effective competitive and improvement strategies – rather than issues of major innovation and new directions of growth. The experience of the advisors has been that, due to the pressure of work, location and lack of opportunity, many SME managers are isolated from other managers and from sources of knowledge and support. This recognition has led to an assessment of the scope for EC to develop a networking component of its activities.

In line with government policy, the managers of the overall EC program have planned a systematic review of the program. This review, based on a methodology designed by Deloitte, will involve extensive surveys of EC clients and parallel surveys of non-clients. Drawing on that methodology, a survey of 450 EC clients was conducted in early 2010 to gain insight into their reasons for entering the program, their experience of the program and the impacts of that engagement. The majority of firms were manufacturing firms in major cities with a turnover of A$2–10 million and 10–50 employees and had been in business for over 10 years.

The experience shows that the availability of the subsidy for accessing professional advisory services was less important than the support to clarify priorities and develop improvement strategies. The firms surveyed had implemented on average four of the recommendations arising from the diagnostic review. The most common reasons for seeking a business review by an EC business advisor were to improve sales or profitability, develop a new strategy and to obtain impartial advice. The firms that had implemented recommendations arising from the reviews said that the Business Advisors had helped to prioritise the key changes and encouraged action. They found the independence and quality of the advisors (and review report) the most valuable element of the EC program.

The firms indicated that the improvements developed in their business, as a result of the engagement with the program, were broadly based, rather than focused on product innovation. In fact, the firms identified improvements in human resources, business strategy and quality as the three most important outcomes. Only a third of the firms cited new product development as a significant area of improvement. Three quarters of the firms surveyed said that they were more productive or efficient due to the role of EC.

Finally, the Minister for Innovation, Industry, Science and Research pledged in his 2010 election platform that the government would draw on the 'Management Matters in Australia' report to develop a new initiative to improve the skills and capabilities of SME managers, which were found wanting in the survey report. Ideally, this would align with a parallel initiative in the Education, Skills and Workplace Relations portfolio to promote the 'workplace of the future' as whole-of-government policy, with reference to international examples of such as those in Finland and Ireland (Green & Walshe 2003; NCPP 2004; Vamos *et al.* 2008).

Summary and overview

In all economies, the majority of firms are small and medium-sized enterprises, and these account for a significant share of output and employment. Many SMEs face difficulties upgrading their capabilities and, as a result, face barriers in implementing new technologies and management practices and are vulnerable to competitive pressure. Consequently, the lack of dynamism in many SMEs reduces the dynamism of the economy, retarding knowledge diffusion and investment in human resource development.

These problems are a concern to most governments. But whether governments have a role in addressing them is controversial. And how to best address them is far from clear.

More recent frameworks developed from the evolutionary economics and innovation systems perspective are pragmatic, emphasising the importance of policy learning in developing effective policy instruments.

Several recent policy reviews in Australia have highlighted the need to raise management capability throughout industry and particularly in SMEs. The Enterprise Connect program, building on earlier initiatives, aims to support capability development in Australian SMEs. The program provides diagnostic and advisory services in response to requests from firms, and may in the future include support for management training and development. The majority of its resources have been focused on relatively small firms and on basic types of capability development, rather than, for example, innovation-related initiatives.

Discussion questions

1) Enterprise Connect is an entitlement program open to all firms. Would it be more effective in pursuing the overall policy objective if it was an investment activity, focused on those firms that are likely to yield the highest growth or improvement in productivity? For example, should EC focus on particular types of firm, like exporters or high growth firms?

2) Much of EC's work goes into helping firms with fairly basic management issues – is this a good use of program resources?

3) How might EC assess whether a firm has an embedded self-driving improvement strategy?

4) How should the program design an internal learning mechanism so that the capabilities of all staff and contracted service providers improve over time?

5) How should the program design a learning mechanism so that the overall design of the program is re-assessed and improved over time?

References

Anderson, T 1998, 'Managing a Systems Approach to Technology and Innovation Policy', in STI Review No. 22, Special Issue on New Rationales and Approaches in Technology and Innovation Policy, Paris: OECD.

Australian Government 2009, *Powering Ideas: An Innovation Agenda for the 21st Century*, Canberra: Department of Innovation, Industry, Science and Research.

BCA (Business Council of Australia) 2006, *New Pathways to Prosperity: A National Innovation Framework for Australia*, Melbourne: Business Council of Australia & Society for Knowledge Economics.

Bloom, N, Dorgan, S Dowdy, J, & Van Reenen, J 2007, *Management Practice & Productivity: Why they matter?*, London: McKinsey & Company and London School of Economics.

Bracks, S 2008, *Review of Australia's Automotive Industry*, Canberra: Department of Innovation, Industry, Science and Research.

Carlsson, B & Jacobsson, S 1997, 'In Search of Useful Public Policies: Key Lessons and Issues for Policy Makers', in Carlsson, B (ed.), *Technological Systems and Industrial Dynamics*, Kluwer Academic Publishers.

Chaminade, C & Edquist, C 2006, 'Rationales for public policy intervention from a systems of innovation approach: the case of VINNOVA', CIRCLE Electronic Working Paper Series Paper no. 2006/04.

Cutler, T 2008, 'Venturous Australia - building strength in innovation', report on the Review of the National Innovation System, Canberra: Department of Innovation, Industry, Science and Research.

Dodgson, M, Hughes, A, Foster, J, & Metcalfe, J 2010, 'Systems thinking, market failure, and the development of innovation policy: The case of Australia', UQ Economics Discussion Paper, No. 403, Department of Economics, University of Queensland; and Centre for Business Research Working Paper N. 397. University of Cambridge, UK.

Green, R & Walshe, E 2003, 'Organisational Model' for the National Forum on the Workplace of the Future, Centre for Innovation & Structural Change. Galway: National University of Ireland

Green, R 2008, *Building Innovative Capability: Review of the Textiles, Clothing and Footwear Industries*, Canberra: Department of Innovation, Industry, Science and Research.

Green, R 2009, 'Management Matters in Australia: Just how productive are we?', findings from the Australian Management Practices and Productivity global benchmarking project, Canberra: Department of Innovation, Industry, Science and Research.

Jones, E 2000, 'The Howard Government's industry policy', Economic Papers 19(3): 60–75.

Jones, E 2005, 'Industry policy in the 1990s: Working Nation, its context and beyond', *Journal of Economic and Social Policy*, 9(2):35–53.

Karpin, D 1995, 'Enterprising Nation: Renewing Australia's managers to meet the challenges of the Asia-Pacific century', Task Force on Leadership and Management Skills, Canberra: Department of Employment, Education and Training.

NCPP (National Centre for Partnership & Performance) 2005, 'Working to our Advantage: A National Workplace Strategy', report of the Forum on the Workplace of the Future, Dublin: Government of Ireland

Nelson, R 1987, 'Roles of government in a mixed economy', *Journal of Policy Analysis and Management*, 6 (Summer): 541-57.

Nicholson, J & Nairn, A 2006, *The Manager of the 21st Century - 2020 VISION*, Boston Consulting Group.

Norgren, L & Hauknes, J 1999, 'Economic Rationales of government involvement in innovation and supply of innovation related services', paper for RISE project, University of Brighton.

Rodrik, D 2004, 'Industrial Policy for the Twenty-First Century', Kennedy School of Government, Harvard University, draft Sept.

Scott-Kemmis D, Jones AJ, Arnold E, Chitravas C & Sardana D 2007, *Absorptive Capacity for Innovation in Australian Industry*, Canberra: Department of Innovation, Industry, Science and Research.

Scott-Kemmis, D 2008, 'Industry Policy for the Knowledge Economy', in Vol. 2 of Green (2008).

Terziovski, M 2010, 'Innovation practice and its performance in small and medium enterprises (SMEs) in the manufacturing sector: A resource-based view', *Strategic Management Journal*, 31: 892-902.

Thorpe, R, Holt, R, McPherson, A & Pittaway, L 2005, 'Using knowledge within small and medium-sized firms: A systematic review of the evidence', *International Journal of Management Reviews*, 7(4):257–281

Vamos, S, Boedeker, C & Green, R 2008, 'Leading Australia to More Innovative, Productive and Fulfilling Workplaces – the Role of Government', Society for Knowledge Economics report, Canberra: Department of Education, Employment & Workplace Relations.

Woolthuis, RK, Lankhuizen, M & Gilsing, V 2005, 'A system failure framework for innovation policy design', *Technovation*, 25(6): 609-619.

Zerbe, R & McCurdy, H 1999, 'The Failure of Market Failure', *Journal of Policy Analysis and Management*, 18(4): 558-578.

Chapter 9

Empowering medical practitioners to innovate: The case of rural primary healthcare in Wellsford, New Zealand

JONATHAN LAZARUS, LISA CALLAGHER AND KENNETH HUSTED

A transdisciplinary approach to Mode 2 innovation uses expertise from a wide range of disciplines and stakeholders to understand and solve societal problems (Mobjörk 2010; Nowotny 2001; Nowotny, Scott & Gibbons 2003; Pohl 2008). A number of factors encourage organisations in the health system towards empowering medical practitioners to participate in transdisciplinary research that creates new solutions for societal health problems. This case examines the individual and team empowerment practices used by Wellsford's Coast-to-Coast Primary Health Organisation to encourage transdisciplinary research.

Wellsford is a rural community whose health services are seriously pressured. Located in the North Island of New Zealand, the closest regional town (Whangarei) is a one-hour drive north and the closest major city (Auckland) is a one-hour drive south. At the last census Wellsford's population was 1,671, with 70 per cent of the population reporting New Zealand-European ethnicity and 28 per cent of the population reporting indigenous Maori ethnicity (Statistics New Zealand 2006).

Coast-to-Coast Primary Health Organisation (CCPHO) is the Primary Health Organisation (PHO) servicing Wellsford and the surrounding rural communities. Funded by Waitemata District Health Board for publicly subsidised services, one of CCPHO's tasks is to deliver primary health services to these communities. Given Wellsford's situation, CCPHO uses transdisciplinary research to deliver primary health services in ways that address the community's health problems with new local solutions. CCPHO believes that empowering individuals and teams to participate in transdisciplinary research can contribute to delivering effective primary health services.

Innovative societal solutions through transdisciplinary research

Sociology of science suggests a radical shift in the way knowledge is created and consumed. Instead of being insular, predominantly relying on strict internal academic quality assurance and being governed by academic norms, science is said to have opened up towards the society and embraced collaborative knowledge production aimed at solving issues relevant for stakeholders.

This shift towards collaborative knowledge production has significant implications for the norms and processes associated with knowledge production. Rather than being exclusively expert-based, strictly discipline-bound and largely self-referential, networked science production transcends disciplinary and institutional boundaries (Nowotny *et al.* 2001), with research agendas and new knowledge production being continuously (re)negotiated and (re)shaped in interaction among stakeholders in localised contexts (Gibbons *et al.* 1994). The strengthened focus on linkages between science and the needs of the wider society also addresses the increasing and explicit societal requirements for more value and clear benefits from publicly funded activities.

Traditional knowledge production systems are organised in a silo-based model referred to as Mode 1. Mode 1 knowledge production is found primarily in academia, where scholars conduct research within disciplinary silos with emphasis on theory development rather than contextual application. In contrast, Mode 2 research is organised around collaboration between heterogeneous teams using diverse skills and experiences to resolve complex context-specific problems (Gibbons1994; Tranfield & Starkey 1998). Although Mode 2 theory explains the value of new knowledge production systems, it provides limited guidance about organising and managing issues associated with collaborative knowledge production for context-specific problems. One approach that can provide guidance is the transdisciplinary research approach.

Transdisciplinary research aims to produce and implement solutions to societal problems. In this case, societal problems concern the need to deliver fast, efficient and equitable primary health services within an increasingly pressured health system – or as one health manager asked,

> *With doctors being a very limited resource up here, how can we provide complete health care for the patient without using GPs?*

Transdisciplinary research use expertise from a wide range of disciplines and perspectives (such as medicine, nursing, psychology and management) and from a range of stakeholders (including health service providers, other community organisations, universities, and governmental agencies) to understand and solve societal problems (Mobjörk 2010; Nowotny 2001; Nowotny, Scott & Gibbons 2003; Pohl 2008).

Three features characterise transdisciplinary research:

- Transdisciplinary research is **problem-focussed** because its explicit intention is to understand (Albrecht, Freeman & Higginbotham 1998) and solve complex problems that cannot be confined to single disciplinary explanations (Horlick-Jones & Sime 2004; Pohl 2005; Wickson, Carew & Russel 2006).

- Given the problem focus, **evolving methodologies** are used to find common features from disciplinary methods and use them to develop tailored tools and methods that solve complex social problems (Mobjörk 2010; Pohl 2008; Robinson 2008; Stokols 2006; Wickson, Carew & Russel 2006).

- **Collaboration** occurs between practitioners, scholars and other stakeholders who bring together knowledge from their different perspectives and use it to develop and implement solutions (Mobjörk 2010). For collaboration to happen there needs to be a willingness on the part of all the participants to be open-minded, tolerant of different world views and opinions, and appreciative of the value of mutual learning. (Stokols 2006; Zierhofer & Burger 2007).

The role of empowerment in transdisciplinary research

Empowerment refers to the process of enhancing individuals' personal beliefs so they can demonstrate their power to influence others (Conger & Kanungo 1988). In organisational settings, empowerment gives individuals and teams the opportunity to develop the knowledge and expertise that can be used to influence collective issues (Kuokkanen & Leino-Kilpi 2000). Empowerment is critical to transdisciplinary research because individuals and teams must be able to influence their colleagues and other stakeholders to adapt different ways of thinking about societal problems and use new tools and methods to solve them.

Factors influencing health systems

To understand why CCPHO empowers individuals and teams to participate in transdisciplinary research, it is useful to appreciate wider influences that put pressure on health systems. These influences are also important because they can affect the practices CCPHO use towards empowering individuals and teams.

Public policy for health service provision

The New Zealand health system is primarily tax-funded and organised through a complex structure that devolves responsibility for managing health services to 20 District Health Boards (DHBs). These boards in turn allocate funding to 81 Primary Health Organisations, of which CCPHO is one. Under the *New Zealand Public Health and Disability Act* 2000, DHBs have a number of statutory objectives including:

- improving, promoting and protecting the health of communities

- promoting the integration of health services, especially primary and secondary care services.

DHBs receive funding from the New Zealand government through the Minister of Health. Funding decisions are based on a formula that takes into account the size of each DHB's population and its needs in regard to health deprivation. When allocating funding, the Minister of Health provides a broad set of instructions to the DHBs about the health services they must provide. These services include:

- public health delivered through public hospitals

- public health screening programs

- health promotion activities

- private health facilities, such as private hospitals, laboratories, medical specialist and radiologist centres

- not-for-profit health agencies, including indigenous Maori-interest groups, Family Planning and Plunket.

From these instructions each DHB is responsible for assessing its population's health needs and managing its services accordingly (King 2001). Thus, through *The New Zealand Public Health and Disability Act* 2000 and the Minister of Health's set of instructions, primary health care can be identified as a priority issue for DHBs.

Waitemata District Health Board (WDHB) is one of 20 DHBs in New Zealand. With approximately 525,000 people in its constituency, WDHB is the largest DHB in New Zealand and services the second fastest growing health district (Ministry of Health 2010). Furthermore, WDHB covers half of Auckland, New Zealand's largest city, and large stretches of rural areas. Of the 525,000 people, the WDHB serves only 1,671 people who reside in Wellsford, although the surrounding community served by the CCPHO is over 14,000. The heterogeneity of WDHB's population presents an ongoing challenge of providing limited health services to a relatively wealthy urban-based segment and a relatively impoverished rural-based segment in an equitable manner (Bennet *et al.* 2009).

Primary healthcare

Primary health care refers to the delivery of health services within the community where patients reside, through community-based medical practitioners providing first point of contact for healthcare assistance (King 2001; National Health Committee 2000). The goal of primary health care is to provide fast, efficient, and accessible generalist health services, which are culturally appropriate and congruent with the community's needs (Hefford, Crampton & Foley 2005). The aim of primary healthcare is to reduce secondary healthcare demands – as they often involve more costly hospital admissions and specialist care – and reduce the rates of premature death associated with delayed healthcare.

Primary health care is supported by The New Zealand Primary Health Care Strategy (2001), which has several foci (King 2001):

- working with local community to organise health services such as medical and healthcare centres, nurse services, health promotion and protection activities that meet local priorities

- identifying and addressing health inequalities such as premature death rates, by restructuring health service delivery methods

- offering comprehensive health services at first points of contact that reflect the priorities and preferences of the local community

- coordinating health services within and across healthcare organisations to ensure improved delivery and effective use of resources

- developing a comprehensive primary health workforce to provide point-of-contact health care in coordinated ways that meets community priorities.

With funding from DHBs, Primary Health Organisations (PHOs) are responsible for implementing The New Zealand Primary Health Care Strategy. This involves PHOs coordinating primary health services across multiple health providers including doctors, nurses, physiotherapists, occupational therapists, indigenous Maori health workers, dieticians, pharmacists and midwives working in public organisations and private practices. To ensure this is achieved, The New Zealand Primary Health Care Strategy puts strong emphasis on partnership with local communities and collaboration across health providers (Abel *et al.* 2005).

Social trends influencing the health system

To appreciate why partnerships and collaboration are critical for PHOs' effective delivery of primary health services, it is necessary to consider broader social trends around the nature of expertise, ageing population and geography of populations that influence the health system.

Nature of healthcare expertise

Increasing specialisation in medical work makes it impossible for individual practitioners to provide comprehensive health care. For doctors, increasing specialisation has been the trend for the past 200 years and this trend is increasingly seen in other areas of medical work (Weisz 2006). In order to provide comprehensive health care, medical practitioners increasingly need to collaborate with other practitioners who have different forms of expertise. Collaboration takes on greater importance when the ageing population and ageing healthcare workforce trends are considered.

Ageing population and ageing healthcare workforce

Within the next 10–20 years health systems worldwide will experience a 'perfect storm'. Populations are ageing and expensive medical technologies that maintain life are contributing to a growing demand for health services. At the same time, the ageing population is retiring and reducing the medical work force. New Zealand is not immune to these trends. It is expected that 16 per cent of New Zealand's population will be over 65 years of age in 2020, with 5 per cent being over 80 years of age at the same time (Anderson & Hussey 2000). The ageing population will place pressure on primary health services (i.e. GPs and nurses) and secondary healthcare (for example, chronic care in hospitals). Adding to this pressure is New Zealand's doctor-to-patient ratio. The current OECD average is 3.1 practising doctors per 1,000 people; New Zealand's ratio is 2.2/1000 and it is predicted to deteriorate further. New Zealand also has the highest proportion of migrant doctors in the OECD. This is mainly due to New Zealand's high rate of medical workforce emigration to the US, UK and Australia (Zurn & Dumont 2008).

Rural geography

As well as social trends, New Zealand's geography presents further hurdles. Generally the country is sparsely populated. Eighty per cent of the population lives in urban areas, and half of those live in the four main cities of Auckland, Hamilton, Wellington and Christchurch. The 20 per cent of the population who live in rural areas are more likely to experience poverty, live in dilapidated housing and be unemployed (Ashton 1996). These factors present serious constraints for people in rural areas who face potential loss of wages, childcare expenses, travel costs and personal stress in order to access health care.

Geographic distance between rural areas and hospitals also has consequences for social relations among medical practitioners and the rural communities where they live and work. In rural communities that are one hour or more drive from a hospital, medical practitioners necessarily assume additional roles including, emergency and after-hours services. These additional roles present significant barriers to recruiting medical practitioners to work in rural communities (Goodyear-Smith & Janes 2008).

CCPHO's transdisciplinary approach to rural primary health service

Given the pressures from increasing work specialisation, ageing population, political expectations, legal obligations and the rural geography, CCPHO chose to use a transdisciplinary research approach to deliver primary health services. This is because transdisciplinary research can produce solutions for societal health problems that are faced in Wellsford, New Zealand. However, transdisciplinary research requires that individuals and teams be empowered to participate. In this section we examine the practices that CCPHO uses to empower individuals and teams to participate in its transdisciplinary initiatives.

Organisational support for empowerment can be demonstrated through clearly defined social support structures that do not bias team members (Kirkman & Rosen 1999; Mathieu, Gilson & Ruddy 2006). To encourage teams to participate in transdisciplinary initiatives, CCPHO facilitate monthly meetings where healthcare and medical practitioners from all health organisations are invited to share their issues related to primary health services in Wellsford.

> *All contacts come to our monthly meetings about continuing education. Those meetings also provide an opportunity to talk about any innovations, any updates, any improvements, any training, and we bring in visiting specialists to come and talk about anything they can provide. For example we had a diabetes specialist come up the other day – that involves everybody. It involves the physiotherapists, occupational therapists, Maori nurses...*

To promote open mindedness and tolerance of different world views and opinions, health practitioners with different expertise take turns are presenting ideas from their disciplinary perspective. For example, the podiatrist will talk about foot care for diabetics, which is then discussed by dieticians, nurses, doctors and occupational therapists to develop new ideas for improving the diabetes management

Organisational support for empowerment can also be demonstrated by creating communication channels where information is exchanged in a psychologically safe environment (Kirkman & Rosen 1999; Mathieu, Gilson & Ruddy 2006). CCPHO's monthly meetings illustrate how this can be done. At the monthly meetings emphasis is put on health practitioners with different disciplinary perspectives having valid ideas to contribute. In this way the contributions of all team members are given consideration.

Support structures can also empower individuals. CCPHO regularly invite staff from Te Ha Oranga to be involved in transdisciplinary initiatives. Te Ha Oranga is the health unit of Te Runanga O Ngati Whatua, a non-government indigenous Maori organisation. Te Ha Organa work with Maori on a daily basis from their clinic in Wellsford. Given that the average Maori health outcomes are worse than that of the general population (King 2001), collaboration with Te Ha Oranga provides a way to better understand Maori health needs and facilitate better solutions.

> *In collaboration [with Te Ha Oranga] it's about there being information that is valuable for GPs when they see their patients and in turn the information from GPs will be valuable for the others when they are looking for the best pathway of care.*

Leadership is important for empowering individuals and teams by creating environments that are conducive to learning. Leadership is also important for encouraging the use of initiative and collaborative decision-making (Kirkman &

Rosen 1999; Mathieu, Gilson & Ruddy 2006). At CCPHO leadership is provided in a number of different ways.

A senior doctor, Dr M, who works at Wellsford Medical Centre, is heavily involved in teaching trainee doctors and nurses about rural primary health care. His hands-on teaching involves working with groups of students to tackle problems that patients present. These students come on field placements to gain experience working in rural health situations, such as minor and emergency surgeries, rural call-outs, supporting people with long-term health conditions and the like.

Managing these types of medical situations is not normally addressed in urban hospital field placements. Dr M encourages the students to interact with the patients so they experience what it is like to work in a rural community where personal knowledge of patients' social lives and histories is the norm. Given the resource limitations in Wellsford, Dr M also encourages the students to think of different ways they might treat patients with the resources at hand. Using a hands-on approach to educating his students, Dr M creates an environment that is conducive to learning about the realities of rural health services in a realistic, yet productive, way.

As well as supporting medical students, Dr M encourages nurses at the Wellsford Medical Centre and those working for other health providers in the community to use their initiative. The Dr says

> With a lack of doctors we are looking at our nurses to have a greater and wider scope in their practice than those who work in urban areas...nurses would like to do more, but they need support, confidence, approval and backing. Let's train nurses and other health workers in the field to see patients needing medium-level care, let's give them guidance and standing orders so as to fill the gap.

To give them confidence and skills to do this, Dr M strongly promotes ongoing professional development. He champions the cause of nurses completing post-graduate studies to support advanced practice and/or register as nurse practitioners, which gives them authority to provide a wider range of care, including prescribing some medicines. In a community that struggles to recruit doctors, having nurse practitioners who can prescribe standard medicines is an important way of using medical practitioners more effectively. One of the nurses says

> He is comfortable with the transition of nurses getting more responsibility and he drives it and those who come and work for us are here as a result of him making them comfortable with it.

Leadership is also provided by non-medical practitioners. The CEO of CCPHO is instrumental in facilitating a collaborative environment. Recognising the value of socialising trainee students into a transdisciplinary mindset, the CEO organised shared accommodation for all students training in Wellsford. The philosophy behind 'the student house' is that by living together students come to realise that open mindedness and tolerance of different world views and opinions are values that can be shared irrespective of their disciplinary training. During their stay, students are expected to live and work together – sharing everything from cooking and cleaning duties to producing team solutions for local health problems they can identify. As one of the trainees says

> *Socially, once you get home to the house – that's when your best networking is done.*

An important aspect of the student house is to facilitate cross training, a method of learning a wide range of skills, some of which may be outside of the individual's normal domain for knowledge (Kirkman & Rosen 1999; Nash *et al.* 2003). By exposing individual students to transdisciplinary team experiences, the CEO aims to enable students to think differently about their roles in health service delivery.

The CCPHO CEO's leadership can also been seen through her support for Wellsford's CarePlus program. CarePlus delivers health services to patients requiring chronic care for pre-existing or long term illnesses. The CEO encourages medical and nursing practitioners in Wellsford's CarePlus team to take a collaborative approach to decisions about patients' care. Rather than each individual making his/her expert assessments and then implementing care for that aspect, the CEO encourages individuals to share their opinions among the team and for the team to make comprehensive decisions about treatment for that patient. In this way patients' treatments are more likely to be coordinated.

> *Our nurses run a chronic care team. CarePlus is a contract we get through our funding. It is broken down into 4 three-monthly appointments for a patient throughout the year. Instead of seeing the same nurse each time, our way of looking at that now is saying – you can see the nurse the first time, to plan your care , but the next time it may be more suitable to see the podiatrist or dietician contributing to your health improvements and outcomes.*

Human resource management practices can play an important role towards empowering individuals (Kirkman & Rosen 1999; London & Smither 1999; Mathieu, Gilson & Ruddy 2006). At CCPHO, recruitment, training and development and rewards practices contribute towards empowering individuals and supporting teams.

In regard to recruitment, CCPHO put effort into attracting medical practitioners whose beliefs fit with transdisciplinary research. Although skills shortages in the labour market and Wellsford's rural location make it difficult to attract medical practitioners, CCPHO are explicit about the value placed on open mindedness and tolerance of different world views and opinions.

> *GPs who come to work for us do have that ethos of giving more power to nurses...there is less of that 'Victorian' way of doing things.*

As might be expected, CCPHO has difficulty with attracting and retaining healthcare practitioners. Consequently, CCPHO has to explore different ways of delivering primary health services. Example, the medical centre has to provide a

24 hour Accident and Emergency service alongside its other primary health care and health promotion services. To address the pressure this activity adds to an already stretched health workforce, CCPHO delivers emergency services through collaboration between the medical centre and the local voluntary St. Johns ambulance service. Although CCPHO are not responsible for recruiting volunteers to the St. Johns ambulance service, they do make an effort to attract medical practitioners to the medical centre who are willing to work within this collaborative arrangement.

As well as recruitment, a number of training and development practices are used that empower individuals. Monthly training sessions provide opportunities for medical practitioners to work with and learn from experts who visit from Auckland. Compared to sending individuals to Auckland, by hosting monthly training in Wellsford CCPHO are able to deliver training to more people and in ways that reinforce its transdisciplinary approach.

Training and development cannot be focused on transdisciplinarity alone. Individual medical practitioners need to participate in formalised professional development activities that enable individuals to equip themselves with skills needed to contribute towards tasks in a timely manner (London & Smither 1999). Professional development is important to maintaining disciplinary skills in order for individuals to contribute to transdisciplinary teams.

As CCPHO has direct relations with a number of New Zealand universities due to the design of medical training programs, it uses these relations to support regular workshops and training days for Wellsford's medical practitioners. As well as travelling to Auckland for these courses, CCPHO also supports individuals to undertake extramural courses and to make use of the experts who occasionally visit Wellsford to provide specialist services.

For individuals who contribute towards the transdisciplinary initiatives, the rewards are both intrinsic and extrinsic. Medical practitioners gain satisfaction associated with learning, addressing complex problems and creating new solutions. They also receive extrinsic rewards through recognition of the greater status that comes with up-skilling and through pay increases that reflect their increased responsibility.

Summary

To address the Wellsford community's health problems, CCPHO took a transdisciplinary research approach to deliver primary health service delivery. Given the nature of transdisciplinary research CCPHO, had to develop management practices that empowered individuals and teams. CCPHO's approach presents a novel case of using a range of perspectives and stakeholders to produce new solutions to important societal issues.

Discussion questions

1) What does this case tell you about the management of innovation?

2) What factors might influence CCPHO's ability to maintain its transdisciplinary initiatives, and why?

3) What factors might influence other health organisations' ability to replicate CCPHO's approach to innovation?

4) How might you evaluate the effectiveness of CCPHO's transdisciplinary initiatives?

References

Abel, S, Gibson, D, Ehau, T & Tipene Leach, D 2005, 'Implementing the Primary Health Care Strategy: A Maori Health Provider Perspective', *Social Policy Journal of New Zealand*, (25), pp .70-87.

Albrecht, G, Freeman, S & Higginbotham, N 1998, 'Complexity and Human Health: The Case for a Transdisciplinary Paradigm', *Culture, Medicine and Psychiatry*, 22(1), pp. 55-92.

Anderson, GF & Hussey, PS 2000, 'Population aging: a comparison among industrialized countries', *Health Affairs*, 19(3), pp. 191-203.

Ashton, T 1996, 'Health Care Systems in Transition: New Zealand', *Journal of Public Health Medicine*, 18(3), pp. 269-273.

Bennet, W, Huakau, J, Latimer, S, Selak, V, Zhou, L 2009, *Waitemata Health Needs Assessment 2009: Health and Health care of Waitemata Residents North Shore City*, Waitemata District Health Board.

Conger, JA & Kanungo, RN 1988, 'The Empowerment Process: Integrating Theory and Practice', *Academy of Management Review*, 13(3), pp. 471-482.

Gibbons, M 1994, *The New Production of Knowledge: The Dynamics of Science and Research in Contemporary Societies*, London: SAGE Publications.

Goodyear-Smith, F & Janes, R 2008, 'New Zealand rural primary health care workforce in 2005: More than just a doctor shortage', *Australian Journal of Rural Health*, 16, pp. 40-46.

Hefford, M, Crampton, P & Foley, J 2005, 'Reducing health disparities through primary care reform: the New Zealand experiment', *Health Policy*, 72(1), pp. 9-23.

Horlick-Jones, T & Sime, J 2004, 'Living on the border: knowledge, risk and transdisciplinarity', *Futures*, 36(4), pp. 441-456.

King, A 2001, *The Primary Health Care Strategy*, Office of the Minister of Health, Wellington, New Zealand.

Kirkman, BL & Rosen, B 1999, 'Beyond Self-Management: Antecedents and Consequences of Team Empowerment', *Academy of Management Journal*, 42(1), pp. 58-74.

Kuokkanen, L & Leino-Kilpi, H 2000, 'Power and empowerment in nursing: three theoretical approaches', *Journal of Advanced Nursing*, 31(1), pp. 235-241.

London, M & Smither, J 1999, 'Empowered Self-Development and Continuous Learning', *Human Resource Management*, 38(1), pp. 3-15.

Mathieu, JE, Gilson, LL & Ruddy, TM 2006, 'Empowerment and Team Effectiveness: An Empirical Test of an Integrated Model', *Journal of Applied Psychology*, 91(1), pp. 97-108.

Ministry of Health, 2010, *About Waitemata District Health Board. Waitemata District Health Board*, available at: http://www.waitematadhb.govt.nz/AboutUs/AboutWaitemataDistrictHealthBoard.aspx, accessed September 24, 2010.

Mobjörk, M 2010, 'Consulting versus participatory transdisciplinarity: A refined classification of transdisciplinary research', *Futures*, 42(8), pp. 866-873.

Nash, J, Collins, B, Loughlin, S, Solbrig, M, Harvey, R, Krishnan-Sarin, S, Unger, J, Miner, C, Rukstalis, M, Shenassa, E, Dube, C., & Spirito, A, 2003, 'Training the transdisciplinary scientist: A general framework applied to tobacco use behaviour', *Nicotine & Tobacco Research*, 5(6), pp. 41-53.

National Health Committee 2000, *Improving Health for New Zealanders by Investing in Primary Health Care*.

Nowotny, H 2001, *Re-Thinking Science: Knowledge and the Public in an Age of Uncertainty*, Cambridge: Polity.

Nowotny, H., Scott, P & Gibbons, M 2003, 'Introduction: 'Mode 2' Revisited: The New Production of Knowledge', *Minerva*, 41(3), pp. 179-194.

Pohl, C 2008, 'From science to policy through transdisciplinary research', *Environmental Science & Policy*, 11(1), pp. 46-53.

Pohl, C 2005, 'Transdisciplinary collaboration in environmental research', *Futures*, 37(10), pp. 1159-1178.

Robinson, J 2008, 'Being undisciplined: Transgressions and intersections in academia and beyond', *Futures*, 40(1), pp. 70-86.

Statistics New Zealand 2006, QuickStats About Wellsford - Statistics New Zealand. Available at: http://www.stats.govt.nz/Census/2006CensusHomePage/QuickStats/AboutAPlace/SnapShot.aspx?type=au&ParentID=1000002&ss=y&tab=Education&id=3505300&p=y&printall=true, accessed September 24, 2010.

Stokols, D 2006, 'Toward a Science of Transdisciplinary Action Research', *American Journal of Community Psychology*, 38(1-2), pp. 63-77.

Tranfield, D & Starkey, K 1998, 'The Nature, Social Organisation and Promotion of Management Research: Towards Policy', *British Journal of Management*, 9(4), 341-353

Weisz, G 2006, *Divide and Conquer: A Comparative History of Medical Specilization*, Oxford: Oxford University Press.

Wickson, F, Carew, A & Russell, A 2006, 'Transdisciplinary research: characteristics, quandaries and quality', *Futures*, 38(9), pp. 1046-1059.

Zierhofer, W & Burger, P 2007, 'Disentangling Transdisciplinarity: An Analysis of Knowledge Integration in Problem-Oriented Research', *Science Studies*, 20(1), pp. 51-74.

Zurn, P & Dumont, J 2008, *Health Workforce and International Migration: Can New Zealand Compete?*, Organisation for Economic Co-operation and Development.

Chapter 10

Applying innovation in information systems management: Ingersoll-Rand Corporation

David O'Sullivan

Innovation is about making changes that can create value for customers and then learning from the process so that it can be repeated continuously. The changes might be both radical and, more often, incremental. Often customers are internal to an organisation and have demands for improved service efficiency, faster response times, lower costs and greater value. Successful innovation requires a deep understanding of the change process. It is necessary to have a method for translating existing and potential customer requirements for greater value, into ideas and projects that can create positive change. Key elements of innovation include a definition of the goals of the innovation, mapping of key value-adding processes, alignment of key ideas with goals, empowerment of innovation teams, monitoring of key results and building an innovation community among all of the stakeholders in the process. This case study concerns the development of an innovation process for an Information Systems Management unit within a large organisation whose customers are mainly other units within the larger corporation. The core objective of the unit can be expressed as 'significant and sustained value creation for all current and future stakeholders'. This case study presents some of the main decisions faced by the unit in building a successful innovation management process.

Background

Ingersoll-Rand is a multinational company comprising six major industrial brands: Clubcar, Hussman, Ingersoll-Rand, Thermo King, Trane and Schlage. It is a commercial products manufacturer whose products include golf carts, refrigeration cabinets, power tools, transport temperature control equipment, security locks and air conditioning systems. It has a turnover of $13 billion and 60,000 employees worldwide. One of its strategic business units (SBU) has responsibility for the design, manufacture and sales of its transport refrigeration products. The SBU has five manufacturing sites, a spare parts distribution centre, a marketing and sales office and an extensive dealer network. The SBU has 2000 employees and a turnover of $1 billion. The Information Systems Unit (ISU) within the SBU is responsible for providing systems and services for all of the organisations including the manufacturing plants, dealers, design and sales offices, spare parts centre, and in addition, some third party strategic suppliers. ISU is also used on special projects around the world by its parent corporation. ISU is divided into four sections: Call Centre, Systems Operations, SBU Projects and Global Projects. Staff are generally multiskilled with primary skills in project management. The non-labour innovation and development budget for ISU is $7 million or 0.7 per cent of annual turnover and can decrease in line with decreases in turnover resulting in the curtailment of some lowly ranked projects. The innovation budget is used to maintain and upgrade existing systems, develop extensions to information systems and design and install new information systems and services. There are also a number of special exploratory projects carried out in collaboration with local research centres, particularly within universities, involving the design and development of new software and hardware systems and sensor networks.

Challenge

The Information Systems Unit faces a number of demands from its major stakeholders. Its corporate parent is demanding better service, greater return on investment and implementation of a 'pay by the drink' service for customers i.e. other units within the SBU have to pay for services and solutions through internal budget transfers. Demands from internal customers include the need for better service, faster response, greater reliability and more leading edge solutions. Staff within ISU have their own demands for more flexible work practices, greater training opportunities, more cutting edge challenges and lower focus on maintenance and help desk activities. ISU is regarded across Ingersoll-Rand for its skills base, friendly service and occasionally novel value-adding projects, but it is also under threat by the trend to outsource IS activities and to centralise and rationalise some IS activities within its corporate headquarters. ISU has a number of major weaknesses including some out-dated skill sets particularly around internet based solutions and a reluctance to take on projects of this nature. Its own internal project management tools are also seen as a bottleneck to managing and controlling some projects. ISU also identifies potential opportunities to expand its services to dealerships and to corporate headquarters that are now beginning to adopt software solutions well known to ISU. Recent acquisitions of other business units that require upgrading of information systems are also seen as potential new 'customers' for ISU. The unit faces two important decisions – to adopt a 'wait and see' approach to its future within Ingersoll-Rand and carefully follow corporate policies regarding the development of information systems; or to embark on an ambitious program of innovation management that could see its value and knowledge base increase within Ingersoll-Rand. This case study follows the endeavours of ISU as they attempt to develop an ambitious program of innovation management that visualises them as becoming the primary provider of services within the SBU and establish themselves as a leading partner in information systems policy and projects across the corporation.

Methodology

ISU embarked on the development of a vision to become the established provider of information services within the SBU and a leading partner in the development of information systems policy across the corporation. Their first decision was to agree on a methodology for change and put in place systems and processes that could support the change or innovation process. The output of this methodology or process was to be a vision, and an agreed set of goals and portfolio of initiatives that could take them towards that vision. The methodology adopted involved five key elements: (i) setting goals, (ii) identifying actions, (iii) engaging teams, (iv) monitoring results, and (v) building communities.

Setting goals

ISU identified a number of key tasks in setting its goals – environment analysis, stakeholder requirements, strategic planning and performance indicators. It began setting goals by conducting an analysis of its internal and external environments that included SWOT analysis, PEST analysis, benchmarking and technology, and process foresight analysis. They took a fresh look at internet based technologies and the development and growth of outsourcing and shared service centres. They looked at their own strengths, weaknesses, threats and opportunities. They could see clearly that weaknesses in one area could easily translate into threats in the future. They could also see that they had overlooked a number of strengths that could become opportunities in the future. Chief among these were the skills they had developed in networking with their internal customers. Benchmarking of other information systems service units was carried out to add new depth to their understanding of their internal environment and included cognate units within the corporation as well as similar units in non-competitive corporations who agreed to share their experiences. They learned that outsourcing may not be a threat and could release their own capacity to do more for the corporation. Following this period of reflection that also included some formal training and attendance at conferences, they began to develop a strong sense of urgency and collegiality around the need for a new vision for ISU that was ambitious and yet credible and realistic. This vision began to form around the need to offer state-of-the-art services in information systems that exceeded their stakeholder requirements and become a leader in new ground-breaking initiatives in collaboration with a local research centre. As the new vision formed, it became easy to communicate to their internal stakeholders at every possible opportunity and to corporate managers as opportunities arose. But, they knew that their vision needed to be backed up with a strong understanding of stakeholder requirements and a strategic plan that was realistic and ambitious.

Significant work followed on gathering high-level requirements of corporate and customers' demands that included face-to-face meetings, focus group discussions and a simple two-question online survey. The survey asked users what five things they liked about ISU services and what five things they would change. They gathered a very large number of suggestions for improvement from users and also discovered that many suggestions overlapped with their own ideas. Later they found it easy to attribute new services and solutions to users. A simple ranking of all of the requirements gathered helped to distil a very large number into the top 20 requirements that needed to be met for ISU to realise part of its vision. The concluding step for ISU in the goal-setting process was the creation of a strategic plan. They decided on a modified version of the 'balanced scorecard' while maintaining its overall method and simplicity. In place of Growth, Processes, Customer and Finance they adopted the strategic thrusts: Engagement, Processes, Customer and Innovation – reserving this latter thrust for goals around significant new processes, services and solutions in the areas of technology, people, processes and information systems. ISU identified strategic objectives and performance measures for each of the four strategic thrusts and then began to communicate their overall plan to all of their users and in particular senior management. They quickly found champions among the senior management group willing to sponsor or at least listen to some of their ideas and proposed actions.

Identifying actions

With a strong vision and clear set of objectives, ISU embarked on creating ideas for change. All staff were encouraged to engage in benchmarking and generating ideas for initiatives that would help them achieve their goals. Ideas emerged, not only for new services and special projects for their external stakeholders, but also for changes to internal processes such as better meeting management and using a collaborative information system for sharing all of their innovation related data. A user survey assisted greatly in underpinning some of the ideas already emerging, but this was not enough. They decided on providing a number of stimuli for staff and some key stakeholders. The stimuli included benchmarking trips to other organisations, conferences, workshops and seminars, in addition to having regular meetings where ideas could be discussed openly and without criticism. One workshop facilitated by an outside consultant proved particularly effective and utilised techniques such as brainstorming, ranking and voting, emphatic design (i.e. looking at users using services) and interviewing users. The role of the facilitator was generally to smooth out the noisy and often cluttered phase of idea generation to a more structured set of firm ideas. Some ideas were isolated and deemed appropriate for further investigation and the investment of time and energy. Of these some ideas were abandoned, some were either merged or put on hold and others were deemed suitable for full-blown implementation. These approved initiatives comprised a number of major groupings that included so called 'quick wins' that could be implemented easily and immediately and more long-term projects. Of the long term projects, there were many that could be seen to have a good reward and be low risk. However, they also selected a small number of projects that were potentially high reward but also high risk. In the fullness of time, some of these projects provided a breakthrough in performance whereas others were simply abandoned as soon as they were seen to be ineffective in meeting the goals of ISU.

This phase of innovation planning methodology produced a portfolio of initiatives that could be ordered, ranked and prioritised using a number of different perspectives. One way was to simply look at initiatives in terms of their cost. Another was to look at initiatives that had low risk or high impact. Another way to rank initiatives was according to their relative impact on ISU goals. An overarching ranking system was tried that took each of these perspectives and assigned a number from 1 to 5. Each perspective was then given a weight from 1 to 5. The ranking number and the weight were then multiplied giving an overall score for each initiative. The portfolio of initiatives could then be sorted by score, illustrating which initiatives scored highly which initiatives did not. In practice, this ranking system was dynamic and scores changed regularly due to changing circumstances and based on lobbying by various individuals. Lobbying, negotiation and compromise was as much a part of the ranking system as was the 'cold facts' regarding costs and benefits of individual ideas and later initiatives.

ISU were anxious to incorporate some element of learning into their project management process since not all initiatives would work in getting them towards their goals. They agreed to document three pieces of information from each initiative as they progressed through their life cycle: highs, lows and actions. Highs were concise comments on what was going well with the initiative at a certain point in time; lows were what was going poorly; and actions were what remedial tasks were going to be done to get the initiative performing well again. Each of these pieces of information was reviewed and discussed from time-to-time and sometimes led to an initiative receiving additional resources and, on occasion, led to an initiative being abandoned.

Engaging teams

Individuals and teams were identified early as the most critical resource of ISU for improving efficiency and increasing value for the corporation. ISU is mainly a project-based organisation and all individuals play either a leadership or support role on various projects in the unit. Individuals represented the intellectual capital of the unit and are a key resource. Some of the guiding principles behind individual staff development included: (i) autonomy and discretion, (ii) sense of meaningful contribution, (iii) opportunity to learn and continue learning on the job, (iv) optimal variety, (v) opportunity to exchange help and respect, and (vi) prospect of a meaningful future. These principles could be applied to any individual within ISU from managers and programmers to systems analysts and administrators. It was acknowledged that not every individual would reach the ideals set out in these principles, but they allowed managers to aspire to putting policies, procedures, training programs, meetings and other resources in place, which would empower their staff to strive for those goals. Every individual was given responsibility for some aspect of the activities within ISU according to their skills, ability and interests. Issues did arise from time-to-time when individuals felt that their skill sets (which had typically increased as a result of additional training and experience while on the job) were out-stripping the skills required for their assigned tasks. These relative skills mismatches called for the careful management of expectations of individuals. Whereas individuals felt that their skills were increasing, certain mundane tasks still needed to be completed effectively.

Individuals were motivated informally through the community that was created by all individuals with ISU, and also formally through a performance appraisal system. The appraisal system was based on so-called SMART objectives i.e. simple, meaningful, accurate, repeatable and targeted. Each year individuals and their immediate supervisors agreed a set of objectives for the individual. These objectives were divided into three categories – ISU objectives, ISU performance indicators and personal goals (for example, skills development by the individual). At the end of the year, each of the objectives and any additional ones agreed during the year were reviewed. In addition, any ideas or projects that the individual was involved with were reviewed. Performance by the individual was openly discussed and immediately followed by an agreement for the following year. Because the system was used throughout the corporation there was widespread acceptance of the review process – although there was occasionally disagreement on the performance of a particular individual.

Another aspect of engaging teams was a significant investment in skills development. This was done mainly through short professional courses but also through more extended courses of study, in particular, part-time degrees at a local university. In general, all staff were encouraged to up-skill where appropriate and skills were monitored using a versatility chart and through the review process described in the previous paragraph.

Monitoring results

ISU decided that regarding the success or otherwise of the innovation management process, there were two important things to monitor on a continuous basis. These were monitoring the regular status of all goals and actions and the periodic monitoring the progress of individuals. The regular status of all goals and actions were reviewed and discussed at bi-weekly innovation planning meetings. Every two weeks all staff met for a brief meeting to discuss key goals, projects, ideas and staff issues. Not all goals and projects were discussed – only those that were highlighted by the individual responsible for monitoring the particular event. A senior member of the staff was allocated responsibility for each particular goal and/or project and for turning their status to green, amber or red. Only activities that had a status equal to red were normally discussed at the meeting. On occasions, other activities could be discussed but usually to celebrate good performance or make early comparisons. The meetings were kept focused and rarely lasted more than one hour. ISU also used a simple online collaboration system for all goals and projects that staff could use to review results of any activity and this was an essential tool for keeping meetings brief and focused.

All individuals were also monitored through the corporate performance appraisal system. Each year individuals agreed goals with their immediate supervisor. These goals included personal and interpersonal skills development, management skills development, specific unit goals assigned to the individual and performance indicators assigned to the individual. Individuals would take clear responsibility for their own personal goals but shared the goals of the unit with others. During the year all individuals met with their supervisor to discuss progress and agree any changes to individual work plans. Also discussed at their interim meetings were any ideas or new projects that were emerging and that could be considered for addition to the overall ideas and project portfolio for the unit. At the end of the year, a formal meeting took place between the supervisor and the individual where the year's activities and goal attainment could be reviewed and where new goals could be set for the following year.

Building communities

The final element in the innovation methodology at ISU was the building of so called 'innovation communities'. These communities began with an online system for managing and sharing all goals and actions within the group. The group choose Microsoft Sharepoint for its ease of use and simplicity. This system had modules for all goals, ideas, projects and other data. This system was supplemented by Sharepoint systems for each individual project team to share project related data. Reports were never written for senior management since the online systems presented a dynamic snap shot of all aspects of innovation at ISU: ideas and problems being logged; a ticket system for the ISU help desk; the entire portfolio of projects; and, the status of strategic objectives and key measures for all of the performance indicators. ISU also created a Sharepoint system for logging complaints and ideas from all major stakeholders that fed directly into the other systems. This knowledge management system was very successful in communicating all important information to all of the key stakeholders within the business unit. In fact it was copied by other project-based functions including engineering and product design. It also received attention from other business units and the wider corporation who could easily see what projects were underway and how easy it was for ISU to take on any corporate project anywhere within the corporation.

Summary

ISU created an innovation management system based on five important areas – defining goals, aligning actions, empowering teams, monitoring results and building communities. Their methodology enabled them to gather together key information regarding change and also show their ability to take on more change anywhere within the corporation. There were a number of important lessons learned along the way. Firstly, innovation needs a method that binds together key pieces of information, in their case – goals, actions, teams and results. This method needs to be simple and easy to understand for both the unit and its stakeholders. Secondly, innovation needs simple and easy to implement online system for managing and sharing key innovation-related information. Such a system not only helps communication within the unit but also between the unit and its key stakeholders. A third lesson is the need for a focus on simple systems, simple data forms, simple processes and simple knowledge management. Simple systems not only support easy communication but also minimise ambiguity and increase collaboration among individuals. Simplicity and conciseness based on a sound methodology became the overall critical success factor that allowed ISU to position itself to add even greater value to the corporation.

Discussion questions

1) What were the main drivers for the innovation plan developed by ISU?

2) What was the response of ISU to the demands from its stakeholders?

3) What are the different types of goals defined by ISU?

4) How did ISU monitor the results of their innovation process?

5) What are the main features of the Sharepoint system?

Further reading

O'Sullivan, D & Dooley, L 2010, 'Collaborative Innovation for the Management of Information Technology Resources', *International Journal Human Capital and Information Technology Professionals*, vol. 1, issue 1, pp. 16-30.

Chapter 11

Becoming an innovative learning organisation

MARGARET TALLOTT, ALMA MCCARTHY AND RACHEL HILLIARD

Background and context

Crann Iorrais Teoranta (CIT) was established in 1987 in Co Mayo in Ireland as a forestry company engaged in a wide range of forestry-based activities for the private, commercial and semi-state sectors throughout Ireland. Since its inception, CIT (now CIET), has quickly grown to become one of Ireland's most reputable contractors for overhead power line infrastructure in the country. CIT's values of consistency, innovation, excellence, and trust act as the cornerstone of the company. The company is continually developing innovative techniques, systems and programs to further enhance its capabilities and achieve its organisational objectives. In 2010, the organisation had 62 highly-skilled employees. CIT represents an interesting example of how a small indigenous company employed the principles of a learning organisation to assist in achieving its strategic and business objectives. This case follows CIT's learning organisation journey over a one year timeframe.

Business development challenges and opportunities at CIT

A number of years ago, the managing director of CIT noticed a cycle: the company was going into decline for a second time, operating in a market where margins were falling while labour prices were rising. He felt the company needed strategic direction and, although having numerous innovative ideas for future development, he had no idea of how to go about systematically assessing these ideas. Customer relations, management policies and systems were absent in the organisation, and there was no meaningful financial information available to the managing director. The management philosophy was reactive in nature and strategic planning was non-existent. There was no underlying vision to propel the company forward. The managing director decided that the company would embark on a mission to engage in strategic planning with the help of an external consultant.

Following the completion of an industry and competitive analysis and a company situational analysis, it was concluded that the line clearance work in Ireland at that time was gradually becoming unattractive. However, the potential to diversify into other markets and provide other services was attractive – particularly opportunities in line clearance work in Northern Ireland and overhead power line construction and refurbishment for Ireland's largest electricity provider (the ESB).

As a result of the on-going strategic management review process, meetings were held between the managing director and an external consultant. The managing director decided to engage in a strategic planning process that would set out a new direction for the business. The learning organisation was identified as a potentially useful framework for enabling the strategic planning exercise. A cross-level and cross-functional team was set up to review and enhance the implementation of the learning organisation at CIT.

The learning organisation principles

The learning organisation is an approach to change management which organisations have used increasingly over the past decade. Learning organisations provide work environments that are open to creative thought and continuous learning, and that embrace employee input and capability. Adopting the learning organisational principles assists organisations to think critically and creatively, to communicate ideas and concepts across the organisation, and to engage with colleagues in the process of inquiry and action (Rheem 1995). As CIT was embarking on a strategic change program, the learning organisation framework was considered most appropriate because it would enable greater employee input and engagement in the change process as well as building on the existing capability within the organisation.

There are five main characteristics or disciplines associated with a learning organisation (Senge 1990):

1. Personal mastery – the commitment by individuals and the organisation to the process of learning. Practising personal mastery clarifies what is important and explores how personal vision can be facilitated by the organisation.

2. Mental models – the assumptions held by individuals and the organisation, which include behaviours, norms and values. Openness, inquiry and trust are important desirable dimensions of mental models in learning organisations.

3. Shared vision – the development of a shared vision is important in motivating staff to learn, as it creates a common identity that provides focus and energy for all staff. It is not solely driven by management or top-down in nature.

4. Team learning – The accumulation of individual learning leads to team learning. The problem-solving capacity of the organisation is improved through better access to knowledge and expertise. Team learning requires individuals to engage in dialogue and discussion. Dialogue requires individual team members to suspend their assumptions in an effort to understand other views. Having heard all the assumptions of team members, discussions can then take place to arrive at the best possible alternative.

5. Systems thinking – allows people to study the business in a holistic manner. This method of thinking assists an organisation to assess how information systems measure the performance of the organisation as a whole and of its various components.

The managing director and team members were consulted and agreed to practise the disciplines; progress was reviewed on a regular basis. All participants were posed the same set of questions at each review meeting:

1. How has this project enabled you to develop your personal mastery?

2. How have your mental models been affected by this project?

3. Are you satisfied that a shared vision has been achieved for this project?

4. In your opinion does this team engage mainly in dialogue or mainly in discussion?

5. Can you identify how systems thinking has been demonstrated in this project, and in terms of the entire organisation?

Towards achieving a learning organisation at CIT

Driving the learning organisation from the top

At the outset of the project, weekly management meetings with the managing director and the company secretary were set up to discuss and advance the strategic planning process at CIT and to assess how the principles of the learning organisation might assist in achieving this.

Discussing how the focus on strategic planning in CIT might enable the managing director to develop his personal mastery, he reflected on how the need to identify new opportunities for the company had caused him to question his vision for the company. However, it had not occurred to him how his vision for the company might enable him to advance his personal goals in life. Although he had been self-employed for almost twenty years, he felt he had not yet achieved the level of fulfilment he wanted. This was causing him greater concern as time passed.

Reflecting on how mental models have been affected by the strategic planning process, the managing director stated that the mental model he held prior to engaging in strategic planning was that, *'strategic planning is a process of constantly applying oneself (i.e. management) to directing activities'*. Being involved in work on the industry and competitive analysis exercise, he claimed, had given him an insight into how strategic planning is carried out. He was happy that he now has a new model of how ideas can be investigated in order to minimise the risk involved. The consultant suggested to the managing director that based on her observations she felt he had a mental model that, *'tells you making a living must be hard work'*. He affirmed that *'yes, I would say that I do'*. The consultant asked the managing director to investigate whether he could countenance changing that model and it was agreed to discuss this at the next meeting.

In attempting to discuss how a shared vision could be achieved for the company, the managing director stated:

> At this point, the company definitely does not have a shared vision. For now I am happy to leave it like that. I want to establish in my own mind first what my personal vision is before I can contemplate discussing it with the rest of the company, or taking on board how their personal visions could be part of the company vision.

It was agreed that while this situation was satisfactory for now, defining a shared vision would be a priority in the near future. The managing director's response when questioned about whether the management team was engaging mainly in dialogue or mainly in discussion was that, *'as the team, in this case, is made up of only three people, with the underlying premise for the project being to advance their goals'*, he felt the team was engaging mainly in dialogue, *'otherwise what would be the point of it all'*, his underlying assumption being that, people will engage in dialogue when working towards a common goal.

Finally, when discussing the systems thinking discipline of the learning organisation, the managing director reported that he could see how the strategic planning process would impact on the company as a system, particularly regarding employees, he commented, *'I know we will have to get the workers on board and include their views'*. In the broader environment, developments in the agricultural sector are seen as presenting issues both in the short term with the 'foot and mouth' crisis and in the long term with the rural environmental protection scheme (REPS) – one of the requirements of farmers participating in REPS is the maintenance of hedgerows, which reduces the need for line clearance. With farmers themselves instrumental in line maintenance, there would be an adverse impact on the core business of CIT due to a decrease in demand.

Three months later

Reflecting on the five disciplines of the learning organisation, the managing director discussed how he was slowly discovering what his personal vision was, following a key strategic decision to try to diversify into other markets: *'being involved in preparing the Northern Ireland Electricity (NIE) Supplier Business Questionnaire for the tendering process gave me a glimpse of how I want to do business in the future'*. He now feels the company can facilitate his personal vision by tendering for larger projects as in the case of the NIE work. This strategy would allow the company to grow and develop. Referring to his personal vision of how he wanted to work, he stated:

> *I want to be involved in strategic partnership with customers and not this short, low-value tendering the company is engaged in at present. I want to grow the company in a balanced way, bringing people along with me and allowing them to develop.*

In questioning the changes in mental models brought about by the strategic planning process, the managing director revealed that his mental model of how business is conducted, and in particular the purchasing process, had been altered dramatically. He elaborates:

> *I didn't even know that business could be conducted in a manner like this. Preparing the Northern Ireland Electricity documentation has exposed me to a different concept of purchasing, one that I had never experienced up to now.*

Following on from the discussion of his mental models at the meeting three months earlier, the consultant asked if his previous assumption of business being hard work had changed in any way. He responded, *'yes, I thought it would be hard work but, I'm actually surprised at how much I'm enjoying it now that I have a better focus on what I want to achieve'*.

Following on from the discussion on shared vision three months earlier, the managing director felt that he was now more comfortable with the idea of a personal vision that could feed into a shared vision for the company. It was time to extend the process to include others in the company. The fact that some projects within the business, such as international tendering and national network renewal work, were looking promising further increased the need to involve more people.

The managing director's recent experience of team learning was leading him to conclude that teams were an ideal structure for learning, *'I see team learning as similar to shared vision, something that we should work towards at CIT'*. He also felt that recent experiments in how ground crew leaders organise their own work schedule and become involved in the tender preparation process resulted in much better outcomes in terms of labour costs and work practices. However, he felt that the process was suffering as a result of insufficient communication between management and staff and between staff themselves and this needed to be addressed. The managing director suggested holding staff meetings at the company offices. The nature of the work was such that ground crews worked in geographically dispersed locations throughout Ireland. Up to that point, none of the ground crew workers had ever visited the company's offices. He felt bringing key people together for such a meeting would provide them with an insight into the administration of the company, its goals and objectives. It was agreed to hold regular team review meetings in order to facilitate implementing the 'learning organisation' throughout the company.

Reflecting on systems thinking, the managing director sees the possibility of the entire country being serviced by one, or a very small number, of contractors – as is the case in Northern Ireland and the UK. From the strategic planning process, it was established that, at that time, CIT held approximately 8 per cent of the Irish line clearance market. While much work had been done on customer relations, it was felt much more needed to be done if the company was to secure a larger share of the Irish market. The managing director again addressed the need to bring all CIT employees into the process stating that, *'we have to try and spread this thing throughout the company, and we need to do it in such a way that there is a bit of fun involved'.*

Driving the learning organisation across the team

A team was established to assist in the implementation of the learning organisation in the context of the change program at CIT. The team consisted of seven members: two company directors (managing director and secretary), the administration assistant, the safety officer, two ground crew team leaders and the consultant. Prior to the first meeting, team members were requested to familiarise themselves with the concept of the learning organisation. Background information together with a brief summary of the concept and the five disciplines of the learning organisation was sent to each team member.

At this first meeting, team members were very enthusiastic about the project. However, concern was expressed about the definition of the learning organisation supplied in the briefing material which was as follows: 'a learning organisation is an organisation skilled at creating, acquiring and transferring knowledge, and at modifying behaviour to reflect new knowledge and insights' (Garvin 1993, p. 4). This matter was discussed and a number of other definitions were presented to the group. The team was briefed on Pedler and Aspinwall's (1998) activity entitled 'Defining Your Learning Organisation'. This activity is designed to help the organisation create a definition of the learning organisation to suit their particular situation. Team members were asked to engage in a brainstorming session where they identified what kind of an organisation CIT would be – what it would look like, feel like, and how it would act – if it were to be a 'learning organisation'. Team members were then asked to forget about the ideal picture and brainstorm ideas of a NON-learning organisation. They were asked to recall past experiences and examples of where learning was avoided. The third stage of the activity was to sort the characteristics into three groups, as follows:

Finally, after discussing and reviewing the features that *must* be present for a learning organisation to exist and the features that *could* assist in achieving a learning organisation, and then identifying features that are counter to a learning organisation and *must not* be present, the following definition of CIT as a learning organisation emerged: 'In CIT what is meant by the learning organisation is an organisation that is continually expanding its capabilities to create a rewarding and successful future'.

The team admitted that before reading the briefing document, nobody had given much thought to his or her personal vision, much less how it could be reflected in the organisational vision. Many examples of mental models and how they can affect judgment were discussed before the team felt it had an adequate understanding of the discipline. The team agreed that shared vision would be explored further in the attempt to define the company's definition of a learning organisation.

Discussing team learning, members admitted they were confused about the difference between discussion and dialogue; again many examples of both were discussed and it was agreed to experiment with dialogue and discussion during the 'definition' activity. Members asked for additional written material on the subject of systems thinking, and in particular systems archetypes, and further information was given to each member. Before the meeting concluded, team members were asked to attempt to practise the five disciplines in everyday tasks and report back at the next review meeting.

Four months later

Four months later, a team meeting took place to discuss progress in achieving the five disciplines of the learning organisation. During the meeting, team members noted that they were becoming more confident in applying and using the principles. However, the main finding of this discussion was that the time span between meetings was too long. Members felt that in order to become adept at practising the disciplines, more regular meetings would be required. This would allow the sharing of experiences in a more timely manner. The team discussed this suggestion and agreed that meetings would be scheduled on a six-week basis and reviewed at each meeting.

Members were anxious to continue the process of developing a shared vision, which would be practical in everyday use. Concern was expressed that the team had no way of knowing if progress was being made by the company towards becoming a learning organisation. To address this issue, the consultant introduced the notion of measuring progress by presenting Pedler and Aspinwall's (1998) profile questionnaire (see Figure 11.1). The team engaged in a discussion about the questionnaire and agreed it would be beneficial to undertake it collectively. Members were asked to consider a number of statements and give their score out of ten for each of the statements listed. A score of 10 would indicate CIT 'is very much like this' and a score of 0 or 1 indicated CIT was 'never or not very much like this'. Team members were also asked to state their underlying assumptions for their scores. Figure 11.1 shows the outcome for 11 features of the learning organisation generated from the scores assigned to these features by the team members.

Figure 11.1 Learning organisation profile at CIT

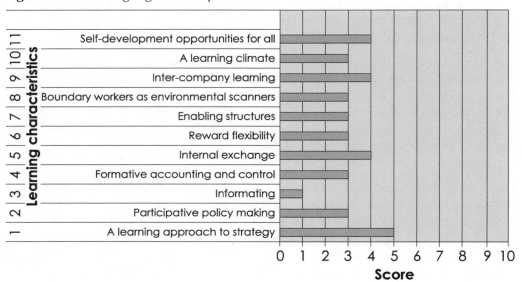

In discussing the result of this activity, members agreed it was a fair analysis of the company in terms of its learning organisation practices. It was suggested that this exercise be repeated twice a year and all members agreed with this. The low score on the subject of informating was highlighted. It was agreed that while there was no intention to withhold information, there was a serious lack of communication across the organisation. This problem had also been raised by the managing director during management meetings. Due to time constraints, it was agreed that the consultant and the managing director would discuss this problem, with a view to having some concrete proposals for discussion at the next meeting.

Six weeks later

Reflecting on the five disciplines six weeks later, team members gave accounts of how their personal mastery had developed. This progress was supported by a report from the managing director regarding how a ground crew leader had picked up extra landscaping work for the company. *'Before these meetings, that would never have happened. The ground worker would not have felt he had the authority to negotiate work on behalf of the company'.* It was agreed that members could see the benefit of how extra work for the company could contribute to their personal vision.

Ground crew leader team members, in particular, noted a change in their mental models resulting from their exposure to financial information at management review meetings. An example of this was given by one ground crew leader when he admitted, *'I thought if you wanted a 10 per cent profit margin, you priced the labour and simply added 10 per cent on top for the profit'.* Members engaged in dialogue and freely exchanged assumptions and ideas about the business. Issues regarding work flow, invoicing, work project completion rates and cash flow were discussed.

Investigation of a particular work flow problem regarding the switch out of power by the national power supplier led to a display of systems thinking when the safety officer advised, *'continuity of power to customers is one of ESB's internal performance measures'*. Expanding on this, team members could also see how the ESB's need for continuity of power in the short term would lead to power disruption in the long term, when lines may be damaged or broken by vegetation. This problem also has serious implications for safety in that contractors may be tempted to cut vegetation too close to power lines in order to have work complete and paid for.

Following-on from the last meeting, the managing director advised the team that he, together with the consultant and the administration assistant, had discussed the problem of informating as identified in Figure 11.1. They proposed additional software and training be acquired to incorporate greater analysis into the accounts system. This proposal was welcomed and it was agreed to try and have this completed within the next four months. During this discussion, members expressed the concern that there was a need to measure progress in a number of areas, not just finance. The use of performance dashboards (Meyers 1998) was identified as a potential solution to this issue. Performance dashboards are graphic tools to measure performance and assist in the learning process for two reasons: (i) learning efforts depend on good performance measurement, and (ii) measurement is meaningless without interpretation and judgment by the people who will make decisions and learn through implementation. This idea was welcomed and the team agreed a set of six performance indicators. In addition to measuring the achievement of the learning organisation profile (as in Figure 11.1), through a process of systems thinking and dialogue, indicators were developed in key business areas including: safety, customer complaints, debtors, successful tenders, and timely 'switch outs' as outlined in Table 11.1.

Concluding this meeting, both the managing director and the consultant commented on the volume of learning that had occurred during the investigation into performance measures and indicators. The degree to which systems thinking was evident in the indicators was noted by all.

Evaluating progress – one year later

One year after the project commenced, the managing director reflected on the progress achieved in CIT's journey towards becoming a learning organisation. At that point, a successful grant application was made to the industrial development authority for Irish speaking regions, which agreed to fund 50 per cent of a feasibility study on Network Renewal as a new strategic direction for the business. The NIE invited the company to respond to a detailed tender submission as part of their strategic sourcing program. CIT was invited to meet with NIE's strategic sourcing team in Belfast to discuss the proposal. NIE complimented the company on their strategic proposal and later advised that while CIT was not successful in securing the contract, this decision was based only on the company's size and scope.

Table 11.1 CIT's performance indicators

Business issue	Process	Performance indicator
Safety	Seen by the company as being of high importance. Used systems thinking and lengthy dialogue to establish training as the key factor in achieving safety.	Training index
Customer complaints	Identified through strategic planning as a key measure of progress.	Customer complaints
Cash flow	A recurring problem, on investigation was related to invoice queries by customers which were not being identified and resolved in time.	Debtors > 20 days
Success in tendering	Management review identified lack of success in one business area; measuring would identify areas where not competitive	% Successful tenders
Switch outs	Line clearance work can require asking the ESB to switch out the power from a line; this can affect job completion rates.	Switch out time delay

The exercise to establish CIT's Learning Organisation Profile outlined in Figure 11.1 was repeated six months later and showed a noticeable improvement in all aspects of the company's learning profile as seen in Figure 11.2.

Reflecting on events and their effect on personal mastery in CIT, the managing director still felt that other business opportunities and value streams should be pursued in order to achieve his personal goals for the business. This is evident from the following comment:

> ... if I were the type of person who was happy to make a living on a small margin with nothing to invest in the company or the people in it, then line clearance would be sufficient, but that is not what I want to do.

The managing director acknowledged the most notable improvement for him being involved in this process was that it, 'restored my personal confidence'. Talking about shared vision, the managing director summarised it as a means by which organisational members will be allowed to achieve personal mastery. He commented, 'we must fulfil members' personal goals if we are to retain key people'.

Figure 11.2 Second learning organisation profile at CIT

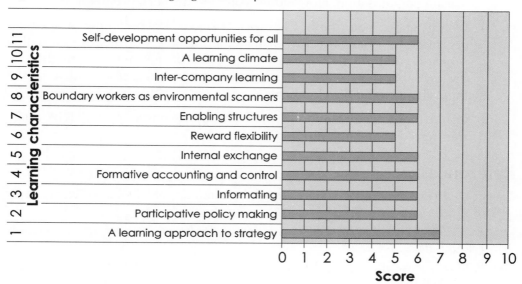

Concluding the discussion on CIT's progress towards achieving the five learning organisation disciplines, the managing director acknowledged they would need further time to develop, stating that, *'I find the concept new, even after working on it for the last year'*. He believed that team learning was very powerful and one of the disciplines that could bring greatest benefit to CIT, and he commented, *'now I know a team is the proper structure to evaluate the worth of any idea that might present itself in the future'*.

Summary

This case study discussed how CIT applied the principles of the learning organisation to facilitate a strategic planning process. The case indicates that the team members were unhappy with conventional definitions of the learning organisation and adapted a definition to suit their needs and goals. The case sets out how senior management and staff across the organisation impact on the achievement of learning organisation principles and shows that this journey is longitudinal in nature. Effective communication at all levels in the organisation is highlighted as a key feature in effecting team learning and other learning organisation disciplines.

Discussion questions

1) Why did CIT decide that the learning organisation was a suitable approach to achieve its strategic objectives?

2) What issues did the review team in CIT have with the definition of the learning organisation and how did they overcome this?

3) The team expressed concern about assessing progress towards achieving a learning organisation. How would you measure such progress?

4) Identify how you think CIT was changed by becoming a learning organisation? Can we say that adopting the learning organisation principles and practices actually caused the changes in CIT or might it be the case that there were other internal or external factors which caused these changes and developments?

5) Could the implementation of the learning organisation at CIT be easily transferred to any organisation?

References

Garvin, D 1993, 'Building a learning organization', *Harvard Business Review*, 71(4): 78-92.

Meyers, C 1998, *"Relentless Growth" How Silicon Valley Innovation Strategies Can Work in Your Business*, Free Press.

Pedler, M & Aspinwall, K 1998, *A Concise Guide to the Learning Organization*, Lemos & Crane, London.

Rheem, H 1995, 'The learning organization', *Harvard Business Review*, 73(2): 10.

Senge, P 1990, *The Fifth Discipline: The Art and Practice of the Learning Organization*, Doubleday Currency, New York.

Part III
Integration, Culture and Change Management

Chapter 12

Changing organisational hierarchies

RORY DONNELLY

KnowledgeCo: Background and context

KnowledgeCo is one of the largest and most successful professional service firms in the world. It has enjoyed almost continuous growth through a combination of mergers, acquisitions and organic expansion. It is active in over a hundred countries from Australia to Zimbabwe; employing thousands of staff and generating multi-billion dollar global revenues. It is a highly respected organisation and consistently features as a top employer to work for in a range of different employee satisfaction and perception surveys.

The firm is very much a knowledge-intensive firm because it engages in the delivery of intangible services rather than the production of physical goods (for further information on knowledge-intensive firms, see Alvesson 2004). These intangible services include assurance, tax advisory, consultancy, legal, actuarial and financial advisory services. Knowledge is the primary input into these services and most of the work undertaken by its employees requires the use of a high level of expertise in order to solve complex client problems and generate innovative solutions.

The firm adopts a partnership structure that is hierarchical in nature. At the point that this study was conducted, the structure in the UK comprised six grades (see following). Each of the six levels in the hierarchy reflected seniority and differences in an individual's status, role and centrality in the firm – as well as in client and professional networks.

This general model was and continues to be adopted despite the tensions generated by this structure within the firm and claims that 'flatter structures' are more appropriate for knowledge-intensive firms (see Castells 2000; Robertson & Swan 2004). Through the analysis of interviews conducted with individuals at every level of the firm across five of its UK offices, this case study examines the countervailing tensions between the removal and retention of the organisational hierarchy.

Partners
Directors
Senior managers
Managers
Consultants
Assistant consultants

Changes to the organisational hierarchy

The interview data revealed that although the organisational hierarchy was firmly embedded across the firm, there was evidence of efforts to gradually move away from the existing structure (outlined above) to suit managerial and organisational interests. For example, in newly established and relatively small departments, distinctions between the responsibilities and the nature of the work performed at each grade were being dismantled in order to flatten the hierarchy and, in doing so, reduce associated salary premiums. This meant that in such departments, staff at the level of consultant faced demands and performed work that was typically undertaken by managers in other departments, but on a consultant-level wage.

The development of these career, pay and working arrangements was also supported by ongoing redundancies at the firm, as well as reductions in the relative availability of high-level positions. In response to these developments, some senior members of the firm identified the need to provide alternative progression opportunities in order to improve staff morale. This included the creation of a series of role types rather than pay-related grades.

However, this strategy was merely being pursued on a localised basis due to differences in the relative performance of individual business areas and the maintenance of comparative structures in competitor firms. There was also concern among some senior members of the firm that such a strategy would negatively affect individuals' motivation and commitment to the firm and the profession. Senior positions conferred internal and external prestige and members would be less able to gauge their position in the professional hierarchy, as traditional 'signposts' would lack relevance.

Professionals typically expect that with time and personal development, they will proceed through the ranks (Maister 1993). Where continued career progression is stifled, it is almost certain to result in lessened motivation, particularly as the reward for going the extra mile is less apparent to individuals. In addition, this is likely to have a negative impact on firm performance and ultimately its profits, despite the impact of the firm's hierarchy in moderating the exchange of knowledge as discussed below.

Tensions over the ownership and exchange of knowledge

Although flatter organisational structures are believed to be more effective in facilitating and promoting the exchange of knowledge, the firm continued to retain a hierarchical structure, which was somewhat counterproductive as it generated tensions between members of the firm. The structure was supported by an up-or-out career progression ethos and so competition between consultants was strongly evident.

This competition extended to the exchange and ownership of knowledge, because of the link between the form and degree of knowledge held by individuals and their hierarchical status and corresponding reward levels. Therefore, members of the firms tended to withhold segments of information/knowledge in order to protect and enhance their position within the firm.

> *The level of knowledge/expertise is what makes the difference between the different levels ... Some people are deliberately obtuse because they don't really want to share their information ... it's like in project work; some people like to keep all the work or knowledge to themselves and don't forward information or emails, so that you do a bad job and the client complains, so that they look better. (Consultant)*

Many consultants consequently retained elements of their tacit knowledge that they perceived to be of importance to their personal and professional advancement. This behaviour can be linked to tensions in the relationships between members of the firm, generated by the hierarchical and competitive nature of the career structure. The exchange of knowledge between levels of the firm was encouraged through team working, networking and coach/apprentice arrangements. However, competition between members of the firm transcended these relations. For example, junior members of the firm reported that their coaches and senior members of staff retained much of their knowledge and only shared information that was needed to perform work to the required standard, and that this was done in order to preserve their competitive advantage. The hierarchy in place also hindered the exchange of knowledge, because an individual's status influenced the nature of the work that they performed. Junior members of the firm tended to be largely office based and so were more active in disseminating and exchanging knowledge. Senior members of the firm, on the other hand, tended to have more client contact and so had less time to spend in the office transferring knowledge thus impacting on the degree of knowledge exchanged and the level of professional development achieved.

The propensity to retain elements of personal knowledge also extended to individuals' engagement with the firm's codification systems. Indeed, the accounts provided by the interviewees revealed that individuals only contributed basic information to the firm's databases, in order to retain ownership of the elements of their knowledge that they perceived to be of value to them as individuals. The firm's databases therefore contained only incomplete and dated segments of information that were of little value either to the firm or its staff, particularly due to constant changes in consultancy knowledge. In addition, members of the firm were reluctant to contribute too much information due to the concern that entries into such databases could expose gaps in an individual's knowledge base.

The hierarchical environment in place accentuated this concern. Junior members of the firm were reluctant to post questions on database forums because this could highlight deficiencies in their knowledge and influence the perceptions that senior members of the firm held of them and their professional competence. They also tended to exchange knowledge with colleagues at a similar level rather than with individuals further up the hierarchy, while senior members of the firm did not wish to be seen to draw on the knowledge of their junior colleagues. These behaviours shaped knowledge flows within the firm.

If the firm adopted a flatter or even a non-hierarchical structure, members might engage in knowledge acquisition and exchange activities more freely. This would improve the efficiency and effectiveness of the firm and its members; however, it would weaken the credibility of the hierarchy and the position of those in more senior grades.

Hierarchies and flexible working

Hierarchical divisions between the grades also became apparent on to the take-up of flexible working arrangements (FWAs). The firm had recently introduced formalised FWAs. Full-time members of the firm were eligible to participate in the scheme, enabling them to vary their office start and finish times within two and a half hour margins of the core hours of 10:00 to 16:00 defined by the firm, so long as they worked a minimum of 7.5 hours per day. Participation in the scheme was subject to business and management requirements and the agreement of an individual's manager.

The interview data revealed that it was primarily junior members of staff that had chosen to take up these arrangements. Many senior members instead elected to retain their informal arrangements. This was due to the demands and nature of the work that they performed and because they believed that informal flexibility offered them greater freedom to structure their work around their own personal needs. They tended to have been with the firm for a considerable amount of time and therefore believed that the firm should have sufficient confidence in their commitment to trust them and enable them to exercise discretion over their working time arrangements.

These patterns in the take-up of FWAs at the firm also reflected gender divisions. The majority of those choosing to operate under the FWAs were women, who were concentrated in junior-level roles. The firm recruited equal proportions of male and female consultants; however, senior positions in the firm were strongly male-dominated. At the level of partner, just 13 per cent were female.

The interview data revealed that the adoption of FWAs negatively impacted on an individual's hierarchical progression. Career advancement was directly linked to billable time and those choosing to work shorter hours were at a relative disadvantage when competing for promotion opportunities. The gendered take-up of flexible working consequently hampered the progress of women. Women often remained in junior roles and performed work that could be accommodated into their working patterns and so was typically less demanding and prestigious. In addition, their hierarchical progression was shaped by the presence of old boys' networks and the glass ceilings in operation at the firm.

The hierarchical structure at the firm was therefore marked by vertical gender segregation. The firm had stated objectives to increase the recruitment and retention of women and to enhance women's representation. These aims were underpinned by increasing equality legislation. However, the link between gender, working hours and this structure has meant that it is unlikely to achieve its diversity and gender equality goals.

The internal and external face of the hierarchy

The salience of the organisational hierarchy varied according to organisational boundaries and played a direct role in shaping external interaction and engagement with clients. Internally, junior members of staff performed much of the work on client projects and even headed-up teams on an informal basis. However, in order to meet client expectations and ensure the appropriate management of the relationship, it was normally only senior and experienced members of staff who engaged with clients. This generated tensions between junior and senior members of staff.

> *I have headed up groups that have had more senior people in than me ... but in a client situation, you always have the most senior person at the top, because the client expects that and most senior people always think that they are the ones with the most knowledge, even if they aren't. (Assistant Consultant)*

In addition, it was mostly the senior members of the firm that engaged in external networking activities. Junior members of the firm tended not to engage in external networking as they typically had little contact with clients and were not necessarily encouraged to network externally. This was because they could potentially interfere with the arrangements that more senior members of the firm had in place.

The organisational hierarchy therefore generated tensions over client engagement and ownership as well as networking activities. However, the removal of this structure would run counter to client expectations and undermine the role and legitimacy of senior staff in generating client work.

Summary

KnowledgeCo is a leading knowledge intensive firm. It seeks to be a dynamic and leading-edge organisation at the forefront of business trends. However, a range of parameters serve to moderate the form and degree of change in its structure, which impacts on its success and performance in a number of key areas. As a consequence, it retains somewhat of a traditional hierarchical structure.

Discussion questions

1) What are the pressures for the retention and removal of the hierarchy?

2) What do you think that this case study tells you about effecting change in an organisation's hierarchy?

3) Why is the hierarchical structure at the firm so resistant to change?

4) Does the retention of this hierarchy make the organisation an attractive company to work for? How might this vary depending on an individual's position?

References

Alvesson, M 2004, *Knowledge Work and Knowledge-Intensive Firms*, Oxford: OUP.

Castells, M 2000, *The Rise of the Network Society*, Oxford: Blackwell.

Maister, DH 1993, *Managing the professional service firm*, New York: MacMillan.

Robertson, M & Swan, J 2004, 'Going Public: The Emergence and Effects of Soft Bureaucracy Within a Knowledge-Intensive Firm', *Organization*, 11 (1): 123 – 148.

Chapter 13

In for the long haul? Family business succession at HaulageCo

ROWENA BARRETT

This is a case about family business succession. Because many successions fail, the 'problem of succession' is a key issue in the family business field (see Aronoff 1998; Bird *et al.* 2002; Dyer & Sanchez 1998; Sharma 2004; Zahra & Sharma 2004). Indeed, from the non-family business literature, we know one third of relay successions – like this case where there is an identified successor – will fail, with the prospective CEO leaving before succeeding the incumbent CEO (Cannella & Shen 2001). Research on next generation family business members is limited. Successor attributes (Chrisman, Chua & Sharma 1998; Sharma & Rao 2000), as well as various characteristics such as socialisation (García-Álvarez, López-Sintas & Gonzalvo 2002) and gender (Haberman & Danes 2007; Vera & Dean 2005) have all been considered to play a role. So too have successor intentions (Stavrou & Swiercz 1998), motivation (Le Breton-Miller, Miller & Steier 2004), commitment (Sharma & Irving 2005) and transformation from follower to leadership (Cater & Justis 2009). In this case, by outlining the socialisation of the successors, explanations of their motivations for joining and their current employment we can begin to see some of the underlying mechanisms at work motivating the next generation to join and stay in the family business.

The business and family contexts

This chapter tells the story of two successors (Matt and Sam) who have jointly succeeded to the management of the one family business. HaulageCo was established in 1954 by the current joint Managing Director's grandfather Gary, after World War II. Prior to World War II, Gary had operated two or three trucks with an A-class licence, which covered those engaged in public haulage or 'hire and reward'. During World War II, when he served in the Army, Gary's wife Rebecca attempted to run the business *'but she couldn't get drivers and they were having problems so father [Gary] decided to park them up and to just put them under tarpaulin sheets' (Fred).* During this time the Road Haulage Organisation (RHO) was set up by the Ministry of War Transport with control over all road freight movements throughout the UK. Three hundred and eighty-eight large haulage firms were taken over on a charter basis with other trucks hired from another 2,700 operators. In all, 34,000 vehicles were controlled by the RHO until August 1946 (Labour Party Transport Policy Document 1954). When Gary came out of the Army in 1946, *'he had lost his licences' (Fred).* From 1947 to 1954 Gary reverted to his building trade qualifications; however, with the election of a conservative government and privatisation of the road haulage industry through the 1952 *Transport Act* (Labour Party Transport Policy Document 1954), he went back into the haulage business with just two vehicles.

Gary operated the business with his wife Rebecca. She made local deliveries, while he drove the longer distances to and from London. As soon as Fred was able he went along with his mother to help with the loading and unloading, explaining *'When I was 14 I used to go with her from school. I was quite a big strong lad and I did the humping for her and as I'd learnt sheeting from my father, I did all that and the roping' (Fred).* While Rebecca stopped driving in 1960, she maintained a role in the business making up the wages and doing the bookkeeping. This established a 'tradition' for the 'business wives' with Gary asking Fred's wife May to take on a similar role in 1973. May said her move into the business was, *'a matter of, you know, you're married into the family now so, no choice'.* Sam's wife April, who would join the company years later, undertook administrative tasks on a part-time basis prior to the birth of their son. This was as a result of the 'opportunity' to work as a consequence of having a family business.

In 1958 Fred started working fulltime in the business after leaving school at 16. He never wanted to drive trucks but his father gave him no choice. As he explained, *'you did as your father told you' (Fred)* and when Gary told Fred, *'we've got you a little wagon out there, go and earn some money',* that's exactly what he did. When he joined the business it was located next to the family home in a Midlands village, which was where it stayed until 1997. In 1997 the business moved to a purpose-built location in a Midlands out of town industrial area with good access to motorways. The move allowed the business to expand.

Sam joined the business in 1984 as an apprentice in the maintenance workshop, while Matt joined in 1997 and had responsibility for the traffic office. At the time of the study, HaulageCo operated 30 vehicles, employed 45 staff and had a £3 million turnover. The company has grown steadily over its history, but most notably since the late 1990s.

The trajectory of HaulageCo differs from others in the industry, which has seen the number of operators fall and the majority operating a fleet of 3.7 vehicles on average (DfT 2006). In this industry, profit margins of no more than 3 per cent are common (RHA 2000) and so economies of scale have driven mergers and acquisitions (M&A). Family firms have not been immune from M&As, for example, in March 2008 Eddie Stobart Ltd, the iconic UK road haulage firm, acquired James Irlam and Sons' from the three brothers representing the firm's second generation owners for £59.9 million.

HaulageCo's strategy focuses on quality service and efficiency while a 'can do' attitude underpins their relationship with customers. All vehicles are equipped with GPS satellite tracking and messaging systems enabling real-time positioning of trucks and loads. Efficient loading and scheduling is also facilitated by use of a leading traffic management software system, which is tailored to meet the specific needs of the business. The business has a number of long-standing customers including a long-term haulage contract with a global transportation manufacturer.

Like many in the industry, HaulageCo faces considerable external pressures, which include the increasing costs of trucks, labour, excise and fuel, which alone is estimated to account for up to 35 per cent of haulage costs (RHA 2000). Other pressures are changing health and safety legislation with increasing regulation on drivers and hours, driver shortages and increasing competition from European firms following the 1998 liberalisation of cabotage enabling foreign registered hauliers take on domestic loads (McKinnon 2007). Debates about road charging are of concern for this industry, and those driving through London can also pay congestion charges and fees associated with London's low emission zone.

Growing up in the family business

The socialisation into the business can start at early childhood for next generation family business members. This was the case for Sam and Matt who grew up with the business that their Grandfather (Gary) founded and in which both their parents worked – their father (Fred) since he was 16 and their mother (May) since Sam and Matt were very small.

Sam and Matt's early socialisation was apparent in their stories of growing up. They spent their childhood living next door to their grandparents in their family home, which was next door to the business. Their evenings, weekends and holidays were spent playing or mucking around in the yard. Both learned to drive at an early age: *'Matt started driving a truck at about seven, didn't you? [Sam asks question to Matt] I was a bit later, I was possibly 11' (Sam).*

May gave a similar account of their childhoods, explaining that because Matt and Sam lived next door to the business, they had grown up in it. She argued that as time went on the boys exercised a free choice to do this, saying,

> *They weren't forced, they used to go out and potter around and, of course, when they could get to drive the wagons. But it was their choice, they weren't forced to go out, they just enjoyed going out and messing around and getting dirty and pottering around (May).*

When Sam was asked how he came to join the business, his response was to say, with a laugh, he was *'press-ganged'*. He went on to explain that the time he'd spent mucking around in the yard and watching the mechanics work on the trucks meant he developed an interest in the engineering side of transport. At school he took subjects like physics, chemistry, maths and metalwork before going on to college for one year to study for his Ordinary National Certificate (ONC).

Having gained his ONC, Sam then planned to start his apprenticeship with another trucking firm. However an apprentice unexpectedly left HaulageCo and Fred employed Sam in the workshop. Despite being the eldest of the two siblings, it was not *a fait accompli* that Sam joined the business first in 1984. For the first two years working at HaulageCo he also studied on day release to complete his engineering apprenticeship in the workshop.

Matt joined HaulageCo in 1996. The story of how he came to join the firm started with Sam explaining,

> *Matt's the brainy one, if you like. Matt looks after the traffic, Matt did school. But in the holidays he was out with the drivers, all that sort of thing. He did his A levels then went to University to study transport.*

Matt was passionate about the business saying that when he was younger he would take any opportunity he could get to go out with his father in one of the trucks. Particularly in the summer school holidays he would say to his father, *'come on Dad there's a job to go to at so-and-so, let's go'*. Looking back he could see that, while for his father the novelty of getting up at four o'clock in the morning to do a job would have worn thin, to Matt it was just fantastic. He would go back to school in September and cheerfully explain what he did on summer holidays as, *'I went driving in a lorry with my Dad!'*.

After completing his degree, Matt took a graduate position with a large transport and distribution firm which led to running one of their warehouses and goods departments. When he joined the family business he took on responsibility for the traffic office and fleet planning.

Matt said he had always planned to join the family business but not straight from school. He wanted to go to university and get a degree that would help with running the family business. He took out a four year undergraduate degree in Transport Management and then went to work for the company where he had spent his placement year. Matt gained considerable experience in the two years he worked for that large company and while he might have stayed longer, the *'reasons for staying changed'* (Matt), and he came to HaulageCo. His father explained that while Matt earned a good salary, he knew he was 'in dead men's shoes' and could see little opportunity for rapid advancement; this was partly why Matt decided to join the family business.

Full-time employment in the family business

Sam: At the time of the interview Sam had been working in the business for 23 years. He had never worked anywhere else. He started as an apprentice in the workshop but had been driving HGVs [Heavy Goods Vehicle] since he got his licence at 21. In his time in the business his 'training' had not taken a defined path, instead, as he explained *'there's no written down path that says in the first three years you will do this, the next three years you will do that or anything like that. It just sort of happens really' (Sam).*

While he had worked in all aspects of the business, his prime responsibility was for the workshop and maintenance of the firm's 30 vehicles, making sure all the vehicles were in good working order and that all drivers met occupational health and safety standards. Over time, he had also taken responsibility for the firm's IT system despite having no formal IT training.

Gary and Fred's philosophy of being 'hands on' and not asking anyone to do something you could not do yourself permeated the firm. It showed in Sam's work experience in all aspects of the business which meant he would drive if there was a shortage of drivers or assist in the workshop if they were busy. As he said, *'You do whatever you need to do. You know, if the toilets are blocked one of us will unblock them, it's as simple as that' (Sam).* This attitude underpinned a good relationship with the 45 staff members and reinforced positive experiences with the family business.

That Sam could say the following also shows his commitment to the business:

> *You know there's some crap things about doing this job – getting up at four o'clock in the morning and the truck's broken down or you've got to get the low-loaders out at two o'clock in the morning and it's cold and wet. It makes you think that there's got to be an easier way. But that's what we're in, isn't it? I don't know anything else. You know, I'm pretty good at what I do and you think yes, I could take them skills somewhere else. As if! I wouldn't last five minutes trying to work for somebody else...*

Sam's wife worked in the business on a part-time basis and his 3-year-old son's joyful enthusiasm for the trucks (witnessed by the author when he visited during Fred's interview) also underpinned his commitment.

Matt: At the time of the interview Matt had been employed in the family business for 11 years. Prior to joining and after finishing his degree in Transport Management Planning he took a graduate position with the large company where he had spent the placement year of his degree. Although he had other job offers he took that position as it offered a range of training. Matt's decision to join the business was influenced by how he interpreted his situation at the large company, as mentioned above, as well as his participation in family discussions about relocating the business and modernising. As Fred explained the family business had outgrown its village location and neighbours were not happy about living next to a 24 hour trucking operation. The family had to choose between selling-up, and moving and growing the business. As a family, they decided on the latter and it was after this time that Matt joined the business and started working in the traffic office. Here he brought with him *'more modern ways of dealing with customers and managing customers' expectations, rather than "well, you'll get it when you get it"' (Matt).*

In explaining his decision to join the business Matt made direct comparisons with his alternatives. For him, the key to his continued motivation to participate was, *'here, what you do directly affects you'*, which was contrasted to what he experienced when he was an employee at the large transport and distribution firm. For him, the motivation for staying hinged on the fact that he could directly affect his earnings and future through the decisions he and his brother made about the firm on a day-to-day basis.

Taking over the reins to the family business

When the data were collected Sam and Matt were titled joint Managing Directors, while Fred was Company Chair. They had each had these titles for a number of years, but what it meant in practice was not at all clear to them. This situation pointed to the problems that could emerge when family business ownership and management became separated. At HaulageCo it meant, *'He* [Fred] *still, controls the bank. He looks at the bank on his computer regularly, and tells us when we've not got enough money in the bank' (Sam).* Indeed, there was an interesting exchange in the joint interview when they were asked who owned the business. Sam responded, *'That's a good question'* and Matt added, *'We don't!'.* With a laugh Sam challenged the researcher, saying, *'If father will talk to you after, you can ask him that question, and then if he tells you the answer, you can tell us!'.*

One of Fred's delights was opening the mail each morning as he could,

> *Learn more from opening the mail sometimes than spending an hour down there [indicating to Sam and Matt's office] ...they won't tell you otherwise, you know, if something happens (Fred).*

But from Sam and Matt's perspectives, this meant that if there was an offer made to buy the business, regardless of who it might be addressed it, their father would put it in the bin.

Fred's behaviour was interesting in light of the stories he told about his father Gary and the bitterness he harboured from his father's inability to delegate decision-making authority. He recounted one incident in particular, which *'put a nasty taste in my mouth for a long, long time'.* Fred was adamant that he would not treat his sons in the same way, but countered that by saying, *'But they've got to have a damn good reason why they'd want to do something. They've got to prove to me that it'll be profitable and how the company would benefit' (Fred).*

When ownership and management are separated, a manager's decisions are constrained by the owners' desires. At HaulageCo, this separation meant it was questionable who ran the company. Fred cast a 'generational shadow' and by staying involved on a day-to-day basis, he had the potential to cause conflict in the future (Davis & Harveston 1999). It also raised interesting questions about the firm's ongoing management and strategy and particularly the likelihood of the family retaining the firm. Fred wanted the company to go forward, saying, *'I've got two grandchildren and I'm here as a caretaker for them - this is my father and mother's legacy'.* However from Sam and Matt's perspectives, there was a series of 'ifs':

If the business is still around and if we still own it and if it's still successful and if we're happy doing it and if they [his and Matt's sons] want to come and show an interest, then yes we'll keep going. But, if, before that, we feel... (Sam)

Shhh...Father...he'll be listening in... (Matt)

... if we want to sell and see an opportunity to do something else, then we shouldn't be hindered from taking that decision because there is a fourth generation. Grandfather did the business for father and him for us, but if we see something else or if we feel it's time to get out, then that is what we'll do (Sam).

There was a question mark over whether Sam and Matt had fully attained the firm's leadership. In what they said and did it was apparent they had internalised the firm's values and goals. Their fit with, interest in and commitment to the business was also apparent while they had good relationships at work and within the family. They had considerable investments in the business and were satisfied with the returns they 'earned' as a result. While it is not possible to predict the future of any business, the commitment of Matt and Sam to HaulageCo would suggest they are there for the long haul.

Discussion questions

1) Sayings like 'clogs to clogs' in three generations highlight the long-term fragility of family businesses, largely generated by poor succession decisions. In your opinion, how fragile is this family business? Do you think Matt and Sam are likely to remain in the family business? Why?

2) In this case the ownership and management control of the business became separated and had the potential to cause problems. What management strategies or practices could be implemented to ensure problems do not arise?

3) A range of factors are likely to impact on family business members' decisions to join, stay or leave a family business. What are those identified in the case and how did they act on the joint successors? What other factors may play a role and how?

References

Aronoff, CE 1998, 'Megatrends in family business', *Family Business Review*, 11, 181-186.

Bird, B, Welsch, H, Astrachan, JH & Pistrui, D 2002, 'Family business research: The evolution of an academic field', *Family Business Review*, 15, 337-350.

Cannella, AA Jnr & Shen, W 2001, 'So close and yet so far: Promotion versus exit for CEO heirs apparent', *Academy of Management Journal*, 44, 252-270.

Cater JJ & Justis RT 2009, 'The development of successors from followers to leaders in small family firms: An exploratory study', *Family Business Review*, 22, 109-124.

Chrisman, JJ, Chua, JH & Sharma, P 1998, 'Important attributes of successors in family businesses: An exploratory study', *Family Business Review*, 11, 19-34.

Davis, PS & Harveston PD 1998, 'The influence of family on the family business succession process: A multi-generational perspective', *Entrepreneurship Theory and Practice*, 22, 3, 31-53.

DfT [Department for Transport] 2006, *Focus on Freight, 2006 Edition*, Transport Statistics, Department for Transport, London.

Dyer, WG Jnr & Sánchez, M 1998, 'Current state of family business theory and practice as reflected in Family Business Review 1998-1997', *Family Business Review*, 11, 287-296.

García-Álvarez, E, López-Sintas, J & Gonzalvo, PS 2002, 'Socialization patterns of successors in first- to second-generation family businesses', *Family Business Review*, 15, 189-203.

Haberman, H & Danes, SM 2007, 'Father-daughter and father-son family business management transfer comparison: family FIRO model application', *Family Business Review*, 20, 163-184.

Labour Party Transport Policy Document 1954, *British Transport,* Labour Party Policy Pamphlet No. 1: Transport House, London.

Le Breton-Miller, I, Miller, D & Steier, LP 2004, 'Toward an integrative model of effective FOB succession', *Entrepreneurship Theory and Practice*, 28, 305-328.

McKinnon, AC 2007, 'Increasing fuel prices and market distortion in a domestic road haulage market: the case of the United Kingdom', *European Transport/Trasporti Europei*, 35, 5-26.

RHA [Road Haulage Association] 2000, Memorandum submitted by the RHA to the UK Government's Select Committee on Trade and Industry, October, available online at www.publications.parliament.uk/pa/cm200001/cmselect/cmtrdind/268/ 01101a02.htmm, accessed 08/01/10.

Sharma, P & Irving GI 2005, 'Four bases of family business succession commitment: Antecedents and consequences', *Entrepreneurship Theory and Practice*, 29, 13-33.

Sharma, P & Rao, SA 2000, 'Successor attributes of Indian and Canadian family firms: A comparative study', *Family Business Review*, 13, 313-330.

Sharma, P 2004, 'An overview of the field of family business studies: Current status and directions for the future', *Family Business Review,* 17, 1-36.

Stavrou, ET & Swiercz, PM 1998, 'Securing the future of the family enterprise: A model of offspring intentions to join the business, *Entrepreneurship Theory and Practice*, 23, 19-39.

Vera, CF & Dean, MA 2005, 'An examination of the challenges daughters face in family business succession', *Family Business Review*, 18, 321-345.

Zahra, SA & Sharma, P 2004, 'Family business research: A strategic reflection', *Family Business Review*, 17, 331-346.

Chapter 14

Workplace wellness within a university framework

RUTH MCPHAIL AND TRISTAN SMITH

Background and context

Since opening its doors in 1975, Grey Gum University has become known as one of Australia's most innovative tertiary institutions and one of the most influential universities in the Asia-Pacific region. Grey Gum University has grown from its inception as a one-campus institution offering a very limited selection of courses, to a multi-campus powerhouse offering over 300 degrees in 10 study areas. The student population is approximately 40,000 with students from over 124 countries. With over 3000 staff employed in academic, general and research capacities across Grey Gum's campuses, servicing the needs of such a large and diverse workforce continues to represent a major challenge that remains as a high priority.

Workplace wellness is a key area of human resource management, which Grey Gum University has focussed upon as an area for improvement. A strong commitment to workplace wellness is thought to assist with: (i) attracting and retaining quality staffing talent, and (ii) improving overall workforce productivity. Grey Gum University has always had a longstanding commitment to workplace wellness but, due to managerial oversight, has never developed a comprehensive and well-coordinated workplace wellness program. The many wellness initiatives available for staff are often fragmented, uncooperative in nature and inadequately promoted, which has resulted in inefficiency and ineffectiveness across the whole workplace wellness program.

Workplace wellness at Grey Gum University

Workplace exercise

Grey Gum University has on-campus gym facilities open to students and staff with a complete range of workout equipment including treadmills, exercise bikes, cross trainers, leg press machines, squat racks, weight benches, rowing machines and much more. With operating hours of 5.30am–9.00pm the exercise facilities can cater to a variation in staff timetables. Gym discounts are available for staff via salary sacrifice, but considering the indisputable benefits of exercise in relation to stress and overall wellbeing, it has been argued that management should initiate more strategies to encourage and incentivise staff participation in on-campus exercise activities.

Grey Gum University also boasts a variety of social sporting clubs including a broad selection of ball sports and athletic options. The Northern University and Australian University Games are held annually and Grey Gum University is a major participant in these events. Some staff have argued that the social sports at Grey Gum are too 'student focussed' and ignore an obvious staff desire to participate. Other staff contend that role inflexibility and time constraints tend to prohibit staff participation in campus sports.

Workplace health

The Health Service at Grey Gum University is committed to (a) promoting and facilitating the prevention and treatment of disease, and (b) empowering students and staff to manage their own health and wellbeing. The services available include emergency and first aid treatment, preventative health measures (flu shots), routine pap smears, sexual health advice, immunisations and overseas travel vaccinations, referrals for x-rays and specialist treatment, pregnancy testing and ancillary health service referrals for psychiatry, optometry, massage and mental health needs. Grey Gum University also offers free short-term counselling for staff members as part of its commitment to improved workforce productivity, reduced absenteeism, decreased accident rates, greater staff retention and higher staff morale.

Once again, the problem is that these health services are poorly promoted to the wider staff population. There is a lack of technical innovation in the delivery of these services and a non-existent focus on tracking program effectiveness. An abundance of literature over the last ten years has highlighted the private sector's shift into constantly evaluating wellness initiatives so that management can justify their existence to shareholders. The higher education sector and Grey Gum University in particular, with its unique in-house resources, might benefit from benchmarking actions such as program tracking and evaluation. The private sector has shown some competency in the evaluation of workplace wellness programs, thereby providing accountability to key stakeholders. It has also shown some capability in demonstrating the efficacy of workplace wellness programs.

Workplace nutrition

Any campus exercise and health program must be complemented with a comprehensive commitment to campus nutrition. Otherwise, the advantages from exercising and 'working out' can be reduced through the consumption of unhealthy foods. Unfortunately, Grey Gum University has a less than desirable record when it comes to campus nutrition. The first problem stems from the strong presence of soft drink and junk food vending machines around campus. Such convenience for staff is a temptation few staff members can resist. Staff members complain that with their workload and time constraints they can't be bothered queuing for scarce resources with students at the main cafeteria. Therefore, the choice then becomes either bringing food from home or snacking from a vending machine that supplies soft drinks, chips, chocolate bars and sweets. Unfortunately, the latter usually wins out.

The university cafeterias themselves are inadequate with very small sections devoted to fruits and salads. What is constantly seen, however, are large heated ovens displaying fried foods and pastries, colossal soft drink fridges filled with an abundance of high energy drinks and long tables filled with sweets and chocolate bars. These snack foods may be appropriate for the ill-disciplined student requiring a sugar hit. However, for highly skilled staff with serious responsibilities to discharge, the provision of highly nutritious food alternatives is best practice – and not only should they be adequately provided for staff, but they also need to be promoted and incentivised by management.

Human resource management policy

Human Resource Management (HRM) policy at Grey Gum University has been developed to foster a work-life balance culture amongst staff. Wide varieties of leave options are available including, sick leave, parental leave, bereavement leave, leave for cultural or family obligations and leave for many other special circumstances. Such a liberal approach to work-life balance extends into offering staff a flexible work year and flexible working hours. Childcare facilities and support services are also offered at Grey Gum University to assist working parents if required.

HRM policy at Grey Gum University does not just cover work-life balance arrangements. There is also a range of staff professional development and manager support initiatives, which can contribute to improvement in both job satisfaction and job performance. Grey Gum University also has strong harassment, bullying and anti-discrimination policies, which give staff a sense of security that they will be emotionally and physically safe at work. Should a grievance present itself, staff are secure in the knowledge that there are mechanisms in place that will seek a just and impartial outcome. Feeling that your employer actually values you as a human being first and as an employee second is a strong driver of not only job satisfaction, workplace productivity and job performance, but also workplace wellness. In summary, Grey Gum University has strived to achieve a suitable work-life balance with its approach to its HRM policy.

Technological innovation in service delivery and tracking

Exercise, health, nutrition and a dedication to best practice are four standard components to include in any workplace wellness program (WWP). But what can positively impact the success of any workplace wellness program is how innovatively the wellness initiatives are delivered. Where technology has, in some instances, complicated our lives by increasing work stress and tightening deadlines, it has also created exciting opportunities to encourage innovation in the field of workplace wellness. Wireless internet technology (embedded in notebooks, laptops, PDAs and mobile phones) has the capacity to transmit information directly between all relevant stakeholders involved in a workplace wellness program. The technology enables organisations to deliver important parts of wellness programs directly to employees and track employee progress via instant progress reporting functions utilised by employees. Password protected wellness portals can be established allowing each employee to access his or her own wellness profile. Employees would then be able to personally update and maintain their records such as physical activity logs in their individualised wellness plan.

Currently, Grey Gum University does not have in place an innovative wireless wellness solution; it relies solely on a workplace wellness website buried deep within the university's workplace health and safety website. Access to the relevant information requires extensive navigation through many web pages before finally clicking onto the relevant area. Overall, this website is hard to access, provides limited information for staff and students, and most importantly, is very poorly promoted around campus. There is great scope for Grey Gum University to explore the wireless options discussed above and to also improve its wellness marketing campaign. Without comprehensive coordination of wellness initiatives, a strong marketing campaign and innovative evaluation / tracking mechanisms, workplace wellness programs can easily be resigned to a fate of inadequacy or worse: abject failure.

Employee attitudes at Grey Gum University

Figure 14.1 represents a sample of employees surveyed about workplace wellness at Grey Gum University. The results indicate both ineffectual promotion and ineffectual delivery of services, which have an unacceptable majority of employees unaware or unsatisfied with university wellness initiatives.

Figure 14.1 Employee attitudes at Grey Gum University

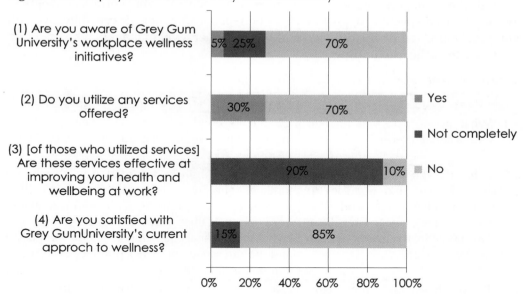

Firstly, question (1) produced an overwhelmingly negative response from the respondents. Over 90% of responses indicated an overall lack of awareness about Grey Gum's current wellness initiatives. Question (2) receives predictable results: given that the majority of respondents are not aware of the services, they subsequently cannot participate in them. A small portion of those unaware respondents (20%), found that when they actively looked up Grey Gum's wellness measures, they unknowingly did actually use some services. This highlights Grey Gum's ineffective promotional strategy. Question (3) finds that of those who utilised Grey Gum's services (30%) around 90% found them 'not completely' effective and 10% of the respondents indicated that they were plainly ineffective. This validates empirical research, which states that un-coordinated services overlook possibilities for mutual synergies and innovative solutions, ultimately resulting in inadequate outcomes (DeVries 2010). Employee dissatisfaction is alarmingly high in this instance. Question (4) conclusively illustrates employee dissatisfaction with 100% of respondents stating they were not completely satisfied or completely unsatisfied with Grey Gum University's current approach to workplace wellness. Common criticisms put forward included: inadequate wellness promotion; a lack of employee consultation; and poor use of innovative technological solutions.

Managers' attitudes at Grey Gum University

To gain an insight into the attitudes of managers at Grey Gum University, managers involved in health and wellbeing programs were surveyed on a broad range of wellness issues. Their responses highlight the obstacles facing the implementation of a comprehensive and well-coordinated workplace wellness program at the university.

Grey Gum's management hierarchy is a large and formidable structure. Even though the managers interviewed do have some control over workplace wellness within their respective departments, when proposing new ideas they are still ultimately affected by the decision making of higher level managers who are often required to authorise funding.

Figure 14.2 Management attitudes at Grey Gum

Question	Response
1. What position do you hold at Grey Gum University?	Of the respondents surveyed their positions included HR advisors, OHS officers/managers and heads of service.
2. What do you consider to have been barriers and obstacles to implementing a total workplace wellness program at Grey Gum University in the past (say, the last five years)?	The primary obstacle recorded was a lack of funding. This was seen to be due to the university's 'student focus' and an inadequate 'staff focus'. Other reasons include a lack of higher-level managerial support for the proposal and the prevalence of higher priorities constantly consuming finite resources.
3. Do you believe in the merits of implementing a comprehensive workplace wellness program at Grey Gum University?	Overwhelmingly, all respondents recorded a 'yes' to this question. Some respondents notably quoting studies that positively correlate workplace wellness with productivity in the workplace.
4. How important would you consider a focus on Return on Investment (ROI) to be when designing a workplace wellness program?	Scale: Insignificant – Some importance – Significant importance – More than significant importance – Central importance The consensus among respondents indicated that a focus on Return of Investment (ROI) be classed as of 'more than significant importance'. The common argument was that management would never adopt a WWP unless it could be reliably proven that a return on investment would follow. Other responses argued that the extent of the focus would be determined by the size of the investment from management. Naturally, a higher investment in wellness would require more detailed ROI modelling.
5. Has Grey Gum (HR or OHS) adopted or developed any ROI mechanisms to track the effectiveness of current wellness initiatives offered by various university departments?	Only one known ROI measurement is currently being trialled and that is in relation to Flu vaccinations. It was documented that such measurements have been extremely difficult to track. Value in such programs is subsequently being measured more by anecdotal evidence regarding improved employee perception of the employer (that is, Grey Gum cares about its staff) rather than quantitative methods.

6. How important would you consider employee consultation to be when designing a comprehensive wellness scheme?	Scale: Insignificant – Some importance – Significant importance – More than significant importance – Central importance This question produced interesting results. Higher level managers were more inclined to answer 'significant importance' whereas HR Advisors and lower level managers considered it to be invariably of 'Central importance'. This shows that perceptions of the importance of employee involvement in decision making changes significantly as the investigation moves higher up the management hierarchy. In this case, the perception of employee involvement changes negatively towards being less significant when investigated towards the top levels of management.
7. What are Grey Gum's strategies for promoting the current wellness initiatives on offer?	The usual answers emerged here with group emails, websites, posters and newsletters being common replies.
8. What are Grey Gum's strategies for encouraging employee participation in the current wellness initiatives?	All respondents indicated the former answer (refer question 7), omitting any reference to the use of incentive schemes or reward initiatives. This shows that management commitment goes no further than email and newsletters to encourage participation. The onus of responsibility is placed firmly in the hands of employees.
9. What role does technology play in delivering and monitoring current wellness initiatives?	Respondents again alluded to the former responses of email and the internet but interestingly all answers contained a suggestion that technology could in fact be used much more effectively. One submission expressed frustration at the fact Grey Gum was not leveraging all technology available including wireless innovations like phone apps, twitter and social networking sites.
10. Into what other areas would you like to see Grey Gum University expand its current wellness operations?	Some important suggestions included visible senior management commitment to workplace wellness; new strategies that support an ageing workforce; stress management and relaxation initiatives; more physical activity at work including Pilates, yoga and walking groups; and more healthy eating options on campus.

ROI and upper management support

The benefits of workplace wellness programs (WWP) have been researched in detail and the majority of authors have concluded that WWP are effective in encouraging employee health and an increase in workplace productivity (Coulson, McKenna & Field 2008; Donaldson 1993; Ho 1997; Kumar, McCalla & Lybeck 2009; Wolfe, Parker & Napier 1994). It seems that the benefits of workplace wellness programs are obvious, but reliably calculating a wellness program's Return on Investment (ROI) when submitting proposals to management can be complex. To illustrate the confusion currently surrounding ROI measurement, Aldana (2001) proposes that for every dollar spent a $3.65-6.05 ROI will result. Chapman (2005) argues average ROI is in fact $6.05 for each dollar spent, and recently Baicker, Cutler and Song (2010) proposed it to be between $2.85 and $3.40. The differences between each of these studies highlight the fact that there is no uniform method for calculating ROI. In summary, there are many interacting variables that can confound the results when calculating ROI, thereby impacting upon the margin for error.

Research by DeVries (2010) highlights the difficulties faced in measuring the benefits of WWP. Further, DeVries (2010) contends that measuring savings and ROI is an extremely difficult challenge because measurement methodologies are complex, costly and time consuming. For example, the most scientifically accurate measurement program would be accomplished through clinical trials that would require the employer to assign one set of employees to the wellness program and another set of employees randomly allocated to a control group. The employer would then monitor health data longitudinally from the two groups of employees for a period of years. At the end of the time frame, the employer would compare the health care costs of the two groups to determine estimated savings and ROI. Very few groups have the financial resources to conduct this type of clinical trial as it would require a department within itself to administer, maintain and analyse the variables.

The best data collection method recommended for organisations without vast resources is to gather as much information about employee health and wellbeing as possible in the employee consultation phase and create an initial benchmark or snapshot of the organisation (DeVries 2010). Using innovative wellness tracking functions (DeVries 2010) it is then possible to compare statistics say, in one years' time, with the initial information gathered to deduce whether improvement has been realised or not. This method is certainly not scientific, but it is a crude and somewhat accurate method of *estimating* a workplace wellness program's value. It is important to remember that many benefits that flow from WWP are in fact intangible and outside the scientific scope of measurement. Measurements for absenteeism, turnover and job satisfaction can all be laboriously calculated if organisations have the resources. However, intangible benefits, which it could be argued are equally valuable, such as cultural improvements and positive shifts in perception among employees, are much harder to scientifically quantify.

The survey results shown in this study indicate that middle management and employees at Grey Gum University all want a coordinated workplace wellness program that is more comprehensive than the current arrangement. The key obstacle seems to be developing a proposal to submit to upper management that categorically demonstrates a positive ROI impact resulting from the implementation of a comprehensive WWP. More research must be completed in Australia in order to develop reliable and accurate workplace wellness ROI calculation methods which will assist institutions such as Grey Gum University to (i) validate their workplace wellness proposals, and thereby (ii) gain upper management support for such initiatives. Until such a time, institutions with limited financial resources such as Grey Gum University will need to rely on methods such as collective petitions to further encourage workplace wellness reform. Petitions that are sent from employees to management could highlight the need to urgently implement a well coordinated WWP.

Summary

In conclusion, workplace wellness programs are integral initiatives which tie employee benefits with workforce productivity. Supporting evidence from the academic literature demonstrates the positive linkage between workplace wellness and workplace productivity. However, measuring a workplace wellness program's official ROI is a complex undertaking. Although there may be academic, employee and middle management support for coordinated workplace wellness programs, until concrete ROI calculations can be accepted with certainty by upper management, then funding for WWP in organisational environments with finite resources will continue to pose a threat to implementation. More research needs to be completed to develop ROI methodologies that are financially viable, practical to administer and ultimately show some level of reliability, validity and overall methodological rigour. Grey Gum University's staff and middle managers must actively champion the benefits of a workplace wellness program and collectively vocalise their support for its change.

Discussion questions

1) Based on the case study, analyse the management and employee attitudes towards workplace wellness programs.

2) What key components must an effective workplace wellness program include for it to be a viable organisational investment?

3) Advise Grey Gum University on better nutritional food and technological innovation arrangements.

4) Can you identify any barriers to success when planning and implementing a coordinated workplace wellness program? Discuss.

Reference List

Aldana, S 2001, 'Financial impact of health promotion programs: a comprehensive review of the literature', *American Journal of Health Promotion*, vol. 15, no. 5, pp. 296-320.

Baicker, K, Cutler, D, & Song, Z 2010, 'Workplace wellness programs can generate savings', *Health Affairs*, vol. 29, no. 2, pp. 304-311.

Chapman, LS 2005, 'Meta-Evaluation of worksite health promotion: 2005 update', *American Journal of Health Promotion*, vol. 19, no. 6, pp. 1-11.

Coulson, JC, McKenna, J, & Field, M 2008, 'Exercising at work and self reported work performance', *International Journal of Workplace Health Management*, vol. 1, no. 3, pp. 176-197.

DeVries, GT 2010, 'Health and productivity innovations in workplace wellness: six new tools to enhance programs and maximize employee health and productivity', *Compensation Benefits Review*, vol. 42, no. 1, pp. 46-51.

Donaldson, SI 1993, 'Effects of lifestyle and stress on the employee and organization: implications for promoting health at work', *Anxiety, Stress and Coping: An International Journal*, vol. 6, no. 3, pp. 64-77.

Ho, TS 1997, 'Corporate wellness programs in Singapore: effect on stress, satisfaction and absenteeism', *Journal of Managerial Psychology*, vol. 12, no. 3, pp. 177-189.

Kumar, S, McCalla, M, & Lybeck, E 2009, 'Operational impact of employee wellness programs: a business case study', *International Journal of Productivity and Performance Management*, vol. 58, no. 6, pp. 581-597.

Wolfe, R, Parker, D, D, & Naper, N 1994, 'Employee health management and organizational performance', *Journal of Applied Behavioural Science*, vol. 30, no.1, pp. 100-122.

Chapter 15

Age discrimination at Virgin Blue Airlines Pty Ltd

BEN FRENCH

This case study explores the Queensland Anti-Discrimination Tribunal's (QADT) decision in *Hopper & Ors v Virgin Blue Airlines Pty Ltd* [2005]. The case was subsequently appealed to the Queensland Supreme Court of Appeal (QSCA), *Virgin Blue Airlines Pty Ltd v Stewart & Ors* [2007] QSC 075. Much of the appeal case addresses issues of legal procedure and technicalities, which are not relevant to this business case study dealing with recruitment and selection processes. In short, the QSCA upheld the decision of the QADT. That is, the QADT had correctly applied the anti-discrimination legislation in determining that the Respondents, (the eight Complainants in the original case before the QADT) were unlawfully discriminated against on the basis of age by Virgin Blue Airlines Pty Ltd (Virgin Blue). The unlawful discrimination occurred when the eight women were treated less favourably than other younger applicants during a group assessment for positions as cabin crew at Virgin Blue. For ease of reference, this case study will primarily focus on the facts as outlined in the original decision *Hopper & Others v Virgin Blue Airlines Pty Ltd* [2005] rather than the legal technicalities of the upheld appeal.

Background

Virgin Blue took to the skies as a new budget domestic passenger airline in Australia during the year 2000. This was in direct competition with the major Australian low cost domestic passenger airlines at the time, Ansett and Qantas. When it commenced operations, Virgin Blue had two aircraft flying one route, employing 200 team members. Since then, Virgin Blue has become one of Australia's leading airline companies, regularly staging airfare price-wars with its competitors, as well as engaging in massive advertising campaigns, emphasising what they believe to be the company's uniqueness and competitive advantage: 'Virgin flair – making the flying experience fun for the customer'.

The company experienced rapid expansion during its early years when one of its major competitors, Ansett Airlines, was placed into voluntary administration. After a period of voluntary administration it became evident that Ansett would not be able to trade out of financial difficulty and it was placed into liquidation. The liquidation of Ansett Airlines resulted in its staff being made redundant, with many of them left with unpaid outstanding entitlements. At the time, this was Australia's largest company failure causing the loss of jobs for approximately 20,000 staff, including 15,000 Ansett staff, plus an estimated 5,000 staff from companies that relied on Ansett Airlines for work (Weller 2006). The news of Ansett Airlines being placed into the hands of administrators was a shock to a great number of its staff who had loyally served the company for a long period of time. Up until about the point of Ansett Airlines' collapse, it was uncommon for experienced staff members from either Ansett or Qantas Airlines to apply for jobs at Virgin Blue. Traditionally the more established older airlines offered far more favourable employment conditions than the new budget carrier, including higher wages and less arduous flight schedules. However with the collapse of Ansett Airlines this all changed, and many of its former staff now unemployed, former staff applied for a variety of jobs with the new budget carrier, Virgin Blue.

Some of the former Ansett Airlines staff who applied to work for Virgin Blue included the eight cabin (flight) attendants ('complainants') that are the subject of this case study. The eight complainants were all females aged between 36 and 56 at the time of their job applications being lodged with Virgin Blue (September 2001 to September 2002 – 'the relevant period'). Although the former Ansett staff had vast experience working in the airline industry as cabin attendants, none of these women were offered positions by Virgin Blue. This led the women to believe that they had been unlawfully discriminated against on the basis of their age. This culminated in the group of eight complainants lodging an anti-discrimination complaint under the provisions of the *Anti-Discrimination Act 1991* (Qld).

Context

Ansett Airlines' demise in 2001 helped bring about the rapid expansion of Virgin Blue during this period. It allowed Virgin Blue to expand its operations by taking over some of the previously owned and controlled Ansett Airline airport terminals across the country. This rapid expansion resulted in Virgin Blue having to screen and recruit a large number of staff members over a short period of time. It also meant that there was an oversupply of labour applying for cabin crew positions with the company. This new labour environment placed a heavy burden on Virgin Blue's ability to effectively manage how its recruitment and selection process was carried out. In particular, its ratio of recruiters to applicants in the group assessment stage was reduced. The situation also resulted in a lack of proper training for the typically young inexperienced recruiters, who were mainly aged between 25 and 34; which is often the case for staff working in recruitment positions. These deficiencies in recruiter training and administration of the behavioural competencies testing resulted in Virgin Blue's recruitment and selection policies (and how they were administered) becoming the subject of legal action. The case went before the Queensland Anti-Discrimination Tribunal and the Queensland Supreme Court of Appeal as noted above.

Facts of the case(s)

The Virgin Blue recruitment and selection process for cabin attendants encompassed several stages. The first stage simply required the completion and electronic lodgement of an employment application form for cabin crew positions. Up until about the time of the collapse of Ansett Airlines, applications to work for Virgin Blue were lodged by postal mail. However, as favourably noted by the QADT, to cope with the significant increase in demand of applications, Virgin Blue changed the employment application process to electronic lodgement. Applications were made via an employment services provider, Staff CV Inc., whose contact details were provided via a link on the Virgin Blue website. Part of the electronic application included a compulsory field on the questionnaire that required applicants to submit their age. There was nothing to suggest that the nominated age details were discriminately used to select young job applicants to attend the next stage of the assessment process, namely the group assessment process. As evidenced by the eight relatively older complainants having passed this stage of the recruitment and selection process.

Although Virgin Blue had traditionally employed more female cabin attendants under the age of 35, it was able to statistically demonstrate that the reason for this was not discriminatory. Rather, Virgin Blue was able to provide evidence that it was because the majority of female applicants applying for cabin crew positions were under the age of 35. Understandably this was reasoned as being due to the nature of the job which included such requirements as being able to travel away from their home base on a regular basis, which often conflicted with family responsibilities – disproportionally affecting female workers.

The nature of the cabin attendants' work conflicting with family responsibilities was not an issue in the case because, similar to most anti-discrimination acts across the western world, the *Anti-Discrimination Act 1991* (Qld) allows for companies to apply a genuine 'occupational requirements exemption' to positions that legitimately require workers to be able to fulfil genuine requirements of the role. Furthermore, there was no contention that the eight applicants were unable to comply with the requirements of the job in this regard. Thus, even though Virgin Blue had requested age specific details at this first stage of the recruitment and selection process, it was not a contentious issue in this case.

In many countries, including Australia, when recruiters are faced with a large number of job applicants it is an established practice for them to use a group assessment procedure rather than interview candidates individually. This was standard practice at Virgin Blue at the preliminary, second stage of the recruitment and selection process. Completing group testing is a recognised recruitment and selection procedure and was therefore not a contentious point in this case. However, the manner in which the group testing was carried out by the Virgin Blue recruiters was pertinent to the complainants' case and became the main legal issue before the tribunal/court.

The second stage of the recruitment and selection process required the chosen applicants to attend a group assessment at Virgin Blue's Brisbane premises. Part of the process required the job applicants to form into groups and demonstrate 'behavioural competencies' aligned to an underlying characteristic that Virgin Blue equated to superior performance at work. The testing assessed assertiveness, team work, communication skills and what was termed 'Virgin flair'. Virgin flair was described in the case as, 'a desire to create a memorable, positive experience for customers. The ability to have fun, making it fun for the customer'.

The group assessment method that was used to assess an applicant's Virgin flair required the job applicants to design and role play several dramatic routines given to them by the Virgin Blue recruitment staff. Whether the applicants had Virgin flair was assessed and rated by the Virgin Blue staff recruiters. Due to the limited number of assessors, it was not possible to have more than one assessor per group and, typically, there was one recruiter per group of ten applicants. Under these conditions it was difficult for the recruiters to assess any individual group member. The group assessment determined which job applicants could progress to the next (3rd) stage of the recruitment process. None of the complainants made it past the second stage of the recruitment and selection process. Thus, the further assessment stages were not required to be discussed in the legal case(s) and are not relevant to this case study.

Basis of complaint

Originally the complainants attempted to argue that the recruitment and selection process itself was flawed because it was 'an elaborate ruse to mask an intentional choice of fact made by the assessors of the most physically attractive employees'. This claim of intentional indirect discrimination could not be supported by a factual basis and therefore was later abandoned by the complainants. It was also contended that the behavioural competencies testing favoured younger candidates. However, the QADT stated that the testing was a standard international assessment procedure used in the aviation industry and that testing had proven that, if used properly by trained recruiters, it produced an 'age neutral' result. Thus the actual testing was not biased in favour of younger candidates.

Importantly, the manner in which the assessors *used* the test to appraise Virgin flair became the major issue in the case. It was argued by the complainants that the recruiters had subconsciously used a 'similar to me' effect when determining the ability to have fun – one of the traits of Virgin flair. QADT Member Douglas Savage SC described the behavioural testing and 'similar to me' effect as follows:

[There is] inevitably, a danger of employing the behavioural competencies system, especially as it required an assessment of 'Virgin flair', was to identify with persons of the same age and experience as the assessors, or what the assessors regarded as, if not of the same age, a 'fun' person. That person was I think likely to be a person of the same age, social class and life experience as the assessor.

Decision

Both the QADT and the QSCA found Virgin Blue's recruitment process at the group assessment stage to be discriminatory and that it had not produced an 'age neutral' result. Although Virgin Blue had not expressly imposed an age restriction on applying for cabin crew positions with the company (except being over the age 18), the 'partly subjective assessment process used for selecting employees – namely the subjective views of the assessors about the behavioural competencies of applicants for employment' had unconsciously imposed age restrictions on applicants.

Tribunal Member Douglas Savage SC was critical of Virgin Blue's attempt to distort its own statistics that in fact demonstrated that age discrimination had occurred. The statistics demonstrated that during the relevant period over 750 people had applied for cabin crew positions with Virgin Blue. Ten per cent of the applicants were over 36 years of age, yet only one of the applicants in this age group was selected for employment. This demonstrated that age discrimination had occurred because there was no other reasonable explanation as to why more applicants in the older age category were not offered employment.

The behavioural testing had resulted in the Virgin Blue recruiters directly discriminating against the applicants on the basis of age by subconsciously showing preference for employing people of similar life experiences and ages to themselves. Although the method of assessment provided lawful criteria, the manner in which it was used, caused by the lack of training and inexperience of the assessors, meant that it was applied in an unlawful and discriminatory manner.

Discussion questions

1) How does the *Tribunal* attempt to strike a balance between protecting the rights of employees and the rights of employers?

2) What are the practical implications of the Virgin Blue decision?

3) Did Virgin Blue make any errors at the first assessment stage?

4) Why is intention irrelevant in determining whether unlawful discrimination has occurred?

5) What other lessons should be learnt from this case study?

Suggested further reading

Weller, S 2006, 'Discrimination, Labour Markets and the Labour prospects of Older Workers: What Can a Legal Case Teach Us?', Working Paper No.31, Centre for Strategic Economic Studies, Victoria University.

Chapter 16

Understanding change: Conflict, resistance and misbehaviour in the workplace

KEITH TOWNSEND

Background and context

Frozone is a relatively new organisation that was created to develop single serve, frozen meals for airlines. It was established without reference to the past, with a focus on new technologies and contemporary management practices. The worksite was designed to use a just-in-time (JIT) production system, in which components are delivered in precise quantities and at the exact time that they are needed in the production process. Under a JIT system, tight quality control is essential because defective or insufficient parts immediately disrupt production.

A significant change objective on the production line was to remove all physical barriers, while still ensuring the safety and integrity of the cooking and storage processes. All processes followed a natural flow, with fresh goods arriving at the eastern side of the plant and storage facilities immediately beside the docks. The goods progressed through the stages of preparation through to packaging, storage and dispatching on the far western side of the plant. Ideally for management, there was no requirement for most employees to go further than 10–20 metres for all the equipment they required, regardless of the section they worked in. Management wanted a plant design that would provide an efficient use of potentially productive time, and as a consequence, limit the (re)appropriation of time (Ackroyd & Thompson 1999). A plant layout where employees are not required to move far from their workspace would limit the possibility of employee 'loafing' and potentially avoid the temptation of employee 'theft of time'.

The worksite can be divided into three main areas. The first is the non-food preparation area, including administrative workspaces, canteen and changing areas/toilets. Secondly, there is the low-risk area of the building where food safety standards are less problematic, as the food was still to be cooked. Low-risk rooms are painted green and employees are required to wear green uniforms and hairnets in this area. The final main area of the processing plant is the high-risk area, where food contamination through poor hygiene or work practices is more likely and potentially very dangerous. Food flows from the cookers which are situated in the low-risk area, pass through the assembly area and then cooked ingredients are assembled into the individual serves and sent through the freezing process. Importantly, the processes in this section are driven by either the technology or upstream processes. This provides the teams working upstream in the process with comparatively higher power due to their ability to control the flow of production. The high-risk area is painted red with red uniforms and hairnets and when considered with the work processes required in this area, is commonly referred to as the 'hell-pit'.

Managerial philosophy

The management team set about establishing a pathway to reaching the vision for the new entity, and employed the services of a *Performance Coaching Consultant*. The Manager of Operations explains that the consultant was employed to assist in the de-programming of the new management so they could *'forget about all the things we thought we knew about managing people and running a business'*. This process involved spending two days a week behind closed doors working through the stages of de-programming and learning each week prior to the opening of the plant.

According to another management team member, they began the process quite cynically before they were 'de-programmed' and became more aware of the opportunities available to them.

> *...after a few months it really started to mean something and I could almost recall the day when we just had this awakening...After that we started to create a mission statement and...make decisions. We wanted a flat structure and to ensure that quality and open communication developed. We wanted to lead not to manage - we wanted to seek guidance from the team members not instruct.*

The project team recognised that all of the management staff had arrived at Frozone from management hierarchies and reporting lines that were very bureaucratic. As the vision developed, the management group was determined to create a business where they could instil 'self-responsibility'[3] in employees at all levels of the business, and as an outcome, create semi-autonomous, high-performance work teams. To do this, an important factor would be a greater

---

[3] A commonly quoted term from management and staff alike.

emphasis on 'open and honest'[4] communication, more sophisticated personnel recruitment processes, payment structured for successful achievement of team goals and multiskilled staff.

Following an extensive and complex recruiting process, where the successful applicants were those who displayed the appropriate team-focussed characteristics, production was underway. The early stages of production saw a much greater than anticipated workload and early success. As a result of the increased workload, managers felt the need to insert another layer of supervision – a team leader role. This increase in managerial authority meant the semi-autonomous work teams were not a reality, and the structure was beginning to look more typical and hierarchical. Nevertheless, there was much optimism from the managers about the culture they were trying to achieve.

Conflict, resistance and misbehaviour at Frozone

While some employees enthused about the team spirit and working environment, many other employees remain cynical at this style of manipulated culture. One employee eloquently summed up the feelings of many at Frozone:

> *The thing we all hate most is the manipulation. Talking about equality, everyone's equal in this place and you can see that because even the boss doesn't have an office, you know? I say, bullshit – when you try living on $390 a week then come back and talk to me about equality because at the moment equality is bullshit, mate.*

What became apparent is that not all employees could see 'the vision' before them. For managers, it is one thing to supervise and guide people who shared the vision and embraced the culture; it is a completely different matter managing people who do not.

There is little doubt that many Frozone employees worked very hard, but when some did not, conflict began to infiltrate the unitarist corporate culture. As one employee stated:

> *...we could be working flat out, you know, 100 per cent and a few people could be slackening off so someone has to pick up the slack. So the choice is either work at 130 per cent or tell these guys to get their shit together.*

Even one team leader was not immune to slackening off according to some employees, *'He's a ripper! We call him Heidi because he's always hiding from the real work'.*

There is a long established literature investigating the way individuals respond to corporate cultures that are created or manipulated. When there are pockets of discontent, the employees will engage in activities that seem rational to them at the time and in the particular context. However, what might seem rational in one context can provide the impetus for escalating conflict.

---

[4] Again, a commonly quoted term from management and staff.

When referring to the team leader previously mentioned, one employee explained that given his attitude, the rest of the team respond accordingly:

> *When we're on nights we can take it a little easy because we know he won't be around all that much. As soon as the big bosses go, he seems to get very busy elsewhere.*

Hence, production in the evening shift was lower than it could have been, based on the collective team's decision that their team leader was not working as hard as them; hence they would also ease back. However, this approach created a great deal of conflict with the morning shift, who had started to feel that they were working harder, with the production numbers supporting that view. One employee explained a feeling shared by many in the morning shift:

> *They are lazy, useless fucks and have no work ethic. They don't get finished at (their work) is left over for the morning staff so we find ourselves working harder because we don't want to be left with anything from the previous day.*

The Production Manager indicated that addressing the conflict between the two shifts is the most difficult aspect of her job. She suggested that the conflict was, to a certain extent 'just an illusion'; however employees see the illusion as their reality. In addition to the slower production in the evening, many employees had started to resist other aspects of management desires, for example, job and shift rotation.

> *...they want to rotate us, but I'm not going. Fuck that, I don't want to go and work in the (assembly teams)...I don't think I'll have to at the moment because there's only six of us that can operate this equipment. If they had more, then I'd...leave (resign) because there's no way I'm going back around there.*

> *They want me to go to the afternoon shift. No way, no way in the world. First of all I've got kids to get home to, and second, I refuse to work with those lazy dogs.*

It would be incorrect to suggest that this conflict and resistance to organisational policies and expectations was the result of one team leader who was not performing his job to the standard expected by others. More accurately, the conflict and resistance is symptomatic of a workplace where a particular corporate culture is desired but the complexities of managing the production process and, more importantly, the complexities of managing the people place strain on a developing system.

Van den Broek and Dundon (2010) offer a typology of resistance and misbehaviour that demonstrates that not all actions can be seen as resistance, rather, the intent behind the actions assists in our understanding. Table 16.1 lists a range of behaviours that Frozone employees engaged in, as well as their stated motivation or target, and a classification of whether their action is more likely to be 'resistance' against managerial or peer controls, or alternatively 'misbehaviour' by way of getting through the day of tedious work. Furthermore, this table provides an analysis of whether the particular acts of resistance and misbehaviour are 'individualistic' or 'collaborative'.

Table 16.1 Misbehaviour and resistance at Frozone

Description of acts causing conflict	Target or motivation	Individual or collaborative	Classification
One employee explains how sometimes she works at a fast pace to create too much stock downstream.	To create problems for other staff with whom the participant had conflict.	Individual	Misbehaviour
A distinct, measurable difference between morning and afternoon shifts' levels of production.	Afternoon shift responding to a team leader they felt was not working hard enough.	Collaborative	Resistance
A small number of employees actively avoid a policy of both job rotation and shift rotation.	To undermine managerial policies aimed to share preferable shifts and jobs.	Individual	Resistance
A number of employees try to take longer meal breaks.	To slow the return to work and as a consequence, production.	Individual and collaborative	Resistance and misbehaviour
Threats of mass resignations.	To force managers to act against an unpopular team leader.	Collaborative	Resistance
An older employee tries to continually avoid team-building activities	Managerial policies designed to create a particular team culture.	Individual	Resistance
Twenty-five per cent of employees did not vote in a supposedly compulsory poll to decide on holiday close-down.	Frustration with the illusion that management had already made the decision before the vote was complete.	Individual and collaborative	Resistance
Horseplay in the cooking area, for example, throwing scraps at other employees.	Motivated by having a little 'harmless fun' while at work.	Collaborative	Misbehaviour

What is evident by the contents of Table 16.1 is that conflict is not always motivated by the same cause. It is not just because of 'poor management' or 'bad employees' or the presence of unions! A range of different factors can cause conflict within organisations. These factors can be individuals acting against managers or co-workers, or collaborative efforts by groups of employees. However, just as prevalent as employees acting against managers and managerial policies is employees who engage in activities that are not accepted by managers but have no malicious intent – just employees letting off a bit of steam or having a bit of fun.

Equally as important to understand is the complexity of employee actions and behaviours when it comes to attempted classifications of a particular behaviour. For instance, employees taking longer meal breaks can be the result of individuals and collaborations and the action can be a concerted effort to disrupt production and managerial control, or equally, can be simply an employee trying to sneak a bit more of their own time from the organisation. Not each example of this same action is equal – if the intent is to harm production, then the action can be considered resistance. Yet if we use Ackroyd and Thompson's (1999) terminology – if it is just the 'reappropriation' of time by an employee, then we are more accurate in describing this same act as misbehaviour. Certainly, by any measure the employee taking additional time from their work schedule will by objective measures be likely to reduce the level of output. Hence, such action will (while potentially on a very small scale) have a negative effect on organisational profitability and consequently be labelled 'sabotage' using the theoretical model provided by Sprouse (1992). Sprouse suggests that sabotage is 'anything you do at work you are not supposed to do' (1992, p. 3).

This chapter is an attempt to go beyond broad sweeping claims about employee behaviour at work, to understand the important nuances that a range of scholars are currently debating and attempting to elucidate greater understanding of employee actions (see for example, Van den Broek & Dundon 2010; Townsend & Richards 2011). With an improved understanding of why employees act the way they do, and the result of those actions, then we can improve the way people are managed for the benefit of all parties – employees, managers and the organisation as a whole.

Discussion questions

1) What does this chapter tell us about the perception and theorisation of 'bad' behaviour from employees?

2) On the basis that there are different motivations behind employee actions and behaviours, how can we better understand why employees take the course of action they do?

3) What role do line managers and team leaders have in influencing the way employees behave in the workplace?

4) How would you evaluate the managers' success in developing the culture for which they aimed?

References

Ackroyd, S & Thompson, P 1999, *Organisational Misbehaviour*, London, Sage.

Sprouse, M 1992 (ed), *Sobotage in the American Workplace*, San Francisco: Pressure Drop Press.

Townsend, K & Richards, J 2011, 'Developing a Contemporary Approach to Conceptualising Employee Actions', in A Wilkinson & K Townsend (eds), *The Future of Employment Relations: New Paradigms, New Approaches*, London: Palgrave.

Van den Broek, D & Dundon, T 2010, 'Up to No Good: Reconfiguring the boundaries of worker resistance and misbehaviour in an increasingly non-union world', *International Labour Process Conference*, Rutgers University, New Jersey, 15th – 17th March

Part IV
Management Leadership

Chapter 17

Leadership during change at Qantas

AMY L COLLINS AND PETER J JORDAN

Background and context

Qantas is one of Australia's leading airlines, providing both domestic and international services. Qantas employs over 30,000 people and produces consistently high profits (Qantas Airways Limited 2010). While it is now regarded as a highly successful business, the history of Qantas, and of the Australian airline industry, does not tell the story of a smooth ride. Since 1990 (after a long period of stability), the Australian airline industry has undergone significant changes, which include the merging and collapse of some of the major airlines, the overturning of the two airline policy that dominated the industry for many years, de-regulation, and the impact of the 1989 pilots' dispute.

In 1920, Qantas (the Queensland and Northern Territory Aerial Services Ltd) was created by two lieutenants returning from service in the Australian Flying Corps in World War 1, as they were convinced that air travel was the most efficient method of travelling across the largely empty landscapes of Australia. Qantas was purchased by the Australian government in 1947, and in 1952, Qantas became an exclusively international airline (Gunn 1999).

Regulation of the airline industry

In 1952, the Australian government passed the *Civil Aviation Agreement Act* which established a strict two airlines policy for the domestic airline industry. This Act prevented the creation of new airline companies. The two airlines policy was created with the stated aim of maintaining the efficiency of the Australian airline industry, and avoiding a monopoly by one of the two major domestic airlines. The policy stabilised the industry and ensured less competition between the two airlines. According to the government, open competition could have been damaging to the industry. The government argued that Australia's small population at this time did not allow economies of scale for more than two airlines (Brogden 1968).The Australian government also heavily regulated the management of Australia's domestic airlines, determining issues such as the capacity of flights, and what fares to charge (Brogden 1968). Australia's two domestic airlines during this period were Australian Airlines (a government owned airline formed in 1946, formerly known as Trans Australian Airlines), and Ansett Airlines (a privately owned company formed in 1935).

In 1981, questions were raised about the use of the two airlines policy. An Australian government inquiry indicated that the public were greatly dissatisfied with the fares the airlines were charging under the *Civil Aviation Agreement Act*. This prompted a more extensive review into the state of the Australian airline industry in 1986, which called for the deregulation of the industry, with the aim of increasing the efficiency of the airlines and reducing the cost of air travel to the public. These findings were further reinforced by the example provided by the USA domestic airline industry, which prospered after its deregulation in 1978.

In 1988, the Australian government announced its intention to deregulate the airline industry, informing both existing domestic companies, Australian Airlines and Ansett Airlines, that after 1990, the two airlines agreement would be dissolved. Airlines would be allowed to choose the routes they would fly and the prices they would charge. Of more significance was the fact that under this policy, new domestic airline carriers could be formed. This decision to deregulate the industry was made on the expectation that a deregulated industry would increase competition between airline companies, which would in turn lead to lower fares, and better service (Hooper & Findlay 1998; Traca 2004).

Australia's airlines in crisis: The domestic pilots' dispute

Leading up to deregulation, an industrial dispute occurred that changed the face of the airline industry and resulted in an unstable environment for the deregulation change planned for the airline carriers (Kain & Webb 2001). Pilots' salaries, while being much higher than the average wages of the time, became a source of discontent for the pilots in the 1980s. The occupation of airline pilot was so specialised and highly trained, that the pilots generally received what they asked for in terms of wage raises. However, the introduction of the National Wage Case Principles by the federal government in the late 1970s restricted the amounts by which wages could increase (Smith 1990). Consequently, pilots were no longer able to achieve the pay increases to which they felt entitled.

The union responsible for the majority of domestic pilots at the time – the Australian Federation of Air Pilots - was formed in 1959, and in the period of the 1980s it represented 100 per cent of the pilots employed at Australian Airlines and Ansett Airlines (Bray & Wailes 1999). In July of 1989, on behalf of its members, the union approached its employers in the domestic airline industry (which at that point included Ansett Airlines, Australian Airlines, East-West Airlines and IPEC aviation) and insisted on an increase in wages of 29.47 per cent, an amount beyond the bounds of the fixed increase rules outlined in the National Wage Case Principles (Smith 1990).

When the airline companies denied the increase and stated they were unwilling to engage in negotiations, the union (who had been given full responsibility by its members to take action to resolve the dispute) responded on 17 August by issuing a directive that instructed its members (over 1600 pilots) to refuse to fly except between the hours of 9.00am and 5.00pm (Smith 1990). For one week, the airlines worked within this limitation; however, the arrangement meant a drastic reduction in operations for the airlines. On 24 August, the airline companies commenced legal action against both the Federation of Air Pilots and the individual pilots who were following the time restriction directive of the Federation. To avoid both the Federation and its individual members being sued for loss of earnings by the airline companies, the Federation responded by orchestrating the resignation of their 1647 members (Smith 1990). The airline industry effectively had no employees that were trained to fly their planes. Without pilots, the industry ground to a halt.

In order to deal with this crisis, the airline companies immediately began a recruitment drive, seeking new pilots from both within Australia and overseas. The general manager of Ansett stated in September of 1989:

> *A dispute doesn't exist, so you don't need an arbitrator. The situation the airline industry finds itself in, is that the pilots have all resigned. The challenge we face is to fill vacant situations and that process is under way. (Gunn 1999, p. 447)*

As a further response to this crisis, the Australian government authorised the use of Australia's international airlines (which were still independent of Australian Airlines and Ansett at this time) as well as a number of military aircrafts, in an attempt to keep the domestic airline industry running. In the weeks following the resignations of pilots, the airline industry was effectively brought to a standstill. By October, however, it was clear that the airlines were managing to operate, albeit with vastly reduced services. By December, the airline companies had built up a large enough workforce of newly employed pilots that were not members of the Federation, that the military aircraft were able to return to their normal duties. This was followed in January by the release of the international aircraft (McDonald 1990).

The dispute ended officially in March of 1990, with the Federation of Air Pilots conceding to the airline companies' new system of rules regarding pilots' employment. These new conditions included individual contracts for pilots that effectively linked any pay increases to increased requirements of flight hours, and removed the Federation as a collective bargaining entity (Smith 1990). By the time the dispute was resolved, each of the companies involved had suffered major financial and reputational losses due to the extended period of halted and reduced operations. The industry was also dealing with a workforce with an underlying level of discontent, as a number of its pilots were being employed under worse contractual conditions than when the dispute began.

Privatisation of airlines

During this period of upheaval within the domestic airline industry, Qantas was also evolving. The government had, in 1991, announced its intention to privatise both the government-owned international airline (Qantas) and the government-owned domestic airline (Australian Airways). In September 1992, Qantas purchased Australian Airlines from the government for $400 million. In March 1993, Qantas was partly privatised, with 25 per cent of its shares going to British Airways, and it was fully privatised in November 1995 (Qantas Airways Limited 2010).

This period of intense change for the Australian airline industry, and more specifically for Qantas, culminating in its merger with Australian Airlines, understandably produced a number of difficulties both within and outside the company. Qantas struggled to integrate the domestic and international airlines, as well as having to deal with the significant changes brought about by the deregulation and privatisation of the industry – and the aftermath of the economic losses resulting from the pilots' dispute. Qantas needed to redefine its business strategies if it was to compete in the vastly changed airline industry.

Timeline for the Australian airline industry

1920	Qantas created as domestic carrier
1935	Ansett Airlines established as a private company
1946	Trans Australian Airlines is created
1947	Qantas taken into public ownership
1953	Two-airline policy established
1952	Qantas operates as an exclusively international airline
1987	Compass Airlines created
1989	August 1989–March 1990 domestic pilots' dispute
1990	Two-airline policy rescinded
1991	Compass Airlines goes into receivership
1992	Qantas buys Australian Airlines
1993	A number of other airlines enter the market as low cost no frills carriers International carriers allowed domestic travel rights in Australia
2000	Open skies agreement between Australia and New Zealand
2001	Qantas purchases Impulse Airlines
2001	Ansett Airlines goes into receivership
2004	Qantas launches Jetstar as a low-cost, no-frills airline

Competition strategy among airline carriers

Competition in the Australian airline industry occurs on different bases. There are a range of options for airlines in deciding on the type of competitive strategy to pursue, from 'full service' to 'low-cost, no-frills'. There are also different markets to be pursued, from leisure travellers to business travellers (Kain & Webb 2003). Each of these decisions will result in changes to the recruitment and training of personnel. It will also impact on the working conditions of both ground staff and flight staff.

Competition decisions were also made by Qantas and Ansett Airlines on the frequency and schedule for services. In the 1990s, Qantas bought a number of new large planes with the aim of providing fewer services but carrying more passengers. While this decision resulted in greater costs in servicing and maintenance, there were reduced costs in terms of personnel and greater economies of scale in flight operations. Ansett Airlines, on the other hand, purchased smaller aircraft that carried fewer passengers, relying on providing more frequent services and attempting to gain market share by being more responsive to passenger needs. While these aircraft were cheaper to run and maintain, Ansett Airlines were not able to achieve the economies of scale that were available to Qantas.

During the 1990s, Qantas was a full service airline that had an extensive network on major national and international routes and feeder routes to regional centres. It was a member of an international network of airlines called One World (Kain & Webb 2003). Ansett Airlines offered a similar service and was a member of an international network of airlines called Star Alliance. Both companies tried to attract business travellers, but Ansett Airlines in particular also tried to market to the leisure traveller. Other airlines that have emerged since this time include Virgin Blue, a low-cost, no-frills airline that initially focussed on younger travellers. Virgin Blue provided a modest schedule and did not have the extensive network of other airlines. The other major airline to emerge was Jetstar, a subsidiary of Qantas developed to provide direct competition to low-cost, no-frills airlines.

Leadership at Qantas during organisational change

Every organisation undergoes change. Despite change occurring regularly in companies, it often results in difficulties for both the organisation and its employees. Whether a change is successful or not depends, to a large extent, on the actions of the organisation's leader. A leader who is able to explain the need for change in an organisation and who is able to explain the link between this change and new policies and new directions, will greatly increase the chances of success of an organisation's change strategy. In order to implement this new direction, the leader also needs to establish a process through which this change will occur.

From the period of 1993 to 2001, James Strong was the CEO and Managing Director of Qantas. He presided over the aftermath of the massive changes in industry brought about by changes in the Australian government policy (including deregulation and privatisation), as well as Qantas' merger with Australian Airlines and the discontent that had emerged following the pilots' dispute.

A major factor contributing to the Qantas Board of Directors' decision to appoint James Strong as CEO was his previous experience and obvious enthusiasm for leading organisations through times of considerable change. Strong was formerly the CEO of Australian Airlines from 1985 to 1989. During his tenure as CEO of Australian Airlines, he instigated a number of major policy changes, including a new focus on customer relations and an emphasis on giving more autonomy to managers and employees.

> *I have always been attracted to situations where the organisation or the board was looking for significant change. I love the concept of trying to be part of convincing people to move in different directions and then trying to get momentum and an acceptance of responsibility instead of opposition. (Strong cited in Turnbull 2006, p. 1)*

Strong's background made him an ideal candidate to oversee Qantas during this difficult period. Qantas at this time was dealing with its recent transformation from public to private enterprise, the addition of domestic routes to their established international routes (a result of its merger with Australian Airlines), increasing competition from new entrants to the market and the lingering resentment of pilots following the pilots' dispute.

Strong knew that a number of changes needed to be implemented if Qantas was to remain a competitive airline in the industry. Through the use of various change strategies, his vision was realised – that of an increased focus on customer needs, an emphasis on cutting costs, and the integration of two airlines through the creation of a new organisational culture.

At the time of the merger in 1992, Qantas and Australian Airlines were vastly different companies, one with an international focus and one with a domestic focus. Therefore, the merger between the two organisations naturally produced difficulties, due to the clash of two very different organisational cultures. The public service culture at Qantas stood in stark contrast to the more business-oriented culture of Australian Airlines. A senior executive in the time period following the merger commented:

> *When I asked the Qantas people who they worked for they said the Board or Mr Ward or the government and when I asked the Australian Airlines people who they worked for they said 'the customer'. (McDonald & Millett 2001, p. 5)*

Privatisation also brought its own challenges. As an airline that had been publically owned with a sole competitor (Ansett Airlines), Qantas was now a commercial business that was expected to make a profit and financially support itself. Previous strategies that Qantas used to manage its business did not apply. The airline industry was still recovering from the large economic losses it suffered during the domestic pilots' dispute in 1989, which made it difficult to make a profit. Finally, increasing competition from both within and outside of Australia meant that Qantas could not just rely on its reputation to ensure its market dominance.

James Strong made a number of staffing changes during his first year as CEO in order to create a team focused on advancing the internal changes that Qantas would be undergoing. Among these was the appointment of an Executive General Manager Staffing and Customer Services (whose responsibilities included overseeing the change process resulting from the merger of the two airlines), and the formation of the Customer/Staff Relations Frontline Teams. New management was also brought in for the Corporate Training and Development Program (McDonald & Millett 2001). These new appointments were a symbolic representation of the need for fresh ideas, and these high-level appointees also provided consistent and visible support for the new policies that Strong would be implementing.

> The biggest task for any CEO is to build a team of people around them because I think we all know that you're not going to be able to do everything yourself at any stage. So it's about building a terrific team of people. (Strong, cited in O'Carroll 2008)

As a result of deregulation, all airlines, including Qantas, were free to set their own policies on their general operations, and differences would emerge between the airlines in terms of price, safety, and customer service. In this increasingly competitive environment, the overall experience of the customer would become a major factor in deciding which airline to support with their patronage. Strong had a clear vision for the future of Qantas. He saw the need for an emphasis on profits, and saw the potential to achieve this through an increased customer focus.

Accordingly, when Strong began his time as CEO, he announced there would be changes made in a number of different areas, including substantial changes to Qantas' customer service policies, which were intended to improve Qantas' image from a transportation service, to a business that guarantees its customers an enjoyable and comfortable experience. Branded as 'A World of Change' (Qantas Airways Limited 1994), the modifications included redesigning the airport lounges and cabin interiors to make them more comfortable, revising the menu for in-flight meals, and also introducing a new, more customer-friendly Frequent Flyer program that rewarded customers for their loyalty to the airline. Correspondingly, Qantas staff training programs were also updated as part of a training strategy known as 'People: Priority One'. These new training programs were designed to reinforce the idea that the purpose of Qantas staff was to provide quality service and to ensure the satisfaction of Qantas customers.

When significant changes are made to the operation of a company (especially when they are initiated by a relatively new CEO), it is not uncommon to encounter resistance from employees, who may resent the inconvenience that can arise from changes in policy – such as having to participate in re-training programs. Strong encouraged an 'out and about' management style that included making regular visits to different branches of Qantas (Hill 1994) and arranging for regular meetings between management and lower level employees. In these meetings, Strong and his management team highlighted the importance of the new proposals so that the employees of Qantas could understand and appreciate the motives behind the changes in policy. Both Strong and members of the senior management team consistently and publically acknowledged the contribution of the employees who had assisted them in the period of change, as the success of the venture greatly depended on the cooperation and enthusiasm of staff at all levels of the organisation.

During James Strong's period as CEO of Qantas, the organisation not only survived during a period of uncertainty and change, but it thrived. Qantas' financial results were consistently improving, and by 2001 (when Strong made the decision to step down as CEO), the organisation had recorded a profit before tax of $597.1 million, employing approximately 31,000 staff and transporting more than 22 million passengers in the period of 2000–2001 (Qantas Airways Limited 2001). This success stands in stark contrast to one of Qantas' chief competitors at the time, Ansett Airlines, which after a period of steady decline, finally collapsed in September 2001 with a debt of $3 billion (Leiper 2002).

Summary

From the late 1980s, the Australian airline industry experienced significant upheaval, which included:

- the domestic pilots' dispute in 1989, which caused the domestic airlines to suffer considerable financial losses

- the deregulation of the industry in 1990, which ended the domestic two-airline policy that had prevented competition from outside airlines

- the privatisation of the airlines in 1991, which led to the merger between Qantas and Australian Airlines in 1992.

The success of Qantas during this period of intense change can be attributed, in part, to the adjustments in both its general approach and specific policies that were implemented under the direction of its CEO and Managing Director, James Strong.

Discussion questions

1) Compare the process of change followed under James Strong's leadership at Qantas during the 1990s to an established theoretical change process.

2) Transformational leadership is a style of leadership that facilitates change. Was James Strong a transformational leader? Why/why not?

3) Describe how the change that occurred at Qantas relates to one or more specific models of contingent change management.

4) How successful do you think the change agents used by Qantas were in facilitating the described outcomes?

References

Bray, M & Wailes, N 1999, 'Reinterpreting the 1989 pilots' dispute: The role of managerial control and labour productivity', *Labour & Industry*, vol. 10, pp. 79-105.

Brogden, S 1968, *Australia's two-airline policy*, Melbourne University Press, Victoria.

Gunn, J 1999, *Contested skies: Trans-Australian airlines; Australian airlines 1946-1992*, Queensland University Press, Queensland.

Hill, L 1994, 'Re-creating Qantas', *Air Transport World*, vol. 31, no. 5, pp. 74-77.

Hooper, P & Findlay, C 1998, 'Developments in Australia's aviation policies and current concerns', *Journal of Air Transport Management*, vol. 4, pp. 169-176.

Kain J & Webb R 2003, Turbulent Times: Australian Airline Industry Issues 2003, Research Paper no. 10 2002-03, Economics, Commerce and Industrial Relations Group, 6 June 2003, Parliament of Australia, http://www.aph.gov.au/library/pubs/rp/2002-03/03RP10.htm.

Kain J & Webb R 2001, Key Australian Aviation Policy Developments: The Ansett Airlines Context 1937–2001 Chronology. Economics, Commerce and Industrial Relations Group, 16 June 2003, Parliament of Australia, http://www.aph.gov.au/library/pubs/online/ansettchron_PartA.htm.

Leiper, N 2002, 'Why Ansett Airlines failed and how to prevent it happening again', *Current Issues in Tourism*, vol. 5, no. 2, pp. 134-148.

McDonald, J 1990, 'Industrial relations strategies in the air pilots' dispute 1989', *Economic and Labour Relations Review*, vol. 1, pp. 121-144.

McDonald, J & Millett, B 2001, *A case study of the role of collective bargaining in corporate change – Qantas Airways Limited*, Business research paper series, pp. 1-21.

O'Carroll, S 2008, *Making the step up from HR to CEO*, Human Resources Magazine, viewed 12th October 2010, http://www.humanresourcesmagazine.com.au/articles/86/0c055886.asp.

Qantas Airways Limited 1994, *1993-94 Annual Report*, Qantas, Sydney.

Qantas Airways Limited 2001, *2001 Annual Report*, Qantas, Sydney.

Qantas Airways Limited 2010, *Qantas through the years*, Qantas, viewed 11th October 2010, http://www.qantas.com.au/travel/airlines/history-through-the-years/global/en.

Smith, GF 1990, 'From consensus to coercion: The Australian air pilots dispute', *Journal of Industrial Relations*, vol. 32, pp. 238-253.

Traca, D 2004, *Virgin Blue: Fighting with national champions*, Insead, Singapore.

Turnbull, J 2006, 'Strong recognised for business endeavours', *AAP Australian National News Wire*.

Chapter 18

Managing leadership talent in creative industries

HERMAN H M TSE

Background and text

Hilton is an international multimedia production company, which is proud of its excellent reputation for designing creative advertisements and producing high-quality animated artworks for more than 10 years. Hilton has been presented with international advertising and film production awards, and the company has been regarded as one of the best in the creative industry over the years. Hilton employs over 2,000 employees serving in different operations around the world, and it has developed a leading position of providing multimedia advertising designs and animated film production to large international companies. In 2008, the company's annual revenue reached a record of $50 million and it has continued to grow with a 15 per cent increase every year.

Hilton's motto is 'Think Global and Act Local' so its management philosophy focuses on creating human capital and ensuring that employees working in the company have both international exposure and local experience in the creative industry. These requirements are important because the nature of the job at Hilton is non-repetitive and design focused. No two advertisements or animated artworks are ever alike, and the job requires a high degree of graphic skills, computer knowledge and marketing experience as well as a strong creative mind-set. The employees are highly trained and experienced in making high-quality multimedia advertisements and animation products. They take great pride in their job for which they are well paid. The emphasis is on quality and innovation, and therefore the employees are given considerable autonomy in how they manage and execute their job requirements. Hilton also provides employees with a relaxing work environment in which they can enjoy free meals, a fitness club, medical services, sport activities, relaxation exercises and hair dressing services as part of their work entitlements. Flexi-time, union practice, and customised work arrangements are available and promoted to employees in the company. As reported in a recent employee engagement survey, more than 80 per cent of employees at Hilton enjoy their job very much and will continue to strive for excellence in their position.

The appointment of a new CEO

In 2010, Hilton appointed a new CEO, David Roger, who had extensive experience in management and leadership. He received his bachelor degree from Cambridge and earned his MBA at Harvard. David started his career as a business analyst of an international consulting firm, and climbed the career ladder to become a partner of the firm after 5 years, when he was approached by a large computer company to be their Director for Asia-pacific regions. He was subsequently promoted to Vice President for Research and Development (R&D), where his duties included the management of all R&D operations located in China, Singapore, UK, Brazil, South Africa, Norway, Australia and Germany. In 2005, David was recruited as CEO of one of the fast moving computer companies in Korea, and under his leadership the company developed a product called i-touch that changed the use of mobile communication in the 21st century.

Since his arrival at Hilton, David has endeavoured to achieve his vision of the company becoming the number one multimedia advertising and computer animation company in the world. As such, he promised the board members that the annual revenue of the company would triple in three years' time. In order to achieve this goal, David needed to choose a new Vice President for the Creative Art and Computer Animation division, which is regarded as a key driver for profit at Hilton. His vision for the division was that employees should be working in different teams, leveraging and sharing their resources, talents, skills and knowledge to develop new services for different types of clients rather than only serving clients with large projects worth over $1 million.

Recruitment process

David set up a recruitment process, searching for an internal candidate to fill the position of Vice President for the Creative Art and Computer Animation division. He identified three potential candidates, each of whom he considered capable of leading the division well. Each candidate was at the same managerial level. David found it difficult to choose between them because each had very strong credentials and a good reputation at Hilton. For example, Peter McKenzie was a loyal employee of Hilton who started as a casual worker in the sales department while in high school, and worked in seven different positions throughout the company before eventually becoming Manager of Web Advertising. While Peter never obtained any formal qualifications in business management, IT or creative art, performance appraisals of Peter's work consistently described him as being very creative, thoughtful and considerate. During his employment at Hilton, Peter helped the company develop a new expertise in creating web advertising for the segment of teenagers aged between 12 and 15. The web advertising division of the company had huge potential to change the management of mobile and electronic commerce, and it had also been highly successful at gaining large accounts, having been responsible for the signing of a number of contracts worth more than $3 million in total. Peter was also known for being very serious about the quality of his own work as well as the standard of work produced by his department. When a project started, he would monitor its progress closely until its completion. The employees in his department were sharp and professional in every aspect of their work.

Another candidate David considered for the position was John Chan, who had been with Hilton for ten years and, at the time, was Manager of Technical Support and Customer Services. John had a reputation for being very bright and industrious. Prior to joining Hilton, he obtained his Bachelor in IT from MIT and a Masters in Electronic Commerce from Cambridge. He was offered a full scholarship to undertake his PhD in IT Management at Harvard. Employees in his department described John as the kind of person who would become an entrepreneur; likely to set up his own company in the future. In terms of his performance evaluations, he was consistently applauded for his IT knowledge, research skills and people management experience. Although John had a strong IT background, he was also good at relationship building with his boss, colleagues and subordinates. For example, he regularly organised social activities for his staff, to ease the pressures they felt in service recovery and customer relationships. None of the employees in his department ever made negative comments about John. Since joining Hilton, John had been successful in retaining business deals with several large accounts because of the high-quality customer support services his department provided.

Melissa Mayfield was the third candidate; she had been working at Hilton for about seven years. She graduated from London Business School with a double degree majoring in Business Management and IT. She had previously been invited to work with the CEO to establish a new structure for Hilton, with the aim of becoming more flexible and responsive to the rapidly changing market. She was often consulted by top management and David Roger regarding the corporate development and strategic directions of Hilton. Before joining Hilton, she worked as a management consultant for a number of large firms and received high regard in the creativity industry. She related to people very well and was very knowledgeable about how to sell aggressive ideas for organisational change. She believed in the core values and operational strategies of Hilton, and actively promoted them to all departments and operations. Honesty and integrity were two important qualities that Melissa often achieved in her performance reviews. Employees who worked under her supervision consistently reported that they felt they could trust Melissa to be fair and consistent with them, and suggested that she is the kind of person who always 'talks the talk and walks the walk'. Melissa was highly respected at Hilton, although she had less experience working in the company than John and Peter. In her tenure at Hilton, Melissa was involved in taking over a small company which had an excellent reputation for creating special computer graphic effects for animal movement. She did an excellent job in merging the company with Hilton by helping to integrate the cultures and operations of both parties. This successful merger enabled Hilton to open up a new market that attracted film production companies to sign business deals with them.

David Roger's decision

After a few months of observation, David Roger decided to choose Melissa Mayfield for the position of Vice President for the Creative Art and Computer Animation Division. After the announcement was made public, there were many comments about this decision. Employees in the departments of Technical Support and Customer Services and Web Advertising expressed regret that neither John nor Peter was chosen for the position, because both of them had more experience working at Hilton than Melissa. Some of the employees also commented that she had more experience and expertise in corporate planning and strategy implementation at the top management level, rather than being qualified to be a Vice President, with the responsibilities of leading a division. Several employees also suspected that Melissa's appointment was somewhat related to her close relationship with David, as the two had been working together over a few projects. The board members noticed the employees' negative reactions and questioned the transparency of David's decision. He did not explain to the board or to his employees why John and Peter failed in the recruitment process. David was confident that Melissa was the right choice for the position, based on her strong credentials and objective evaluation. However, because of the pressure David received from the board, he was determined that Melissa should prove that he made the right decision by achieving the goal of tripling revenue within three years.

Melissa Mayfield's management and leadership

Melissa, as the newly appointed Vice President of the Creative Art and Computer Animation Division, had the responsibility of overseeing 150 employees, 50 of whom had worked for the small company that Melissa was involved in taking over previously. In line with David's vision for the division, Melissa worked to reform the division to ensure that Hilton could expand the coverage of its clients, managing both large and small accounts effectively. The Creative Art and Computer Animation Division consisted of five major account teams responsible for 60 per cent of the overall revenue at Hilton. These account teams were headed by Sammy, Grace, Andrew, Sally and Kenneth who reported directly to Melissa about the daily operation of their team. Each team had about thirty employees, including a chief creative director, two associate creative directors, three copywriters, two art directors, five computer graphic designers, six computer animation designers, three computer programmers, four digital musicians and three team assistants.

Sammy and his team got along really well with Melissa, largely because the team included some employees who were working in the small company that was taken over by Melissa previously. Such employees know her quite well and had already formed good relationships with Melissa. The team had an outstanding track record of producing high-quality work for their clients, and the clients in turn had positive comments on the excellence of the advertisements and animated art-works it produced. Thus, Melissa made sure that Sammy's team is always provided with extra resources and challenging jobs so that team members could improve on their talents and abilities to the highest level. Among all the teams, Melissa trusted and relied on Sammy's team the most because she felt it is the most creative and talented and the most willing to go the extra mile. Sammy and his team members felt comfortable with Melissa's leadership; she was not afraid to give them free rein on their accounts, as they always came through for her. As a result, the team generated a good record of revenue which accounted for 40 per cent of the divisional target.

Andrew and his team also performed very well for the division, but Andrew often felt uncomfortable with how Melissa treated his team in terms of psychological support and resource allocation. Andrew felt that Melissa was not fair and consistent, favouring Sammy's team by providing them with the most talented employees and additional resources. Andrew saw that Melissa paid more attention to Sammy's team and seemed to be more interested in the performance of his team than any of the others. At the end of Melissa's first year, Sammy and his team members received a higher bonus and commission because they had been given more opportunities to serve large accounts than the other teams. In terms of performance, Andrew and his team managed many medium accounts, contributing 35 per cent of revenue to the overall divisional target. Recently, a creative animated artwork of Andrew's team had won an international design award because two of their clients had nominated it for selection. Andrew and his team felt that Melissa didn't recognise their achievement, giving Sammy's team the best accounts, projects, resources and budgets. Because of this, Andrew found it hard to hold back the animosity and frustration he experienced toward Melissa's leadership and management.

Similarly, Grace was also concerned that her team was not part of Melissa's inner circle, and did not have close relationships with the other teams. She has also noticed that Melissa showed favouritism to the other teams, especially those managed by Sammy and Andrew, as she was often engaging in social activities with those teams after office hours. Grace also saw Melissa giving more attention to the projects of Andrew and Sammy's teams, providing them additional resources and manpower to complete their assignments. For example, whenever new employees joined the division, Andrew and Sammy always got the best graphic designers and computer programmers. Grace couldn't understand why Melissa didn't notice her team or try to help it achieve higher standards of work. She felt Melissa undervalued her team – because the *quality* of her team's work was unquestionable. Grace and her team were confident they could achieve better results than the other teams if they were given the same opportunities, resources and talented employees.

Sally agreed with Grace's perceptions about what was happening in the division. Sally and her team also didn't have a good relationship with Melissa because her team was too far away from the inner circle. Sally's team was always assigned less valuable projects and smaller accounts that other teams didn't want to take. Sally felt anger, resentment and jealousy towards Andrew and Sammy because their teams were well looked-after by Melissa and their work always attracted client attention and praises. The CEO recognised their effort by rewarding them with more bonuses and commission. Because of this resentment, Sally and her team found it difficult to work with Andrew and Sammy's teams to complete a large project assigned by the CEO. Her team members felt reluctant to share important information with Andrew and Sammy's teams because their contribution to the project would not be noticed by Melissa.

Although Kenneth seemed to agree with Andrew and Grace's observations about Melissa, he did not feel any negative reactions to Melissa's leadership in the division. Kenneth had worked for the division for five years, and nothing seemed to bother him very much. His account teams had never been outstanding, but they had never been problematic either. Kenneth viewed his team and its work more as a basic operation, in which the team is given an assignment and carries it out. Being in Melissa's in-group would entail bearing more responsibilities that require extra time in the evening or on weekends to get the assignments done to a higher standard. Kenneth felt this would create too much pressure on him and his team. His working philosophy was that, 'the more responsibilities you take, the more likely you are to make mistakes'. He felt it is better to complete what you are assigned and enjoy the work you are doing. Therefore, Kenneth was happy with his role as it was, and had little interest in trying to be part of Melissa's inner circle, or in requesting more opportunities, resources or manpower to do earth-shaking projects for large accounts.

David Roger, the CEO of Hilton who was responsible for Melissa's selection as Vice President of the division, received some negative comments about Melissa's unfair treatment and imbalanced resource allocation in the division. David felt surprised about the comments because employees in her old department reported that Melissa was fair and consistent, and that she relates to people well. In a recent performance review, Melissa explained that she felt under a great deal of pressure to achieve the goal of tripling revenue in three years. She found it difficult to implement the strategy of balanced resource allocation to all the teams because each had different levels of expertise and talent. Melissa felt that each team should focus on a particular type of account rather than managing both large and small accounts at the same time. Furthermore, Melissa declared that she had limited time and resources to develop an equal relationship with each of the team account leaders, and it is unavoidable that the team leaders would feel they have different quality of relationships with her.

Summary

Overall, Hilton has undergone significant changes to achieve the goal of increasing revenue. The changes include appointing a new CEO and selecting a new Vice President for the Creative Art and Computer Animation Division, which has resulted in inter-group conflict and team ineffectiveness.

Discussion questions

1) What leadership and management models or theories are relevant to this case study?

2) Do you agree with David Roger's decision to choose Melissa Mayfield for the Vice President position? Why?

3) How would you evaluate the leadership effectiveness of Melissa Mayfield in the Creative Art and Computer Animation Division?

4) To what extent are Melissa's relationships with the five team leaders and their team members effective or ineffective to the overall goal of the division?

5) Do you think Melissa should change her leadership approach toward the team leaders and their members? If so, what should she do specifically?

Bibliography

Northouse, PG 2006, *Leadership Theory and Practice,* 4th edn, Sage Publication.

Yukl G 2007, *Leadership in Organisations,* 7th edn, New York: Prentice Hall.

Chapter 19

Leading change at all levels of Defence Signals Directorate

TERESA MARCHANT AND CRAIG CARDINAL

Background and context of the organisation

The Defence Signals Directorate (DSD) is an intelligence agency in the Australian Government Department of Defence, with its headquarters in Canberra. The DSD mission is to reveal their secrets and protect our own, and thus DSD is both poacher and gamekeeper when it comes to telecommunications. The history of DSD begins in the Second World War, when Australian Navy, Army and Air Force personnel were brought together to support General MacArthur's South-West Pacific campaign by intercepting and decoding Japanese radio signals. DSD was established in 1947 and its current roles are:

- collecting and analysing foreign signals intelligence (Sigint)
- providing advice and assistance on information and communications security (InfoSec).

The Sigint role involves work for the Australian Defence Force (ADF) and Australian Government and is highly sensitive. DSD also provides information, security advice and services mainly to Australian federal and state government agencies. DSD also works closely with industry to develop and deploy secure cryptographic products. The purposes of the organisation are to provide counter-terrorism capability, support military operations and detect electronic attack against Australian government networks. Recent years have seen a dramatic expansion of DSD's InfoSec role as a result of the internet's explosive growth and moves to online service delivery by Australian governments. The organisation's work is critical in protecting and supporting national interests.

Organisation details

There are over one thousand members of the DSD dispersed around Australia including in the nation's capital, Canberra, as well as states that are remote from the capital: the Northern Territory and Western Australia. Members are also based in international locations. Both military and civilian personnel constitute the organisation's members. They work closely with a number of stakeholders including other organisations who use the intelligence produced by DSD. The Army, Navy and Air Force are powerful, key stakeholders. The Australian Public Service Commission (APSC) has and the Department of Defence have an overarching interest in good people management practices, and DSD also works closely with private sector providers of maintenance, operations and human resources capability development.

The organisation has become more operationally focused over the years, supporting counter terrorism and Australian military operations such as in Iraq and Afghanistan. DSD is a highly operational agency where decisions need to be made quickly. The consequences of these decisions can be immediate and significant, sometimes meaning the difference between life and death. It is important that DSD members understand that the work they do saves the lives of Australians.

The DSD workforce is young compared to the public sector average and the ageing Australian workforce in general. On average, DSD members are six years junior to their public sector counterparts. The predominance of younger members at DSD is increasing due to a proactive but exacting graduate recruitment program that accepts around one in ten applicants.

Responding to demands for change in the public sector environment

This case study explains how DSD went about culture change, including altering how leadership was perceived and executed in the organisation. Australian public sector leaders are being forced to embark on rapid and significant change in leadership style, driving contemporary leaders to analyse how to transform vision into outcomes and adopt more effective leadership traits and behaviours in an environment of significant flux. These variables include an ever-increasing generational divide, a shift towards a flatter post-bureaucratic public sector hierarchy and continuing advancements in information and communication technology (ICT). Each of these variables is contemporary in nature and increasing in intensity. Leaders need to adopt fewer command and control styles, and less hierarchical organisation structures, in order to create flexibility and responsiveness in an ever-changing and volatile service delivery environment.

DSD was originally based in Melbourne and had a strong, distinctive culture that had some of the characteristics of a small business. The challenge for the organisation was to keep and build on aspects of the culture which produced high performance, and let go of other aspects of the culture in order to transition to a large, modern and supremely professional organisation. In 2003, DSD launched an extensive organisational change that lasted for several years. At the time, it was Australia's largest and most secretive intelligence agency. Comprising over one thousand civilian officers, DSD had one of the youngest average workforces by six years and was the most technologically advanced department in Australia. Most of DSD's work highly classified and the skills and training cannot be bought commercially. DSD faced a need to break down hierarchical management structures and inter-department silos in order to deliver outcomes. In particular these outcomes included counter terrorism in the wake of the terrorist attacks on the US on 11 September 2001 and the Bali bombings, and military support to deployed forces in Iraq and Afghanistan. Thus, it faced a leadership challenge comprising of the three important variables facing public sector leaders: generational change, technology and post-bureaucracy, all in the face of increased security threats which rendered the organisation's work more significant.

In seeking to transform the organisation so that it could effectively respond to these challenges, the organisation's senior leadership placed the objective of empowering employees to exhibit leadership at all levels at the centre of a culture change strategy. DSD's (then) Director, Steve Merchant, saw effective leadership as pivotal to ensuring the organisation's effectiveness and embarked on a four year leadership development plan. The aim was also to break down barriers between different parts of the organisation and create the cross discipline teams that the organisation desperately needed.

Leading change: Profile of the change leader

There were several aspects of Steve Merchant's profile that suggested leading a change process all about transforming people and culture in a thousand strong organisation might not come naturally to him. It was very different from anything he had done before. He had spent most of his career working with small teams, the largest being only 38 members, before he joined DSD. He was previously head of a strategic analysis branch in another Australian public sector agency, working on issues that involved in-depth analytical thinking about deep and hidden issues. He was a self-described quiet, reserved, Arts graduate in his fifties, with a tendency to being a perfectionist.

However, the Director understood the significance of leaders 'walking the walk':

> We need to understand that the leadership team's actions and decisions have a powerful symbolic impact, often beyond what may be intended. The team inevitably casts a 'long shadow' in DSD. The leadership team's behaviour – our individual and collective decisions; how we use our time; how we interact with others; our willingness to share knowledge and work across organisational boundaries; the time we devote to mentoring and developing our staff – will send powerful signals about what is important.

DSD made a conscious effort to incorporate complementary skills in the senior leadership team. One of the challenges for Steve Merchant was to open up his own personal values for scrutiny. He was willing to spend face time with his team whenever possible. Of the transformation he achieved, Steve Merchant found the overall experience to be challenging, but enjoyable.

Developing the values

The Director had reservations about promoting a set of values which served little purpose and were not acted on in practice:

> I had previously been a sceptic about organisations that display values on their walls. As a person, I've always had very strong values and believed them to be very powerful, much more powerful than rules. As one of my colleagues once put it, rules determine how people behave when they know they are being observed. Values determine how we behave when we think no-one is watching. So I never doubted their power.

> But I'd become cynical about organisations that publicly proclaim their values, because I kept seeing behaviour that was inconsistent with those values. Moreover, that contradictory behaviour was not only tolerated but sometimes rewarded.

Nonetheless, the change process did lead to a clear set of values that were promulgated and serve the purpose of guiding DSD members' behaviours. These values became prominent after the Director consulted with staff about what they liked and didn't like about working for DSD in a series of over 20 'Have Your Say' sessions. The values captured what people said they liked about DSD. They were:

- we make a difference
- we strive for excellence
- we belong to a great team
- we are audacious in concept
- we are meticulous in execution.

From an employee perspective:

> The values remain exactly as they were defined back then. We noticed that once they were defined they started appearing in placards all over the walls. Although they were short, anybody in the organisation knew the exact context of what they meant. It did not matter where you worked as they applied to all. From these values we knew that we not only had our say – but everybody was listened to and we had a set of values that demonstrated what was important to the organisation as a whole.

Interestingly, the Director found it useful to reframe his questions in these sessions from a negative perspective, which mainly produced tactical criticisms and a critical session that was confronting, to more positive strategic considerations.

Organisation processes to achieve change

With a young and talented Gen Y workforce with some of the most powerful IT infrastructure in the world at their fingertips, and charged with providing real-time intelligence for counter-terrorism and support to military operations, the workforce needed more than a vision and values.

As a believer of leadership at all levels, Steve Merchant led an organisation-wide change and development strategy that enabled a highly technical workforce to be leaders in their own right.

> *...we were certainly not looking for ICT experts who can also write the next Defence White Paper. Rather, we were looking for ICT experts who can also think how we can use ICT more effectively to progress the business we're in.*

Three processes were developed to achieve the required changes. The overriding emphasis was on communication, consultation and engagement with DSD members:

Establishing new strategic priorities, values and culture The mission statement of DSD was clear and significant: reveal their secrets and protect our own. However there was still considerable effort expended on determining what the strategic priorities would be. This was based on Stephen Covey's seven habits of highly effective people, who would think about what epitaph they wanted on their grave and made sure they lived their lives accordingly. In a similar vein, the senior management pondered what legacy they wanted to leave at DSD. This helped the team to identify its strategic priorities.

Reducing leadership to its essence Change at DSD encompassed improving leadership, dispersing it more widely though the organisation, challenging technical staff to embrace leadership and to relate their work to the wider strategy of the organisation. To achieve this, the essence of leadership was identified as how we influence the behaviour of others.

> *In DSD we have consciously tried to de-mystify this thing called leadership. We've tried to capture the essence of leadership in a simple statement that everyone can connect with. This has proved to be very powerful. Reducing leadership to its core activity in that way immediately enabled a crucial related point to be made: everyone does it. Everyone exercises leadership to some extent. People say they understand why I have been on about 'the leadership thing' and they're up for it.*

Diagonal-slice To develop and enable leadership of this nature, DSD implemented a diagonal-slice program where a cross section of the organisation attended a four day residential program entitled Building the DSD Team. This program was a massive commitment of time and other resources, including from the executive. For example, every program had a mentor from the Senior Executive Service or Senior Australian Defence Force equivalent, the Director spoke at every program as did the Deputy Secretary (Intelligence and Security). More than 800 DSD members went through the program in less than three years.

This diagonal-slice concept is unique, as it consisted of a truly representational section from the organisation. For example, for the civilian members this meant one from the Senior Executive Service, two from Executive Level 2, four from Executive Level 1, twelve from Australian Public Service Level 6 and so on, down through the ranks until all staff were proportionally represented. A similar arrangement applied for the military participants. Still today, most leadership development programs focus on developing individuals by virtue of their position or grade. It is rare, if not unique, to see the organisation as whole embark on leadership development. Indeed, it was considered a brave experiment, but it worked, according to independent evaluations.

The program took all participants through the organisation's history, values and behaviours as well as the application of emotional intelligence and leadership theory. Each participant had a 360 degree evaluation that was analysed at length. Further, as part of the program, groups based on the diagonal slice presented innovative solutions they thought would help drive the organisation forward, whether it be human resources (HR) or complex intelligence solutions. Irrespective of grade or position, everybody was empowered to put forward and champion innovative solutions. The program generated long-lasting capabilities that were born from very junior members. This in itself delivered a very powerful message to the organisation's workforce: everybody is a leader and can influence positive outcomes:

> The message I took from this was that there was a level of sincerity and commitment to driving the organisation forward. That we are all an important part of this and have something to offer. The transformational behaviour was that we were valued and we had a say in shaping our future.

> For most of us, the outcomes from the program were immediately positive. I am sure there was the exception but for the most part, we all left the program feeling part of this incredible team. We believed that in our own way, we could influence the organisation and help shape it to meet the demands of the future. There were obviously still bureaucratic structures, but across the teams they were flattened and we were all potential leaders in this regard.

The program not only reiterated the vision, values and behaviours, but equally important, it empowered all DSD members to be part of the leadership process. This was critical to breaking down internal stovepipes and providing fluent internal networks.

> From a personal perspective, it provided a very exciting and rewarding environment to work in. My role within the organisation changed a few times during this period, but irrespective of the position it was a great sense of everybody belonging to an important team. I cannot speak for everyone but my memories as a Target Manager in a Military Support role are of perpetual tiredness mixed with empowerment and excitement. It felt as though we could take on anything and nothing was out of reach. If you had valid argument then you could lead the change to deliver the capability framework to support it. I believe this was the conscious outcome from this period of change.

Role of Results Consulting in the change

Results Consulting) is a reasonably small consulting firm based in Canberra with staff, in the main, having solid public sector backgrounds. Results initially responded to the DSD tender for what became the 'Building the DSD Team' program and were shortlisted for interview.

> *At the interview we were informed that the program would consist of a diagonal slice of staff from all levels, and, considering this, we were asked would we still be interested in working with DSD? Initially a little sceptical, we indicated we would and it was one of the best decisions that we made.*

The project was challenging, involving multiple cultures and levels of understanding and knowledge within the organisation.

The program was designed in close cooperation with Directorate staff to develop and foster leadership and teamwork skills to take DSD into the future. Focussing on self-awareness, emotional intelligence and team skills, the program was piloted, evaluated and then modified based on the results of the pilot. Since the pilot the program has been delivered over 40 times within the organisation. Through a process of continual review and evaluation the program has been updated to reflect the changing needs of DSD. As a result of the program remaining relevant to the organisations needs, and by working in close partnership with DSD, this program has proven to be a major success story.

In addition, the program was the subject of a major external evaluation generally unusual for programs of this type. This evaluation found that the program has demonstrated significant long-term results for the organisation in both changes in behaviour and understanding of organisational direction.

Apart from the formal evaluation, DSD's staff survey results were able to demonstrate a direct correlation between a deeper understanding of organisational direction and required leadership behaviour and attendance at the program.

The Building the DSD Team program includes the application of assessment tools such as the Team Management Profile (TMP) and 360 feedback to support individual understanding of self and others. Results Consulting understood the required theory for achieving the changes, but, as important, used it to deliver down-to-earth, no nonsense programs.

From the perspective of Results Consulting, there were a number of aspects that were unique apart from the diagonal slice. These were, the significant level of ownership by the Director DSD (he attended every one), the level of access that the consultants were afforded to the Director to deal with issues or concerns and the commitment the organisation demonstrated in providing the additional administrative backing to make the program work. DSD and the Director actively modelled the behaviour that they talked about and truly partnered with Results. They demonstrated this by always giving Results a 'heads up' on issues that may impact them, keeping them informed about outside influences or changes that they should know about, and managing the relationship proactively. Results, in turn, alerted the Director and others in the organisation to emerging issues or concerns that may have surfaced during the programs. This engendered high levels of trust above and beyond what might normally be seen in a commercial relationship. Results noted that they felt they were truly a partner with DSD in the change process.

HRM strategies to support the change

The Human Resources section of DSD had a substantial role in the change, beyond just delivering HR services. They took a strategic role in building the most important capability of DSD via the People Strategy Plan and an excellent HR management information system.

People Capability Development Framework Working closely with the APSC, this framework set out the type and level of skills expected of staff across all the public service levels. These skills encompassed both leadership qualities and professional technical skills across the thirteen professional streams in DSD. Each was headed by a designated stream leader who had particular responsibility for the health of their streams, as well as their normal day job. Setting out clear expectations for members at each level allowed them to make better informed decisions on their own career development initiatives.

Learning and development Members of DSD felt affirmed by the idea of leadership at all levels. The organisation supported this by providing extensive learning and development opportunities such as quality in-house training programs, and courses offered by the Department of Defence, the Australian Public Service Commission and the prestigious Australian Government School of Management. DSD also established a Signals Intelligence Academy with a small permanent staff of highly respected analysts and adjunct staff who ensured that training kept pace with the rapidly changing intelligence demands on the organisation.

Regular and systematic reviews, focus and communication

Processes were also established to sustain the change. They included monthly meetings to review strategy), culture and management as well as annual offsite leadership team meetings to consider the next twelve month's focus. There are also annual 'State of the Directorate' presentations in multiple locations and an annual staff survey.

Resistance to change

DSD traditionally valued technical excellence. Not every member of DSD was comfortable with the new ideas about leadership. Some found them challenging and confronting. The new culture recognised and rewarded people for their leadership excellence. Some members argued that these innovations devalued technical skills and individual brilliance, but as Steve Merchant elaborated:

I went to great lengths to explain this was not the case. This was not a zero-sum game where we had to trade off technical skills for leadership qualities. I was demanding both. I wanted our brilliant crypto-mathematicians to be inspiring and nurturing our next generation of brilliant crypto-mathematicians. I don't think I am now looked on with suspicion as that guy who'd destroyed our technical expertise. The thing that clinched that turnaround was not my protestations of innocence, but the re-investment we made in technical training.

Summary and overview

DSD operates in a demanding context due to its specific Defence mission and the more general changes in the public sector environment – and this context is not static. The organisation is perhaps uncharacteristically young in terms of its workforce and also highly specialised. Leadership at all levels, from the whole workforce, was conceived of as one solution to these challenges. The Director, not a natural candidate for transformational change, embarked on a daring program of reform over four years. The predominant focus was on soft skills: demanding positive influence, innovation, input and collaboration. The changes were supported by extensive learning and development opportunities as well as other integrated HRM processes. The leadership team at DSD promulgated the values with passion about making DSD a stronger and more effective organisation. This was based on being intelligent and learned, as one would expect from an organisation of this nature, but which isn't always so evident in practice. In this organisation it does seem that the leaders actually walked the walk instead of just talking the talk.

Discussion questions

1) What do you think this case study tells you about theories of leading change in a large public sector organisation?

2) How would you describe the main change agent? How does this description fit with what the change literature says about the leader in a change situation?

3) DSD employees are predominantly technical experts with qualifications in ICT among other areas. The literature would describe these as hard skills, yet DSD changed to become an organisation that also valued soft skills such as leadership, communication, participation, vision and values. How was this achieved at DSD and why was it successful?

4) The case presents a mostly positive perspective on change at DSD. Given that resistance to change is relatively common, what might have been some of the sources of resistance to change and what strategies for overcoming resistance to change were evident?

5) DSD is a unique organisation in terms of its nature and role. How likely is it that these changes would be transferable to other organisations in the public, private or non-government sectors?

References

APSC 2010, 'About the Commission and the APS', <http://www.apsc.gov.au/index.html>, accessed October 24 2010.

Bolden, R 2004, 'What is leadership?', Centre for Leadership Studies, University of Exeter, <http://www.leadership-studies.com/documents/what_is_leadership.pdf>, accessed August 28 2010.

Bolden, R, Denison, P, Gosling, J & Marturano, A 2003, 'A review of leadership theory and competency frameworks', Centre for Leadership Studies, University of Exeter, Exeter, <http://centres.exeter.ac.uk/cls/research/abstract.php?id=29>, accessed October 24 2010.

Dalglish, C & Miller, P 2010, *Leadership: Understanding its global impact*, Tilde University Press, Melbourne.

Dunphy, D & Griffiths, A 2006, *The sustainable corporation: Organisational renewal in Australia*, Allen and Unwin, St Leonards.

DSD 2010, 'About DSD', <http://www.dsd.gov.au/aboutdsd/index.htm>, accessed October 20 2010.

Dunphy, D & Stace, D 1993, 'The strategic management of corporate change', *Human Relations*, vol. 46, no. 8, pp. 905-921.

Kotter, JP & Schlesinger, LA 1979, 'Choosing strategies for change', *Harvard Business Review*, vol. 57, March-April, pp. 109-112.

Limerick, D & Cunnington, B 1993, *Managing the new organisation: A blueprint for networks and strategic alliances*, Business & Professional Publishing, Sydney.

McKenzie, I 2010, 'Speech to National Security Australia Conference', Canberra, ACT, February 26 2010, <http://www.dsd.gov.au>, accessed October 17 2010.

Merchant, S 2006, Presentation to APSC, SES Breakfast Seminar, Canberra, ACT, August 24 2006.

Robbins, SP, Judge, TA, Millett, B & Waters-Marsh, T 2008, *Organisational behaviour*, 5th edn, Pearson Education Australia, Frenchs Forest NSW.

Robbins, SP, Waters-Marsh, T, Cacioppe, R & Millett, B 1994, *Organisational behaviour, concepts, controversies and applications*, Prentice Hall, Brisbane.

Stace, D & Dunphy, D 2001, *Beyond the boundaries: leading and re-creating the successful enterprise*, 2nd edn, McGraw-Hill, Sydney.

Acknowledgements

Thank you to Stephen Merchant for providing a very useful account of the changes and for graciously agreeing for his description of the change to be taken to a wider audience. Mr Merchant has long experience in the Australian Intelligence Community and in the Department of Defence, principally in the analysis of international strategic issues and the development of Australian

Defence policies. He is currently Deputy Secretary Intelligence and Security within Defence and was recently awarded the Public Service Medal 'For outstanding public service in the fields of Defence strategic and international policy and intelligence collection and analysis'.

Thank you also to Chris Morely – Managing Director, Results Consulting (Australia). Chris and Paulene Cahill facilitated the programs and worked in partnership with DSD. Chris and Paulene had long careers in the public sector before moving into consulting. They are experienced facilitators and change practitioners.

Chapter 20

Leadership and motivational challenges in the Australian IT sector

JANE P MURRAY

Company background and context

In early 1997, two young Australian IT graduates hatched a plan. Instead of working 9-5 in a large IT organisation, they decided they would like to start up their own software development company. After a lengthy period of discussion and planning, the pair began operations in the garage of one of their suburban Australian homes. In order to get the business up and running, they both continued their regular jobs by day and worked on their new business venture after hours. A first milestone occurred not long after the company began when the pair successfully tendered for, and secured, software development work for a major Australian television network. Their work began with the pair programming systems that would run hardware for two popular children's television game shows. Following their success on this project, the duo then won a second tender from the network to create real-time statistical scoring software for a major international sporting event. At this point they were still a workforce of two.

As the company became more firmly established it became necessary to hire more staff. In particular, an artist and an additional programmer were needed to complete the contract work with the television network. The first two employees to join the organisation were friends and colleagues of the founders. These individuals were a perfect fit within the organisation as they shared the vision of their friends in creating a small but successful IT firm. The two new employees had no issue with working long hours out of a suburban double-garage. The group of four continued to work for the television network but at the same time began discussing their collective desire to enter the game-production market. The owners soon found that they did not have the capacity or the resources to create and build a game on their own, so they began to talk with other small IT companies that were looking to branch out into the same area of software development. It was at this point that the founders visited America and began a joint venture to produce a children's computer game with another small IT company. The relationship continued for almost four years until the game was published and distributed to multiple international markets; however, despite the efforts of both organisations, the game never reached the level of success that both parties had envisaged.

By the beginning of 2002, the founders had come to a point where an important decision would need to be made – would they close down the business, or would they keep trying to make it successful? After a period of much discussion, one of the directors opted to leave the company and return to university to further his education. The remaining founder decided to change the direction of the company and focus fully on the opportunities that were available in the realm of on-line gaming (gambling). The company had begun to do small projects in this area during the previous four years with any funds received being ploughed straight back into internally funded and IP owned games projects. This decision has since proved to be a wise one. A major result of this change in direction is that the company has grown significantly both in numbers and stability.

Fourteen years later there is a very different story for this organisation. The company is no longer operated out of a suburban double-garage. Over the years its success has been built upon continually increasing its pool of experienced employees. The company now provides employment to over 40 staff including quality engineers and software developers experienced in a variety of the latest technologies, processes, paradigms and tools. At present, the company's clientele includes many successful international companies, including publicly listed organisations. The company now boasts significant expertise across several domains and technologies, including internet multiplayer immersive games, online casino management systems and slot gaming systems and environments. In addition, their core competency lies in gaming and game technologies.

Motivational challenges

Much of the expansion that has occurred within this organisation has been in the last five years. As a result, the motivational practices that were successfully used in the past are very different to those that are required now. In the beginning, workers shared the dream of the founders and were happy to be paid lower wages and work longer hours to be involved in the making of a successful organisation. As mentioned, many of the early employees were not only colleagues, but also friends of the founders. This created a very close-knit culture where employees routinely performed over and above what would be expected of an employee in another organisation. It was this commitment that enabled the organisation to keep operating through the tough periods outlined above.

However as the organisation grew, the owner realised he needed to look outside of his personal networks to attract and retain staff. This is where the challenge of keeping this growing workforce first came about. Also, when the company changed its direction from retail fun games to gambling, many of the original staff struggled with the moral question this change in direction raised. From its humble beginnings where motivating employees was not a real issue (the founders were intrinsically motivated to achieve success), the company now faces many motivational challenges. Five major challenges currently impacting the organisation are outlined below.

Challenge 1: From dynamic flexibility to process-driven consistency

In the early days, many contracts were secured because of the dynamic flexibility of the organisation. If employees needed to work for 18 hours per day, seven days per week for six months to meet a deadline or to ensure the organisation successfully won tenders - that was just part of the job. Internal peer pressure was high and the small group of programmers and artists would willingly work all hours to ensure successful outcomes. It was this pressure to conform that allowed the organisation to flourish. The owner of the organisation credits this dynamic flexibility as *'integral in ensuring the organisation stayed in business...many of our larger competitors just couldn't achieve what we were able to achieve in incredible timeframes'*. Not only did this approach help to keep the company afloat, but the organisation's reputation amongst its major clients was built on this flexible model of operating and the final quality of its product.

However in the current organisational environment, these flexible work practices are no longer sustainable. As the company has grown, the ability to be flexible and move quickly to client demands has diminished. Employees within the organisation have other interests outside of the organisation and will not commit to 18-hour workdays being the norm when working on projects, or react immediately to an international client's request at 2am in the morning week in, week out. Yes, employees are happy to put in additional hours to reach deadlines when required, but the acceptance of this culture has changed as the organisation has grown from its small quorum of original staff to a medium-sized organisation. This current situation has not only caused internal problems, but has also impacted client relationships. The company that the clients know and love has changed, and in their eyes it is not entirely for the better. The customers do accept that the increased process is essential due to the growth and scale of operations; however they still desire the benefits of both worlds.

Challenge 2: Graduates come, graduates go

A second key tool that allowed the organisation to remain competitive was the use of graduate student labour. Over a period of 10 years the organisation has built a strong relationship with both universities and IT focused technical training institutions within Australia. These relationships assisted the organisation to interview and offer internship programs on meaningful and relevant projects as well as employment to some of the best and most talented graduates prior to them completing their degrees and being snapped-up by larger, wealthier organisations. These graduates were the best and most talented from their cohorts and the organisation was able to employ them at rates much lower than what would be paid for an experienced worker in the same position. These graduates would then gain experience at a very fast pace, way beyond their years out of university or what could be gained in the equivalent timeframe elsewhere. However as the company has grown and begun to be noticed by its competitors, the level of experience held by these graduates has made them very marketable to competing organisations. Many of these employees are subsequently offered higher positions and higher salaries in larger organisations and, although they struggle with leaving an enjoyable workplace, they are ambitious to extend their skills and knowledge and are keen face the challenges a new workplace would offer.

Challenge 3: Remuneration lags the market

Related to the above issues with graduate retention, the organisation has traditionally used a strategy of opportunistic and good-value hiring processes. This means that the company knowingly lags the market in terms of the remuneration it provides to its staff. This was a clear strategy at the company's inception, and has been a major factor in the company's survival – it simply could not afford to pay market rates. As a result of this, performance appraisals were avoided because staff would (rightfully) expect to be awarded substantial pay rises relative to their appraisal results. And at this point, the company just did not have the funds available to be able to give these rises. As a result, average performers could work anywhere between 2 and 3 years without having a scheduled and formal appraisal review. The staff that were well looked-after in terms of remuneration were the key employees who were employed in critical jobs. In these cases, the organisation would do what it could to keep remuneration at market rates, but if employee requests were more than the organisation could meet, then the staff would often leave for the better paying jobs in other companies. During this period the organisation relied on the fact that it worked on interesting projects, used cutting edge technologies, and had a small-business culture (flexible hours, casual dress, direct relationships with the owners and managers), to help retain staff. These benefits were seen to offset issues relating to salaries because money was often not the highest priority for staff.

In the last two years the company has become more financially secure; however, there is still the inherent mindset of the company founder to keep staffing costs as low as possible. This is in case the company should fall on hard times again (interestingly in the organisation's history only three staff members have ever been retrenched). Now, out of a natural sense of fairness, the owner would like to start changing the remuneration structure within the organisation because many loyal employees have become integral to the success of the business. Currently, many staff are naturally looking at the market and asking the question *'given the company is doing well, why shouldn't I be paid as well as my friends who work for other IT firms?'* This is an issue that the company would like to resolve as soon as possible, but it is having problems deciding on how this should and could be done in an equitable way.

Challenge 4: Multiple employees in multiple locations

A further challenge that has resulted from the growth of the organisation is that there are now four separate company offices located within close proximity of each other. As the company began to grow, the owner still had major concerns over the long-term financial viability of the organisation and wanted to remain conservative in making commitments. Taking this into account, in 2005 the owner opted to rent additional office space across the road from its original office as the number of employees increased. There were three reasons for this decision. First, the process of moving offices for all staff would take time and during this period employees would not be productive (the company had no excess funds to cover this down time). Second, the owner reasoned that should the company have to contract in size, the lease for the second office could easily be terminated. Third, the current office is located in a busy town centre with ample transport, eating and shopping options for staff. Moving to larger premises would mean moving away from this level of convenience for staff.

Over the subsequent five years and as the company has continued to expand, the owner has rented a further two office spaces in the vicinity of the first two offices. Again, the decision to expand office space in this way was the same as the reasons outlined above. The major issue with this office configuration is that although staff are still located in close proximity to each other, there are now essentially four different organisational sub-cultures forming. In addition, the interaction between members of different work teams has begun to suffer. The owner has tried to combat this by having end of week drinks and occasional functions; however, the distance between workers still seems to be on the increase.

Challenge 5: Which leader do I follow?

When the company first began operating in 1997 there were two founders who led the company. These two individuals were, in general, equally charismatic, possessed equal leadership skills, had equal technical abilities and had equal business skills. On balance the duo worked very well together. As the organisation was small, messages sent from both leaders to employees were mostly consistent. If there was a discrepancy, a resolution could quickly be found. However, when one of the founders left, the remaining founder realised that a replacement leader was needed to assist him to successfully run the business. The owner strategically decided to employ a 'grey-haired CEO'. This was done to maintain credibility with existing customers and to gain further sales, deal-making and business development experience.

During this period, the company was once again led by two strong leaders. Any shortcomings of one leader was compensated for by the other. However, the same problem existed: as the company grew the leaders would often cause confusion by frequently communicating two different points of view, giving different directions and using differing leadership styles. Behind closed doors these differing styles enabled well-rounded analysis and debate of opportunities; however, many staff felt that there had been many instances where two different messages were being conveyed. This situation continues to cause motivational issues within the organisation as staff often comment that they are given two different opinions on how to perform a task, and that often progression on projects can be slowed due to the time it takes to clarify which leader's direction is correct.

Summary

In summary, although the organisation is in a very strong position to continue its current growth and success, there are key issues within the company that are currently impacting employee motivation and preventing the organisation from being as successful as it could be. The challenge from here is to provide solutions to these issues so that the company can ensure its success into the future. The main challenges that have been outlined include a change in company culture from dynamism to consistency, graduate retention issues, remuneration lagging the market, multiple office sites creating 'distance' between employees, and problems arising from having two engaged, passionate and charismatic leaders giving differing direction within the organisation.

Discussion questions

1) What suggestions would you make to the owner of this organisation to maintain and increase the motivation of its staff as the company continues to grow?

2) How would you suggest the organisation manages the conflicting expectations of staff and existing clients regarding flexibility and availability?

3) What motivational strategies might the company employ to help keep its graduate employees?

4) How would you suggest the company should approach the issue of remuneration while ensuring that employees consider the new arrangements are equitable?

5) How would you solve the 'multiple offices problem', which is causing employees to become less engaged with each other?

6) What other motivational challenges do you see on the horizon for this organisation?

7) Identify the range of different motivational theories and concepts that are evident in this case study.

Chapter 21

Transformational leadership in a public sector agency

Hani G Abdalla and Ashly Pinnington

Introduction

The government agency investigated in this case study is one of the leading agencies in Abu Dhabi. It is responsible for the assessment of, and granting permission for, projects and industrial facilities in the Emirate of Abu Dhabi. The agency was established in 1999, although operations did not start until late 2001. The main aim of establishing the organisation was to assess new and existing projects and industrial facilities in the Emirate of Abu Dhabi. It evaluates the impacts of major projects and provides instructions in order to minimise negative effects and remove identified obstacles. The purpose of these activities is to ensure successful operations and protect the future interests of the Emirate.

During its short life span, the agency has contributed to some reshaping of traditional management practices in the public sector. This organisational change has been achieved through designing and implementing new processes based on best international practices. New leadership styles have been introduced and are supported by an intensive mentoring and training program for managers and employees. The agency's leadership has moved the emphasis of the organisation from focusing on the task and the traditional way of doing things to concentrating on employees' wellbeing and customer satisfaction.

Problems

There are several problems relating to employee motivation, performance and retention that have challenged the agency and its leadership. These HR problems are far from unique to the organisation and to a large extent are shared by many other public sector organisations in the country.

The rapid growth of Abu Dhabi's economy during the past few years has, in general, led to a considerable increase in workloads and raised the level of stress experienced by many employees. Furthermore, greater job mobility and growing rates of inflation in Abu Dhabi have been accompanied by a decrease in employee commitment and a reduction in typical periods of employee service in organisations.

The higher rate of employee turnover in the agency has created shortages in several categories of skilled employee and is considered to have been partly responsible for the concomitant reduction in overall organisational performance, combined with growth in the number of customer complaints.

Change in the macro environment and in the public sector

The initial structure of the agency was hierarchical and subdivided into functional departments, which has been the standard structure for organisations in the government sector in Abu Dhabi. A simplified version of the organisational structure of the agency is presented in Figure 21.1.

This type of organisational structure can be characterised by an autocratic style of leadership because decision making is highly centralised and the communication channels are primarily top-down. Horizontal communication between the different sectors of the organisation is minimal. Response to external and internal changes is slow and lengthy due to the process of centralised decision making.

Furthermore, the structure does not focus on client satisfaction. Employees working in such structures can become characterised by low levels of motivation due in part to poor chances of obtaining promotion. These types of structure inhibit employees' creativity and innovation since employees are simply expected to do what they are told. Employee participation in decision making is minimal to non-existent. This often encourages a weak sense of loyalty to the organisation.

Figure 21.1 Agency organisational structure 2001

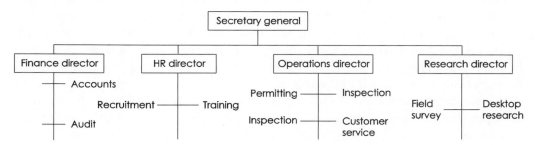

Organisations with a functional organisational structure are not always characterised by a high level of employee turnover and this was not previously the situation in the Abu Dhabi government sector. Government jobs in the UAE culture were considered as 'jobs for life' and this was understood to provide subordinates with the necessary job security to maintain high levels of organisational commitment. In addition, there were many disadvantages associated with working in the private sector in the UAE, including low wages, less concern for the employee in contrast with concern for production, long working hours and inability to move freely between jobs. Consequently, these negative factors encouraged government employees in the past to retain rather than change their jobs.

Another major factor that stimulated the preference for an autocratic leadership style in Abu Dhabi and across the United Arab Emirates government sector has been said to be the multicultural nature of organisations. The composition of the population in the United Arab Emirates is diverse, and it exhibits a high level of multiculturalism. Multicultural organisations provide a challenge for leaders to find a suitable leadership style that is universal to all cultures within the organisation (Jung & Avolio 1999). One of the ways of coping with contextual complexity when managing cultural diversity is to practise an autocratic leadership style. Application of this style of leadership ostensibly guarantees similar treatment for all employees regardless of their nationality or culture, and therefore, is considered by some people as likely to reduce the chance of conflicts arising between employees.

The autocratic leadership style of governmental organisations was previously believed to be suitable for public and quasi-public sector organisations. This general attitude changed dramatically, however, during the exponential rise of the UAE economy commencing in 2006. The economic boom led to a substantial revitalisation of the UAE public sector and growth in visa entry permits for job vacancies in all sectors of employment. Major constraints on employees working in the private sector were significantly reduced as private businesses became more able to pay global rates for experienced and well-qualified international expertise. The boom led to a considerable increase in the wages offered to technical specialists and professionals employed in the private sector.

Recently, the UAE has attracted a large number of international organisations that have relocated their headquarters to the country to participate in the munificent environment. The inward movement of multinational firms has encouraged greater interest amongst locals in the introduction of western styles of leadership to the UAE work culture. During the first three years of the current global recession, the Abu Dhabi economy managed to maintain growth due to increases in oil prices. There has also been a further influx of European and Western organisations to Abu Dhabi in search of new markets that are more buoyant than their own domestic markets. This business growth has contributed to increased job opportunities and growth in employee job mobility specifically within the emirate of Abu Dhabi, making it difficult to attract and retain experts within the government sector. Increased employee mobility and skill scarcity in specialised occupations has become one of the main driving forces for change in the traditional leadership and management practices of the government sector.

The nature of organisational structure in the government sector is often characterised by a slow response to external changes in the environment. The public sector's inability to maintain pace with the economic and technical development of the private sector in the UAE has led to a large number of valuable employees considering leaving their organisation to join the private sector. This has caused a major problem with the government sector losing a high percentage of its best technical expertise to the private sector, and this is considered to have contributed substantially to lower levels of work performance and reduced levels of customer satisfaction. The problem was less one of volume of potential applicants and more around recruiting and retaining highly skilled people in specialised positions and occupations. Some specialist roles remained vacant for several months or witnessed turnover of a rapid succession of viable occupants. In order to overcome these serious difficulties with recruitment and retainment, the Abu Dhabi government had to act and improve working conditions and employment opportunities in the government sector. One concerted response by the government in tackling this dilemma has been the launch and implementation of the Abu Dhabi Governmental Excellence Award program.

The Abu Dhabi Award for Excellence in Government Performance is an award program developed to provide governmental bodies with the expertise and techniques required to enhance organisational performance. This is achieved through capacity building, process improvement and simplification. His Excellency Mahammed Ahmed Al-Bawardi, Secretary General of the Executive Council of Abu Dhabi, described the move towards launching the program as:

> *A natural response to the inevitable need for change required by the Government leadership to achieve Excellence in organizational performance in terms of the services given to all stakeholders. The provision of excellent government services leading to people and employee satisfaction will inevitably contribute to overall society satisfaction through creating a positive impact on it, socially, economically, environmentally and politically.* (General Secretariat of Executive Council 2010, p. 7)

The model developed by the award program identified leadership as one of the major criteria for the success of the initiative. This perspective is consistent with the management and leadership literature which emphasises the relationship between leadership and organisational performance (Eden, Avolio & Shamir 2002; MacKenzie, Podsakoff & Rich 2001). Leaders have the ability to motivate subordinates by increasing their level of satisfaction and involvement within the organisation, which then can lead to higher levels of performance and organisational commitment (Limsila & Ogunlana 2008).

This policy initiative made it necessary for the executive leaders of government agencies to devise new approaches that would enhance employees' levels of commitment and productivity, leading to improvements in overall organisational performance. The need for change to the agency's normal mode of operations was understood as urgent and it was agreed that a change in leadership behaviour was required in order to manage change in HR activities and work operations. Executive leaders and managers had to shift their focus from mainly concentrating on the task to focusing on employees. Two new styles of leadership were introduced: the transactional and the transformational leadership styles

(Bass *et al.* 2003). One route taken to introduce these new styles of leadership was to recruit brand name leaders with substantial previous experience in managing change in large organisations. The second approach was to emphasise leadership training for all employees.

The agency's approach

The first step towards implementation of the change was to identify the organisation's vision, mission and values. The second step was to develop and then communicate a strategic plan for achieving the agency's vision. In June 2007, the agency retained an American consultancy company specialised in the provision of management solutions.

The main objectives of the consultancy company were to evaluate the current practices of the agency and provide recommendations based on best international practices for improvements to the system. The consultancy company first studied the current practices of the organisation to gain an understanding of the roles and responsibilities of the agency and the type of services provided. The next step was to evaluate the international best practices applied by government organisations around the world to learn from their experiences. The results of the international best practices study were then presented to the agency's top management in order to set the vision and mission of the organisation. The consultancy company provided a gap analysis report to top management to identify the resources required for achieving the vision of the agency. Finally, a strategic plan was agreed and set in place to guide the change process.

The first stage of the strategic plan involved a complete restructuring of the agency. The new proposed organisational structure was flatter than the traditional structure. The structure provided direct managers with more authority than did the previous one. The roles, responsibilities and competencies for each position in the organisation's structure were identified. The next stage involved meetings with managers and individuals within the organisation to determine their competencies and identify the need for additional training required by those managers.

The roles and responsibilities for each job position were clarified and specified through job analysis. Individuals' expertise and competencies were evaluated according to their position descriptions. Furthermore, employees' level of satisfaction was assessed through interviews with managers and individuals. The consultancy company then worked with the human resources department to develop a new employee rewards program. The objective of the new rewards program was to provide additional sources of motivation for employees in order to increase the level of employee satisfaction and strengthen levels of organisational commitment, and hence improve organisational performance.

The new program is based on a contingent reward leadership model. The objectives of each employee are identified at the beginning of each fiscal year. The performance of employees is then evaluated by direct mangers in order to evaluate every employee's individual achievement according to assigned objectives. The appraisal and evaluation of performance is based on a clear and contingent rewards system. The amount of reward obtained is therefore based on each employee's assessed level of individual achievement.

The next step was to introduce a new leadership style complementing the new human resource management system of motivation and reward. The consultancy company introduced two styles of leadership; transactional and transformational. Their introduction was combined with an empirical examination of which leadership style was more suitable for implementation in the agency. The contingent reward transactional style of leadership was thought by many to be culturally most suited to the needs of employees and was introduced to the majority of the functional departments of the organisation, such as the Human Resources, Finance, Awareness and Research departments. Managers were provided with extensive training in order to be able to apply this leadership style.

The transformational style of leadership was adopted on a smaller scale and applied to the Operations department within the agency. This department is central to the strategic operations of the organisation and is responsible for the assessment, permitting, inspections and handling of hazardous material. Application of transformational leadership styles is new to the UAE culture and requires an extensive training program for both managers and employees. It was therefore seen as involving a higher degree of risk and uncertainty, but potentially also was regarded as having greater pay-off. Transformation leadership was viewed as more capable of resolving the problems of employee motivation, performance and retention that have challenged the agency and its leadership. The agency outsourced the management of this department to a western based organisation and the type of contract with the consultancy company was classified as a strategic partnership.

The purpose of the strategic partnership was to introduce new management practices to the operational department based on best international practices. Three managers from the outsourced company headquarters were transferred to the agency to manage the operations department. The main responsibilities listed in the strategic partnership program included:

- introduce a new management/leadership style to the department
- assess the current practices of the department and provide recommendations for improvements
- ensure continuous operation of the department
- provide technical and capacity building training for department employees to ensure successful operation upon completion of the strategic partnership contract.

The first step in introducing the transformational leadership style to the operations department was to develop a new organisation structure for the department that would complement the new style of leadership as shown in Figure 21.2. The new structure placed the three selected managers who were deployed through the strategic partnership at the top of the organisation tree.

Then four Project Leaders (see Figure 21.2) representing the four main units of the department were selected. Their main responsibility was to ensure successful completion of projects within their units. All projects leaders were provided with training on the application of the transformational leadership style.

Figure 21.2 Operations department organisation structure

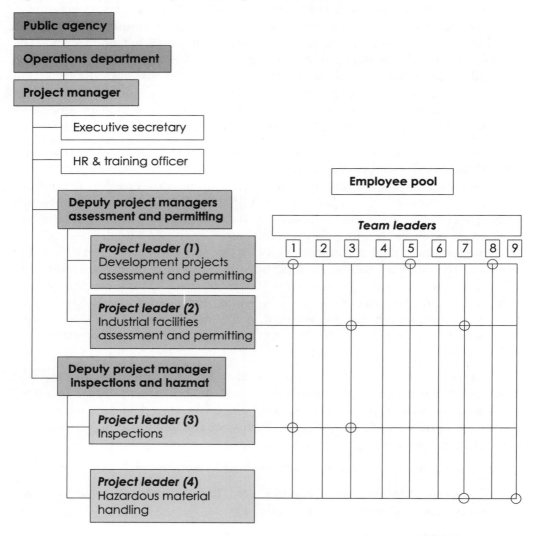

Finally, the department's employees were placed in a 'pool' system within the organisation structure. The pool system is a project-based organisation structure and HR system where employees are not exclusively assigned to any specific unit within the department. Instead, employees are employed on the basis that they are available to work on a number of different projects within the department. The advantages of the pool system are that it facilitates flexibility and job rotation contributing to the elimination of some of the more unnecessary routine work associated with government operations. A major strength of the system is that it enables project leaders to utilise the technical expertise of all employees within the department according to the needs of particular projects and project goals.

Within each unit in the Operations department, the project leader (see Figure 21.2) is responsible for selecting the project teams and defines the work-hours contribution required by each team member. Then, a team leader is selected for each project within the unit. The team leader is responsible for managing the project team and ensuring successful completion of the project. A major HR advantage of flexibly selecting the team leader is that it provides all employees with the opportunity to lead a team in order to practice and develop their leadership skills. Another benefit of this particular system of rotation of the team leader role is that it stimulates increased horizontal and vertical channels of communication within the department. Extensive training on the application of the new transformational leadership style is provided to all employees. Additional advantages of the new project matrix structure include the following:

- ensures equal distribution of work and responsibilities within the department

- provides additional flexibility for employee movement within the units in order to cope with the increasing work load of the department

- ensures that each employee is aware of different operations within each unit of the department and understands their individual contribution to the success of the department

- identifies skills and competencies of employees, and individual training programs can be designed accordingly.

Review of the transformational and transactional leadership approaches

The new approach developed by the agency was evaluated after two years of application in order to identify the leadership style most suitable to ensure higher employee commitment and performance. Leadership behaviours and their impact on employee satisfaction were measured using Bass and Avolio's (2004) Multifactor Leadership Questionnaire (MLQ form 5X). Employee performance was measured from the agency quarterly employee evaluations and employee commitment was measured using Suliman's (2002; 2009) organisation commitment questionnaire survey.

Results of the leadership behaviour survey

The review identified a strong association between implementation of transformational leadership and higher levels of employee performance and commitment. This is consistent with findings reported in the literature on leadership and management. The transformational leadership factor known as 'Individualised Consideration' had the highest influence on employee performance and commitment. This shows that by appealing to subordinates' individual needs, transformational leaders in the agency were more able than previous leaders to inspire and motivate employees and thereby enhance their levels of organisational commitment and work performance.

Implementation of the contingent reward transactional leadership style was also positively associated with improved employee performance and organisational commitment. This is also consistent with findings conveyed in the literature on transactional leadership and contingent rewards systems. However, the results of the review showed a stronger influence of transformational leadership on organisational outcomes than transactional styles.

Other styles of leadership not involving transformational approaches, known as 'management-by-exception' (active and passive) and 'laissez-faire' leadership styles showed a negative impact on organisational outcomes. These styles of leadership are defined as avoidant styles. Management-by-exception (active) is where the leader provides some guidance to subordinates on goals and objectives and intervenes responsively whenever problems arise. Management-by-exception (passive) is as its name suggests a less proactive approach. The laissez-faire leadership style is where the leader simply leaves people to get on with things without exercising any leadership initiative. These styles were all found, in the review, to lead to low levels of employee satisfaction and impact negatively on individual commitment and work performance.

The findings of the review imply that the agency's new leadership approach in enhancing employee commitment and performance has been successful. It further suggests that western theories of leadership can, to some extent, be transferred to other cultures. It is worth noting, however, that the level of influence was not as strong as that observed in western cultures. This was particularly evident in the statistical analysis of the survey data which showed that subordinates in the UAE culture do not make a clear distinction between the transformational and the contingent reward transactional leadership styles. This factor analysis can be interpreted as showing that cultural values will moderate the relationship between leadership style and organisational outcomes. The results from the review are consistent with the leadership literature which states that transformational leadership can be utilised in different cultures, taking into consideration the dominant national culture (Jung & Avolio 1999).

Conclusion and new challenges

The new system of leadership (transactional contingent reward and transformational) was applied in June 2008 throughout the agency. Quarterly performance evaluations and employee satisfaction surveys were conducted to monitor the effectiveness of the new system. Customer satisfaction surveys were redesigned and implemented on an annual basis in order to assess the overall performance of the agency.

A considerable increase in both employee performance and customer satisfaction was noticed in the first year for all departments of the government agency. Both transactional and transformational leadership styles continued to have a positive influence on employee performance. These findings were expected since application of both styles shifted the focus of management from daily operations to being more considerate of employees' needs and wellbeing.

Recently it has, however, become more difficult to determine exactly which leadership style is most suitable. Since rolling out full implementation of the program across the agency, the cultural significance of the application of styles of leadership has again become evident. A larger number of employees have reported no noticeable change in leadership styles of their managers. Instead, they claim that the new contingent reward system is the main driving force motivating their improved performance.

A principal challenge facing the executive leadership and HR specialists within the agency, therefore is to determine how best to improve the effectiveness of the leadership styles of project leaders and team leaders. Indeed, what further changes should be made to the structure, culture and HR policies and practices of the organisation? Clearly, the highest levels of organisational performance in relation to international best practice can only be achieved and sustained through implementation of leadership styles that positively influence motivation, individual work performance and long-term employee retention.

Discussion questions

1) In what different ways has the macro-environment influenced HRM in the UAE public sector?

2) What are the characteristics of transformational and transactional leadership styles?

3) How might two different styles of leadership be implemented in the UAE public sector and achieve similar outcomes?

4) What are the main issues facing the agency in long-term organisational change?

5) How can HRM assist with transformational leadership and transformational organisational change?

References

Bass, B, Avolio, B, Jung, D & Berson, Y 2003, 'On predicting unit performance by assessing transformational and transactional leadership', *Journal of Applied Psychology*, 88(2): 207-218.

Eden, T, Avolio, B & Shamir, B 2002, 'On impact of transformational leadership on follower development and performance: A field experiment', *Academy of Management Journal*, 45(4): 735-744.

General Secretariat of the Executive Council 2010, Category 1 – Awards and Entities Handbook and Guideline 3rd Cycle 2010-2011, in: Abu Dhabi Award for Excellence in Government Performance Programme [online].

http://www.adaep.ae/En/MediaCenter/Pages/ViewPublication.aspx?PB=Category%201%20Awards%20-%20Entities%20(Handbook%20and%20Guidelines)%20-%203rd%20cycle%20(2010-2011)&NPB=NaN&PPB=Category%201%20Awards%20-%20Entities%20-%20Preparation%20Guidelines%20(Best%20Practice%20Submission)-%203rd%20cycle%20(2010-2011) Abu Dhabi, UAE Nov 2008, Inive pp. 1-45.

Jung, D & Avolio, B 1999, 'On effects of leadership style and followers' cultural orientation on performance in group and individual task conditions', *Academy of Management Journal*, 42(2): 208-218.

Limsila, K & Ogunlana, S 2008, 'On performance and leadership outcome correlates of leadership styles and subordinate commitment', *Engineering, Construction and Architectural Management*, 15(2): 164-184.

MacKenzie, S, Podsakoff, P & Rich, G 2001, 'On transformational leadership and salesperson performance', *Journal of Academy of Marketing Science*, 29(2): 115-134.

Suliman, A 2002, 'Is it really a mediating construct? The mediating role of organizational commitment in the work climate-performance relationship', *Journal of Management Development*, 21(3): 170-183.

Suliman, A 2009, Draft research questionnaire survey for measuring organizational commitment and job satisfaction.

Part V
People Management and HRM

Chapter 22

McDonald's UK: Enhancing corporate reputation and developing an employer brand

STEPHEN TAYLOR

Background and context

During the last years of the 20th century and the first few years of the 21st, the reputation of the McDonald's restaurant business in the UK suffered a serious decline. Despite the company enjoying very considerable commercial success during this period, press coverage was uniformly negative. Rarely did a week go by without hostile headlines appearing in newspapers linking McDonald's to stories about unhealthy eating, rising obesity rates, poor employment practices or unethical business practices of one kind or another. As the most high-profile and fastest expanding restaurant chain in the country, the company had become the natural target for campaigners who disapproved of the fast-food industry, large multinational corporations in general and American multinational corporations in particular.

At the same time, negative impressions about McDonald's as an employer were fuelled in the UK, as elsewhere, by the growth in usage of the term 'McJob' as a generic label for low-status occupations. The term first appeared in 1991 in the bestselling novel *Generation X* written by the Canadian writer Douglas Coupland, where it is defined as 'a low-pay, low-dignity, low-benefit, no-future job in the service sector'. Aside from being used very widely in the press and in other media, it went on to be used to describe a deeply pessimistic development in one of the most influential recent articles that has been published on the UK labour market – 'McJobs and Macjobs: the growing polarisation of jobs in the UK' by Maarten Goos and Alan Manning (2003). In the same year, the term McJob appeared in the Oxford English Dictionary for the first time, defined as 'an unstimulating, low-paid job with few prospects, especially one created by the expansion of the service sector'. The decision by lexicographers to include McJob in this most prestigious of dictionaries, not only confirmed that the term had entered common parlance in the UK, but also appeared to confer on the definition a new (and high) level of legitimacy.

It is important to stress that the term McJob does not mean 'a job in McDonald's', but can refer to any job in the food service sector. However, because it has negative associations, its increased usage in the 1990s and more recently has very seriously damaged the company's reputation as an employer. In his book, *My Secret Life on the McJob* (2007), the American academic Jerry Newman described spending a fourteen month sabbatical working 'undercover' in a variety of fast-food outlets in the US, only one of which was a McDonald's restaurant. In fact his experiences working there were far from negative, but the title of his book served to reinforce the widely-held impression that working at McDonald's is something that educated and discerning people tend to avoid doing.

McDonald's UK operation has tended to suffer from negative connotations about its employment practices more than was the case in most of the other countries where the company operates. This is partly because food service work in general tends to be accorded less prestige in the UK than is the case elsewhere in the world and partly because of the extraordinary growth that McDonald's enjoyed in the country during the 1980s and 1990s – when the company opened between fifty and a hundred new restaurants each year. This mass expansion was accompanied by limited central direction as far as employment practices were concerned. Local managers and franchisees were given responsibility for staffing-up their restaurants, leading to the adoption of inconsistent approaches. They often struggled to recruit and retain effective employees and were not always particularly choosey when deciding who to hire. This led to the development of the widely-held view that anybody could get a job 'flipping burgers' at their local McDonald's just by turning up and asking it. Such impressions were then reinforced and amplified by journalists writing articles that frequently used the term McJob and always used it negatively. As a result, perceptions of the company as an employer became poor among the public in general. When people were asked in an opinion survey in 2004 whether or not they thought that McDonald's was a good employer, fewer than 20% said 'yes'.

McDonalds' own staff attitude survey found that the popular characterisation of its jobs was by no means accurate. In 2004: 74% of the company's employees reported being satisfied with their jobs and happy to 'recommend working at McDonald's to a friend'; 77% stated that they were committed to their work; while 86% were happy with the training and skills development opportunities they were given. Staff were particularly positive about the flexibility that their jobs gave them to juggle work and home responsibilities, the career-paths that were provided for them to follow and the enjoyment they got from working as a member of a team. The definition accorded to the term McJob was, therefore, not perhaps a fair or correct reflection of the lived reality for a good majority of people actually working in the company's 1,200 UK restaurants.

However, the survey also revealed that staff were generally dissatisfied with their pay and that only 60% agreed with the statement 'I am proud to work at McDonald's'. Staff turnover was also running at very high levels in 2004. The annual rate had reached over 80%, while the 90 day turnover rate (i.e. the proportion of new starters leaving before they have completed three months' service) was running at 24.5%. It appeared that poor hiring decisions were being made too often and that the company was not effectively managing the expectations of new starters about exactly what their jobs would involve on a day to day basis.

Thus the company had plenty of scope to improve its HR operations and its poor reputation as an employer. While McDonald's had always taken strong action to defend its reputation as a restaurant business when attacked, it had tended not to retaliate when it received negative media coverage of its reputation as an employer. Managers resigned themselves to the fact that most people thought that jobs in McDonald's restaurants were of a low quality. The trouble was that this perception was damaging the capacity of the company to recruit and retain good people in an increasingly tight labour market. Moreover, because confident, well-motivated staff are key to the commercial success of the restaurants, the poor reputation was serving to damage sales and to limit the potential profitability of the company's UK operations. Surveys of staff opinion also demonstrated how irritated McDonalds' employees themselves were with the persistence of these misconceptions about them and their jobs.

Employer branding initiatives

In the years since 2004, managers in McDonald's UK have brought forward a series of initiatives designed to address the problems outlined above. In many respects the company has led the way in developing approaches to employee resourcing which have since been imitated by other large employers. Central to the approach taken has been the development of a very thoughtful, well-resourced strategy aimed at improving the reputation of McDonald's as an employer. Managers have sought to regain the initiative and actively to manage their reputation rather than to allow the media to define it unfairly and unfavourably as had happened in the past. The approach taken can in many ways be characterised as a textbook case of the adoption of approaches associated with employer branding theories.

The term 'employer branding' was first coined in the early 1990s by a London-based consultant called Simon Barrow whose career had been spent working both in marketing and management functions. Since then the concept has attracted a good deal of attention and has been extensively developed by HR managers and consultants, by professional bodies such as the Chartered Institute of Personnel and Development (CIPD) in the UK and by some academic researchers. Despite being widely dismissed by critics as being no more than a 'passing fad', the underpinning ideas behind employer branding have proven to be both compelling and resilient. The approach involves the HR function borrowing approaches that have long been used to market goods and services to groups of customers and applying them to the management of relationships between organisations and their labour markets. A common misconception of employer branding is that it is primarily concerned with improving the effectiveness of recruitment advertising. This is not the case. It is a far broader and more strategic activity, which is concerned with developing and enhancing over time an employer reputation that is both positive and distinctive. At its heart is an understanding that labour markets are competitive and that to recruit and retain the most talented staff, organisations need to differentiate what they are able to offer employees from the offerings of competitor organisations.

There are two major stages involved in establishing a strong and effective employer brand. The first stage requires the organisation to develop what is often known as a compelling 'employee value proposition' (EVP). Having achieved this, the next stage involves its communication to employees, would-be employees, potential employees and people who have some influence over the job choices that people make (for example, careers services in schools and universities). In the case of large corporations such as McDonald's, who suffer from relatively poor reputations as employers, there is a further need to communicate the EVP to opinion-formers in media organisations.

A long-established and very true mantra quoted by successful marketing managers is 'to your own brand be true' – the implication being that no marketing campaign will be truly effective if it is either dishonest or not wholly honest about the product or service that is being marketed. Making exaggerated claims about the qualities of what is on offer may raise sales in the short term, but over time such an approach has the effect of dashing consumer expectations and reducing trust in the brand that has been developed. The same principle applies to employer branding activities. What is communicated about a workplace must reflect the reality of working there. In other words, to be effective over the long term, an employer branding exercise must effectively communicate a genuine, and not merely an aspirational, employee value proposition.

The approach taken by McDonald's UK fully met these requirements, effectively putting the theory into practice. The starting point was therefore to work out and gain a good understanding of what employees did and didn't like about working for McDonald's. The aim was to establish in what ways the working experience positively differed from that offered by other equivalent organisations. Considerable investment would then be put into further enhancing the positive elements and addressing those about which employees tended to be more negative.

Forming the employee value proposition

The 2004 staff survey demonstrated that there were three major aspects of the experience of being a McDonald's employee in the UK that staff liked. The first, labelled 'family and friends' by managers, was the satisfaction that people derived from working as part of a team and the way that effective teamworking energised them, creating a positive atmosphere at work. Secondly, staff voiced their appreciation for the flexible working systems the company operates in its restaurants. McDonald's has, for example, long made use of term-time contracts, which allow people with children of school age to take extensive periods of time off during the school holidays, their posts being occupied while they are away by students looking for vacation work. Thirdly, it was clear that staff were positive about the training and career opportunities provided to them – a particular strength of McDonald's since it was first founded in the USA during the 1950s. On the negative side, the survey revealed a fair amount of dissatisfaction about pay levels, deep frustration about the negative image associated with working for the company and also a lack of confidence and pride in their employer and in themselves as McDonald's employees. Over the following few years each of these points was addressed by the company so as to enhance its EVP – a process that is ongoing at the time of writing (2011).

Employees rarely express satisfaction with their pay, even when they are generally satisfied with other aspects of their jobs, and in this respect McDonald's is no exception. Pay rates in restaurants have to remain relatively low to ensure that the business remains profitable and competitive, but the company has always aimed to pay higher rates than its key competitors and always pays at a level above the National Minimum Wage. While there was relatively little room to manoeuvre on pay rates, the company was able to use its market muscle to introduce a very extensive staff discount scheme, which now includes 1,600 retailers within its remit. McDonald's staff are able to use vouchers to purchase goods and services at a considerably reduced cost. The most widely used vouchers give discounts of between 10% and 30% off the costs of mobile phones, Apple products, holidays and driving lessons. Just under £1 million a month is now collectively saved by McDonald's employees in the UK as a result of this scheme.

The company has also taken steps to offer more flexible working opportunities, pioneering the use of software which enables employees to swap shifts themselves by arrangement with each other without the need to ask permission from their managers. In 2006, family contracts were introduced, which allow two or more members of the same family to work for the same restaurant and to decide between themselves who works each allocated shift. Two years later the scheme was extended to groups of friends, enabling staff to combine working for the company with the unpredictable business of studying and looking after children and other dependent relatives. These schemes make it possible for staff to demonstrate high levels of commitment in both their work and home lives by permitting them to decide for themselves when they work. Survey evidence shows that the flexible working schemes are the main reason why a good number of the company's staff choose to remain as McDonald's employees over a long period of time.

Another major area of activity in recent years has been the enhancement of the training and development opportunities that are made available to McDonald's staff. In 2007 the company successfully applied to the Qualifications and

Curriculum Authority (QCA) and gained status as an awarding body. As a result it is now able to certify its training courses at different levels and has developed a hierarchy of in-house qualifications, which are gained through a mixture of online study and attendance at taught training events. A vocational apprenticeship scheme has been launched which it is intended will soon enrol 10,000 people each year. Higher level qualifications include a diploma in shift management (at level 3) and a further management program taught at level 4 (i.e.: foundation degree level). All in all, £30 million are invested on training each year, enabling the company to maintain a very well-equipped training centre (known as the McDonald's University) that provides outstanding, state-of-the art learning facilities. Moreover, to enable staff who do not have a home computer to participate, every McDonald's restaurant in the UK now has a PC installed in its staff room.

An important aim of the training programs, in addition to enhancing the employee value proposition, is to improve the employees' levels of confidence. Building personal confidence as well as professional competence is seen as a priority by McDonald's because their research has found that the two work together in combination to help generate the positive business outcomes being sought, namely the delivery of high levels of 'quality, service and cleanliness' in the company's restaurants.

Because a good proportion of the restaurants are located in relatively deprived neighbourhoods and are staffed by local people, many employees have left school without gaining any qualifications. The company provides opportunities for them to gain GCSEs in English and Maths through participation in its training schemes. The company also enrols staff in a program that leads to a certificate in financial management, which equips them better to organise their own personal finances. Further initiatives aimed at confidence-building include the decision to commission the fashion designer Bruce Oldfield to design a new range of uniforms in 2008 and encouraging team leaders to take their crews out several times a year to undertake a variety of organised leisure activities.

Communication initiatives

Having formed and started to consistently deliver this 'employee value proposition', the company needs to find effective ways of communicating it to its employees, would-be employees and the world generally, in order to improve its reputation as an employer. An early decision was to do this using language that lacked brashness or aggression. The prejudices that many held against the company were partly a function of the manner in which it had tended to communicate in the past.

A softer, more conciliatory and humble tone was adopted and the company has found it to be much more effective. This was then used in a series of initiatives that aimed to disrupt popular preconceptions of working at McDonald's. An early initiative was a poster and advertising campaign in which a series of facts about careers in McDonald's were stated alongside the slogan 'Not Bad for a McJob'.

This was followed later by a further campaign based around the slogan 'My McJob'. Both these initiatives attracted positive press coverage, as did the launch of a petition urging the Oxford English Dictionary to change its inappropriate definition of the term 'McJob'. The petition ultimately gathered 120,000 at a series of roadshows held around the country which were extensively covered by the local press. More recent campaigns have focused on celebrating the diversity of the McDonald's workforce in the UK and on seeking to persuade opinion formers, particularly those working in education, that McDonald's is a good employer that provides excellent career development opportunities for its people. To that end, a series of high profile advertisements have recently appeared in up-market publications such as the Guardian, The Economist and the Times Educational Supplement.

In order to enhance the effectiveness of internal communication, extensive use has been made of a website called 'Our Lounge' which is used both by existing and former staff. The site has been designed in such a way as to downplay the presence of corporate logos and 'official' top-down communication. It looks interesting and attracts a lot of use by staff when they at home. It contains employee blogs and photos posted by staff, and it is highly interactive. People use it to discuss issues with each other, but it is also used to reinforce the opportunities the company seeks to provide for its people (discount scheme, wellbeing initiatives, training and educational opportunities etc.) and is hence a tool of employee engagement as well as a means by which the company seeks to build its reputation as an employer.

McDonald's UK also uses its website to communicate with potential employees, having shifted all its recruitment online in 2008. Restaurant managers post their vacancies there and continue to make the ultimate decision about who they hire, but all applications now go through the website, enabling a standard set of messages to be communicated. Central is an online test that all would-be restaurant staff complete which is personality-based and designed to ensure that only people with the attributes that the company is looking for (happy working in a team, comfortable interacting with customers etc.) are interviewed. Through this website the company is able to communicate its expectations and also to let people know what it seeks to offer them as an employer.

Evaluation

Managers at McDonald's in the UK are generally very happy with the impact that their initiatives have had. Whereas ten years ago all press coverage about the company as an employer was negative, positive stories are now just as common to read. As a result, the staff are much more willing to voice confidence about their jobs and their employer than they were. The annual staff attitude surveys are a good guide as these are anonymous and are completed by 90% of the company's employees. Between 2004 and 2010 the percentage of staff stating that they were committed to the company increased from 77% to 88%, while the percentage of those stating that they are proud to work for McDonald's went up from 60% to

84%. Increased staff satisfaction is also reflected in the figures for employee turnover. The crude annual turnover rate for staff working in McDonald's restaurants has declined steeply in recent years, most of it well before the recession of 2008–9. In 2004 the figure was 80.2%. By 2010 it had fallen to 37.9%, high by national standards but very much in line with the turnover rates that are typically recorded across the catering and retail sectors.

Managers are particularly pleased with the reduction they have seen in their 90-day turnover rate, a measure of the number of new staff leaving within the first three months. This stood at 24.5% in 2004, reflecting the tendency for people to have false expectations about what their jobs would involve and the number of unsuitable people that managers were hiring. By 2010 this had fallen to just 2.4%. The company has also established that 164,000 people use the Our Lounge website, including over 80,000 former employees and that the site is visited 42,000 times each day.

In addition, McDonald's has seen a substantial increase in the number of people applying for jobs in its restaurants. Across the UK it now attracts 2,000–3,000 online applications every day. Of these only around 1 in 15 are ultimately successful, enabling the company to be a great deal more selective about who it employs than it was previously able to be. This has been achieved despite the company expanding its total headcount from 67,000 to over 80,000 between 2004 and 2010. A knock-on effect has been an increase in the customer service ratings recorded by 'mystery shoppers' who judge restaurants on their cleanliness, quality and the time they take to serve food. Negative scores have more than halved since 2005.

Progress has also been made more generally in improving the company's reputation as an employer. Since 2007, extensive research has been commissioned each quarter among the general public asking the question 'Do you think that McDonald's is a good employer?' In 2007 only 21% agreed that it was. Three years later the figure was 34%. This is by no means a good overall result as it demonstrates that a majority still have to be persuaded that McJobs are not what they are popularly perceived to be, but it represents a significant improvement in a short period of time.

Summary

This case study represents a good example of a company applying all the principles that are associated with effective employer branding initiatives. Whereas ten years ago McDonald's in the UK had lost control of the image it portrayed in the labour market, it now manages its reputation carefully and has started to decontaminate its damagingly negative brand image as an employer. This is ongoing work, but to date the investment it has put in to improving the experience of working at McDonald's, and particularly in communicating its employee value proposition, has yielded very positive results.

Discussion questions

1) In what different ways do you think that McDonald's has benefited financially from the substantial investment it has put into improving its reputation as an employer in the UK?

2) What other methods might be used over time to evaluate the impact of the various employer branding initiatives described in this case study and other similar future initiatives? Why might other approaches be more beneficial?

3) What are the major lessons that other organisations might learn from the experience of McDonald's when seeking to improve their employer brand images?

References

Goos, M & Manning, A 2003, 'McJobs and Macjobs: the growing polarisation of jobs in the UK, in R Dickens, P Gregg & J Wadsworth (eds), *The Labour Market Under New Labour*, Basingstoke, Palgrave.

Newman, J 2007, *My Secret Life on the McJob*, New York, McGraw Hill.

Chapter 23

'Unhappy families': Job and reward strategies in a college theatre

GLEN JENKINS

The College Theatre is at the cultural heart of the university and opens its doors throughout the year to an eclectic program of events including cinema screenings, a wide variety of live performances (dance, drama, jazz and world music), as well as an extensive program of lectures, and it is a celebrated venue for one act plays. The theatre, unlike the academic departments in the university, is open seven days a week with both matinee and evening performances.

The emphasis at The College Theatre is on quality and innovation – providing a service to staff, students and the wider community and acting as a regional centre of excellence in the performing arts and culture. Thanks to increased funding from the Arts Council, as well as events within the theatre complex, productions have moved outside of the theatre to include an annual dance festival in the city centre, touring home-produced, one-act plays and other co-productions to venues across the UK.

The 330 seat auditorium offers a range of excellent facilities with video, 35mm and 16mm projection facilities, a professional lighting and sound system, radio microphones, and a range of facilities for people with disabilities including an infrared hearing system, loop system and specialised wheelchair facilities. Also, the theatre has a bar and restaurant, exhibition space and theatre shop including box office all within the theatre complex.

To provide service excellence, the theatre is run by the Artistic Director, Priscilla Boddington CBE, who has turned the theatre into one of the most profitable areas of the university. As a regional university with a purpose-built campus, the university prides itself on its people management policies and practices. Traditionally, as in many other universities, the employees form three main groups: academic staff (lecturers, research workers and visiting lecturers); support staff (administration, technical and operational support); and senior managers. Each group is traditionally employed on different terms and conditions, with different pay and benefits packages, and the way pay is determined varies markedly from group to group. Pay for academic staff is determined by national level collective bargaining between the Universities and Colleges Employers Association (UCEA) and the University and College Union (UCU). Whereas pay for support staff is negotiated locally with UNISON. All senior managers are employed on personal contracts and their pay is negotiated on an individual basis. In determining pay levels for its employees, the university carries out extensive local and national benchmarking and is recognised in the local community as a 'good' employer. Employees benefits are organised on similar lines but vary slightly for each group – for example, senior managers are eligible for a performance-related pay scheme linked to a range of factors including income generation, research and teaching excellence and efficiency, as well as private medical insurance and death-in-service benefits. The benefits package is harmonised for all staff and all are eligible for a variety of benefits including: final salary pension schemes into which the university makes significant contributions; generous family-friendly benefits including a crèche; holiday entitlements above the local market median; and flexible working arrangements.

The theatre itself is organised in three sections:

1. Administration – staffed by the artistic director, a general manager, head of marketing and sales, three box office staff, four porters, three security staff and two clerical officers

2. Auditorium – staffed by two front-of-house managers and seven full-time stewards, plus the technical services manager and three full-time theatre technicians all trained in sound, vision and stage design.

3. Customer services – staffed by the bar and restaurant manager together with three chefs, twelve part-time waiters and five bar staff; the shop and box office manager and two assistants.

Financial and Human Resource Management services for the theatre are provided by the university's central administration.

Although run independently from the university, the theatre's terms and conditions of employment are defined by the university's HRM policies and practices, which in turn define the theatre's employee reward policies and practices. However, partly because of recent changes and financial constraints, the relationship between the university's senior management and Priscilla (the Artistic Director) has become strained. The main cause of the tension in Priscilla's view is the lack of flexibility in the university's total reward strategy, which fails to recognise the business needs of the theatre. In particular, it does not recognise the unique needs of the theatre's employees and the roles they have to play.

All full-time support staff within the theatre are members of UNISON, but part-time staff rarely join – being made up primarily of students who work during their studies. Apart from the part-time staff, turnover had been traditionally very low and satisfaction surveys have shown the level of engagement to be high, with the majority of employees focused on the theatre's quality and innovation strategy.

The problem

The problem began five years ago when the university negotiated flexible working arrangements with UNISON that consisted of a new pay structure and flexible contracts. The university successfully argued that this change was necessary to improve employment flexibility in the university and that working practices needed to change because of the new economic circumstances the university now faced.

To bring greater transparency and flexibility to its reward structure, the university integrated seven different job families, based on seniority, into the existing broad banded pay structure and linked this to the job evaluation scheme. The families were:

- executive
- senior management
- management, professional and specialist
- teaching and research
- administrative
- technical
- operational

According to Armstrong and Stephens:

> Job family structures resemble career structures in that separate families are identified and levels of knowledge, skills and competency requirements defined for each level, thus indicating career paths and providing the basis for grading jobs by matching role profiles to level definitions. (2005 p. 195)

All roles in the new structure were given generic descriptions that clearly set out the skills and behaviours required to progress through a family. Furthermore, it was argued that the new structure would increase transferability of skills and improve career progression – be it upwards or across at the same level but in a different family.

UNISON, in its attempt to protect the conditions of service of existing staff, argued successfully that while it supported the new pay structure, other changes in flexibility should be on appointment thus creating a two tier structure between new staff and those with longer service. Hence, all new staff appointments were to be put on new flexible contracts. The new flexible contracts removed some long standing terms and conditions particularly for support staff – including the removal of local agreements on unsocial hours, reduced overtime rates and the introduction of performance-related pay when merited. However, technical staff who worked primarily in the university laboratories retained the unsocial hours agreement and were treated as a special case. In order to improve laboratory use, technicians also benefited from team-based, performance-related pay linked to student and research staff satisfaction surveys of the use of laboratories. Also, a number of performance-related pay schemes were introduced for operational staff to promote efficiency and customer service. Included in these were: conference staff received performance-related pay linked to participant satisfaction at conferences; bar and restaurant staff received performance-related pay based on customer satisfaction surveys; and all campus shops and retail outlets including box office received performance-related pay based on the achievement of sales targets.

Apart from the performance-related pay elements for technicians and shop and box office staff, the new pay structure initially had limited effect on the theatre staff. However, unlike other managerial staff (general manager, bar and restaurant manager, the shop and box office manager and the front-of-house manager) the artistic director and the head of marketing and sales were placed under the management, professional and specialist job family. The other managers were placed in the administration family. While administration was a lower grade, this had little immediate effect on the terms and conditions of these staff as their salaries were protected. Stewards, porters, security, box office, shop, restaurant and bar staff were moved to the operational family and technicians to the technical family.

At the time the local agreement was signed, the artistic director felt that the change would have little impact as staff turnover was low, but coinciding with this change, the two front-of-house managers moved away from the area and new appointments were made under the revised flexible contract. The changes in terms and conditions for the new front-of-house manager are described below:

	Old contract	New flexible contract
Rates of pay	Pay comparable with local market rates	Pay comparable with grade in job family linked to local market rates
Working time	**Flexible with pay for unsocial hours:** Monday to Friday additional 1/10th between 8 and 10 pm, 1/5th after 10.00 pm. **Overtime payments:** time and half pay for Saturday and double time for Sunday. Weekly hours	Flexible 24/7 contract. Unsocial hours abolished. If employee works overtime, can take time off in lieu. Annual hours
Duties and responsibilities	Manage stewards and porters, health and safety of auditorium and backstage environments	Deputise for artistic director in the evenings, manage stewards and porters, health and safety of auditorium and backstage environments, responsible for box office staff in the evenings in the absence of the artistic director
Work location	Auditorium	Theatre complex

Under the new flexible contract, the front-of-house manager took on more duties and responsibilities. For example, it was essential that a key person should be responsible for the theatre complex at all times, particularly for health and safety reasons. Indeed, in the absence of the artistic director, such as on the weekend, it was only the front-of-house manager who had the authority to close the theatre in an emergency. The front-of-house manager was usually the only manager present at weekends and on the weekday evenings and responsibility for the theatre complex rested with her at this time. The role was far removed from the traditional administrative role in the university and required direct contact with customers and performers. Indeed, the front-of-house manager was also responsible for promotion and ticket sales at evening and weekend performances and invariably, problems with box office receipts or ticketing problems were referred to her. The role also required providing support to performers and addressing customer grievances when they arose. In addition, the front-of-house manager was the last to leave the theatre in the evening, transferring responsibility for the theatre complex to the university's security staff when the venue closed. This meant occasionally that on late evening performances the front-of-house manager left the complex just before midnight. There was always difficulty in recruiting suitably qualified people to the role who were prepared to work the unsocial hours that the theatre demanded and at the last selection panel only two applicants were felt to have the necessary skills, knowledge and aptitudes the role required.

Shortly after the new flexible contract was implemented, it soon became apparent that the front-of-house manager was paid less than other managers in the theatre complex partly because they remained on the old contract but also because of the new performance-related pay element in their pay.

The front-of-house manager, in discussions with her own staff, soon found out that Saturday and Sunday evening performances invariably went on after 10.00 pm. As a consequence, the front-of-house manager on duty soon discovered that she was being paid less per hour than the stewards she supervised. This arose because of the overtime and unsocial allowances that the longer-serving stewards accrued under the old contractual arrangements and the reduced grade of the front-of-house manager position.

Box office staff received a monthly bonus when tickets sales achieved approved targets and, given the success of the theatre, this bonus became a regular payment. However, the front-of-house manager was excluded from any performance element and despite being involved in promotion, marketing and sales as well as the supervision of box office staff, no bonus was paid.

Also, unlike the university's laboratory technicians, the theatre technicians worked on a shift basis with one week in three being from 2.00–10.00 pm. During these shifts, theatre technicians benefited considerably from the unsocial hours agreement and the technicians' performance-related pay element became an added financial reward. In practice, this group's performance-related pay, together with the unsocial hours payment, meant that a technician too received more pay per annum than the front-of-house manager. In short, of the staff working in the auditorium on the weekend, the front-of-house manager was invariably one of the poorest paid employees.

The matter came to a head when, on finding out the disparities in reward between box office staff, stewards, technicians and the front-of-house manager, a newly appointed front-of-house manager left after only one week on the job, citing in her exit interview unfairness in pay as the reason for leaving.

Discussion questions

1) Critically evaluate the use of job families as a method of structuring pay within the university. Why has the pay structure failed in this case?

2) Consider the role of pay determination in the creation of the flexible employment contract of the front-of-house manager and the performance-related pay of other workers. What changes to the local agreement would you recommend to prevent problems like this arising in future?

3) What reward interventions would you recommend to improve team work and the recruitment and retention of front-of-house managers within the theatre?

References

Armstrong, A & Stephens, T 2005, *A Handbook of Employee Reward and Management Practice*, London: Kogan Page.

Blyton, P, Martinez, LM 1995, 'Industrial relations and the management of flexibility: factors shaping developments in Spain and the United Kingdom', *International Journal of Human Resource Management*, May 1995, Vol. 6, Issue 2, p. 271-291.

Green, C, Kler, P & Leeves, G 2010, 'Flexible Contract Workers in Inferior Jobs: Reappraising the Evidence', *British Journal of Industrial Relations*, London, Sept 2010, Vol. 48, Iss. 3, pp. 605-629.

Kelliher, C & Anderson, D 2008, 'For better or for worse? An analysis of how flexible working practices influence employees' perceptions of job quality', *International Journal of Human Resource Management*; March 2008, Vol. 19, Issue 3, p. 419-431.

Long, RJ 2001, 'Pay Systems and Organizational Flexibility', *Canadian Journal of Administrative Sciences*, March 2001, Vol. 18, Issue 1, pp. 25-33.

Perkins, SJ & White, G 2011, *Reward Management: Alternatives, Consequences and Contexts*, 2nd edn, London, Chartered Institute of Personnel and Development.

Wright A 2004, *Reward Management in Context*, London, Chartered Institute of Personnel and Development.

Chapter 24

The role of line managers and employee voice in the restaurant industry

JANE SUTER AND MICK MARCHINGTON

Background and context

RestaurantCo is a large non-unionised restaurant company with more than 300 branches across the UK, employing more than 7000 staff. The company is a good example of a large organisation with employees distributed throughout numerous smaller establishments, characterising a large proportion of the hotel and restaurant sector (Forth *et al.* 2006). This case study highlights how the individual styles of branch managers and the informal culture developed at each establishment is likely to take prominence over formal, top-down HR policies and practices and head quarters' (HQ) attempts to create a more standardised organisational culture (Head & Lucas 2004). It focuses on front line managers and their use of a participative management style and informal employee involvement and participation (EIP). Because the restaurants operate long opening hours, seven days a week and have unpredictable trade patterns, there is a need for complex shift patterns and a workforce primarily on non-standard contracts. This context demands close working relationships between front line managers and employees, highlighting management motivation towards a more informal, open management style.

RestaurantCo developed from a small family owned business in the 1960s to a relatively modest collection of franchised operations following a period of rapid growth in the 1990s. Over the next few years, these franchised operations were brought back in-house and the company became a privately owned branded chain. Subsequently, RestaurantCo experienced further changes in its corporate governance with floatation on the stock market, a return to private ownership and a re-floatation a few years ago. The recent changes in ownership led to a refocused business strategy aimed at building company value alongside increased investment in the restaurant environment, with a program of refurbishments and new restaurant openings. The food and drink menus were expanded significantly for the first time in many years. Cost savings were also made through integrating the supply chain with other restaurants owned by the group. Overall, this was a huge organisational change and inevitably caused a number of problems, with restaurant managers complaining about less efficient deliveries and mistakes with the ordering and supply of ingredients. At the same time, initiatives aimed at improving customer service were introduced to improve all aspects of the 'RestaurantCo Experience', including the introduction of a 'Mystery Customer' program where random visits by assessors monitored aspects of customer service at each restaurant. The overall ratings from mystery customers were then linked to a performance-related bonus for local managers. This centralised monitoring of service highlights a degree of head office control which, as we see below, contradicts the supposed autonomy of branch managers at local level.

The company is regarded as a high quality restaurant business that 'prides itself on serving quality food, in pleasant surroundings with high standards of customer service'. From the turn of the 21st century, it experienced strong growth in the number of customers and is the market leader in its sector. Company literature indicates a strong focus on positive employee relations, with RestaurantCo acknowledging that employees 'are part of our assets'. The small family business origin of RestaurantCo is reflected in a history of an informal employment relations approach, and as the organisation has grown senior management attempted to maintain the individuality of restaurant branches. Yet, with recent changes to ownership, there has been more focus on improving the management of human resources and a more strategic approach. As a result, the HR function expanded rapidly and developed new policies and practices. Recent developments at RestaurantCo sought to make the HR function more strategic, with it becoming 'business partners' to operations managers and 'practical commercially focussed HR'. This is in contrast to much of the sector which historically has not been known for taking a strategic approach to HRM (Lucas 2009).

Organisational change was managed through initiatives that focussed on motivating and energising staff. Regional road-shows for management and key staff members – such as waiter trainers and senior chefs – were conducted to help HR and senior management communicate detailed plans and key initiatives. Business planning and internal communication processes were transformed, with a much stronger focus on formal EIP, with numerous top-down communications and regular team briefings across all levels of the organisation. Financial participation for more senior managers, including longer serving branch managers, was introduced and was linked to improvements in company performance.

A number of management development programs were launched – they were designed to recruit, retain and develop managers. One of these was implemented to develop leadership skills and to aid in the progression of managers from branch to operational roles. There was a renewed focus on building teams and increasing interaction between the centralised support functions and branch establishments. Company recruitment literature suggests that managers are recruited on the basis of their 'ideas and commitment', and a new management capability framework was put in place to reflect this.

The role of line managers

A branch manager and usually one or two assistants ran each restaurant establishment. The company had the view that branch managers should 'treat the restaurant as if it were their own small business'; thus line managers had a large amount of discretion in how they implemented HR practices. In addition, a large part of the role was as shift supervisor and these 'supervisory responsibilities' did not vary significantly from those of the assistant manager. Indeed, due to long operating hours and the shift system, the manager on duty would take on the role of supervising employees, a role that was shared between both branch and assistant managers. Although there was an assistant manager between the branch manager and the shop floor, employees still reported directly to the branch manager. The manager on duty would deal with more immediate problems and issues for employees; whereas wider issues were referred directly to the branch managers. Moreover, branch managers took on a number of HR functions such as appraisals, pay reviews, personal development plans and objective setting.

Branch managers were given a wide range of responsibilities, for other members of staff, customers, property and finances. Key amongst these were the day-to-day running of the restaurant; developing and motivating a team; ordering and controlling stock/supplies; looking after finances; operating the payroll system; disciplinary actions; checking health and safety for customers and staff; ensuring food safety; checking product quality and service standards. The key qualities looked for in recruiting managers are:

- a keen service mentality
- the ability to work autonomously
- strong self-motivation
- the capacity to think strategically
- first-rate leadership skills
- a flexible approach to your work
- the ability to relate to people

Managers who had been with RestaurantCo for some time had experienced a change in the role and skills of the branch manager. They believed that more was now expected from them, more responsibilities had been devolved and that work had been intensified. Indeed, HR policies had become more sophisticated and formalised with more selective recruitment, the introduction of employee and management competencies and more formalised EIP. One of the branch managers described how the skills required by them had changed recently:

In the last three years they have started asking more of the managers, probably more than they have ever done – to come up with marketing initiatives, forecasting labour budgets, things that they have never done before and probably with very little support or no guidelines of how to actually do these things themselves.

Each branch had a large amount of autonomy from the centralised head office function for the day-to-day running of the restaurants. Although restaurants were controlled within a traditional organisational hierarchy, each unit had similarities to a franchise. A key characteristic within the capability framework was for managers to take ownership for the delivery and performance of their branch, so they were supposedly allowed a fair degree of autonomy in how to manage their own unit. Head office or 'Restaurant Support' was made up of departments such as Human Resources, Training, Marketing, IT, Supply chain and Payroll. Attitudes towards restaurant support were often fairly negative, as the departments were perceived as having little understanding of the restaurant context or the perspective of managers. There was also a clash of operating cultures between the small, informal restaurant setting with long operating hours and direct customer contact, and Restaurant Support – a large 9–5 office-based workplace. Restaurant managers often complained about being unable to get support at times that suited them or being contacted for information at times when the branch was busy.

Branch managers preferred to view the restaurant and its employment relations as informal; whereas head-office emphasised the need for more professional management and over-rated the formality of policy implemented at branch level. The branch structure of RestaurantCo makes it necessary for many HR responsibilities to be devolved to front line managers and points to the need for them to be trained in people handling skills. Yet, in a large organisation where employees are distributed throughout numerous smaller establishments, the impact of formal policies imposed by head office was inconsistent between branches. For example, the regularity of team meetings varied at the discretion of the branch manager and there were differences in the types of information presented on staff notice boards.

Managers at branch level spoke of making decisions with little, if any, consultation with their operations managers, and some claimed that senior operations management had no impact on their decision making. Yet these decisions related to operational issues about the day-to-day running of the branch; whereas more senior management took company-wide operational decisions, such as the menu and suppliers, budgets and service controls such as the mystery diner, with little or no input from branch level. This led to negative attitudes as managers spoke of being given responsibility to run restaurants and yet not being trusted to make certain decisions, which they believed they were in a better position to make. One example was a cost-cutting strategy to reduce non-consumable supplies where, instead of trusting managers to reduce costs, they were simply excluded from the decision-making process. Managers could no longer order directly from suppliers, with all orders instead being redirected through the supply chain department, which in turn dealt with each supplier on behalf of the individual branches. This not only impacted on morale but also frustrated managers who felt that mistakes had been made because the supply chain department had a limited understanding of individual branch needs. See Mabey and Finch-Lees (2008) and Storey (2004) for further information on management and leadership studies.

Line management style and informal EIP

In an industry characterised by small establishments, the style and behaviour of front line managers has major significance for the way staff are managed (Liden, Bauer & Erdogan 2004). Where formal bureaucratic control becomes difficult, as is often the case in interactive service industries, informal management-worker relationships come to the forefront. The role of leadership is critical to organisational success as a top-down autocratic approach to managing teams of customer service employees can lead to poor customer relations (Guest & Conway 2004; Kiger 2002). Managers at RestaurantCo described their style as 'leading by example' or 'leading from the front'. This leadership description translated to a very hands-on approach, where most managers participated in all work tasks if required; it often meant managers working in the kitchen alongside chefs or assisting waiting staff on the restaurant floor. Inevitably, this led to close contact between staff and management and aided in promoting informal EIP with day-to-day work tasks (Stinglhamber & Vandenberghe 2003). As one manager stated, *'You can't help but talk when you are on shift'.*

Table 24.1 The RestaurantCo capability framework

Capability	Definition of key skill	Positive behavioural indicators that relate to informal EIP
Inspiring leadership	Creates confident, performing teams	Ensures people know why tasks are important Sets stretching but motivating goals Makes sure people feel involved Allocates responsibilities fairly
Harnessing potential	Ensuring RestaurantCo gets the best from its people	Empowers people to develop their own solutions Gives candid, helpful feedback Knows what makes people tick, and uses this to motivate others.
Belonging	Creates an organisation that works as one	Listens to and encourages the contribution of everybody Works collaboratively with other restaurant managers
Innovation	Ensures RestaurantCo remains leader of the industry	Constantly looks for new ideas Feeds ideas up the organisation Is receptive to new ideas Shares successful ideas with other managers

Source: RestaurantCo Management Capability Framework

A propensity toward a more participative style was supported by management recruitment and development tools based around the RestaurantCo Capability Framework. This identifies the key skills, attributes, characteristics and knowledge required for successful performance in both assistant and branch manager roles. Of the eight capabilities, four relate specifically to informal EIP.

At RestaurantCo, informal EIP was highly significant to workers and valued by branch managers. Managers revealed that the use of EIP recognised that positive relationships with their staff were vital in gaining employee compliance, eliciting discretionary behaviour, ensuring good customer interaction and gaining commitment both to them as managers and to the RestaurantCo brand. EIP was therefore less of a tool for consultation and more of a solution for the difficulties managers had in maintaining control over employee-customer interactions; as such it was a method for persuading and committing employees to company and branch values and objectives. Despite apparent support for a participative management style and autonomy for branch managers, it was clear that RestaurantCo still used centralised controls to impose more formal policies and standardised practices which failed to embed a participative culture throughout the organisation (Cox, Marchington & Suter 2009).

Contextual pressures shaped the uptake and implementation of different forms of EIP, thus requiring managers to choose how to mix formal and/or informal EIP. These choices were shaped by the appropriateness of the method to a particular situation or the type of issue, and at RestaurantCo operational issues in the service environment tended to constrain EIP. For example, the fact that customers are there at point of sale and workers are on varying shift patterns seemed to both constrain and promote different forms of EIP. When managers were under pressure due to increased trade, there was less time to use both types of EIP, particularly formal. Moreover, the cost of team meetings were often referred to in terms of additional staffing costs which is particularly relevant in a labour-intensive context and to managers who were under pressure to control and reduce labour costs wherever possible. Such restrictions on labour expenditure became a major barrier in enabling managers to hold regular shift briefings. This was further amplified by external HQ budget controls leaving branch managers powerless to increase their labour budgets to accommodate staff meetings and little senior support to do so. This is perhaps why team meetings at the branches were often seen as a fairly major event.

Formal EIP was emphasised more strongly by managers in larger busy branches; indeed this may be a key factor as branch managers indicated that they had less time to involve employees informally and so relied on communicating with them through formal methods. Interestingly, in smaller branches formal EIP played a less significant role because informal EIP seemed to work well and was perceived as more appropriate and adequate by managers. In larger branches formal EIP was more necessary to ensure all employees were covered.

Despite displaying positive attitudes towards informality, line managers were reluctant to rely completely on one method of EIP and instead utilised a combination of both formal and informal EIP to complement each other. One option for managers was to operate formal and informal EIP in parallel in order to ensure full employee coverage. Regardless of a desire to use informal EIP, the level of trade still put limits on its use and so more formal methods were utilised to ensure key messages were communicated direct to all employees. Furthermore, combining formal and informal EIP ensured that key messages were delivered to all employees, including those part-time workers who branch managers may not see regularly. For example, managers used notice boards to ensure that all staff, especially those they did not encounter on the same shift, were kept informed. This implies that although there may be a preference for informal EIP, formal mechanisms are necessary as a safety net.

The subject matter or type of issue also influences management's choice of a particular method of EIP. Strategic or wider company issues were more likely to be communicated through formal methods. Managers tended to utilise notice boards to provide a reference system to reinforce training messages, company standards, staff capabilities or legal requirements. Team meetings were viewed as more appropriate for communicating top down information which might need to be explained more fully to staff; whereas day-to-day operational issues were dealt with more informally to give employees greater scope for decision making relating to their work roles. For example, workers often influenced or even determined issues relating to how many people would be needed on particular shifts, the selection of work tasks or how to organise work areas. Informal face-to-face interaction was also seen as more appropriate where issues required more honest feedback and better problem solving from employees. Managers thought employees were in a better position to generate new ideas and solve problems for issues that directly related to their job roles.

Another option was to combine formal and informal EIP in sequence, with the latter being used to improve the quality of information provision through formal methods. For example, team meetings were used to explain a service issue problem or deliver key operational changes and this was complemented by managers using face-to-face discussions to further employee understanding or to obtain employee feedback. Although this often took the form of a formal method followed by informal, it is equally possible that informal EIP may precede formal EIP. The sequential interaction between formal and informal EIP was observed in managers utilising each form to serve different functions and therefore capture different types of employee contribution. For example, formal EIP can forewarn employees of change or be used as a tool for top-down information provision. Informal EIP may follow on by getting employees on board with management agendas, gaining more comprehensive input and cementing employee engagement, or embedding information provided via formal methods.

Summary and overview

This case study of RestaurantCo highlights the importance of front line managers as the focal point for managing teams and the vital link between senior management and frontline employees (Purcell & Hutchinson 2007). It also shows that their role is extremely broad and includes both a supervisory and a business management function. The role has also expanded in recent years as more elements of HRM have been devolved to the branch. This is comparable to other research highlighting the expanding and changing role of the front line manager (Hales 2005). The case study illustrates that, despite so-called management autonomy, branch managers were restricted to operational decisions relating to the day-to-day running of the branch; whereas more senior management took company-wide operational and strategic decisions, which were imposed at branch level. This raises concerns about quality of decision making and any subsequent implementation. The tension between management autonomy and head office control also undermines informal EIP at branch level as both line managers and employees have limited power and influence (Ferner *et al.* 2004). Indeed it has long been recognised that the experience of managers on the front line is often under-utilised, despite their unique knowledge-base and ability to integrate both strategic and operational issues (Becker & Huselid 2006; Currie & Proctor 2005; Nehles *et al.* 2006).

Informal EIP achieves prominence in the hotel and restaurant sector where an informal and almost familial element exists in the employment relationship due to the small size of most establishments (Wilkinson, Dundon & Grugulis 2007). Although informal and formal EIP are likely to support and complement each other, the former is likely to take prominence in contexts where line managers work alongside their staff, where there is plenty of interaction between them and where formal procedures for EIP and HRM more generally are less significant. The levels of informality found in this sector illustrate the vital role of informal EIP within the manager-employee relationship (Gerhart 2005). In addition, the close physical proximity of managers to employees in small establishments can make the restaurant environment more conducive to informal discussions.

The case study also highlights the challenges faced by hospitality managers, not just in relation to EIP but more generally in attempts to integrate different HRM practices into an effective bundle (Kepes & Delerey 2007). Moreover, there are limits to formality in a service environment, thus making informal methods particularly conducive to a busy restaurant environment. In the face of complex employee shift patterns and unpredictable levels of trade, line managers tend to find informal methods less time consuming, more immediate for dealing with day-to-day issues, more useful where matters arise that are only relevant to certain individuals or workgroups, and less disruptive to business. Yet, despite their preference for informality, front line managers did not jettison formal methods completely; indeed, formal and informal methods were typically combined, operating either in sequence or in parallel, depending on contingent factors. Given the importance of formal and informal methods in HRM more generally, it is critical that front line managers are selected, trained and appraised on their people management skills as well as their operational abilities (Marchington & Wilkinson 2008).

Discussion questions

1) The case study demonstrates tensions between centralisation and decentralisation, in particular in the attempt to impose buying decisions on the branches whilst at the same time emphasising that branch managers were given lots of autonomy. Identify the main points in this tension and how are they played out. How would you seek to minimise the contradictions exhibited here?

2) How effective do you think the capability framework was in providing a competency-based HR system for branch managers? What advice would you give to RestaurantCo to ensure that its HR system is integrated across recruitment and selection, training and development, pay and reward, and employment relations?

3) How do you think formal and informal EIP link together and what can line managers do to make sure that it works well? Provide examples to support your answer.

4) Informality is clearly central to the role of line managers in this context, but do you think this style would work as effectively in other sectors? Why/why not?

References

Becker, B & Huselid, M 2006, 'Strategic Human Resources Management: Where do we go from here?', *Journal of Management*, 32 (6), pp. 898-925.

Cox, A, Marchington, M & Suter, J 2009, 'Employee involvement and participation: developing the concept of institutional embeddedness using WERS 2004', *International Journal of Human Resource Management*, 20(10), pp. 2150-68.

Currie, G & Proctor, S 2005, 'The antecedents of middle manager's strategic contribution: The case of a professional bureaucracy', *Journal of Management Studies,* 42(7), pp. 1325-1356.

Forth, J, Bewley, H & Bryson, A 2006, *Small and medium-sized enterprises: findings from the 2004 Workplace Employee Relations Survey*, DTI: London.

Ferner, A, Almond, P, Clark, I, Colling, T, Holden, L, Edwards, T & Muller-Camen, M 2004, 'The dynamics of central control and subsidiary autonomy in the management of human resources: Case-study evidence from US MNCs in the UK', *Organization Studies*, 25(3), pp. 363–391.

Gerhart, B 2005, 'Human resources and business performance: Findings, unanswered questions, and an alternative approach', *Management Revue*, 16(2), pp. 174-185.

Guest, D & Conway, N 2004, *Employee Well-being and the Psychological Contract*, CIPD: London.

Hales, C 2005, 'Rooted in Supervision, Branching into Management: Continuity and Change in the Role of First-Line Manager', *Journal of Management Studies,* 42(3), pp. 471-506.

Head, J & Lucas, R 2004, 'Does individual employment legislation constrain the ability of hospitality employers to "hire and fire"?', *International Journal of Hospitality Management*, 23(3), pp. 239-254.

Kepes, S & Delerey, J 2007, 'HRM systems and the problem of internal fit', in Boxall, P, Purcell, J & Wright, P (eds), *The Oxford Handbook of Human Resource Management*, Oxford, Oxford University Press.

Kiger, PJ 2002, 'Why customer satisfaction starts with HR', *Workforce*, 81(5), pp. 26-32.

Liden, R, Bauer, T & Erdogan, B 2004, 'The role of leader-member exchange in the dynamic relationship between employer and employee: implications for employee socialization, leaders, and organizations', in L Shore, S Taylor, J Coyle-Shapiro & L Tetrick (eds.), *The Employment Relationship: examining psychological and contextual perspectives*, Oxford: Oxford University Press, pp. 226-252.

Lucas, R 2009, 'Is low unionism in the British hospitality industry due to industry characteristics?' *International Journal of Hospitality Management*, 28(1), pp. 42-52.

Mabey, C & Finch-Lees, T 2008, *Management and Leadership Development*, London: Sage.

Marchington, M & Wilkinson, A 2008, *Human Resource Management at Work*, London, Chartered Institute of Personnel and Development, Fourth edition.

Nehles, A, van Riemsdijk, M, Kok, I & Looise, J 2006, 'Implementing Human Resource Management successfully: A first-line management challenge', *Management Revue*, 17(3), pp. 256-273.

Purcell, J & Hutchinson, S 2007, 'Front-line managers as agents in the HRM performance causal chain: theory, analysis and evidence', *Human Resource Management Journal*, 17(1), pp.3–20.

Stinglhamber, F & Vandenberghe, C 2003, 'Organisations and supervisors as sources of support and targets of commitment', *Journal of Organisational Behaviour*, 24: 251-70.

Storey, J (ed) 2004, *Leadership in Organisations: Current issues and key trends*, London, Routledge.

Wilkinson, A, Dundon, T & Grugulis, I 2007, 'Information but not consultation: exploring employee involvement in SMEs', *The International Journal of Human Resource Management*, 18(7), pp. 1279-1297.

Chapter 25

Union and non-union employee representation at BritCo Ireland

NIALL CULLINANE AND JIMMY DONAGHEY

Background and context

BritCo is a British-owned multinational corporation operating in more than 170 countries. It was one of the first public utilities privatised under the Thatcher government in the 1980s. Since the early 1990s, BritCo has expanded into international markets. In 1990, for example, BritCo entered the Republic of Ireland market through a joint commercial venture with an Irish semi-state company. In 2000, BritCo acquired this joint-venture company and also purchased another leading Irish private sector organisation, IndyCo. Consequently, the company became a key player in its sector in the Republic and a major rival to the Irish market leader, a former state monopoly, EireCo. In the aftermath of this acquisition in 2005, BritCo's UK head office decided to separate the Northern Ireland operation, previously part of BritCo UK, and merge it with the Republic of Ireland operation on an all-Ireland basis. BritCo Ireland was born, employing close to 3,000 employees (2,000 in the Republic and 1,000 in Northern Ireland).

Despite being formally one operation, there is a marked distinction in the inherited legacies and culture of the organisation on both sides of the border. BritCo in Northern Ireland has a very different, and much longer, history in contrast to the company's operations in the Republic. The company had operated in Northern Ireland for many decades previously during BritCo's reign as a state-owned monopoly. There is a long tradition of heavy unionisation and collective bargaining. Two trade unions are formally recognised with a membership density of over 90 per cent of the work force: *Managerial Union*, representing managerial grades and *Operative Union*, representing operational-level employees, principally engineers but also some clerical employees in the call centre functions. Notably, the arrangements with unions in Northern Ireland operate as a subset of BritCo

UK industrial relations structures. Collective bargaining and the determination of terms and conditions for Northern Ireland are primarily conducted at the UK group level, which is at corporate headquarters in London. This places constraints on the ability of unions to bargain at local level in Northern Ireland, where their role is more consultative, albeit with some limited scope for negotiation on the application of particular policies and practices affecting membership.

In contrast, BritCo operations in the Republic had been entirely non-union and the practice of employee relations was very much coloured by a non-union 'enterprise culture'. However the actual merger of BritCo on an all-Ireland basis in 2005 had a negative impact on employment relations in the Republic as a number of departments and operations closed down and were moved to Northern Ireland. Fears of redundancy were common amongst employees. This was aggravated further as employees felt that redundancy terms were low by industry standard in the Republic and behind those offered by *BritCo* in Northern Ireland: a 'no compulsory redundancy' agreement existed in Northern Ireland dating from BritCo's UK public ownership days. Underlying employee grievances in the Republic was a general sense of injustice revolving around BritCo employees lacking union recognition rights in the Republic in comparison to the arrangement in Northern Ireland. A perception existed amongst employees in the Republic that Northern Irish staff experienced superior employee voice because of this representation, as well as improved terms and conditions on issues like redundancy pay, time-off and benefits. This led to a trade union drive amongst employees in the Republic and a campaign for recognition. BritCo management opposed recognition, however, and in response to the campaign for trade union recognition, sought to enhance existing employee voice arrangements in the company.

The arrangements for employee voice in BritCo Ireland: Northern Ireland

Due to the distinction between employment relations traditions across the two jurisdictions, BritCo has run significantly different employee voice regimes in the Republic of Ireland to those existing in Northern Ireland. Within Northern Ireland, BritCo utilises a wide range of both indirect and direct employee voice methods.

The main indirect employee voice methods include:

- *bi-monthly meetings* with representatives of the two recognised trade unions
- twice-yearly *Joint Consultative Committees* (JCCs).

The main direct methods of employee voice include:

- a weekly newspaper

- a staff email/intranet
- an annual company-wide survey.

Indirect voice

Every second month, trade union representatives in BritCo Ireland in Northern Ireland meet with key members of the human resource and senior management team to discuss any noteworthy organisational developments that may impact employees. To a large extent these meetings are managerially-led: the bulk of the discussion revolves around what management identify as necessary changes in particular business units, often in an attempt to reduce operating costs, and how they plan to proceed with such changes. In this context, the unions serve as a 'funnel'; they then pass the relevant information down to their members. In other respects, the unions in these meetings serve as 'sounding boards' in the sense that management outline possible changes and consult the unions on how employees might react to such change. However, while predominately management-led, these meetings also offer opportunities for union representatives to articulate any issues of concern which may be unsettling members. These indirect meetings typically provide a platform for further direct communications as, in light of what is consulted at such meetings, management go and meet with the individuals affected as a group and subsequently on a one-to-one basis.

Company-based JCCs meet at the start of the financial year in April. These involve the company CEO; the human resource, finance and line directors; local union representatives; and, on occasion, national level full-time union officials. The JCC deals with broad financial matters relevant to company operations in Northern Ireland, for example, what the quality planning budget for the year might be or the overall financial scenario facing the company. Specifics from each of the different lines of business are then addressed by the director of that particular line. For example, the Director or Head of Engineers will outline the business plan for the year in that area. The same process will be replicated with marketing, sales, IT solutions and so on. Whilst the formal constitution of the JCC specifies that union representatives should only comprise one representative from each business area, local-level representatives often seek to bring full-time national level officials for support. Union representatives cannot set the agenda and typically do not know what will issues will be up for discussion. They can, however, raise issues of concern in the 'any other business' section of the agenda. Although the JCC is formally designated to meet twice yearly, under the stewardship of the new CEO, they have taken place on a more regular basis.

Irrespective of these meetings at high level, both unions meet with HR management on an ad hoc basis in relation to particular issues like sick absence cases, discipline and grievances. Much of this will often take place on an informal level, with managers and union reps 'chatting off-the-record' before going into any formal procedures.

Direct information and communication

In recent years there has been a shift in emphasis within BritCo in Northern Ireland towards direct information and communication mechanisms. This has been particularly sponsored by the arrival of a new CEO, strongly committed to generating high levels of management-employee communication. The main indirect mechanisms revolve around a weekly internal company newsletter called *Retail Read*. This provides staff with updates on business developments and performance across the company in Northern Ireland. Alongside this has been a fairly long-standing staff email and intranet service, the latter providing a range of information on various human resource management policies such as disciplinary procedures, pension matters and so on. A more recent innovation, spurred on by the CEO, was a weekly 'All Hands Call', where the CEO makes a phone call to all employees on business and financial developments within the company. If they wish, employees may listen-in live and actually respond – or they may opt to listen to a recorded version later. A final direct voice mechanism is the annual Employee Engagement Survey. This is a company-wide survey of employees that attempts to track employees' overall job satisfaction and commitment to the company. Once the survey has been collected and the results collated, sub-groups are informally set up, comprising a mix of management and employees, to assess the results and consider why people may be engaged or not.

The dynamics of voice in BritCo Ireland: Northern Ireland

Whilst there is a considerable breadth of voice mechanisms existing in BritCo in Northern Ireland, how do they operate in practice? One way to answer this question is to explore how key organisational issues have been addressed in the company in recent times.

Although BritCo management report very positively on their relationship to the trade unions in Northern Ireland, they stress that they are in a process of 'redefining' the trade union role in the company. This has been most evident in senior management endeavours to integrate employment relations practices more closely with other elements of corporate strategy to ensure greater customer responsiveness and match the degree of labour flexibility achieved by many of the company's non-union competitors. There has been a progressive drive by the company to alter agreements on working practices and working hours to provide for greater management control over the deployment of employees and the re-scheduling of their activities.

This dynamic has been notable in relation to engineers' shift attendance. Since 2005, BritCo has sought to change engineer attendance patterns across the company in Northern Ireland. Traditionally work attendance patterns varied across the company, with many employees availing of start/finish day shift early schemes. Employees adhered strictly to a fixed roster, rarely, if at all, working beyond contracted hours. Management increasingly found that such practices were untenable in light of market demands. Company clients were frequently unhappy as they did not want BritCo engineers to be on their site at 8am if they would not be open at that time. Perhaps more problematically was the tendency for engineers to 'down tools' and leave the job as soon as their hours for that day had been completed – regardless of whether the job had been finished or not. BritCo management sought to restructure the working day of the engineers and broaden the pattern of work so that engineers would work later into the evenings. Management attempted to broaden the working day from 4pm to 6pm and then later to further expand this to 8pm. For engineers this was a source of some contention and the issue became something of a 'hot potato' between management and the operational union for the best part of four years. This matter was addressed largely through the bi-monthly meetings described above. At these meetings, the relevant operational managers would present to union representatives the data supporting the need for change and the proposed re-scheduling of work shifts. Then, over a 12 week period, union representatives fed this information back to, and consulted with, their members outlining their respective options. Through this process of indirect consultation, the change-over process in work shifts was achieved, albeit not without some dissatisfaction amongst the engineers. For management, the manner in which the process was addressed represented the crux of their approach to employee voice in Northern Ireland:

> That would be the principle of any consultation we do: present the facts, the rationale on what needs to change, proposals for how we are going to go about it, listen to what people say and maybe change anything that comes from that. (Human Resource Manager)

Yet on this particular matter, union representatives tended to be less sanguine. Whilst acknowledging that management gave their members' opportunities to voice concerns, unions were doubtful that this impacted upon management's subsequent actions:

> Our views didn't change what the company wanted to do. During the whole process, we were telling BritCo senior managers that we are getting inundated with calls with concerns, with people worried about how was it going to affect their life, from child care arrangements, from caring for parents. Suddenly management wanted people to be able to fulfil these new arrangements. We were told there would always be exceptions to rule that people could appeal and people did appeal. I think I'd be right in saying that of everybody who did appeal, I think only one person won the appeal. (Trade Union Representative)

Despite this, management are perceived by both the unions and employees to be excellent in communicating on various business and financial developments. It is in the area of adequate consultation and negotiation, however, that concerns remain. In many respects, the unions are conscious of a progressive withering away of their substantive influence to jointly determine policy within the company nationally. Whilst unions are provided with formal opportunities for consultative voice on proposed organisational change, there is dissatisfaction over management's reluctance to allow this to extend into meaningful influence of policy:

> *Do we have any influence on management? Honest truth? Very little. In the last four years whenever I've been involved in any major project, no. When it's first presented to us till we go through the whole process, up to implementation, any changes we have been making or any gains we've made for our members has been small. It's going to be implemented nearly to the letter of what we first received. (Trade Union Representative)*

The arrangements for employee voice in BritCo Ireland: Republic of Ireland

Within the Republic of Ireland, BritCo utilises a wide range of both indirect and direct employee voice methods. The direct methods of voice replicate those mechanisms existing in Northern Ireland. Unlike Northern Ireland, where the emphasis on direct voice mechanisms is of new vintage, the direct mechanisms in the Republic have been in place since the beginning. They have, however, been progressively enhanced by the arrival of the new CEO who, as noted above, appeared to be heavily committed to increasing levels of communication between management and employees. Whilst the direct voice schemes largely converge across both jurisdictions, the main indirect employee voice methods in the Republic of Ireland are however substantially different from Northern Ireland, incorporating:

- 'BritCo Vocal', a non-union employee representation forum covering the whole Republic

- the 'Southern Works Committee' (SWC), a non-union employee representation forum designed for BritCo Dublin engineering site to deal with issues specific to this site with company-wide issues being treated through BritCo Vocal.

BritCo Vocal stemmed from a forum established a few years previously to meet the requirements of the European Union's Information and Consultation Directive. It had however become dormant due to a lack of activity and management interest. The forum was revamped under the title of 'BritCo Vocal' – largely in response to a growing union recognition drive in the company during 2007. Whereas no coherent electoral system existed for the previous forum, under Vocal, employee representatives are chosen through election, with typically one representative per 100 employees. The electoral constituencies are designed to allow for each business area to have one representative, although the engineering and call centre section of the business are allowed to elect three representatives due to their being over 300 people employed in each of those sections. Employees either self-nominate or are sponsored by colleagues. Where more than one representative comes forward, an election takes place. Whereas the previous forum was little more than a presentation by the former CEO on the financial performance of the company, Vocal, at least initially, is a more expansive affair, beginning with the HR Director outlining current developments in the company, followed by a financial and market update by the CEO, with the remainder of the meeting set aside for employee representatives to raise pertinent issues and discuss matters of concern. Employee representatives then report back to their constituents on the detail and outcomes of the meetings, mostly through email and notice boards.

The SWC emerged when it was felt that too many issues from an engineering plant in Dublin were dominating the agenda of Vocal. This plant in particular had been subject to a number of revisions in employee car policy. Many engineers at this site lost access to company cars, had to change company cars for vans or, in some cases, went from a fully expensed company car to an allowance; the dynamics of rolling out this change process had generated a range of employee grievances. Creating the SWC, which mirrored the same institutional features of Vocal, was BritCo management's response to the issue.

The dynamics of voice in BritCo Ireland: Republic of Ireland

BritCo Ireland appears to have gone to considerable effort to deliver non-union forms of employee voice in the Republic of Ireland, but how are these mechanisms evaluated by employees and management? Again, it is useful to look at how key organisational issues have been addressed through the forums.

One key issue of concern for employees was the potential redundancy payments on offer at BritCo Ireland in comparison to Northern Ireland. Through Vocal, management explained that the terms presented in the company handbook in the Republic had simply been replicated from those which existed in the acquired firm, IndyCo. Terms were low, management conceded, because as a relatively young company IndyCo staff would not have held long service. Management accepted that the handbook should be re-written by HR in consultation with the employee representatives on Vocal. Employee representatives were given a month to review the final handbook through meetings with their constituents on pertinent issues that arose from the review process. The outcome from the review initiative was that aspects of the Northern Irish redundancy program were introduced into the Republic; principally, the practice of a redundancy pool wherein employees at risk of redundancy are given eight weeks to secure a new position and/or project in the company. Representatives and employees interviewed across BritCo Ireland in the Republic expressed satisfaction with the manner in which this issue was addressed through Vocal – and the subsequent outcome.

The outcome in relation to how redundancy was addressed through the non-union forum in the Republic is pointed in other ways. Employee representatives on the Vocal forum felt that once management attempted to solve underlying grievances that had prompted union demands to the company, and once the momentum of the union organising campaign wore off, the range and scope of issues at Vocal meetings, and employees' capacity to have influence in policy, substantially narrowed. Attempts at raising other substantive issues have been claimed by Vocal representatives to be either written off the agenda or glossed over by management in meetings. This led to two employee representatives dropping out of the forum. As one Vocal representative noted:

We get listened to, but whether we have substantial influence, no I doubt it.
(Vocal Employee Representative)

Initial management promises of robust involvement in policy-making matters have become steadily confined to the management of facilities-type issues. Progressively, Vocal was found to become a vessel for the downward communication of information from senior management. Training for the role has been described as superficial and ad hoc, with many representatives claiming that they have not received sufficient advice on how to handle grievances from their relevant constituents. From the perspective of employees at BritCo in the Republic, this has led to a number of representatives being identified as weak and unable to effectively advance employee concerns.

The dynamics of the SWC in practice have been somewhat similar. The first year of the SWC was marked by an ongoing exchange between management and employee representatives over the terms of reference for the forum i.e. what was appropriate for SWC and which issues should be advanced to Vocal. In this time, the grievance that had largely engendered the SWC – the car policy – was slowly resolved by management independently of the forum. When both management and employee representatives agreed that the SWC should deal with strictly local-level Dublin South issues, the SWC primarily found itself dealing with numerous facilities management issues, something that proved a the disappointment to many of SWC representatives. Again, a perception existed amongst representatives that they would have a voice in shaping policy issues in Dublin South, yet much to their disenchantment, the kinds of issues that became a feature of forum meetings were minor grievances over car parking spaces and the lack of adequate smoking shelter facilities. However, there was one instance where an issue of more weighty import was raised before the forum – unfair management appraisals of employee performance – but it appears that a number of the SWC representatives lacked confidence in handling it. Many SWC representatives felt they lacked adequate training in handling matters of such gravity given their potential impact on individuals' careers. Rather than give employees advice, for which SWC representatives felt they had not been trained, they would simply show employees the relevant human resource information on the company website and indicate to them the relevant steps to follow before bringing a grievance.

Despite the continuing concern over performance management, within two years of the SWC being introduced activity began to steadily fall off. Such has been the level of fall-off in activity that the forum was wound-up by management. Management tended to describe the wind-up being due to a lack of widespread collective issues of concern at the plant since the resolution of grievances over the car policy change. However, SWC representatives portray a different picture.

Over time, a number of representatives began to absent themselves from meetings, primarily as a result of losing interest in handling 'tea and toilet roll' issues:

> *Would I say we were really listened to and had a say? No. I thought it would be more about being involved in important policy and getting your voice across on it, but that certainly never happened. (SWC Employee Representative)*

More importantly, however, the workload advanced to SWC representatives effectively declined, as employees stopped bringing grievances to representatives. In part, this was due to a number of SWC representatives being promoted into line management positions and being viewed by their constituents as 'too close' to management.

Summary

Overall, despite the existence of numerous mechanisms across the organisation, the delivery of employee voice in BritCo Ireland has been uneven. In Northern Ireland, BritCo Ireland has managed to maintain direct and indirect systems of voice and has largely used them as conduit to roll out corporate strategy. This has, however, impacted upon the union system of voice which is being progressively redefined to adapt to an increasingly managerially-driven agenda. In the Republic of Ireland, management sought to deliver indirect, non-union, employee voice schemes. Whilst the new indirect mechanism displayed evidence of some success as consultative mechanisms, their impact in the Republic has declined over time.

Discussion questions

1) Compare and contrast the outcomes derived from management and union exchanges in Northern Ireland with the exchanges of management and non-union employee representatives in the Republic of Ireland. Are there significant differences in the outcomes across the different types of voice regimes? Why might this be so?

2) Given that BritCo Ireland management adopt a positive attitude to recognised unions in Northern Ireland, why might they have been opposed to the extension of a union-based voice regime in the Republic?

3) On the basis of this case, can you identify differences in how management might understand the concept of employee voice in contrast to how it is understood by employees or unions?

4) What lessons might be drawn from the management of non-union employee forums from the evidence presented in this case?

Chapter 26

Learning on the job in UK TV production

Irena Grugulis and Dimitrinka Stoyanova

Until the 1990s, TV production in the UK was dominated by the major terrestrial broadcasters. Most of the schedule consisted of output that was commissioned, produced and broadcast in-house. The employment systems reflected this and strong internal labour markets developed, supported by union membership. Trainees were recruited after formal education and both vocational training and work systems (of assistants, placements and structured traineeships) supported extensive skill development. Skills were learned on the job and clearly understood progression routes existed to facilitate movement up the various occupational hierarchies.

The political reforms of the 1990s changed this structure dramatically as the major broadcasters were required to outsource a growing proportion of their production to independent companies and freelance workers. In order to create this labour market, many professionals were made redundant then hired back as freelancers. Skills development and learning was not a problem for this 'first generation' of freelancers because internals, who were already familiar with each broadcaster's system and whose skills had been honed 'in-house', had simply been transformed into externals. However, over two decades have passed since these reforms took effect and TV production is now dominated by freelance labour such that the majority of those entering the industry today can expect to spend their careers on freelance contracts. Given this, it is important to ensure that skills can be sustained. Accordingly, this case study compares and contrasts the experiences of those who learned in-house with that of their freelance successors.

Internal labour markets and the 'community of practice' before 1990

Novices were employed full time on low level work. They helped to carry the equipment, made teas and coffees and held umbrellas over the camera to keep it dry. These were necessary tasks and they were important in two ways: they gave novices opportunities to watch what happened and learn from it; and performing the tasks meant that novices became part of the production team, a process Lave and Wenger (1991) call 'legitimate peripheral participation'. This allowed newcomers to gradually develop their understanding of the processes in the context of actual productions.

Technical skills were developed alongside an appreciation of the way that the various specialisms interacted. Working on a production is a complex project and each professional had to be aware in some detail of the work done by the others involved as well as the impact these could have on their own work. Cameramen relied on the grips to set the rails accurately so their pictures hit the mark; directors relied on the observations of the continuity people to ensure that action flowed smoothly from scene to scene, regardless of which take made the final cut; and everyone depended on the location manager and their assistants to ensure that no strangers wandered on set during takes. Edward, a sound recordist explained:

> [Y]ou have got to know the camera operator's job, what he wants; the lighting cameraman's job because where his lights are going to go you have got to be able to work out where you are going to go to get the sound. And know what the editor needs in the cutting room when it gets that far. You know, if you see somebody's back of head, I'm struggling to get that line, but it is back of head so I don't need it. So, it is knowing what you can get away with and what will be covered on other shots as well. So it is actually, knowing how a film is going to be put together as you are shooting it. You know well you are not going to need that line because it will be on a close up at that point or a different angle… it is just experience, really, of how people work and how a film is shot and put together. It is just experience that you can only get on the shopfloor, I think. They can't teach you that in a classroom I don't think.

Hugh, a camera operator agreed:

> And the other really important thing I suppose, which is what I tell a lot of other cameramen and directors, young directors or - you know - not young but new directors, is to go into the edits. See what shots they are [using], see how long the shots last, see what type of shots that they use, you know. And I did that myself, I sat in, as painful as it was, because you are looking at your own filming, you are looking at your own work and seeing how the editor and the director use your filming to make the program, to make sense of the program. And you quickly learn what is good and what is bad, and why on earth did you do that. Because it seems so, when you are in front of the screen it seems so logical that you would have done a particular move or something, you know.

Novices also learned the professional etiquette. Watching how senior colleagues acted in different situations helped develop an understanding of the specific ways of behaving and interacting within the community. An experienced director of photography (the most senior person on the camera team) gave an example of this in relation to working with actors: a clapper loader may stand in the eye line of the actors who will then stop 'the take'. Sometimes, however, actors would use this as an excuse, if they had, for example, forgotten their lines. An experienced clapper loader familiar with the professional etiquette would simply apologise and continue with the work rather than contradict the actor. This 'protocol' or context-dependent behaviour is the type of knowledge developed through exposure and observation. Being a legitimate peripheral participant in a community of practice did not simply mean becoming competent in performing a set of specific tasks. It also meant becoming a part of the social practice of television. A novice did not simply learn how to handle jobs, but also how to behave, how to interact with others, how to interpret situations in context as they happen and how to relate to people performing different types of roles.

The structure of the labour process facilitated these informal ways of learning. Work was unevenly paced, with long periods of preparation and often a great deal of time between 'takes' while sets were changed and technical settings adjusted. These were used by people to talk to each other and novices could ask questions about the technical or other aspects of the work and experienced colleagues were usually happy to answer. They could also extend their repertoire of tasks.

> *What happened was that the people ... the thing about it was you have to remember in the old days when you were an assistant editor... there was an editor and an assistant so people would meet you, you know...what would happen as an assistant was that you would pal up with a producer actually. Because the editor would be working ... would be editing away and there would be quite a lot of periods when you and the producer would just sit chatting at the back or sorting out, looking for rushes, or just chatting, actually. So what happened was then you got friendly with a producer and then you might ... you might do a bit of editing whilst the editor was away or something, or cut a sequence, or something like that. And then in my case I got friendly with a couple of producers of the editor who I was assisting, used to cut films for, and they asked me to cut films. But I had to go and edit a bit of other stuff first. So I went and did this ... particularly this current affairs and a thing that was...I think that was the first sort of formal editing I did, actually. And after that I came back and edited these 60 minute films, yes. (Mark, editor)*

In addition to learning on the job, novices had access to a range of formal courses as well as a range of productions.

> *I was working in television so I was learning rapidly about those sorts of skills for working in television sound. And it was a great place to learn because in those days, I joined the sound department as a trainee in about 1981, I think... [and] was introduced to a vast and broad range of subjects from studio drama to news gathering to post production and to location filming and got a, you know, a great range of experience in all those over a couple of years. (Sam, sound recordist)*

> *Well I was only actually at the BBC in Bristol for about just over two years. I was a trainee cameraman for a year and then I was a floor manager for regional television for a year and then… the BBC has this fantastic system called 'attachments' . . . if you are staff at the BBC you can apply to do an attachment for 6 months where you get to do somebody else's job …like I was a regional floor manager in Bristol and these attachments were advertised every week. So I applied for all the ones that were for assistant producers (what the job was called in those days). So I applied for all the assistant producer jobs, or the attachments, that came up, and you basically …the idea is that you can go and try the job out for 6 months and if they like you, then they'll offer you a full time job. Or you might find you are no good at it you know and so on. But luckily I did (Alexander, producer-director)*

This exposed junior staff members to a multitude of settings and experiences, enriching their knowledge of contexts and professionals and helping to build an all-round profile.

> *You need the time, you need turnover of programs, you need to do programs, you need difficult circumstances, you just need experience I think. You just need that experience…. I think it is getting less and less. I think it is probably getting less because people seem to be getting younger. I don't know whether it is me getting older, I am not sure, but I think it would be unusual these days to spend the best part of ten years before you start producing/directing your own stuff. (Robert, producer-director)*

Novices had access to experienced professionals whose practice embodied the professional standards, norms of interaction and the skills and knowledge required. They had the opportunities to observe productions from start to finish and were encouraged to learn about specialisms beyond their own to help the work process. They attended formal courses and benefitted from internal transfers.

Fragmented labour markets and learning on the job after 1990

More than 20 years have passed since the original reforms and today the majority of workers in TV production are freelancers. Most new entrants are graduates and some (though by no means all) hold degrees such as media studies, journalism or drama, which have given them exposure to TV production. Entry is not restricted to those fortunate enough to gain a job with a major broadcaster, but there are few full-time positions. The most common entry-route is through unpaid 'internships' in which novices spend time in independent production companies. These may lead to paid work but often they don't.

> *In some sectors of the industry, the way it is perceived to be for young people, is that you make yourself available to work for nothing or next to nothing. And because there aren't formal structures, it's not as if you can reliably say 'well I know I have got to do this because everybody does it but I also know that having, in a sense, won my spurs, I will move up, I will get paid*

employment'. It is a lottery, I mean that might happen, but very often it doesn't happen. And the reputation you get is as an eager young person who will work for nothing rather than as somebody who is really good and deserves, you know, a leg up (Simon, BECTU official)

In some specialisms, clear progression routes can still be observed, notably camera departments on big productions. These use elaborate technical gear, which requires a team to operate.

Trainee yes, I mean … well it is kind of an unofficial apprenticeship, really, so normally one person will know somebody who is trying to get into the industry and who has done some short films as a sort of loader or something and wants to get into slightly bigger projects. And they will just come in to shadow the loader and the assistant, really. And they'll help you know they will help organise the gear and I'll make sure you know if someone needs to go sometime and get something he will do it and he will assist generally. But he is very much aware he has a shadowing role rather than anything else. (Arthur, Director of Photography)

Outside feature film and TV drama the development of new lightweight equipment means that productions no longer require a team of camera operators, focus pullers and grips. Crew members often take on more than one role and it is common to have a sound recording camera operator or a producer-director. Some productions do not employ trained operators. In those that do, pressure on budgets and the flexibility of freelance contracts mean that specialists are hired for the minimum possible time rather than the duration of the production

There is physically less things to do. You often could do with an assistant and it has sort of become the norm that you don't get anybody to help you and so therefore it is written … you know, the budget… there is no room in the budget to get someone to help you. And so you normally don't get an assistant. (Mark, editor)

Trainees are still employed to carry-out basic tasks but, unlike their predecessors, those who are fortunate enough to get paid work or long-term placements in the industry often discover that they are separated from the action on set and that their support work rarely gives them access to production professionals.

Because they had done a lot of production and they had all - all the producers were freelance and they have left all the paperwork to do. Like, you need to go through the program and find out what archive is in there, what music is being used and it should all have been cleared beforehand but it really hadn't been. I think they had an intense period where they had got all this work in, but the thing with producers is they want to get out when they have finished…. So there was all this work to do and not much - you know, and not many people wanting to do it because it is not something that people really enjoy doing. (Britney, production assistant, small independent production company)

This has two implications for novices. Firstly and most fundamentally, when production teams shrink the first jobs to go tend to be those of the runners and the tea boys who are least necessary to the current project so there simply is no place on set for them. Secondly, even when they do gain access to filming, the fragmented labour market and short-term contracts mean that there are fewer people around to observe or question and less time for such observations. These implications are at odds with the idea of legitimate peripheral participation and communities of learning, which require time, stable mentoring provision, exposure to variable projects and legitimate learning status. Commercial pressures affect both access to opportunities to learn and the learning experience itself.

Novices respond in a number of ways. They teach themselves technical skills by borrowing equipment from firms or persuading affluent relatives to fund a production:

> *Initially we used to work on film and that is when I was an assistant and worked alongside an editor. Once we shifted over to computers, this thing called an Avid [editing software], you don't get an assistant. So I didn't work alongside anybody else, they just taught me how to do it and then you just go off and do it. (Mark, editor)*

Others simply attempt to find work in their chosen occupation. This is difficult enough for established freelancers with proven skills and extensive networks to draw on. Indeed some estimates reveal that freelancers spend only an average of a third of the year in work (Randle 2008, p. 1251). Producers are vividly aware of the extent to which productions depend on the expertise of those who make them and are reluctant to risk a commission by hiring an inexperienced trainee to perform a key task.

> *And there are no assistant editors any more in fact so I don't really know where you learn the trade. So people come to us and say 'I want to be an editor' and you say 'well, I can't throw you in at the deep end, you have got no experience'. And they say 'well, where do I get it from?', you say 'I don't know. I really …but I can't take a risk with a network program that you can cut it when you've not done it'. (George, company owner)*

At the same time, industry fragmentation has shattered the traditional progression routes and lengthy training periods. The standard set of career steps, minimum experience requirements and clearly understood job titles have gone. Both entry and subsequent progression is unregulated and small firms often use the prospects of enhanced 'credits' (job titles) to persuade individuals to accept lower pay, so job titles are rarely a good indication of competence. This means that few people in the industry trust formal lists of credits and that it is difficult to offer newcomers career guidance.

> *I think, you know, the thing to remember is in today's world it is much more difficult to go through a structured sort of regime of moving up the ladder….
> It used to be, in the sort of days when the studios were much more in control, you used to very much join as a camera trainee, and then a clapper loader and then a focus puller and then an operator and then a DP [director of photography]; and it was a set way of doing things and you would generally*

do it over a set amount of time but that doesn't really exist anymore. So I think it's very difficult for people to know which direction to come in to … and I think the most common question I'm asked by people starting in the industry is what should I do next? It is difficult. (Arthur, Director of Photography)

For those in employment, skills can be acquired on the job, just as they were before:

The only …the subsequent training I have had really has only been that once I moved to London I worked in a mixture of different companies with more experienced producers and production managers, I suppose, who …who I actually…because then I felt I was in a community where I could ask questions and learn from other people. And a couple of …in my career there have been a couple of positions where I have actually had a really good producer I am working with who I have been able to ask a lot of questions of. (Claire, production manager)

But freelance labour means that employment is less long, less stable and rarely continuous.

I never got a permanent job but I would have loved you know …that way I would have really trained on the job properly but you know I ended up having to learn by myself because I always was freelance. Which is …I think an ideal scenario is for your first job is to have a permanent position so that you know, you are learning all the different projects that that company is doing. (Claudia, production manager)

Smaller teams, different equipment and caps on budgets limit the opportunities that novices have to learn while increasing numbers of novices (because there are no-longer gatekeepers restricting entry) putting pressure on jobs and pay rates. For some, lengthy productions and paid positions provide positive learning experiences but they are not the majority.

Summary and overview

The last few decades have seen major changes in TV production. The focus of this case study, the labour market, has shifted from one in which lifetime employment was the norm to the standard experience being gaining work through a series of fragmented freelance contracts. This has major implications for the way skills are learned. Well established internal systems of learning on the job, supported by formal training and placements still exist in the major terrestrial broadcasters – but for the majority, who work outside these companies, their experience is very different.

Discussion questions

1) What were the experiences of trainees before and after the changes of (a) learning, and (b) work?

2) What type of skills and what sort of knowledge did novices gain on the job?

3) What are the external factors influencing learning in UK TV production today?

4) Most studies of learning at work only look at structures and incidents *within* a firm. How does extending analysis *beyond* the organisational boundaries help us understand this case?

5) Are efficiency/productivity and learning mutually incompatible?

Useful readings

Antcliff, V, Saundry, R & Stuart, M 2007, 'Networks and social capital in the UK television industry: the weakness of weak ties', *Human Relations,* 60(2):371 - 393.

Bechky, B 2006, 'Gaffers, Gofers, and Grips: Role-Based Coordination in Temporary Organizations', *Organization Science* 17:3-21.

De Fillippi, R & Arthur, M 1998, "Paradox in Project-Based Enterprise: The Case of Film-Making." *California Management Review,* 40(2):125 - 139.

Grugulis, I & Stoyanova, D 2009, ''I don't know where you learn them' skills in film and TV', pp. 135 - 155 in *Creative Labour: working in the creative industries,* edited by A McKinlay & C Smith, Houndsmills: Palgrave Macmillan.

Grugulis, I & Stoyanova, D 2011, 'The missing middle: communities of practice in a freelance labour market', *Work, Employment and Society,* 25(2).

Holgate, J & Mckay, S 2007, 'Institutional barriers to recruitment and employment in the audio-visual industries', London: Working Lives Research Institute.

Lave, J & Wenger, E 1991, *Situated Learning: legitimate peripheral participation,* Cambridge: Cambridge University Press.

Leadbeater, C &. Oakley, K 1999, *The Independents: Britain's New Cultural Entrepreneurs,* London: Demos.

McKinlay, A & Quinn, B 1999, 'Management, Technology and Work in Commercial Broadcasting, c. 1979-98', *New Technology, Work and Employment,* 14(1):2-17.

Paterson, R 2001, 'Work Histories in Television', *Media Culture Society,* 23(4):495-520.

Storey, J, Salaman, G & Platman, K 2005, 'Living with enterprise in an enterprise economy: freelance and contract workers in the media', *Human Relations,* 58(8):1033 - 1054.

Tempest, S, McKinlay, A & Starkey, K 2004, 'Careerring Alone: Careers and Social Capital in the Financial Services and Television Industries', *Human Relations,* 57(12):1523-1545.

References

Randle, K, Wing-Fai, L & Kurian, J 2008, 'Creating Difference: overcoming barriers to diversity in UK film and television employment', Hatfied, Hertfordshire: Creative Industries Research and Consultancy Unit, University of Hertfordshire.

Chapter 27

Diversity and policing: Doing gender at Victoria Police

JULIE WOLFRAM COX AND GEORGINA CAILLARD

Background and context

Established in 1853, Victoria Police has employed women since 1917 but representation of female staff remained fairly low for many years. During 1999 and 2000, the then Chief Commissioner, Neil Comrie, aimed to recruit and promote more female staff and introduced equity training. Efforts to increase the attraction, retention and progression of female staff were stepped up during the subsequent period when Christine Nixon was Victoria's (first female) Chief Commissioner of Police (2001–2009). Over the past twelve years Victoria Police has developed a series of initiatives to increase the diversity of its workforce, including the introduction and extension of flexible work initiatives (since 2007) and changes to applicant fitness and agility requirements to increase the accessibility of Victoria Police careers to female and to older applicants. Some of these initiatives have recently been reviewed. Victoria Police is currently encouraging applications from indigenous Australians and people from multicultural backgrounds.

Strategies, policies, plans and initiatives

Gender initiatives at Victoria Police need to be understood in relation to Australia's equal opportunity frameworks and to its own diversity strategies and policies, a summary of which now follows. Within this summary we highlight key terms in order to display some of the important emphases of the organisation in recent times. For example, Ms Nixon developed the first Victoria Police Diversity Strategy, which aimed to develop infrastructure and systems to support what was termed *diversity capability* and was linked to an Equity and Diversity Corporate Plan (2003–2008). The organisation's website emphasises the importance of attracting people who are *diversity-competent*: who understand and respect that everyone has characteristics that make them unique, including awareness that people may approach or experience things differently because of their religious or cultural backgrounds and beliefs. The importance of promoting harmonious community relationships based on *mutual respect, tolerance and trust* is stressed as a particular focus at Victoria Police. The organisation's current five-year strategic plan, *The Way Ahead 2008–2013*, is published in many languages and emphasises *safety, community connections* and the importance of *valuing our people*.

Multiculturalism is also important to Victoria Police, as articulated in its Multicultural Policy Statement (for 2006–2008). This statement affirms the importance of Victoria Police's workforce needing to *reflect* the diverse communities of Victoria and to *provide flexible services* to all Victorians with respect for particular needs. It states that constructive community engagement and proactive policing will build *social capital* and assist *social cohesion and community strengthening and safety*. This represents a move away from the crime-fighting/remedial policing emphasis of the past and was aligned with Victoria Police's (temporary) dropping of the terms [Police] *Force* and [Executive] *Command* and introducing a very flexible uniform policy – including more casual items such as polar fleeces and baseball caps and inclusion of variations that respected the dress codes of those in religious minorities. The policy states that Victoria Police aims to promote an inclusive community that respects and celebrates diversity in its many forms. Both Ms Nixon and the subsequent Chief Commissioner, Simon Overland, took part in Victoria's annual Gay Pride March, Overland allowing officers to join him in uniform and on paid time if they were on duty and received permission from their supervisors.

The organisation's (now regionalised) Multicultural Advisory Unit promoted and facilitated engagement between police and culturally diverse communities and both Multicultural and New and Emerging Community Liaison Officers continue to assist this work. The Multicultural Policy Statement gives priority to the development of multicultural plans to reflect regional and local priorities and to be underpinned by recognition of several *generic principles*: equity, diversity, access, responsiveness, communication, participation, and accountability. Recognition of the importance of basic *human rights* is also of importance and Victoria Police's website states that applicants should be aware that Victoria has a charter of Human Rights and Responsibilities and that Victoria Police's Human Rights Unit aligns the principles of policing with that charter. Earlier, in 2003–2004, Victoria Police identified six *key values*: open-mindedness, difference, tolerance and understanding were included within the valuing of flexibility and of respect.

Researchers Isabel Metz and Carol Kulik described Victoria Police's efforts to develop a *diversity-inclusive organisational culture* in a 2008 article in the journal *Human Resource Management*. They presented arguments that police forces tend to be *male hegemonic* in that masculine attributes such as strength, authority and power are assumed within organisational structure and that access and progress of women and minorities is limited. They commented on how Christine Nixon disrupted this hegemony through her consultative and inclusive approach to leadership and through her emphasis on accessibility of senior staff. The latter was effected through some delayering of the senior management structure, inclusion of community representatives on key committees, a requirement that senior officers regularly spend time in operational work and by her own invitation to staff to email her directly and to 'call me Christine'. Her emphasis on evidence-based rather than authoritarian decision making was also particularly important here.

Multiple measures

A variety of indicators of the success of such initiatives can be used, and in the following sections we briefly illustrate this range by describing some measures of Victoria Police's progress with respect to the recruitment and status of its female employees.

Statistics

Operating in one of Australia's most populous states, Victoria Police currently employs a total of nearly 15,000 staff, of whom 33% were female on 30 June 2010. This is high in comparison with the national average, where the proportion of females to total police employees remained at about 20% until 2006. Thirty-five per cent of new full-time recruits to Victoria Police were female in 2010. By then females constituted 27% of its total full-time ongoing staff workforce, compared with 14% in 1995, 13% 2000 and 17% in 2005. The proportion of females was much higher among part-time and fixed-term staff than among full-time ongoing/continuing staff. For example, 82% of ongoing part-time police officers were female in 2010, as were 63% total fixed-term staff. While females represented a minority (20%) of sworn/operational full-time staff in 2010, they represented a majority (65%) of unsworn full-time public servant staff.

Behaviours and attitudes

Several cases of gender discrimination occurred at Victoria Police toward the end of the last century and reports of sexual harassment and negative attitudes toward women continued through the early 2000s. Despite comprehensive legal frameworks, subtle forms of discrimination can remain. For example, in an article in *Journal of Management and Organization*, Alberto Melgoza and Julie Wolfram Cox (2009) found that in one Australian policing organisation, male police officers felt more strongly (both negatively and positively) toward other males than toward female police officers. This was interpreted as an illustration of how females may be perceived as less central or normal than males and as 'others' within the organisation. Such 'othering' may be a particular issue for part-time female officers. Victoria Police has supported several studies of its part-time workforce since the introduction of a pilot part-time program in 1992 and a formal part-time employment policy in 1996.

As argued by Janet Chan, Sally Doran and Christina Marel in a 2010 issue of *Theoretical Criminology*, barriers to the integration of women within Australian police forces have remained even after decades of equal employment laws and policies. They argued that it is important to examine the processes and mechanisms that accomplish how gender is 'done' in policing and how gender is a social accomplishment and not only an individual attribute.

Gender Talk

Over the last four years the authors have worked as part of a team on an Australian Research Council project co-funded by Victoria Police into its governance and accountability mechanisms. One part of this project included a series of interviews, and during the first wave of briefings and interviews with a total of 41 staff there were many (unprompted) references to the diversity initiatives that took place during Christine Nixon's tenure at Victoria Police. We argue that such references aid understanding of the complex and gendered nature of police identity and show how the image of the fit, young, Anglo male police recruit constituted a norm, or perhaps a nostalgic reference point, for several interviewees, both female and male. They also show how issues of gender are entangled with other aspects of diversity and difference.

For example:

> [O]lder people, they don't want to socialise as much as well. So, you get older people with families that that's where they go home to and that's understandable but the big thing years ago was when you did have a, say a bad day or a major incident, people would all get together and talk about it and socialise better and I think overcome adversity better by just being together and talking about it and we had a – morale was a lot closer than it is today. I think, as we have here, we have probably over 50% females now. I don't think that's a good thing. I'm not anti-female by any means but even yesterday we had four females here that were on the two units and even one of them said at times it's wrong. We should have some males here.... I think the fitness side of things is lowered. So, but that you would have to probably get from the Academy itself but I think the Academy standard and I think also the standard of the older people coming in where they see it as maybe just a five-year job because they've already had a career and it's something that they want to do and so it's a five-year job, they don't have the same career goals and drive as someone that's probably coming in in their early 20s.... There's too many females in comparison to males and we're now having problems with older females then not wanting to be operational members when they get to the age of 40 or 45 or 50, we're having females in regards to getting pregnant and wanting to be part-time and a lot of part-time causes those problems as well. A lot of stations have problems with too many part-timers, so the organisation's changed due to those factors as well. (Male, Sergeant).

> I'm an advocate for recruiting young people. I don't want a 40 year old to join. Okay? I don't think we need them. And it's purely because working the

van, and that's what they've got to do, is a young person's job. It's hard to fit in with family life, the stresses and strains involved, and I just think that young people cope better with it, with the night shifts and weekend work and all those sort of things. Whereas if you're an established person with an established family, it's very hard to (1) accommodate those people and (2) for them to understand the concepts and for them to have the same sort of loyalty I think to the organisation.... So I think that, the philosophy that [Nixon] brought with all that recruitment I think really affected us. And really stagnated, I thought, the organisation.... And I notice now they're all coming through quite young again, so we've sort of gone back to that younger type person. So I think her bringing that sort of philosophy really didn't help us at all. We had a lot of people turned away that were quite good and would have been good for the organisation. But due to gender or due to, you know, oh you need more life experience, come back. People will come back maybe once, maybe twice, and then after that they say I'll go and do something else... I'm probably bordering on a sexist comment here, but, I'll say it anyway, all of a sudden, the woman's way of doing things became the way that everything will be done.

Interviewer: *What do you mean by the woman's way?*

Softly, softly. Warning after warning after warning after warning and no consequence for action. (Male, Sergeant)

It's a definite boys' club... In [working with] my police officers I often have to take on the bloke. If I don't do the blokey, I don't get through to them. So I find myself taking on the bloke culture... And I can relate to most of them quite easily, but I've got to do the blokey stuff. And I'm not a blokey girl, but I have to do it, and I find it works when I do... It was very interesting; because during the time that [Nixon] was Chief I saw a change in people's attitude towards her. It went from 'who the hell does she think she is, she's trying to turn us all into warm fuzzy fairies' to 'oh, well, you know, maybe she's, yeah, maybe it's ok' to 'who the hell does she think she was, she's tried to turn us all into warm fuzzy fairies'. So it kind of went full circle I think, and that was most interesting... My idea of a policeman is a big bloke... So I can't get over these 2'6" baby little girls who weigh about 40 kgs, you know, what the hell are they doing being police officers, but anyway, I'm sure they know how to do it. ...I think the guys, the general force is pleased that there's a guy back in charge again[5]. (Female, Administrator)

However, others were far more positive about the progress that had been made on gender:

Look, the growth in females has changed, numbers have changed the organisation a great deal. It used to be a blokey sort of an organisation. Far more considerate now. And I think that those who broke the ice initially did a fantastic job. Looking back 25 years ago there was sort of a growth in recruiting...I remember the first policewomen came along, but they are

---

[5] A reference to then Chief Commissioner of Police Simon Overland.

terrific, they are really good. And they proved obviously they could do the job and they're reasonable people and, you know, all that sort of stuff, and they command respect and they were good...I think we learned to communicate better I think in terms of reasoning and discussion and all that sort of stuff. In the old days you just didn't do it. But then it became more of a considerate approach. I think that was a big thing. And an appreciation too of the risks that, you know, they were encountering. So policing became more of a considerate approach to our operations. Rather than crash and bash it was, you know, think about these things. (Male; Assistant Commissioner or above)

You couldn't get in to be a trainee unless you could scale like a nine foot wall and that meant that women basically couldn't get in. I mean some of the tests were so indirectly discriminatory that they just excluded women from the start. Ironically some of the most significant objectives to the changes [Nixon] made at that time were actually women who'd got through the process under that model and now felt that it was diluting the test ..., but nonetheless those changes have been made. And then there's a whole lot of recruitment targets around women and there's a whole lot of flexibility in the employment models now to allow them to balance particularly childcare or parental care responsibilities which seem to rest with women in most cases. And a whole lot of advertising completely changed from sort of more aggressive male dominated models with the guns and the cars and the helicopters to more of the relationship-type police initiatives. (Male; Briefing meeting)

Embodiment

The changes brought about by Christine Nixon were at least to some extent embodied by her, as has been discussed by Metz and Kulik and by Sinclair. It is notable that Nixon was an outsider who was highly educated and recruited to Victoria Police after working her way up to senior staff positions at NSW Police.

I think it's fair to say that Christine was faced with a challenge. Not only was she from New South Wales, and outside of Victoria Police, it doesn't matter that it's New South Wales, but not only was she external to Victoria Police, she was a woman, and there'd never been a woman as the Commissioner of Police before. So there was [sic] these two challenges. And I think she handled it magnificently. She didn't come in with a big stick and, you know, you'll obey me because I'm the Chief Commissioner etc.. She came in to build her credibility in the organisation. Credibility in that she was there to listen to people, understand the organisation, and then build a team of people that she had the confidence in who could take the organisation along the path that she believed it needed to go. (Male, Assistant Commissioner and above)

Christine Nixon came along and it was like Mum, Mum in the kitchen. And she would chat away, very knowledgeable and that, a couple of changes she bought in upset a lot of the people.

Interviewer: *What were they?*

One was the [Gay] Pride march. Yeah, people were entitled to their whatever their viewpoint is but a lot of – like me in particular - was offended by the fact that the uniform was seen to be in the parade and that appeared to the general public as 'oh yes, well they agree with this'. It's not an agreement – it's a uniform to do the role of keeping the community in order. Once you start aligning yourself, and that's what it came across as, you're seen to be taking alliance with whatever interest of the day…on the street [is] where half the arguments start because people have no respect for the uniform. (Male, Sergeant)

However:

Policing is policing, no matter who the boss is. However, when she marched in the gay/lesbian thing at St Kilda and sent an email out that any member can join in the march and it will be on duty, many members felt that it was a disgraceful thing to do… She seemed to be siding with too many minority groups but maybe that's just a personal opinion…. A certain percentage resented the fact that it was female being the Chief. I kept an open mind and I found in her favour. (Male, Senior Constable)

Soft policing?

The association of Christine Nixon and her policies designed to assist the recruitment and development of female staff at Victoria Police with a 'softer' style of community and preventative policing were, for many of our more conservative interviewees, quite problematic. The notion of 'soft' policing was a gendered notion and was criticised in comparison with that of 'real' policing and 'catching crooks'. Given this context Victoria Police's current emphasis on hardening its approach to certain crimes and reinstating fitness requirements and a 'more streamlined' and darker uniform from 2012 may be considered, at least to some extent, as a re-masculinisation of the organisation.

Summary and overview

Overall, the increasing proportion of female staff at Victoria Police needs to be understood as one of many indicators of increasing diversity and as the result of a series of strategic and policy initiatives. In addition to the collection of such quantitative indicators, qualitative research has revealed that the role of the police officer remains gendered, if not feminised, and the subject of strong and diverse opinions.

Discussion questions

1) What additional statistics are important for a thorough assessment of whether or not efforts to increase the proportion of females at Victoria Police have been successful?

2) Why is the proportion of full-time female staff (and police recruits) of particular importance?

3) How and why is selection for fitness and agility a gendered issue?

4) What different logics and approaches to diversity management are apparent at Victoria Police? To what extent are these approaches complementary or conflicting? Are there other approaches that could be utilised in this organisation?

5) Explain the notions of doing (and undoing) gender. What sort of research is likely to be able to help us to understand these notions? Why is this the case?

Acknowledgements

The research presented here was partly funded by an Australian Research Council Linkage Project Grant and by Victoria Police, for whose continued support we are most grateful. The arguments presented in this chapter do not necessarily reflect those of Victoria Police.

References

Chan, J, Doran, S & Marel, C 2010, 'Doing and undoing gender in policing', *Theoretical Criminology*, 14(4): 425-446.

Melgoza, AR & Wolfram Cox, J 2009, 'Subtle sexism: Re-informing intergroup bias and regulating emotion in an Australian police organization', *Journal of Management and Organization*, 15(5): 652-666.

Metz, I & Kulik, CT 2008, 'Making public organizations more inclusive: A case study of the Victoria Police Force', *Human Resource Management*, 47(2): 369-387.

Sinclair, A 2005, 'Body possibilities in leadership', *Leadership*, 1(4): 387-406.

Chapter 28

A high performance work system in a multi-stakeholder context

EVA KNIES, PETER LEISINK AND PAUL BOSELIE

Introduction

The focus of this chapter is on the renewal of HR policies and practices, which resulted in a High Performance Work System (HPWS), at the Dutch insurance company Achmea. The majority of publications on HPWSs are based on studies of Fortune 500 companies, mainly from an Anglo-Saxon perspective (Keegan & Boselie 2006). Creating shareholder value is the main objective for these companies, and little attention is generally paid to the interests of other stakeholders (for example, employees, trade unions, society). Mainstream HPWS approaches tend to focus on multinational companies such as General Electric, Google, IBM, Microsoft and Toyota. There are of course many other relevant organisations operating in various institutional contexts. The case study of Achmea is appealing for various reasons: a range of stakeholders were involved in the creation of the HPWS (a characteristic of the Rhineland model of capitalism); Achmea is not quoted on the stock exchange; and the healthcare sector in the Netherlands, which is the major area of Achmea's activities, is subject to major reforms resulting from economic and political developments. By studying the HPWS presented in this case study, one will gain insights into the impact of various contextual factors (Rhineland model of capitalism, healthcare sector) on the shaping of HPWSs, the relevant characteristics of an HPWS design, the different actors involved (stakeholders) and their interests and the outcomes related to the implementation of HPWSs.

Setting the stage

Achmea is a large insurance company located in the Netherlands. It employs over 20,000 people. The corporation has seven divisions which provide services to both corporate and individual clients customers. The organisation is the market leader in the field of health insurance. The organisation has a long tradition of innovative HR policies (such as introducing a 'cafeteria reward system'[6] in the 1980s and 'teleworking' in the 1990s) and stakeholder value management. These stakeholders include customers, 'shareholders', distribution partners and employees. The term shareholder is put between quotation marks because Achmea is not publicly listed and has only two institutional shareholders, namely the cooperative Rabobank and the foundation Achmea. Achmea adopts a partnership approach, meaning that the organisation places considerable value on its relationship with employees through their trade unions and the works council.

Sense of urgency

The healthcare sector in the Netherlands has been subject to many reforms, including the gradual introduction of market mechanisms. Since 2006, all Dutch citizens have been legally obliged to take out health insurance. The law makes it mandatory for insurance companies to accept all citizens as clients. Health insurance companies negotiate with healthcare providers about the provision of healthcare and, to an increasing extent, insurance companies bargain for special arrangements. All these developments have resulted in increased competition which challenges insurance companies to deliver better service at less cost than their direct competitors. Such reforms affect organisations and their employees and raise new challenges for human resource management (HRM) policies and practices.

In addition to these changes in the market, organisations in the Netherlands are confronted with an increasing number of challenges as a result of demographic changes in the workforce (Verworn, Schwarz & Herstatt 2009). Although the problems related to a tight labour market have been pushed into the background by the recent economic downturn, labour issues remain relevant. Western countries see an ageing population and, moreover, the workforce is becoming increasingly diverse, partly as a result of women and immigrants having a larger share of the labour market. Facing a tight future labour market and a growing diversity within the workforce, organisations face the challenge of recruiting and retaining highly motivated and competent employees if they are to maintain a high level of service delivery. The way in which organisations take up this challenge is influenced by the wider institutional environment. This makes it relevant to go briefly into the Rhineland model of capitalism that prevails in northern continental Europe.

The Rhineland model and context

The Rhineland model represents an institutional environment that pays special attention to a range of stakeholders, including trade unions and government, and that puts value on trusted relationships, consultation and participation of 'social

---

[6] Also known as a 'flexible employee benefit scheme'.

partners' (Leisink & Greenwood 2007; Paauwe & Boselie 2003). High performance from a Rhineland perspective is represented by superior levels of individual, organisational and societal outcomes. From this perspective, a high performance work system will be aimed at satisfying the needs of various stakeholders (for example works councils, trade unions and the government) and will be aligned with the institutional context, for example with regard to labour legislation and societal norms and values. This appears to be the situation in the Achmea case study presented in this chapter. The Achmea case study shows the introduction of an HPWS involving multiple stakeholders with an underlying approach that could be characterised as adopting a Rhineland perspective, incorporating multiple goals (individual, organisational and societal).

A new HR policy focus

Facing the challenges described above, Achmea decided to create a new high performance work system (HPWS). This decision was also inspired by the merger of Achmea with Interpolis, another insurance company. Achmea did not want to simply harmonise employment policies, it wanted to more fundamentally innovate its HR policies. Therefore, Achmea negotiated an agreement with the trade unions and the works council to design a new HPWS.[7] A short overview of the theory of high performance organisations (HPOs) and high performance work systems (HPWSs) can be found in Box 28.1.

Box 28.1: High performance organisations and high performance work systems

High performance organisations

Many contemporary organisations struggle to survive in a global arena faced with increased competition, dynamics and complexity. Superior performance to other organisations (often direct competitors) operating in the same population or industry is a necessity for organisational survival (Boxall & Purcell 2008). Superior organisational performance is often linked to notions of the High Performance Organisation (HPO). An HPO can be characterised by the following aspects (Kirby 2005, in Paauwe 2007):

- mission, values and pride (communicating)

- creating a collective state of mindfulness

- entrepreneurial spirit

- seeking consistent alignment

- leadership at all levels, hands-on and value-driven management

---

[7] Such an agreement, that is part of a collective labour agreement, is legally binding under the Dutch labour law framework.

- sticking to the knitting, core business

- employee empowerment, sense of ownership

- process and metrics, performance management.

The majority of these HPO characteristics are closely related to human resource management policies and practices, in particular leadership style, employee empowerment and performance management. In reality, perhaps only few organisations in a given population or industry will ever fully achieve all the aspects of an HPO summarised above (Boselie 2010). The concept of an HPO is closely related to what is known as a high performance work system (HPWS) in human resource management. A high performance work system is a special type of HRM aimed at achieving superior organisational performance through the realisation of HR outcomes.

High performance work systems

A high performance work system can be defined as a bundle of specific HR practices that creates employee abilities in terms of knowledge and skills, employee motivation through a sophisticated incentive structure, and employee opportunity to participate in decision making (Appelbaum *et al.* 2000). The alignment of individual HR practices within a bundle or system of practices is thought to create synergetic effects (Delery 1998). In other words, a fit between individual HR practices will strengthen the impact of HRM on performance outcomes. An internal fit between the individual HR practices, creating a coherent and consistent human resource system, is assumed to lead to higher performance than the sum of the individual HR practices (Kepes & Delery 2007). The underlying theory for the high performance work system, including the notions on internal fit, is known as the AMO theory. The AMO model builds on the notion that HR practices can be bundled to enhance ability, motivation and opportunity to perform (Appelbaum *et al.* 2000; Wall & Wood 2005).

At the start of the design process at Achmea, there was no blueprint available for an HPWS design. A bottom-up approach was adopted to determine the main focus of the HR policy and practices. Various stakeholders were interviewed to explore the challenges they were facing, and their perspectives on the aims of the innovation process and any preconditions to achieve these aims. Based on interviews with members of the executive board, top managers, HR managers, employees and representatives of the works council and the trade unions, the HR department phrased the main focus of the new HR policy as follows:

> *Employment in Achmea is aimed at developing, using and rewarding your talents as an employee. We believe in the strength of the individual. Every employee is different. Think of differences with regard to gender, ethnic background, life stage, knowledge and experience, and the way in which you see life. Achmea wants to use the strength of these differences. We want to use your talents at the right moment for activities that fit with your talents, your wishes and your life stage.*

From policy to practices

Several months later, all the stakeholders involved in the process attended a works conference to discuss the interview findings and to begin the translation of this umbrella view into concrete action plans. To assure the link between HR outcomes and the business goals of each division, divisions were able to prioritise some practices over others. During the process of designing and implementing the HR practices, two deliberative bodies played an important role: the HR staff at corporate and division levels on the one hand, and the tripartite talks between Achmea as the employer, trade unions and the works council on the other. On a regular basis, the translation of the vision into various HR practices and the overall progress were discussed. After three years, the result was a mix of practices laid down in HR policies as well as in the collective agreement (see Box 28.2). Note that this categorisation into ability, motivation and opportunity practices is slightly arbitrary since some practices could be classified into more than one category.

Box 28.2: Achmea's high performance work practices

Ability practices

- team budgets for training and development (including extra budgets for teams/departments facing reorganisation)

- special attention to the recruitment of minorities (including refugees, immigrants and disabled people)

- encouragement of employees and supervisors to make personal development plans

- introduction of 'My Career' (virtual career centre on the intranet)

- health checks.

Motivation practices

- continuous dialogue between employees and their supervisors (evaluation and feedback)

- information about and support for internal promotion

- flexible working hours and distribution of hours over the year (collective labour agreement)

- opportunities to work from home.

Opportunity practices

- possibilities for job rotation

- networking opportunities (for example through networks for women, young professionals and lesbian, gay, transgender and bisexual employees)

- encouragement of employees to reflect upon their daily work practices and to come up with changes in work processes to improve the quality of service to customers (kaizen principle)[8]

- possibilities for voluntary community aid (collective labour agreement)

- maternity coaching to support women pursuing their career after return from maternity leave.

Results

The results of implementing these new HR practices are monitored using an annual survey. The results of this study show that an increasing number of employees are reporting that their talents are being recognised and used by the organisation. For example, more employees indicate that they have a job that fits their abilities and that they get more opportunities for personal development. Moreover, employees are more positive about the opportunities that Achmea provides to achieve a good work-life balance. The level of perceived work pressures has remained the same. These results indicate that employees are positive about the implemented HR practices. However, the survey results also show some downsides of these new practices – in particular the introduction of the principles of 'lean production' – with approximately 40 per cent of all employees reporting that the same amount of work has to be done with fewer people than a year earlier. The question is how these changes have affected employee and organisational outcomes.

Results from a different survey provide the opportunity to answer this question. Employees report that they are more satisfied with various aspects of their job (challenges in their work, pay, work pleasure, opportunities for development and promotion) than before the introduction of the new HR practices. Further, employees report that they are more willing to exert effort at work. Both employees and supervisors indicate that team performance has improved, meaning that customers get better value for money. These results indicate that both employees and Achmea have benefited (in terms of wellbeing and performance) from the implementation of these HR practices. In Box 28.3 the relationship between HPWSs and performance is elaborated upon using AMO theory.

Overall, the works council and trade unions assess these changes positively. They continue to evaluate the progress and negotiate on measures in the collective agreement that guarantee and facilitate employees' employability.

---

[8] The introduction of the kaizen principle is a part of the lean production system (Dankbaar 1997; Niepce & Molleman 1998). Generally, it is assumed that lean production does not fit an HPWS approach, because of its focus on standardised work processes. However, the kaizen principle does offer employees the opportunity to participate in decision making, which is a characteristic of an HPWS.

Box 28.3: HPWSs, AMO theory and performance

AMO theory

Boxall and Purcell (2003, p. 20) argue that, according to the AMO model, 'people perform well when:

- They are able to do so (they can do the job because they possess the necessary knowledge and skills);

- They have the motivation to do so (they will do the job because they want to and are adequately incentivised);

- Their work environment provides the necessary support and avenues for expression (for example, functioning technology and the opportunity to be heard when problems occur).'

Ability practices include selective recruitment and selection (getting the right people) and training and development (developing skills, knowledge and abilities). Motivation practices include performance appraisal (evaluation and feedback), performance-related pay, coaching and mentoring, employment security, internal promotion opportunities, fair pay and employee benefits. Opportunity practices include autonomy, employee involvement, job rotation, job enlargement, job enrichment, self-directed teamwork, communication and decentralisation of decision making.

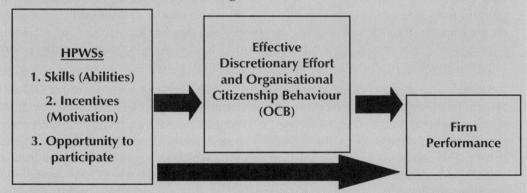

Source: adapted from Appelbaum, E, Bailey T, Berg P & Kalleberg, A 2000, *Manufacturing advantage: why high-performance work systems pay off*, Cornell University Press, Ithaca, p. 27.

HPWSs, AMO theory and Performance

A high performance work system that builds on the AMO theory is assumed to increase employee in-role and extra-role behaviour (Organ 1994; Williams & Anderson 1991). In other words, specific HR practices that increase employee abilities, that contribute to employee motivation and that stimulate opportunities to participate have a positive effect on discretionary effort in task performance (in-role behaviour) and 'the willingness of employees to walk the extra mile' without additional rewards (organisational citizenship behaviour (OCB) or extra-role behaviour) (Boselie 2010).

These OCB outcomes have the potential to positively enhance firm performance as defined by Beer *et al.* (1984) in terms of achieving organisational, individual and societal goals. There is also a direct relationship between HPWSs and employee outcomes. For example, employees who are offered the opportunity for training and development, or who are well paid, will be more satisfied with their jobs. Conversely, Appelbaum *et al.* (2000) report some potential downsides to implementing HPWSs: they suggest that some employees may experience greater stress and pressures of work.

Top managers and frontline supervisors

Two groups of internal stakeholders proved to be very important in the implementation of these practices at Achmea: frontline supervisors and top managers. Frontline supervisors are responsible for the enactment of HR practices. We also found that frontline supervisors who have better people management skills and are more motivated to support their employees are assessed more positively by their subordinates (see also Leisink & Knies 2011). The results of the above-mentioned survey also indicated that supervisors provided more support for their employees when they themselves were supported by their superiors. This finding encouraged the HR department and the executive board of Achmea to introduce employee-related targets. Supervisors are now not only evaluated on the financial targets they achieve, but also on their people management performance. This performance is measured by asking employees in the annual survey to assess the leadership behaviour of their supervisor. To improve the support provided to their employees, all supervisors received training in improving people management skills.

Achmea's top management showed their support by not only introducing soft targets (such as the supervisor's score for employee support as perceived by their team members) but also in other ways. When Achmea was facing the economic recession, the chairman of the executive board announced that Achmea would continue to renew its HR practices because this was a prerequisite for growth and stakeholder-value management. Through this, he acted as a role model: in showing leadership support he demonstrated that he practised what Achmea preaches.

Important aspects in creating an HPWS

HPWS

The Achmea case study is a clear example of the development of an HPWS that is aimed at achieving a sustained competitive advantage in a changing, highly competitive market. Appelbaum *et al.* (2000) define an HPWS as a bundle of HR practices aimed at creating employee abilities (A), motivation (M) and opportunities to participate (O). All three types of practices can be found in Achmea's HR system. Ability practices include team budgets allocated for training and development (intensive employee training and development), special attention for diversity in the recruitment process, the encouragement of employees and their supervisors to make personal development plans, the introduction of a virtual career centre on the intranet and the opportunity to apply for a health check. Motivational practices include continuous dialogue between employees and their supervisors (evaluation and feedback), opportunities for internal promotion and opportunities to work from home. Moreover, in the collective agreement, provisions are laid down for flexible working hours and the redistribution of hours across the year. Opportunity practices include possibilities for job rotation, network opportunities and the introduction of kaizen principles.

The notion of 'internal fit' is an important feature of an HPWS. The alignment of individual HR practices, within a bundle or system of practices, is thought to create synergy (Delery 1998). In other words, a fit between individual HR practices will strengthen the impact of HRM on performance outcomes. An internal fit between the individual HR practices in a coherent and consistent human resource system is assumed to lead to a higher performance than the sum of the individual HR practices (Kepes & Delery 2007). In the case of Achmea, the alignment of individual practices is effectively guaranteed because all practices are in line with the main vision. An example of a fit between individual HR practices that strengthens the impact on performance is the encouragement to make personal development plans in combination with budgets for training and development, opportunities for job rotation and internal promotion. As such, the system assures that all practices contribute to developing, using and rewarding the talents of all employees, regardless of their gender, ethnic background, life stage, knowledge and experience and the way in which they see life.

Comparing Achmea's HPWS to the list of possible HR practices provided by Boselie (2010, p. 134), it is noteworthy that Achmea did not include all possible AMO practices. Nevertheless, their approach still delivered positive outcomes. This observation is in line with the idea of so-called 'mini-bundles'. Based on extensive research, Guest, Conway & Dewe (2004) concluded that a limited set of HR practices can also result in heightened performance. The example of Achmea shows that creating an HPWS is not simply a matter of going through a checklist – it is important to align specific practices that fit with the overall HR strategy.

Contextual factors

Overall, the implementation of this HPWS resulted in positive employee and organisational outcomes. This success is partly rooted in the adoption of a partnership approach – a characteristic of the Rhineland model of capitalism which aims to create value for a range of diverse stakeholders (for example, shareholders, employees, trade unions and society) (Leisink & Greenwood 2007; Paauwe & Boselie 2003). Achmea decided, inspired by its cooperative roots, to involve representatives of the trade unions and the works council in the process, and to aim not only for high performance but also for employee wellbeing. Survey results confirm the working of the mutual gains principle: employees who are more satisfied with their jobs – and are therefore more willing to exert effort in their job – report that their teams perform better. Further, this is a mutually reinforcing mechanism: employees working in high performing teams report greater satisfaction. Having a customer-oriented focus contributed to these outcomes. For example, the introduction of 'lean production' principles was aimed at creating added value for customers but, at the same time, it also created opportunities for employees to participate more fully.

Taking a partnership approach has resulted in an HPWS that is firmly embedded in Achmea's HR strategy. HR practices are not only laid down in the organisation's HR policies, but also in the collective agreement. Achmea's innovation process shows that, contrary to what is often assumed, adopting a partnership approach not only involves dealing with constraints, it also requires sufficient leeway to make strategic choices (Boxall & Purcell 2003; Child 1997).

Process

About one year prior to the change process, Achmea agreed with the trade unions and the works council to renew their HR policies and practices, although a detailed blueprint that mapped out the changes was not yet available. This was because the HR department decided not to take a top-down approach but, rather, to involve various stakeholders in the process. This bottom-up approach included interviewing employees, employees' representatives and HR and other managers, installing a tripartite steering committee and allowing teams and departments to differentiate in their implementation of the HR practices. These elements all contributed to a sense of ownership by the different stakeholders, making them more willing to invest in the process. The HR department put a lot of effort into managing the relationship with the various stakeholders. For example, when some managers felt that the changes were more about employees than about the business, the HR team emphasised the consistency within the multiple goals. Moreover, they gave permission to send out a survey on the implementation to all employees and supervisors to demonstrate the win-win situation.

Actors in the implementation

Apart from the HR department, two other actors were critical in the implementation process: frontline managers and top managers. Line managers are responsible for implementing the HR policies and practices and, as such, employees' perceptions of the HPWS are heavily dependent on their supervisors' actions. Achmea has established conditions that contribute to an effective translation from HR rhetoric into reality. For example, all supervisors were trained to improve their people management skills, and employee-related targets were introduced to stimulate people management activities. Achmea's top management not only approved the introduction of soft targets, they also continued to show their support for the innovation process when Achmea was facing the economic recession. All these aspects continue to contribute to Achmea's high performance, a fact demonstrated by Achmea's second place in the ranking of best employers in the Netherlands.

To conclude, our study of Achmea shows that an HPWS's contribution to superior organisational performance is not only about the HR practices included but also about the process and the context. According to Kirby (2005, in Paauwe 2007), High Performance Organisations (HPOs) share some important features. Many of these are also characteristic of Achmea's approach to renewing its HR policy and practices. By taking a partnership approach and involving a range of stakeholders from the start of the process, a sense of ownership was created, as well as a collective state of mindfulness. By formulating an overarching HR philosophy, a shared mission was created. By acknowledging the crucial role of line managers in the implementation, it was recognised that leadership at all levels is important. These elements are all linked by the underlying ambition to create value for customers, employees, shareholders and society, and thereby contributed to the unique nature of Achmea's renewal of its HR policy and practices.

Discussion questions

1) Identify specific human resource practices within Achmea that serve multiple stakeholders' interests (mutual gains). Further, name at least two practices that have potential downsides for one or more stakeholders.

2) In what ways did the works council and trade unions assist in the design and introduction of the HPWS? What is your opinion about this type of employee representative participation in decision making (something that is a characteristic of the Rhineland model of capitalism)?

3) What factors contributed to the support from Achmea's top management for the organisational change process described?

4) Did any barriers exist that could have prevented the implementation of the HPWS by frontline managers? If so, what were these, and how could they be overcome?

References

Appelbaum, E, Bailey, T, Berg, P & Kalleberg, A 2000, *Manufacturing advantage: why high-performance work systems pay off*, Cornell University Press, Ithaca.

Beer, M, Spector, B, Lawrence, P, Mills, DQ & Walton, R 1984, *Human Resource Management: A General Manager's Perspective*, Free Press, New York.

Boselie, P 2010, *Strategic human resource management: A balanced approach*, McGraw-Hill, London.

Boxall, P & Purcell, J 2003, *Strategy and human resource management*, Palgrave Macmillan, New York.

Boxall, P & Purcell, J 2008, *Strategy and human resource management*, 2nd edn, Palgrave Macmillan, New York.

Child, J 1997, 'Strategic choice in the analysis of action, structure, organizations and environment: retrospect and prospect', *Organization Studies*, 18 (1): 43-76.

Dankbaar, B 1997, 'Lean production: denial, confirmation or extension of sociotechnical systems design?', *Human Relations*, 50: 567-583.

Delery, JE 1998, 'Issues of fit in strategic human resource management: Implications for research', *Human Resource Management Review,* 8 (3): 289-309.

Guest, D, Conway, N & Dewe, P 2004, 'Using sequential tree analysis to search for 'bundles' of HR practices', *Human Resource Management Journal,* 14 (1): 79-96.

Keegan, A & Boselie, P 2006, 'The lack of impact of dissensus inspired analysis on developments in the field of human resource management', *Journal of Management Studies,* 43 (7): 1492-1511.

Kepes, S & Delery, J 2007, 'HRM systems and the problem of internal fit', in P Boxall, J Purcell & PM Wright (eds), *The Oxford handbook of human resource management,* Oxford University Press, Oxford, pp. 385-404.

Kirby, J 2005, 'Toward a theory of high performance', *Harvard Business Review*: 30-40.

Leisink, P & Greenwood, I 2007, 'Company-level Strategies for Raising Basic Skills: A Comparison of Corus Netherlands and UK', *European Journal of Industrial Relations,* 13 (3): 341-360.

Leisink, P & Knies, E 2011, 'Line managers' support for older workers', *International Journal of Human Resource Management,* 22 (9): 1902-1917.

Niepce, W & Molleman, E 1998, 'Work design issues in Lean production from a sociotechnical systems perspective: neo-Taylorism or the next step in sociotechnical design?', *Human Relations,* 51: 259-287.

Organ, DW 1994, 'Organizational citizenship behavior and the good soldier', in M Rumsey, C Walker & J Harris (eds), *Personnel selection and classification,* Lawrence Erlbaum, Hillsdale, pp. 53-67.

Paauwe, J 2007, *HRM and Performance: In Search of Balance,* Inaugural lecture, Tilburg University, Tilburg.

Paauwe, J & Boselie, P 2003, 'Challenging 'strategic HRM' and the relevance of the institutional setting', *Human Resource Management Journal,* 13 (3): 56-70.

Verworn, B, Schwarz, D & Herstatt, C 2009, 'Changing workforce demographics: strategies derived from the resource-based view of HRM', *International Journal of Human Resources Development and Management,* 9 (2/3): 149-161.

Wall, TD & Wood, SJ 2005, 'The romance of human resource management and business performance, and the case for big science', *Human Relations,* 58 (4): 429-462.

Williams, LJ & Anderson, S 1991, 'Job satisfaction and organizational commitment as predictors of organizational citizenship and in-role behavior', *Journal of Management,* 17 (3): 601-617.

Part VI
Global Innovation, Strategy and People Management

Chapter 29

Reuters: Human Resource Management in global perspective

PAUL SPARROW AND CHRIS BREWSTER

Introduction

A critical challenge for organisations in the 21st century is the need to operate across national borders. Competing demands of global integration and local differentiation have highlighted the need to develop human resources as a source of competitive advantage (Brewster *et al.* 2008; Schuler, Dowling & De Cieri 1993; Taylor *et al.* 1998). Functional-level globalisation studies, such as this study of the management of human resource management, concentrate on different mechanisms of people, information, formalisation or centralisation-based integration, organisation design features and attitudinal orientations (Kim, Park, & Prescott 2003; Malbright 1995; Yip 1995). Human resource management is known (Rosenzweig & Nohria 1994) to be the aspect of management that is most localised, but here too the benefits of standardisation are enormous.

How do major international businesses deal with these complexities? What is happening to HRM in a global context? Can we build on existing models of IHRM in order better to capture the complexity of modern approaches to the topic? To shed light on such questions, this case study focuses on firm-level processes associated with the globalisation of the HRM function (Brewster, Sparrow & Harris 2005: Sparrow, Brewster & Harris 2004). The case study signals four substantive issues in managing the globalisation process at this level of analysis:

- the need to be pragmatic in strategy

- the challenge of keeping Global HRM aligned with the business context

- the need to accommodate reverse globalisation processes

- the need to nuance the regional role.

Reuters context

Reuters in 2008 was an important multinational in the high-technology information industry, providing financial information and more general news to the financial sector and to news organisations. It had grown, and continued to grow, through acquisitions. With revenues of over £2.5 billion it employed around 17,000 staff in over 100 countries and had nearly 200 in-country sites and establishments. It had a population of over 800 expatriates which, at around five per cent of the workforce, signified the high levels of international mobility needed. There were three regional headquarters: Europe, Middle East and Africa (Regional HQ in Switzerland); the Americas (Regional HQ in the USA); and Asia/Pacific (Regional HQ in Singapore). It operated through business divisions, a series of geographic sales and service channels and shared resources operations.

This had not always been the case. Before 2001, Reuters described itself as a 'confederation'. It went public in the mid-1980s and this was followed by very rapid growth. It was predominantly a geography-focused business. Each national senior company officer was seen as a 'master of the universe'. Accountability for profit and loss was held by country managers. There were a number of atomised mini-businesses that each 'owned' their sales, marketing, product development, finance and HRM. There were a few global groups, for example in the consulting and legal operations. The problem was that this structure led to 'autonomy with scale'. For example, the business had over 70 development centres located in high cost countries. There were over 1,300 products based on dozens of different technical delivery architectures, 300 offices around the world (often with multiple offices in the same country), and 26 different client billing databases processing invoices. In a similar vein, HRM had 34 different HRM information systems, 21 performance appraisal forms and 8 grading structures. In order to address this, from 2003 to 2005 there was a large and extensive change program designed to reinvigorate the culture and behaviour and based on the motto of 'Fix It, Strengthen It, Grow It'.

Standardising the HRM organisation and structure was a key part of the change process. Before 2001, HRM had a disaggregated and largely regional structure. Budget and headcount was held locally and there was little global process or coordination. The focus was very much on transactional aspects of HRM, and this administrative requirement was delivered principally through HRM generalists. There was no HRM representation on most of the senior leadership teams. The only corporate centre specialists were in remuneration, international assignments, executive development and recruitment.

However, a degree of regionalisation of both the businesses and HRM were also needed. Organisations must consider cost efficiencies in the delivery of their HRM services across different geographical areas. And, they have to identify the new HRM coordination needs as they move from line-of-country reporting arrangements towards global lines of business. It is necessary to provide the systems to support HRM strategies that are being executed on a global basis. In Reuters, there was a managed process of migration, often initially towards regional HRM service centres, with an aspiration of eventually moving towards global ones. This meant that the HRM function had to understand which of their processes really had to be different – should remain localised - and which ones must be core to all countries. Making these decisions was not easy.

Being pragmatic in strategy

When the HRM function started to standardise its processes it faced four challenges: managers were busy working on the general business transformation; HRM was already stretched managing redundancies and change; there was no appetite for any new HRM process; and there was no budget for the work.

The change process was therefore driven by pragmatic concerns, starting with changes to create a globally consistent performance management process, followed by talent assessment, then compensation processes.

The change management processes were owned by the business and supported by HRM, so were positioned and embedded in the cycle of business activities, forming part of an annual HRM 'roadmap'.

Reuters believed it was better to set strategy globally, and then let the regions drive the agenda that suited them. The global/local divide was driven by the following prerogatives:

- high level strategy was set globally

- HRM Business Partners worked with leadership teams globally and nationally to develop a talent pipeline in the right context for their needs

- some central initiatives (e.g. reverse mentoring for senior leaders) were replicated locally as required

- accountability was taken by the line, with overall ownership held by the group leadership team

- regions took responsibility for leading initiatives that resonated with local needs

- support and budget was given to local employee groups to encourage mutual support of activities.

The organisation became increasingly aware of the need for global consistency – they could not afford for the information that they provided to vary depending upon source. They had structured their business model to reflect this globalised reality and invested heavily in a globally applicable management information system with a strong electronic HRM component. The objective was for every manager and every employee to have access to the HRM information they needed from the website and for the global HRM function to have information on all aspects of HRM around the business, wherever located.

Keeping global HRM aligned with the business context

Reuters introduced a centralised policy but within a geographically dispersed finance and HRM organisation. In parallel to the overall globalisation strategy, decisions were taken on the business model, sourcing and shoring options. This had implications for what was and should be the retained HRM organisation. Many corporate functions were centralised, but finance, business service processing and software development activity was sourced to emerging markets. Despite a clear direction of travel for the global HRM function, the agenda evolved as the challenges of execution developed.

Reuters created offshore transactional centres in lower cost locations. This involved a large deployment into India, Bangkok, and Beijing. Its service centre provided blended finance and HRM support covering areas such as commission, payroll and maintenance of the core systems structure. The intention was to move up the value-chain to perform activities beyond those of a transactional nature.

> ... The HRM team ...have a hybrid structure at the moment... regional shared service centres and they feel that that's working. Standardisation is ...the challenge... harmonisation of benefits, contracts etc. That's much easier to do in a finance environment than in an HRM environment, because of the consultation practice... [but when] we picked up payroll and tried to find a common way of doing things, it's just virtually impossible. Given just the requirement of each particular geographic or legal location, the advantages of trying to drive a single harmonised process becomes less obvious. (Global Head of Finance, Group and Shared Services)

For HRM professionals, the issue of return on investment in e-enablement was nuanced:

> ... it depends on which part of the agenda you're talking about... for organisation design... effectiveness, the answer is probably no... Areas like employee engagement, diversity or culture change, there's a lot you can do with technology... In diversity... we've done some really cool stuff... putting together a website and reference materials ...internal blogs to have dialogue... ... hosted chats with senior leaders... technology (for survey data) where all of the HRM business partners access reports themselves and run analysis locally. (Global Head of Organisation Development)

Accommodating reverse processes

Reuters' HRM function also found that the offshoring process in itself created a need for close alignment of HRM and the business:

> ...We started...a major transformation program to define the organisational footprint that we were going to have, narrowed the number of software development sites we have...moved a material amount of work off to lower cost centres both in Bangkok, but also in Beijing, where we are building up... so we've got quite a bit of experience in setting up offshore centres... we're really quite good at that. We've got a very sophisticated HRM person, based

in Asia, who oversees that. This is all quite bespoke... immersed in the transformation program... and the HRM intervention is defined on the basis of what is happening there. (Global Head of HR and Business Divisions)

The HRM role in managing offshoring to the Indian, Thai and Chinese sites created its own range of policy decisions and activities, which had to be layered into the overall globalisation strategy, including:

- aggressively recruiting and building up centres

- hiring in, and later 'creating', managers with the relevant capabilities

- supporting downsizing in other parts of the business

- knowledge sharing

- knowledge transfer

- pursuing a broad learning and development support effort

- redefining roles to change the conditioning and nature of key job roles

- extending career paths

- managing the entrepreneurship challenge: creating new businesses in the context of large existing businesses

- making decisions about the level of flexibility in HRM process standardisation: creating what was called 'HRM lite'.

This led to some reverse pressures and a need to re-localise in some areas:

... we... recognised that in order for us to properly grow businesses within the broader context, we needed to set up a framework that was... 'HRM lite'. Lighten up on our approaches to compensation, how we go about recruiting people, even down to the application form they would fill out... Instead of having a new business always be some sort of frustrating exception to the rule.... as we go through very fast paced growth in a new area where we haven't had people before... we recognise that it is different environment, and configure our HRM policies and approaches in that way. We worked closely with the business leader on... his (sic) business needs... and put together a framework looking to external best practice with other companies that have configured their internal growth agenda in this way (Global Head of HR and Business Divisions)

[From a business perspective] We... need to be more sensitive... that one size doesn't fit all from a remuneration perspective... as much as we need a global philosophy, we need to recognise that either on a regional or a business level there may be a need to determine whether or not the programme works inside that and if it doesn't what's the variance and allow for some of that flexibility, because what happens is, it becomes very frustrating for the managers and its perceived that HRM is just impeding their need to retain people. (Regional HRM)

Nuancing the regional role

The main drive at the time of the research was towards globalisation, but clearly with the need for some regional nuancing, as a buffer to avoid the trap of over-centralisation. As one regional specialist put it:

> The best way to say it is, everything is done on a global basis from an HRM strategy perspective to make sure the global focusing on the key deliverables if you will, on a consistent basis across the board and philosophy is the same, So that's the overall framework. And then on a regional basis, we look at what's unique in the local environment that needs to be factored in. I don't think of it as a strategy; I think of it as a sort of hands-on engagement with the business, I'm trying to think of holes in it now. (Regional HRM)

The dangers of over-centralisation were mentioned a number of times:

> In order to rationalise things across the world… we were forced to increase our fixed costs base salaries [in some geographies], and reduce our variable costs on commissions to get more in line. Well that was really non-productive, more expensive, but it did fit the global framework. (HQ Director)

The regional layer would hopefully overcome these difficulties. But, this role was not always understood. The changes were creating a complex organisational structure. In some cases responsibilities were not clear or, even where they were, certain key managers were not happy with them:

> It's a very complex business….I've tried for many years to think of a more complicated business, how could you make a business more complicated?

> And that's the problem with any part of the business, if you centralise everything too much and make blanket statements for the world. It will in fact damage the parts of the world that you are not living in. So we have a centralised thing called the Global Role Framework, which to me is not instigated by HRM maybe. But it's a complete nonsense. The global role framework leaves less flexibility for people to create teams that are relevant to their local market place, and secondly it makes sure that no one has 100% of the job….so actually nobody is accountable for anything….the global role framework is a disaster. (HQ Director)

As a consequence the role of the regional offices was creating some concern.

> We are over-matrixed. HQ does not understand our situation; there have to be exceptions for this market. Regional is strange for us. Imagine trying to run the US from Mexico in Spanish, no-one would do it – but that's what happens here in Japan. I generally go direct to HQ. (Subsidiary CEO)

Some HRM specialists simply by-passed the regional office, or at least did not seem to even think about them when they were explaining their role:

> My main responsibility is to implement the corporate mission in our country as well as to coordinate the local HRM practices and local management. Just me and someone else here. In this sense our role is quite generalist. At the

local level we just contact HQ every time we need specialist support. *(Country HRM manager)*

Here is one country-level specialist explaining her HRM approach, and making the assumption that the main dialogue was between central and country units only:

> *What drives our strategy is… growth, at least locally. HRM has to support this strategy… Our main goal in HR is attract, retain and motivate those people who are able to make the organisation in the best condition to achieve its strategy. Most of the guidelines of our strategy, culture and philosophy come from abroad. At HQ they develop HRM policies and then they ask us to adapt them to our local context… We are supposed to adapt them to our legislation… The main responsibility for the development of HRM policies relies on the central unit of the company… All the HRM processes are elaborated (there)… at the local level we just implement the decisions they take… They elaborate global frameworks, but in doing that they always take into account the specificity of each country. (Country HRM)*

Being reminded of the regional level, she said:

> *From an HRM point of view region is not so relevant. (Country HRM)*

This apparent invisibility of the regional layer did not apply everywhere. In those countries where there were few HRM resources, usually the smaller countries, the HRM expertise provided by the regional centre was in fact much appreciated:

> *When you…are entering into new markets you need the talent to really operate in these markets…So the question…is how do we attract this talent… convince a potential candidate that we have the right strategy… in this market… the proliferation of many competitors in countries where salary conditions are better…[means] we have talent retention and… talent nurturing and growth issues. It is on these kinds of issues where the Regional HRM operation comes into its own. (Regional Director)*

Even here, it might be observed that the regional role can be pushed towards the transactional rather than strategic.

Summary and overview

So what can be learned by examining the HRM function globalisation process?

1. The IHRM function has to work through the structural and organisation design issues that changes in the organisation's business model have invoked. It needs to analyse what decisions on the business model, sourcing and shoring mean for the retained HRM organisation.

2. The global HRM function has to structure itself and design its service offerings in a way that enables it to support these wider business changes, but also to apply the learning from this to the decisions it makes about its own operations. HRM specialists do not just need to understand global strategy but, importantly, they also need to

        understand the new globally-executed business models that have become possible.

3.   For the HRM department, facilitating global sourcing and shoring options creates a significant agenda for the function. This agenda, however, also creates a unique set of pressures on the HRM function's globalisation path. Although an organisation might be pursuing a strategy based in global standardisation, managing offshoring can create a separate and counter force for re-localisation.

4.   To unravel these complexities, it is important to understand the different arguments that are used to demonstrate the value associated with key developments such as offshoring. This could be seen in three ways: creating value, leveraging value and protecting and improving value.

5.   Although the HRM strategy may be designed on a global basis to ensure a focus on key deliverables, this often just sets an overall framework. On a regional basis, attention shifts to what is unique in the local environment. This factoring in local insight does not constitute a strategy, but rather a hands-on engagement with the business. This is inevitably associated with complex organisational structures, meaning that in some cases, responsibilities are not clear and the ability to create teams that are relevant to their local market place becomes more difficult. These tensions have to be borne however as there are many dangers to over-centralisation.

Discussion questions

1) How closely has Reuters been able to mirror the business structure in its HRM structure?

2) How successful was Reuters in handling the standardisation/ differentiation conundrum?

3) What steps could the global HRM function take to make it work better?

4) What tensions does the current system create and how could they be resolved?

5) What changes might be anticipated if business turns down?

6) What is the role of the regional HRM office? Is this a useful reflection of the business organisation, or is it in fact a costly redundancy? How could the regional HRM office make a bigger contribution?

References

Adler, NJ & Ghadar, F 1990, 'Strategic human resource management: a global perspective', in R Pieper (ed.), *Human Resource Management in International Comparison*, De Gruyter, Berlin/New York.

Ashkenas, R, Ulrich, D, Jick, T & Kerr, S 1995, *The Boundaryless Organization*, Jossey-Bass, San Francisco, CA

Bartlett, CA & Ghoshal, S 1989, *Managing Across Borders: The Transnational Solution*, Harvard Business School Press, Boston, MA.

Birkinshaw, JM & Morrison, AJ 1995, 'Configurations of strategy and structure in subsidiaries of multinational corporations', *Journal of International Business Studies*, 4: 729-753.

Brewster, C, Sparrow, PR & Vernon, G 2007, *International Human Resource Management*. 2nd edn, CIPD, Wimbledon.

Brewster, C, Carey, L, Dowling, P, Grobler, P, Holland, P & Warnich, S 2008, *Contemporary Issues in Human Resource Management: Gaining a Competitive Advantage*, 3rd edn, Oxford University Press, South Africa, Cape Town.

Brewster, C, Sparrow, PR & Harris, H 2005, 'Towards a New Model of Globalising HRM', *International Journal of Human Resource Management*, 16 (6): 949-970.

Edwards, T & Rees, C 2006, *International Human Resource Management*, Pearson, London.

Evans, PAL, Pucik, V & Barsoux, J-L 2002. *The Global Challenge: Frameworks for International Human Resource Management*, McGraw-Hill Irwin, Boston.

Kim, K, Park, J-H & Prescott, JE 2003, 'The global integration of business functions: a study of multinational businesses in integrated global industries', *Journal of International Business Studies*, 34: 327-344,

Levitt, T 1983, 'The Globalization of the Markets', *Harvard Business Review*, 3: 92-102.

Malbright, T 1995, 'Globalisation of an ethnographic firm', *Strategic Management Journal*, 16: 119-141.

Porter, ME 1990, *The competitive advantage of nations*, MacMillan Press, London.

Prahalad, CK & Doz, Y 1987, *The multinational mission: Balancing global demands and global vision*, Free Press, New York.

Rosenzweig, PM & Nohria, N 1994, 'Influences on Human Resource Development Practices in Multinational Corporations', *Journal of International Business Studies*, 25 (2): 229-251.

Rugman, AM & Collinson, S 2008, *International Business*, Financial Times/Prentice Hall, London.

Schuler, RS, Dowling, PJ & De Cieri, H 1993, 'An integrative framework of strategic international human resource management', *International Journal of Human Resource Management* 4(4): 717- 764.

Sparrow, PR, Brewster, C & Harris, H 2004, *Globalizing Human Resource Management*, Routledge, London.

Taylor, S, Beechler, S, Najjar, M & Ghosh, BC 1998, 'A partial test of a model of strategic international human resource management', *Advances in International Comparative Management*, 12: 207-36.

Yip, GS 1995, *Total global strategy*, Prentice-Hall, Englewood Cliffs, NJ.

Acknowledgements

We would like to thank the line management and HRM specialists and staff of Reuters (pre ThomsonReuters), at headquarters and at six major national and regional subsidiaries, for the time they spent with us, for completing the network analyses and the questionnaires and for their interest in our work.

Chapter 30

Implementing HRM within multinational corporations: Localisation or global standardisation?

Anastasia Kynighou

Background

BankCo[9] is a large Northern European bank – its three key businesses are: retail banking and financial services; global investment management and services; and corporate and investment banking. BankCo was founded more than 120 years ago and is well into the maturity stage of its life cycle. Currently the firm employs over 100,000 staff worldwide in more than 80 countries. In the late 1990s, a subsidiary company, FinanceCo, was created. The aim of FinanceCo was to focus on BankCo's operation outside the country-of-origin. Overall, BankCo's corporate mission is to increase its profitability through an effective growth strategy. The basis for this vision, as it has been claimed, is a vigorous model that the parent company attempts to diffuse to all parts of the Multinational Corporation (MNC). BankCo also aims to disseminate a set of core corporate values to all employees in all subsidiaries. The goal is that these values will govern world-wide operations, even if practices differ among subsidiaries. The values are professionalism, team spirit and innovation.

BankCo expanded in Eastern Europe and Africa through the acquisition of local banks. Thus, BankCo prefers to acquire local knowledge and expertise since the banking sector is sensitive to local and global market pressures and is frequently controlled by national central banks.

---

[9] Guide to Respondents: Head of Administration and Finance Domain (HAF), Head of Human Resources (HHR), HR Officer I (HRI), HR Officer II (HRII).

History of the local sub-unit

BankCo started operating in Cyprus in the early 80s through a partnership between BankCo and two other foreign banks. In the early 90s BankCo purchased the shares from one of its two partners, hence increasing its participation to 51 per cent. Subsequently, the name of the parent company was adopted in Cyprus in an attempt to transfer the former's model to the Cypriot market. Under the legal status of an 'offshore' company, BankCo only served non-Cypriot clients. During this time, the banking sector's trade union had no legal rights in the workplace.

BankCo - Cyprus Limited started operating ten years later as a fully licensed local bank, catering to residents in addition to non-resident clientele. BankCo in Cyprus provides financial services, such as corporate banking, retail banking and private banking. As argued in corporate documents, BankCo Cyprus aims to use capabilities found at both the top and local level in order to provide creative solutions that cater to the needs of the local market. Hence, in this case customer needs seem to drive local strategy. However, the opposing drive comes from FinanceCo, whose reason-for-being is to *control* subsidiaries (through explicit guidelines and set targets) and ensure that the brand-image is preserved.

Size and market position

The Cypriot subsidiaries, like all subsidiaries outside the country-of-origin, are also part of FinanceCo. Currently, BankCo employs close to 200 people in seven branches around Cyprus. The general manager (GM) is a home-country national, and to be appointed to that post a person is required to have at least five years of international work experience. This is a strategic choice by the parent company which appoints home-country nationals to the positions of GM and deputy GM in all foreign subsidiaries (Bartlett & Ghoshal 1989; Mohan 2006; Perlmutter 1969). Moreover, ten non-Cypriots, who are now Cypriot nationals because they are married to Cypriots, work at BankCo. This indicates that the vast majority of employees and top management are Cypriots and even non-Cypriots have personal reasons for living in the island and are not part of expatriate missions or international assignments – bar the GM and his deputy.

BankCo's actual market position is difficult to pinpoint; however, it competes in a sector that is dominated by two big Cypriot banks; Bank of Cyprus and Marfin Popular Bank. This sector has seen a significant number (considering the Cypriot market's size) of foreign banks, some of them Greek, entering in recent years – especially since 2004 when Cyprus entered the EU. Indeed the EU put pressure on Cyprus to promote competition between firms and limit oligopolistic or monopolistic tactics used until then.

In turn, competition for staff among banks has changed because, until recently, there had been a 'gentlemen's agreement' among the banks. The implicit expectation was that 'you don't touch my employees, I don't touch yours'. As competition became fiercer, this agreement collapsed and employees are now allowed and expected to move from one bank to another. This new development now affects employment decisions especially regarding workforce size, employee turnover and labour costs. BankCo's employee turnover reached 10 per cent in 2008, which is considered to be quite high due to the sectoral mobility of staff.

HR department and HR philosophy

Interestingly enough, employees own seven per cent of the firm's capital; thus they are significant stakeholder group. As such, BankCo's HRM philosophy, as explained by the top management of the subsidiary, is that the bank be staffed with high calibre individuals who will lead the firm to more successful paths. As a result, learning and development is extremely important for BankCo, and the aim of the HR Department is to develop its staff since their expertise will affect the services provided to clients.

HR within BankCo is no longer seen merely as a low-level management tool and has acquired a more strategic role in recent years. This is reflected in the sub-unit's new structure and hence indicates that HRM is currently perceived as strategic.

> Last year I was reporting to the administration and support director. The HR was perceived as something administrative, something bureaucratic. This year I am reporting straight to the GM - because he believes in the strategic role the HR has to play in the sub – and am also part of the management committee. Still, we are more of an HR function at the moment rather than HRM but things are changing. (HHR)

One limitation in adopting more sophisticated HR practices lies in the fact that the HR department is comparatively small. It comprises the head of HR, a staff facilitator (who is responsible for financial loans provided to BankCo's staff), one training officer and two recruitment and performance officers. This is summarised in the Figure 30.1:

Figure 30.1 Structure of HR department – BankCo

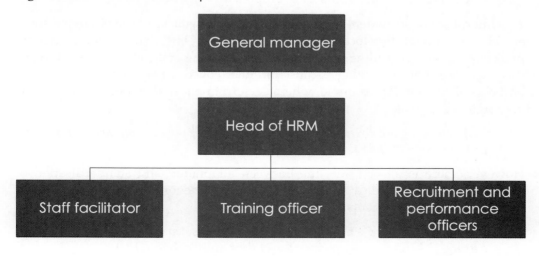

The local workplace of BankCo Cyprus is also greatly affected by the presence of Enosi Trapezikon Ypallilon Kyprou (ETYK); the banking sector trade union. In fact, more than 95 per cent of the workforce are members of ETYK, and as HHR claims,

> ETYK is so strong so there is not really much point in managers trying to resist them. It's a matter of 'if you can't beat them, join them.'

The biggest conflict that occurred between local and home country management concerned the working hours of the Cypriot workforce.

> Headquarters (HQ) said that we have to work 8am-5pm like everyone else in Europe and the answer from Cyprus was simple: NO. Collective agreement says bank's employees have to work between 7.30am and 2.30pm and it was very hard for them to accept that. They would ask us 'but when do you actually work then?' This is actually one of the things that makes the bank sector attractive for employees and there was nothing that BankCo could do to change it (sic).

Implementation of HRM practices: Localisation v standardisation

The major question when examining HR implementation within MNCs is the extent to which HR practices are adopted from the top level (standardisation) or adapted to local contingencies (localisation).

In the case of BankCo, and according to local managers, guidelines are imposed by HQ but the application of the practices follows local rules. At the same time, the relationship between the subsidiary's management and HQ is very formal and the GM of Cyprus reports directly to the board of directors and the retail banking manager of BankCo. This depicts how home and host country effects interplay to shape local HRM (Bjorkman & Lervik 2007; Edwards, Colling & Ferner 2007; Pulignano 2006; Rees & Edwards 2009; Sippola & Smale 2007).

This interplay is also evident when comparing the key tasks of the HR department at the top and at the local level. The corporate HR department is mainly preoccupied with recruiting, promoting and retaining staff. However, in Cyprus this logic does not exist either because of either collective agreements or because of the local culture. For example, whereas recruitment in the country-of-origin is very rigid, in Cyprus,

> [...] you still get calls from people who put [social] pressure on you to hire their daughter or their nephew etc. (HAF, sic)

However, there is a very fine line between adaptation and standardisation of practices and this is not a straightforward phenomenon as one would expect. Despite the above comments, it was also claimed that

> The main framework is the same. Minor adaptations depend on differences in culture. [...] HQ gives us an overview of their expectations. (HRI)

These indicate there is potentially extensive scope for adaptation of internal procedures. This is welcomed by HQ as long as the final outcome is consistent with standards set out in the main framework. Adaptations often take place in Cyprus since most line managers are host-country nationals. This is, in turn, due to increased local educational levels of local managers which allows them greater understanding of global targets. In contrast, in countries like Greece where culture is quite similar but the business system is quite different, all line managers are expatriate managers, and are '*planted*' there by the parent company (HAF).

In addition, many control mechanisms are employed by the parent company and are applied to all subsidiaries. For example, HQ controls all subsidiaries through 'audit missions', where people from the country-of-origin or FinanceCo visit Cyprus in regular intervals. Moreover, once per year there is a general audit where each department prepares reports that are then sent to HQ. Results from each subsidiary are then compared to those of other subsidiaries. This benchmarking technique creates internal competition among subsidiaries but also sets performance standards throughout the organisation.

The (expatriate) general managers have functional roles in all subsidiaries and are expected to carry out the same tasks in all locations. In fact, HAF claims that

> If the GM changes, this will not affect how the bank will work at all. Their approach might be different but practices will remain the same. They actually try to have the least possible impact on you as possible.

From this statement and based on the local managers' perceptions, it can be assumed that GMs are used as yet another control mechanism. They allow local managers to shape their practices according to the demands of the local market/workforce. However, at the same time they play a critical role in ultimately validating procedures so as to ensure that service standards and strategic objectives are met.

Nonetheless, local HR practices are also shaped by a global framework called the Operations Directive. This framework, which is diffused to all parts of the organisation, includes all guidelines of BankCo under which all subsidiaries should operate. In addition, it provides frameworks which local managers need to use when developing their local HR policies and explicitly outlines key objectives and tasks, which are standardised in all subsidiaries. This is especially important since the firm is growing through mergers and acquisitions. When acquiring brownfield sites these usually carry with them their own culture, practices and business system; hence a common framework exists to ensure internal consistency.

The Operations Directive has three main uses. First, it can be used by subsidiaries as a tool for communication between FinanceCo business departments and the various subsidiaries in order to exchange support on the company's topics and projects, shared concepts and vocabulary. In addition, it is used as a tool of organisation, to help in setting up organisational projects and drafting job descriptions, and to provide a style guide for writing instructions and procedures. Third, it is a tool to assist in change management, and is used for training support when putting in place new principles of organisation, or for the implementation of information systems etc.

BankCo also uses training as a mechanism to increase consistency throughout subsidiaries. Training courses for the local trainers are frequently organised either in the home country or in other countries (like Slovenia or Czech Republic). Their purpose is to support local subsidiaries, to assist in developing their respective levels of expertise, to diffuse 'best practices' to subsidiaries and to keep people up-to-date. To sum up, FinanceCo provides strong frameworks/tools that local managers use to accommodate the needs of their own subsidiaries, while at the same time meeting FinanceCo's objectives and leading to increased consistency of internal processes within the MNC.

Examples of HR practices that are adjusted to suit local standards include recruitment and training. For instance, the Staff Training Guide (which is inspired by the Guide to Training prepared by FinanceCo) states that regardless of the local unit's size or structure, and over and above the local regulations, the efficient implementation of a training plan requires the involvement of a number of key players. Still, 'players' refers to local managers. General management, along with HR, set the priority objectives of the company and domains, while HR itself is responsible for delivering the training issued in the evaluation.

Thereafter, HR works with the Heads of the Domains and Functions in order to identify the collective needs of the functions, as well as needs of individual employees. These are then prioritised and in turn a training plan is established. General management, the management team and HR then validate the training plan which is then implemented and evaluated by HR. It is evident that local managers (i.e. Heads of Domains) make decisions based on the local department's needs. Nonetheless, these needs derive from the strategic planning set by and validated by general management in Cyprus. Keeping in mind that the GM is always an expatriate, the attempt by HQ to exercise control on how these needs are shaped and to control the plans before being implemented becomes apparent.

Likewise, for staff recruitment, the policy states that the HR function of the bank holds the responsibility for all matters relating to the recruitment of new staff. However, this department/function is always performed in consultation with the relevant head(s) of domain(s) of the Bank, i.e. the line managers. Eventually, for a practice to be implemented, the approval of the general manager is required. Again, the role of the GM as a 'gatekeeper' is evident.

Summary

The case study of BankCo Cyprus illustrates how different pressures are exercised on the MNC to ultimately shape HRM at the local level. In addition, it was made evident that these influences can be both internal to the firm (or even internal to the specific sub-unit) as well as external. The case study highlights how the MNC strives to legitimise its actions in the host environment, while ensuring that internal procedures and processes are consistent in all parts of the organisation (Kostova & Roth 2002; Rosenzweig & Nohria 1994). On the one hand, the use of a number of internal control mechanisms (i.e. global policies, expatriate managers etc.) facilitate attempts to transfer practices from the top (HQ) to the bottom (subsidiary) level of the organisation. These mechanisms not only make local managers accountable to HQ but can also been seen as a benchmarking technique, which might create internal competition between various parts of the MNC. Moreover, expatriate managers play a critical role, not so much in shaping locally implemented practices, but in ensuring that these are within corporate expectations and that they do not bare any financial or other liability. In addition, evidence from this case study highlights how internal parameters, such as the subsidiary's own age, size or even type of ownership, can have a significant role in moulding HR practices.

Further, external contingencies such as the national culture and institutions shape the implementation of HRM. Despite distinctive attempts by HQ to transfer certain employment practices to Cyprus (i.e. working hours), this initiative was undermined by the presence and relative strength that the sectoral TU enjoys. Yet, it appears that sectoral patterns are changing due to global pressures. Moreover, the host-country's national culture, sometimes implicitly, affects how employment decisions are made in the local subsidiary. Customer expectations, employee expectations, employee preferences and ultimately the demand and supply of workforce, are shaped to a certain extent by local culture and this will be reflected in the choices of local management as well. As such, the expatriate manager's role is to ensure that either the local culture or institutions will not jeopardise the local unit's performance or damage the MNC's global brand.

Hence, actors at both the top and local level should appreciate how these various factors interplay together to ultimately shape the set of HR practices implemented in foreign parts of MNCs.

Discussion questions

1) A number of factors appear to influence the implementation of HRM within local sub-units of MNCs. Literature tends to classify these into institutional, cultural and organisational factors. Identify the key influences, whether internal or external, that shape HRM at the local level of a MNC and classify them according to these clusters.

2) In your opinion, how does the MNC achieve internal consistency while at the same time remaining legitimate in the host-country environment? Do you think that there is a conflict between these two pressures?

3) Critically assess the role of expatriate managers in the local unit. Do you think they facilitate or hinder any attempts by the MNC to transfer HR practices? Why?

References

Bartlett, CA & Ghoshal, S 1989, *Managing across borders: The transnational solution*, Boston, MA: Harvard Business School Press.

Bjorkman, I & Lervik, JEB 2007, "Transferring HR practices within Multinational Corporations", *Human Resource Management Journal*, 17(4): 320-335.

Edwards, T, Colling, T & Ferner, A 2007, "Conceptual approaches to the transfer of employment practices in multinational companies: an integrated approach", *Human Resource Management Journal*, 17(3): 201 – 217.

Kostova, T & Roth, K 2002, "Adoption of an organizational practice by subsidiaries of multinational corporations: Institutional and relational effects", *Academy of Management Journal*, 45(1): 215 – 233.

Mohan, A 2006, "Variation of practices across multiple levels within transnational corporations", in M Geppert & M Mayer (eds), *Global, National and Local practices in multinational companies*, London: Palgrave Macmillan.

Perlmutter, H 1969, "The tortuous evolution of the multinational corporation", *Columbia Journal of World Business*, January-February: 9- 18.

Pulignano, V 2006, "The diffusion of employment practices of US-based multinationals in Europe. A case study comparison of British- and Italian-based subsidiaries", *British Journal of Industrial Relations*, 44(3): 497 – 518.

Rees, C & Edwards, T 2009, "Management strategy and HR in international mergers: choice, constraint and pragmatism", *Human Resource Management Journal*.

Rosenzweig, PM & Nohria, N 1994, "Influences on Human Resource Management Practices in Multinational Corporations", *Journal of International Business Studies*, 25: 229 – 251.

Sippola, A & Smale, A 2007, "The global integration of diversity management: a longitudinal case study", *International Journal of Human Resource Management*, 18: 1895-1916.

Chapter 31

Managing international talent in a highly decentralised multinational enterprise

ANTHONY MCDONNELL AND HUGH SCULLION

Introduction

This case explores some of the key issues and challenges faced by a European-owned, building materials sector multinational enterprise (MNE), which has grown rapidly over the past 40 years based largely on an international strategy of cross-border acquisitions. The case will highlight links between business strategy and global talent management and more particularly, the role of the corporate HR function in the context of a company with a culture committed to delivering superior performance through a highly decentralised approach to managing international business operations. This case will highlight the complexity of staffing and talent management issues in this context both in developed markets and also in the growing emerging markets in Central and Eastern Europe and Asia. The talent management challenges are arguably more acute in these regions due to greater cultural and institutional differences, resulting in a particular demand for a distinctive type of managerial talent that can operate effectively in these culturally complex and geographically distant markets (Scullion & Collings 2011)

Background and context

European Buildings Materials Company[10] (EBMC) is a large, publicly listed, European headquartered MNE, operating in the building materials industry. In particular, EBMC targets three core businesses covering both residential and non-residential customer bases:

---

[10] This is a pseudonym to protect the company's identity.

1. Primary materials (e.g. cement, aggregates, asphalts)

2. Building products (e.g. precast concrete products, fencing)

3. Distribution (e.g. builder's merchants and specialist distribution).

The EBMC strategy is one of vertical integration in terms of manufacturing and horizontal integration through servicing the breadth of building material product customers. EBMC operates multiple organisational structures consisting of global business functions, geographic regions and international product divisions. Each of the three core businesses report to a European or American structure who report to the seven group functions (finance, human resources, risk management, corporate social responsibility, investor relations, environment, and health and safety). These functions then report to the chief executive officer. There is a mixed product and region-based organisation structure, which fits well with the decentralised approach allowing for a high level of flexibility for local conditions. This approach is essential for building materials companies due to the localised nature of the industry. Consequently, the development of strong management sensitive to the local market and cultural context is critical.

Over the past 40 years the company has developed from a small local player to a global enterprise with operations in more than 30 countries with a global workforce of approximately 80,000 people. Some 90 per cent of this employment is accounted for outside of EBMC's home country. The company has developed a major presence in mature markets in Western Europe and North America, which accounts for approximately 85 per cent of business, and more recently there has also been considerable growth in a number of emerging markets including Central and Eastern Europe (CEE), South America and Asia with a growing focus on the Chinese and Indian markets. The relatively limited nature of these operations in developing regions is illustrated by the organisational structure which sees the Indian and Chinese operations reporting to the European division.

International business growth strategy

Since the formation of the company in the early 1970s, EBMC have followed a focussed and consistent business development and growth path with a strong emphasis on performance and results that has involved internal/organic growth. However, the main engine of growth has come through the success of the cross-border acquisitions strategy which has taken place across regions and products. Over the past decade, the level of growth has been remarkable, witnessing the emergence of the company as a global leader in the industry, which is reflected in its rise to the top 100 non-financial services MNEs in the world. In recent years, acquisition activity has been in the range of 70 to 75 per annum, primarily small- to medium-sized firms. However due to the global recession there has been less emphasis on riskier acquisitions and more of a focus on operational and commercial competiveness.

The company has a well-developed methodology in selecting companies for acquisition. First, target companies must be market leaders commanding first or second position in their domestic market. Second, they should preferably be mid-sized, high performing companies. Third, the quality of the local management team should be high and the local managers committed to growing the business. While the main foreign market entry strategy has been acquisitions of wholly-owned subsidiaries, international joint ventures have also been used on occasion as a stepping stage to full ownership, particularly in the emerging markets where investments are riskier. There is a high failure rate of Cross Border Mergers and Acquisitions (CBMAs) with around 70% of deals failing to achieve the desired results (Capron 1999). Research highlights that the main reasons for failure in CBMAs are related to cross-cultural and HRM issues (Dowling, Festing & Engle 2008) and hence cross cultural management and HRM are increasingly viewed as critical to the successful implementation of CBMAs. This reflects the complexity of integrating the HRM systems from the different organisations and national contexts. Generally in the implementation phase of CBMAs, the tensions between the need for global integration and local responsiveness, influences issues such as the level of integration the acquirer seeks and the extent to which the parent company seeks to introduce a common corporate culture. However, in our case study, the company operated a highly hands-off approach to senior subsidiary management allowing local managers a very high degree of autonomy to develop the business using their local knowledge and networks. The role of the corporate HR function in this context was limited to a few key areas which we examine below.

The corporate HR function

As organisations internationalise, the corporate HR function is faced with the challenge of establishing effective structures and processes. This may take one of three forms (Scullion & Starkey 2000): centralised, decentralised or transition HR. EBMC operates a highly decentralised approach with a very small corporate HR staff at headquarters who undertake a narrower range of functions than centralised global firms. This reflects the highly decentralised, corporate structure that has been in place at EBMC since the early days of internationalisation. As the company operates in a relatively simple, locally based industry, HR policies and practices are devolved to the business unit level to support the business strategy, and senior management recognise that sustainable competitive advantage will derive from securing high quality local management who are able to respond effectively to changing conditions in each host environment. Consequently, the overall role of the corporate HQ is one primarily of support services and coordination.

Shortages of managerial and professional talent have emerged as the key HR challenge facing the majority of MNEs (McDonnell, Lamare, Gunnigle & Lavelle, 2010), and the growing difficulty of recruiting and retaining managerial talent has been a significant constraint on the successful implementation of global strategies (Stahl *et al.* 2007). MNEs increasingly need managers with the skills to operate in the new market conditions faced in foreign operations both in developed and emerging markets. Inherent in EBMC's market-driven growth approach is an acknowledgment of the importance of having a sufficient level and calibre of talent to grow the international businesses. Indeed, talent management is one of three identified strategic themes under the company's human resources strategy (the other two being organisation development and systems and processes). EBMC operate three different leadership programs, aimed at employees at different levels, to ensure there is a talent pipeline that will deliver the leadership capability to run an international business for 5 to 10 years in the future. There are strong links between all three strategic themes, the business strategy and the corporate HR function. Recently, there has been more focus on organisational development as the organisation begins to shift from a portfolio or conglomerate approach towards a more complex, integrated global organisation form. This will pose a new challenge for the corporate HR function and the need to ensure the balance between global integration and local responsiveness will become even more critical, particularly as the changing business environment is increasingly driving the structure of the business and the HR agenda.

Managing international talent in EBMC

MNEs have three options with respect to staffing their foreign operations: employ parent country nationals (PCNs), employ host country nationals (HCNs) or employ third country nationals (TCNs). It is quite common for MNEs to use PCNs in the early years of a foreign operation to help transfer the company's culture and establish the preferred reporting and control systems of the parent company, and for purposes of establishing control in the foreign market (Dowling, Festing & Engle 2008). This approach is also used by EBMC mainly in the early stages of internationalisation in some of the emerging markets where typically PCNs fill the top two or three positions in the foreign subsidiary. However, it has also been argued that the staffing policy needs to evolve with the firm's strategic evolution (Schuler, Dowling & De Cieri 1993). For instance, the continued use of an ethnocentric management approach with the use of PCNs in the top positions is likely to limit an organisation's ability to attract and retain high calibre local managers and professionals. The staffing approach will also vary depending on whether an organisation enters the foreign market through establishing a new greenfield site or through acquisition. In addition, the location of the foreign operation may have a very practical effect on the staffing strategy.

Research suggests a growing need for MNEs to recruit managers with distinctive competencies, and a desire to manage in culturally and geographically distant emerging markets (Bjorkman & Xiucheng 2002). However, there may be staff availability issues in terms of high-quality managers and professionals in some emerging markets. Also, it is more difficult to get PCNs to accept assignments in some emerging markets and the preparedness of leadership talent to move to new strategic markets cannot be guaranteed. Research suggests that mobility across borders, and particularly to higher risk locations such as Africa, Russia and China, is proving increasingly difficult to achieve (Yeung, Warner & Rowley 2008).

Talent management in high-growth acquisition MNEs

The growth of interest in global talent management reflects the growing recognition of the critical role played by international managerial talent in ensuring the success of MNEs. This also reflects the intensification of global competition and the greater need for international learning and innovation in MNEs (Bartlett & Ghoshal 1989). Recent research argues that MNEs increasingly need to manage talent on a global basis to remain competitive, and that talent can be located in different parts of their global operations (Stahl *et al.* 2007). The difficulties of implementing effective global talent management (GTM) strategies are accentuated in highly decentralised MNEs adopting a rapid-growth, acquisition-based business strategy model. When a firm is acquired, they come with staff that may or not be wanted by the acquired firm. EBMC's acquisition strategy involves specifically targeting high performing companies with high quality local management. EBMC's post acquisition staffing strategy is generally to continue with the existing local management as they usually have a demonstrated track record and strong entrepreneurial flair. Hence, a key element of the talent management strategy in EBMC the acquisition of good managerial and leadership talent, and indeed the availability of high quality local management is one of the key criteria used when selecting companies for acquisition.

In practice, the acquired firm's management are allowed a very high degree of autonomy to run the subsidiary operation – so long as they reach the performance targets that reflect the local nature of the industry and the highly decentralised approach of EBMC. This approach has consistently produced high performance and growth to date. However, one corporate initiative was the introduction of a performance incentive scheme, which seeks both to reward senior local managers and to retain them as their know-how, networks and knowledge would be attractive to other MNEs. There seems to be little issue that the HCN managers are relatively unknown to HQ management and there is little indication of the loyalty of these employees to the company. Also, there is very limited mobility of managers between the HQ and the subsidiary which may limit international management development opportunities and the ability to develop talent at the global or regional levels. However, as long as the GTM strategy continues to support the business strategy and the present business model is achieving excellent results, there is little pressure on EBMC to change. However, as the company increasingly looks to the emerging markets as the high potential areas for business growth, there may be a greater need in the short term to use more expatriates to establish the business in the foreign markets. In saying that though, there is little evidence that an overall approach, which depends on high quality local management to grow the market with very successful results, will significantly change in the near future. The particular GTM challenges in the emerging markets are discussed below.

Talent management in developing economies

The increasing investment in the emerging markets by EBMC in recent years has resulted in a growing demand for a distinctive type of managerial talent that can operate effectively in these challenging markets (Scullion, Collings & Gunnigle 2007). The talent management challenges for EBMC are more complex and acute in these emerging markets. While these markets have high-growth potential, they also involve higher risk. These cultures are considerably different to the home culture of EBMC and indeed much of their other foreign operations. A means by which EBMC have sought to reduce some of the risks of development in these countries is to engage in international joint ventures before then looking at a full acquisition.

However, despite the growth of unemployment in recent years in countries like India and China due to the global recession, recent research suggests there is still a scarcity of high-level knowledge in these countries and that the demand for talent remains relatively high (Teagarden, Meyer & Jones 2008). In addition, the inability of these countries to produce graduates of the quality needed by MNEs has resulted in acute skill shortages in key areas (Farndale, Scullion & Sparrow 2010). Reports have highlighted that MNEs in India only take between 15 and 20 per cent of available graduates because they do not fit the requirements of western economy MNEs. The retention of managers and professionals in their emerging markets is a major talent management challenge for EBMC. There is intense competition for scarce managerial and leadership talent in these markets and the tight labour market for such talent allows individual managers to move easily to other MNEs or even to domestic organisations. Finally, organisational loyalty is not particularly strong in some of the emerging markets with, for example, turnover rates of 45 per cent reported in key sectors of the economy in India (Bhatnagar 2007).

In the mature markets of North America and Europe, the vast majority of EBMC's senior managers are now HCNs, reflecting the company strategy to localise the management By contrast, the emerging market operations have a number of expatriates, particularly in the early years, as a means to develop the markets and also for control purposes. The Central and Eastern European (CEE) region is an area of growing importance for the company since the first investment into Poland, which was made in the mid-1990s. Expatriates have been used in this region to develop the market, but more recently there has been a greater drive to implement a localisation strategy. In recent years EBMC have developed businesses in a number of other CEE countries and, interestingly, have used Polish graduates who were integral players in developing the Polish operations to lead the development of these markets (a localisation strategy would follow the initial set-up of the market). This suggests an emerging talent strategy of moving high potential managers between countries of a particular region (TCNs), namely the CEE region. However, there was virtually no mobility of managers between different regions of the world, which is an issue EBMC may need to address if they wish to evolve from being a highly decentralised conglomerate organisation to more of an integrated international business.

The selection criteria for managers in the emerging markets involve a number of elements. Effective cross-cultural management skills and a strong motivation and desire to go and work (not solely monetary) in the emerging markets are important. In addition, managers accepted for these international assignments must be on the high potential list as the developmental aspect of these assignments is increasingly important for developing international leadership capability. In EBMC, 'high potentials' are individuals having the potential to be promoted two levels or crossing two functional areas. A key element of global talent management in EBMC is that mobility did not always mean moving upwards but could involve sideways moves. EBMC wish to see lateral moves becoming more important as it helps give individuals a better understanding of the entire business and positions them better for taking on a range of roles rather than a very narrow role. Also in a highly competitive business where cost reduction is increasing important, lateral mobility allows development opportunities and develops a team approach.

One talent management challenge facing EBMC and many other MNEs is the increasing difficulty in getting people to take up overseas postings. There is growing evidence that families are less willing to accept the disruption of family and social lives associated with international assignments. Dual career issues (Harvey 1997) are increasingly seen as a worldwide trend that can pose significant restrictions on the career plans of multinationals. In the EBMC case, a particular challenge was the failure to persuade US managers to move to other regions of the world. This reflects their polycentric approach to international management where, until now, managers were not expected to move across regional frontiers. Another peculiar feature of the case study company is that repatriation is not regarded as a problem issue. The practice of repatriation remains something relatively rare in EBMC. One important factor here seems to be the small size of the corporate head office. Also important is the balance of employees between domestic and international operations. In EBMC, over 90 per cent of employees are based outside the home country. In practice, international assignments are essentially a one way ticket and opportunities for a post in the parent country following an international assignment are extremely limited. Hence, the company is very careful not to raise expectations about the prospects of a job on return from international assignments.

Summary

EBMC has been a huge international success story through its high-growth acquisition development strategy. A highly decentralised management approach has been adopted thus far in the management of its international operations. With high-quality international managers an increasingly scarce resource, the acquisition of high-performing companies with high calibre managers and employees has many benefits, although it also brings many challenges. There is little doubt that their highly decentralised international management approach has stood them well. However, with the worldwide economy in a state of flux and the greatest business growth opportunities in diverse, culturally different developing economies there are question marks over whether the current approach is best suited in the future.

Discussion questions

1) What are the strengths and weaknesses of the decentralised management approach adopted in EBMC?

2) EBMC tends to favour a polycentric staffing approach with high utilisation of HCNs. What are the disadvantages of a polycentric approach? What strategies could be used to overcome these?

3) What are the benefits and weaknesses of the 'one-way ticket' approach to the use of PCNs?

4) A key part of EBCM's international business strategy is acquiring high performing subsidiaries with high calibre employees. What systems and practices should EBCM consider putting in place to ensure its key employees are motivated and retained?

5) How may EBCM look to diffuse key knowledge from their foreign subsidiaries to other operations and to HQ to ensure a more encompassing global perspective?

6) Discuss the talent management challenges which may arise from the shift from a conglomerate to a more integrated regional or global operation.

References

Bartlett, CA & Ghoshal, S 1989, *Managing Across Borders: the Transnational Solution*, Boston: Harvard Business School Press.

Bhatnagar, J 2007, 'Talent management strategy of employee engagement in Indian ITES employees: Key to retention', *Employee Relations*, 29: 640-663.

Bjorkman, I & Lervick, JE 2007, 'Transferring HR practices within multinational corporations', *Human Resource Management Journal*, 17(4): 320-335.

Bjorkman, I & F Xiucheng 2002, 'Human resource management and the performance of Western firms in China', *International Journal of Human Resource Management*, 13(6): 853-864.

Capron, L 1999, 'The Long Term Performance of Horizontal Acquisitions', *Strategic Management Journal*, 20(11): 987-1018.

Dowling, PJ, Festing, M & Engle, AD 2008, *International Human Resource Management*, 5th edn, Thomson: London.

Farndale, E, Scullion, H & Sparrow, P 2010, 'The role of the corporate HR function in global talent management', *Journal of World Business*, 45(2): 161-168.

Harvey, M 1997, 'Dual-Career Expatriates: Expectations, Adjustment and Satisfaction with International Relocation', *Journal of International Business Studies*, 28(3): 627-658.

McDonnell, A, Lamare, R, Gunnigle, P & Lavelle, J 2010, 'Developing tomorrow's leaders – evidence of global talent management in multinational enterprises', *Journal of World Business*, 45(2): 150-160.

Schuler, R, Dowling, PJ & De Cieri, H 1993, 'An integrative framework of strategic international human resource management', *International Journal of Human Resource Management*, 4(4): 717-764.

Scullion, H & Starkey, K 2000, 'In search of the changing role of the corporate HR role in the international firm', *International Journal of Human Resource Management*, 11(6): 1061-1081.

Scullion, H, Collings, DG & Gunnigle, P 2007, 'International HRM in the 21st Century: Emerging themes and contemporary debates', *Human Resource Management Journal*, 17: 309-319.

Scullion, H & Collings, DG 2011, *Global Talent Management*, London: Routledge.

Stahl, GK, Bjorkman, I, Farndale, E, Morris, SS, Stiles, P, Trevor, J & Wright, PM 2007, *Global Talent Management: How Leading Multinationals Build and Sustain Their Talent Pipeline*, Faculty & Research Working Paper, Fontainebleau, France: INSEAD.

Teagarden, MB, Meyer, J & Jones, D 2008, 'Knowledge – sharing among high-tech MNCs in China and India: Invisible barriers, best practices and next steps', *Organizational Dynamics*, 37(2): 190- 202.

Yeung, AK, Warner, M & Rowley, C 2008, 'Growth and Globalization: Evolution of human resource practices in Asia', *Human Resource Management*, 47: 1-13.

Chapter 32

From local to global: Cross-cultural adaptation at Ainsley Accoutrements

KATE HUTCHINGS

Background and context

Ainsley Accoutrements was established by Jane Jones after she completed her studies in fashion design at the Royal Melbourne Institute of Technology in Australia in 1992. The firm sells designer-inspired shoes, handbags, scarves and gloves, as well as hats for the summer and winter horse racing carnivals – which have until recently been imported exclusively from Italy and Spain. Ainsley Accoutrements has found a niche in the accessories market, providing for upper-middle class professional women and the 'charity lunches' fraternity. Since beginning with one store in the fashion conscious High Street of Malvern in Melbourne's inner eastern suburbs, Jane Jones rapidly expanded her fashion empire to 24 stores across Australia, employing a total of 320 staff. As well as being general manager and having responsibility for overseeing a group of 8 human resources and communications/marketing staff, Jane had undertaken 4 buying trips to Florence, Milan, and Madrid each year to source the requisite goods for sale across her chain of boutiques.

As the global financial crisis (GFC) began to be felt throughout the world in late 2008, sales started to slow dramatically for Ainsley Accoutrements, with some of the long-standing customers losing lucrative jobs in the finance sector and wealthy housewives suffering the effects of stock market losses. Jane Jones realised that she would need to make some quick decisions about how to keep all her stores open and maintain her position in the market. Clearly, the only choice was to reduce the gross cost of her stock; savings which could then be passed on to the consumer. In early 2010 Jane Jones approached her Business Development Manager at the State Bank with a plan to trade out of her difficulties by designing her own accessories and having them manufactured in China. State Bank quickly embraced the idea and loaned Jane Jones a little over $1 million to establish a factory in Southern China, close to Hong Kong. This was a logical choice as it provided quick access from the factory to Ainsley Accoutrements' distribution centre in Melbourne. Wanting to establish an operation as quickly as possible, Jane Jones decided on a wholly foreign-owned subsidiary, which had been permissible under Chinese law since the late 1980s, rather than a joint venture with a local Chinese partner or established factory.

Establishing the factory in China

Prior to sourcing a site to open a factory in China, Jane Jones phoned her old friend Crystal Wang, whom she studied with at design school in the late 1980s. Crystal was one of the first Chinese people to study in Australia as an international student and stayed on after design school, eventually gaining permanent residency and rising to the ranks of senior designer clothing buyer for the Australia-wide Marilyn department store chain. Jane asked Crystal for some initial suggestions about establishing a factory in China. Crystal advised Jane that rather than going through the very time-consuming process of purchasing land and building a new factory, it would be better to purchase an existing factory. Crystal further put Jane in touch with a friend in China, Wenjing Chen, to assist her with the early stages of production. Jane thought that she needed some advice from a local Chinese national, so she arranged to fly to China to meet with Wenjing. She put her on a one month contract to assist with establishing the new factory and making contact with suppliers.

Jane could only stay in China for two days and quickly dismissed Wenjing's attempts at 'small talk' about family and friends. Wenjing owed a favour to her old friend Crystal and their families had been friends and business partners for three generations. Also, she had much experience dealing with Western businesspeople and hence she tried hard to ignore Jane's lack of interest in developing a friendship, learning about Chinese history, or her offer to sightsee the beautiful gardens of Southern China. Wenjing said that she had good contacts with local officials and could assist Jane with rapid negotiations to purchase an old factory which had been built by the Portuguese in the 1800s and to get planning permission to convert it into the requisite production premises. Additionally, Wenjing highlighted that she had strong contacts with local leather manufacturers and silk producers and would provide these contacts to Jane and her China-based manager once the factory had been re-modelled.

Pleased with the outcome of the discussions and that all had been formalised, Jane flew back to Melbourne, and one month later, Wenjing contacted Jane to advise that the factory was ready and that she had recruited almost 100 employees with prior clothing and textile industry experience, to operate the production line. Wenjing also advised that she had recruited a former colleague, who had a good standard of English, Quan Yang, to be factory foreman. Jane was delighted at how seamlessly the operations had been established. She provided Wenjing with a bonus, thanked her for her time and said that an Australian manager would arrive at the factory in two weeks to meet with Quan.

Appointing an Australian manager to the Chinese operations

Jane then called in her most senior employee, Robert Delgarno, to ask him to take an international appointment to China for six months to oversee the early production stages and to recruit a local Chinese manager to take over the operations from him once production was in full swing. Jane wanted Robert to move to China in two weeks, so to make the deal more attractive she offered him a very appealing salary, four times that of his current income, and said that she would cover all housing expenses, and that he would receive a completion bonus when he returned to Australia six months hence. Robert was keen for the salary and the excitement of the experience and eagerly agreed to the opportunity as he had never travelled outside of Australia.

Two weeks later, with 40 kilograms of luggage, Robert, and his wife Sharon, boarded the Cathay Pacific and Dragon Air flights to China via a two day stopover at the Keminiski Hotel in downtown Hong Kong. Though Sharon was not able to obtain a work permit, she agreed to take leave from her accountancy career and also seemed fervent about the experience of living in another culture. Jane felt confident that she could rely on Robert to effectively manage the Chinese operations as he had worked for her for eight years, rising from the position of sales assistant in the Pacific Fair store on Queensland's sub-tropical Gold Coast, and had previously been self-employed as a milliner. Jane felt he was very knowledgeable about the fashion design business and eminently suitable for the position of managing the factory in China.

Poor quality manufacturing and poor quality international management

Two months into operations in China things were not going well. Performing his regular inspection of the factory production line one day, Robert was very unimpressed with the quality of the goods being manufactured. The workers sensed that he was dissatisfied and started talking amongst themselves in Mandarin. Robert could not understand anything that they were saying and angrily walked back to his office, on the way signalling to the local Chinese factory foreman, Quan, to follow him up to his office to discuss the problems.

> *'Quan, what is going on here?'* Robert implored, *'I told you to tell them that I would offer performance bonuses for those that produced in excess of quota but they have not even met the minimum targets we set out when we started production two months ago... and... for this last batch of shoes and handbags the stitching is terribly uneven and the appliqués have not been transferred correctly...– we certainly cannot sell these items as high end goods in Australia. And I am supposed to have had these shipped to*

Australia next week. What is wrong with the leather – we had an agreement with Wenjing that we would receive top quality leather from the suppliers and this looks like it comes from some very tired old buffalo – it is certainly not the finest quality calfskin!'

'I am very sorry Mr Robert,' started Quan. *'Sorry'* said Robert *'How does sorry fix things – I want you to explain why you were supposed to take care of supplies and manage the factory floor and all the products look so bad. I have been counting on you to manage day-to-day operations while I liaise with Jane at headquarters. Why haven't you been in there helping them fix the problems?'* *'But Mr Robert',* said Quan, *'I am sorry, sorry but all the pattern designs that were sent to us from Australia were written in English and there were only some very few pictures and it was very difficult for the workers to understand exactly what your Australian designers wanted. Though I speak English okay from my time studying in America, I am not a trained designer so I could not really understand the patterns either. Besides, the workers would not respect my position if I sat down on the sewing machine and helped them finish their work. Maybe if you could come and talk to the workers – I know you are very busy but when you sit up there on the third floor in your office, the workers feel they do not know you and (this is very difficult for me to say, because I do not want to embarrass you)...but the workers do not think you care about them'.*

'Yes, yes, all very well', argued Robert, *'maybe we can re-do some of the work if you can quickly get me a new batch of leather and silk supplies'.* *'Again, I am so sorry Mr Robert',* replied Quan, *'but I am having problems with the suppliers – they will not send us the best quality fabrics and the orders are taking a long time to process. The suppliers are not happy that you said that you did not have time to go to their banquets with them. They understand that business needs to be much more quick in China these days to ensure international competitiveness, but they gave their best materials to people who made an effort to build a relationship with them. . Also, the workers, well they feel a bit unsure about where you are with them. You did not provide them with a bus to travel to/from work or organise a canteen for their lunches. When you did have an ad hoc meeting with the employees one month ago one asked if you could install a canteen. You said you would but when I reminded you a week ago, you said that it didn't matter – so long as there were no accidents at work'.* With dismay Robert retorted *'I just do not have time for dinners with suppliers – I am working with Lisa at headquarters to refine the designs. And I do not understand why the workers care about a free lunch – I suppose we can do this if it will make them work more efficiently. I guess I just did not realise that China is so much hard work!'.*

Adding spousal non-adaption into the mix

Feeling overwhelmed and more than a little despondent, Robert left the factory early to meet Sharon at their company-rented, Western-style, large, garden-view apartment, ready to have dinner and cocktails at Ling Ling's Late Night Lounge

Bar in the nearby, fashionable district. When he met Sharon at the door she was not dressed for an evening of dining and dancing. She immediately burst into tears and screamed

> *Robert I just cannot take this anymore – I am so bored with spending most of my time sitting in this apartment. And when I do go out it is to these tedious tennis parties and lunches with the expat wives. I miss my friends in Australia and having a proper conversation about something that matters to me. I really miss my job and feeling useful. And I am sick of going down to the markets to do the shopping but not knowing what half the stuff is ...and hardly anyone speaks English and I don't know what they are talking about and they don't understand me. The air is so polluted here and I just wish I could do for a run in the park like I did at Fitzroy Gardens near home. Jane said that she would pay for me to do some study by distance education but today when I contacted Margaret in HR at Ainsley Accoutrements in Melbourne she said that there was no longer a budget for this. I am so bored, bored, bored. I hate it here. Why did you bring me here? I just want to go back home to Melbourne".*

Robert stood there perplexed as he had no idea that Sharon had been struggling to adjust to life in China and thought she was actually enjoying the career break and the shopping expeditions. *'What about me?'* he retorted,

> *I somehow need to phone Jane at HQ and let her know that everything is a mess here. The factory workers have done a poor job with the first batch of materials and now the new supply of leather has arrived and it is third rate quality and we just cannot use it to produce products that are anything like what we used to buy from Spain and Italy. The last two months has been a complete waste of time and money. How can I tell Jane that I have failed totally? I thought China was becoming so Westernised and I thought it would be just like working in Australia. My career is on the line – how can I ever explain to Jane?*

Later than night Robert garnered the courage to call Jane in Australia. Jane answered the phone and before Robert had a chance to say anything, Jane said how glad she was to hear from him and spoke in raptures about having recently brokered a deal to open 6 new stores in Australia and two in New Zealand.

Summary

Ainsley Accoutrements has experienced rapid change, and consequent challenges, in moving from importing products to sell in its high-end boutiques to establishing a production facility in a country where the company had no prior experience. Numerous cross-cultural problems have arisen in managing in China, yet the company has profited from a degree of goodwill from Jane Jones' contacts in China – who have tried to adapt to the Western culture and style of management. Despite all their current difficulties, these displays of goodwill auger well for the company's future prospects if the Australian manager can learn from some of his mistakes and work towards understanding Chinese business and culture.

Discussion questions

1) What does this case study tell you about the challenges of establishing international operations?

2) What are the key cross-cultural problems Robert is having in managing the workforce in China?

3) Identify the problems being experienced by Sharon and what you believe could have been done to minimise her difficulties?

4) Can this situation be salvaged?

Chapter 33

Managing diverse workgroups in Islamic cultures

EBRAHIM SOLTANI

Background and context

Azar Ltd was founded in Tehran's suburbs, Iran, in 1970, to make brick in its multitude of forms. In 1983 the company underwent huge changes where the management decided to invest in modern brick-production equipment. The investment proved very lucrative and two years later the company moved to a large site and recruited more people with the skills to operate and make most of the new brick-making machinery and equipment. As a result of the economic boom of construction sector, and bricks being the most common building material, the company established production facilities in the suburbs of two major cities of the country where bricks had traditionally been used in construction for the past several centuries. The boom stimulated the firm to rethink and revisit its recruitment strategy across the three sites, and the decision to recruit cheaper sources of labour has been core to the human resource management (HRM) strategy of the firm since 1990.

According to the HR manager, cheaper sources of labour imply a low or unskilled workforce, coming mainly from rural and remote regions of the country or being refugees from the neighbouring countries. The adopted recruitment policy of the firm has resulted in a greater workforce diversity, where the employees are different in terms of race, age, education, culture, religion, disabilities, and language – to name but a few. Such a focus on diverse work groups as described in this case is regarded as a common practice and perceived to be cost-effective, profitable and rewarding for management. Several HR managers have noted that the construction sector in general and their own firms particularly have enjoyed higher annual productivity growth rates largely because of their employment strategy of hiring diverse workgroups. Despite such an optimistic view of recruiting a diverse workforce as a major source of higher productivity and thereby controlling labour costs and maximising profit, the trend in productivity of diverse workgroups shows a decline over the past several years. Indeed, several HR managers recognise a need on the part of the management team to not only perceive the tangible benefits of a diverse workforce, but also to put into place some objective measures where the value of the heterogeneity of the group is recognised, the potential of group members is realised, and more importantly, personal needs are attended to.

The company quest for diverse workgroups

The economic boom that started in the late 1980s was propelled by the need to reconstruct cities that had been severely damaged during the eight-year Iran-Iraq war. To accommodate the capacity needed for the booming economy and generate more revenue from the existing opportunities, Azar Ltd had gone through extensive restructuring of its HRM strategies with a focus primarily on recruiting cheap but diverse workforce. Like other firms across the industry, Azar Ltd faced severe difficulty in recruiting employees in 1990s. In addition to post-war Iran reconstruction policies, which resulted in a whole economy demand for more domestic workforce, the recruitment difficulties were primarily attributed to the nature of brick-making and brick-burning jobs. A majority of the workforce perceived their job to be rather meaningless as it was repetitive, tough, and hard manual work.

Due to the nature of construction and brick-making jobs and the fact that they are very low-paid and contain an unpleasant element of hazard and risk for the worker, these manual jobs appeared to be rather unattractive to the local unskilled workforce. As a result of the decline in the number of local recruits, Azar Ltd recognised the diversity with an equality policy based on the premise that 'anyone, from anywhere, with any background' is offered the opportunity to join the company. The introduction of the so-called 'diversity and equality policy' helped the company to attract and recruit a huge number of foreign workers, which accounted for over 68 per cent of its workforce. The profile of the workforce shows that they are different and very diverse in terms of several criteria, namely: religion, ethnic breakdown, cultural background, language and dialect spoken, and age structure.

Whilst the management of Azar Ltd claim a genuine and true diversity and equality pronouncement, the externally imposed governmental legislation is in fact more relevant. Indeed, the brick-making sector has been a real haven for numerous low or unskilled refugees and those local workers who were from rural and remote parts of the country and left no option but to join (to quote the words of a worker) the 'unwanted job'. The primary interest of this workforce in brick-making jobs is mainly the basic need of seeking food and shelter (i.e. physiological needs) rather than achieving a higher level of development or so-called transcendence or spiritual needs for cosmic identification.

Diverse workforce's perception of diversity and equality

For the management of Azar Ltd, diversity and equality practices are viewed as a means of achieving two sets of interconnected and interlinked objectives at two levels, organisation and individual employee. At an organisational level, the main reason for adopting and implementing an equality and diversity policy is clearly rooted in its strength to drive overall organisational performance, and more specifically, impact favourably on the bottom-line results. At the individual level, diversity and equality is emphasised as a competitive resource for creating an organisational environment wherein not only the full potential of the ethnic minority cadre is maximised, but also both the ethnic minority and majority groups can work shoulder to shoulder regardless of their individual differences to improve the overall organisational performance. For the employees, however, the recruitment of diverse workgroups and adoption of any associated policies has been seen to be primarily driven by the dire state of construction and manufacturing sectors in recent years and the need for a mechanism to fit only the management priorities.

The combination of diverse ethnic workgroups and the passive management approach to diversity and equality have resulted in ethnic segregation of the workforce across the three branches. The reality of diversity and equality practices does not seem to vary between the three branches. With the exception of the initial pronouncement of recruiting the available workforce from any background, there has then not been any evidence of adopting and implementing any sign of diversity and equality. Such overt managerial and organisational ignorance has in turn left no better option for the diverse workgroups but to protect themselves against any inequality at work. As part of their self-protection mechanism strategy against workplace inequality, the diverse workgroups seem to focus on shared language. To alleviate their dissatisfaction with the way management handled their basic employment needs, the diverse workgroups appear to use language similarity as an important and immediate means of recognition, identity and a wider informal protection. Whilst Persian (Farsi) is the common language in workplaces, each ethnic diverse workgroup prefers to speak their own dialect, a means of sharing work-related problems and finding how to best cope with them. Diverse workgroups use their common language and dialect as a means to find a sympathetic hearing among their fellow co-workers. Indeed, the importance of a common language seems to win support from both local and foreign workers.

Manipulating the diverse workgroups: A mechanism for fitting management priorities

Despite the boom in the construction and manufacturing industries over the past years, there has not been sufficient evidence to suggest that the growing market for the two heavily labour-intensive sectors has any tangible ramifications for the diverse workgroups. For a majority of the diverse workforce, the management of Azar is characterised by a top-down, authoritarian managerial approach and a purely cost-driven organisational mindset. The authoritarian managerial approach serves to work against the diverse workgroups in terms of their basic employee rights. And the top-down management approach appears to fall into disfavour at the very early stage of employment – i.e. the point of employee selection. As one experienced non-local supervisor tellingly pronounces:

> They [management] know that we need the job and have no any additional source of income. They also know that we may not have legal residency status. At the beginning of our employment they do not ask about such issues as our visa status and work expedience. So they offer us a job and we think that they treat everyone in the same manner because we are very different. But once we have started to work, they then put pressure on us and threaten to fire us or report us to police.

Most tellingly, perhaps, is a foreign worker who comments:

> We are selected from different backgrounds in terms of, for example, language, nationality, religion, and culture. We all have no formal qualification and are not aware of our basic rights. If we want to leave the job they would highly likely report us to the police as most of us do not have proper work visa. I have five children here with me. So I cannot do anything but to comply with whatever they [managers] say.

The key to management success in pursuing such a command and control approach is reported to lie at the reality of diversity in workgroups across the sector. As one ethnic minority worker states:

> We are too diverse; each 10 to 12 of us has something in common and are different from others. We are not big enough to make our voice heard. We are therefore very vulnerable to any management's action.

The underlying theme for most diverse workgroups is the fact that the dominant coercive management approach results in a serious rise in the level of hostility among the members of ethnic groups. Such open hostile attitudes of diverse workgroup members seems to encourage excessive competition, which only favours the management's intent to exercise manipulative power and make most of their workforce's hard work. Such intent, however, lacks one strategic element of diversity and equality initiatives: it neither contributes to the realisation of the full potential of the diverse groups nor results in encouraging and enhancing creativity and innovation. Indeed, the adopted approach to managing diverse workgroups is partially compatible with the rationale of the business case for diversity and equality and the antithesis of the notion of equality and diversity in the sense that diversity and equality policies bring about recognition for the diverse workgroup members.

As construction and brick-making jobs are generally perceived as low-skilled or unskilled tasks, the two sectors are mostly staffed by foreign workers from neighbouring countries and local unskilled ethnic minority workers. A review of the documentary evidence and general financial information of the cases reveals that the adopted business logic for employing diverse workgroups contributes significantly to the overall organisational performance and the bottom-line results.

The initial and primary impetus for management to recruit diverse workgroups stems from the fact that the ethnic minority workers have low expectations in terms of pay, promotion, training and development. And more importantly, the workforce are expected to be submissive. These characteristics, as well as strict scrutiny of workers' performance, have led to better bottom-line results. This cultivates a management approach of controlling the workers, which forces any worker to be whipped into a desired shape to serve only management priorities or be dismissed in the case of failure to do so. It is widely recognised across the three branches that (to quote one of the brick-making workers),

> Management expectations of the diverse workgroups are too high. They do not tolerate not only any sort of complaint but also any suggestion for work improvement. We do not have the right to question our management's decisions.

This is indeed a major concern for most of the diverse workgroups and an essential element contributing to their unspoken dissatisfaction with the management.

Summary

In a nutshell, Azar Ltd has placed a heavy emphasis of equality and diversity for individual recognition and promotion of diverse personal values as a means to higher productivity. However, the current management does not seem to uphold to such promises. Instead, it has created an environment in which a systematic injustice and inequality of ethnicity has reached a crescendo, or as a 61-year old non-local worker put it,

> I think this is the management who is a real threat to our equal treatment. All they [management team] see in our individual differences is how to make more profit out of us. If we were not diverse we could speak with one voice and be united on everything. Now each group of us has to act in a different but unhealthy way in order to keep the management happy.

Discussion questions

1) What is your take from this case study in terms of the definition of diversity and equality?

2) What are the dominant approaches to utilising diverse workforce and equality practices?

3) Do you agree with the management of Azar in terms of their treatment of the diverse workforce? Are the workforce treated equally? If not, discuss why?

4) What are the major problems of effective management of diverse workgroups in non-Western organisational contexts? Why is it perceived to be more effective in the Western organisations?

Further reading

Ogbonna, E & Harris, LC 2006, 'The dynamics of employee relationships in an ethnically diverse workforce', *Human relations,* 59(3):379-407.

Ogbonna, E & Noon, M 1995, 'Experiencing inequality: Ethnic minorities and the employment training scheme', *Work, Employment & Society*, 9(3): 537–58.

Ogbonna, E 1998, K ethnic minorities and employment training: Redressing or extending disadvantage?, *International Journal of Training and Development*, 2(1): 28–41.

Özbilgin, F & Nishii, L 2007, 'Global Diversity Management: towards a conceptual framework', *International Journal of Human Resource Management*, 18 (11): 1883-1894.

Özbilgin, F & Syed, J 2008, *Diversity Management in Asia*, Cheltenham and New York: Edward Elgar Press.

Soltani, E 2010, 'The overlooked variable in managing human resources of Iranian organizations: workforce diversity – some evidence', *The International Journal of Human Resource Management,* 21(1): 84-108.

Soltani, E, Syed, J, Liao, YY & Shahisough, N (in press), 'Tackling one-sidedness in equality and diversity research: Characteristics of the current dominant approach to managing diverse workgroups in Iran', *Asia Pacific Journal of Management*, DOI 10.1007/s10490-011-9259-3.

Soltani, E, Scullion, H & Collings, D 2010, 'Managing diverse work groups: the case of less developed countries', in Özbilgin, M & Syed, J. (Eds), *Diversity Management in Asia*, pp. 352-372, Edward Elgar: London.

Chapter 34

Strategy and people management in China: The case of a large, private auto plant

Fang Lee Cooke

Background and context

AutopartCo is a large family-owned company that specialised in designing and manufacturing automotive parts. It is located in a large city in northern China. Initially set up by three family members in the 1980s as a small smelting firm, AutopartCo emerged in the mid-1990s and has grown rapidly into one of the largest privately-owned firms in the local area. By 2009, it employed over 2,600 employees, 80 per cent of whom were shopfloor workers. The company is managed by a number of family-member managers at the senior level. Managers at the middle and lower levels are either recruited externally or promoted internally.

As one of the major wheel manufacturing firms in China, AutopartCo targets foreign-owned automotive firms as their corporate clients by supplying aluminium wheels at the upper end of the product market. These foreign-owned automotive client firms come from both China and abroad. This product market orientation means that AutopartCo needs to be at the forefront of the technology in both design and manufacturing. It also needs to be proactive in predicting new trends and fashions in the automotive industry in order to be able to design new wheel products to meet the technical and aesthetic requirements of new vehicle models. Automotive component supply is a highly competitive business; firms need to bid for business contracts using their design, price and speed of delivery as selling-points. Being able to build relationships with, and win trust from, the automotive corporate clients is an added important element to secure new businesses.

AutopartCo has a relatively sophisticated website and a strong marketing team. It employs consultancy firms to provide advice on marketing strategy and human resource management (HRM) practices. The company also has a proactive green policy and is actively engaging in energy-saving, recycling and environment protection activities as part of its corporate social responsibility (CSR) commitment. It is a major employer in the local area and has won many awards, such as quality assurance awards and model enterprise awards, at the municipal and provincial levels. AutopartCo's strategic intent is to continue to expand its business in China and more so overseas. In the mid-2000s, it set up a branch office in Singapore to facilitate business development in the Asia-Pacific region. It is anticipated that an increasing proportion of the company's business revenue will come from overseas, making the firm one of the major wheel manufacturers in the region.

Professionalisation of managers

Like many family-owned businesses in China, the family members were the only managers at AutopartCo during the start-up stage. As the business grew, non-family-member (professional) managers were recruited. However, the family-member managers remain in charge of the key positions, with one of them being the CEO. There are over 30 senior and mid-ranking managers at the wheel manufacturing plant – some of them were recruited because they were friends of the family members and deemed more trustworthy in key managerial positions. This was despite that fact that they may not be the most competent managers. Others were recruited for their competence to fill a gap in in-house expertise. As the firm was expanding rapidly there became a serious shortage of managerial staff, and this was partly due to the difficulty in recruiting managers from the labour market. Those managers developed in-house were promoted so fast that they were not properly groomed before taking on the role. This is a common problem that many firms in China face due to the shortage of managerial talent. Indulged by the tight labour market, managers hold significant bargaining power against their employer. Many of them are able to dictate terms and conditions of employment and control the way they work.

It is not surprising that the owner-CEO felt that in the current business environment, professional managers tend to have a low level of commitment to the firm. Some are even guilty of serious misconduct (see below for example). In choosing managers, trustworthiness is therefore deemed more important than competence in AutopartCo. This preference for trustworthiness reduces the perceived fairness by staff in the promotion and staffing of managerial positions, despite the fact that internal promotions are generally based on competence and performance in the firm.

In addition, the performance appraisal system is only implemented for non-family-member managers, as it is considered difficult to evaluate family-member managers. The latter also enjoy a higher level of remuneration than the former. Management remuneration and bonuses are distributed in a non-transparent manner, which reinforces the perception of inequality between the family-member and non-family-member groups of managers. This differential treatment invokes a strong 'outsiders' feeling amongst the professional managers and further reduces their commitment and effort, leading to opportunistic behaviour and problems in managerial performance and retention. These problems reinforce resistance from the owner-managers to separate ownership from the business management through the deployment of professional managers. Instead, owner-managers continue to be highly involved in all strategic as well as operational matters of the firm at all levels. This not only makes their working life overburdened, but also puts professional managers in an awkward position as their plans and decisions may be overruled by owner-managers any time without due process. With the constant interventions from owner-managers, professional managers feel bound and lack of space to operate.

Paradoxically, the high level of involvement of owner-managers in the business management has not stemmed opportunistic behaviour by non-family managers. The biggest problem is in the sales and purchasing area. The company has four sales managers. Two of them are very astute but dishonest in that they take tens of thousands of yuan in commissions privately – both from selling products and purchasing materials each year. But their sales volume is high, and they bring in good revenue for the company. They have worked for the company for ten years and are two of the longest serving employees of the firm. The other two sales managers have worked for the company for just two years. They are not as competent as the other two and have a much lower sales volume. But they are honest and in fact resent the corrupt behaviour of the other two dishonest managers. These non-family sales managers reported theft incidents to the owner-managers of the company because taking commissions is against the company's code of conduct.

The family-member managers had suspected that something unethical had been going on with the two corrupt managers, but were nevertheless disappointed to see their suspicion confirmed. The CEO could not understand why the two managers behaved like this, as he felt that the company has treated them very kindly. And they were already well rewarded, receiving performance-related bonuses in addition to company stock options. The company has been making good profits in the last ten years, so the overall income of the managers has been rather handsome. The owner-managers now face the dilemma of whether to dismiss the two corrupt sales managers. If they do, then the company will lose a significant share of its business as these two managers, who are very familiar with the business, are well-connected in the market and have developed good relationships with the clients. Worse still, they may take a number of key staff with them when they leave the firm, hence causing further losses. On the other hand, such unethical behaviour, if tolerated, sends a signal to the rest of the workforce that gross misconduct may go unpunished and therefore encourage the rest to follow suit.

In fact, dishonest behaviour is not uncommon amongst sales employees. Wilkinson *et al.*'s (2005) study also revealed the problems of HRM and relationship management encountered by the British multinational corporations (MNCs) that had sourcing partnerships with indigenous Chinese supplier firms. Difficulties in recruitment and retention, corrupt behaviour, cultural and communication problems, and poor working practices of the supplier firms were some of the major problems faced when managing key staff in the purchasing function.

Engagement of shopfloor employees

On the shopfloor, production activities are divided into four processes, each being contained in one workshop. Within each workshop, work process is further divided into simple tasks. Production occurs around the clock and employees work eight-hour shifts. Work routines are simple and highly repetitive. There is no job rotation within or across the workshops. For example, one worker's task is to lift a wheel from one belt to another manually, a task which he needs to repeat for the whole shift and in every shift. Job rotation was considered inappropriate by the owner-managers. It was felt that workers did not want to be doing different tasks in one shift to alleviate their boredom because it would slow down their working speed and reduce their earning – workers are paid in two parts: basic wage and piece rate wage/bonus.

The workshops are spacious, clean and tidy, but not well illuminated to save energy. The 5S program (sort, straighten, shine, standard and sustain), a Japanese shopfloor management concept to create space and improve efficiency, has been implemented. However, there is no employee involvement program in place to pull together ideas to improve working conditions or productivity because the managers feel that the workers are not interested in doing anything extra beyond their work tasks. The work environment is noisy but workers do not wear the ear muffs that are provided by the company for protection because they feel uncomfortable. In the summer, the temperature in the workshop can be in the high 30s (degrees C). Electric fans are available, but not air conditioning. Like many other Chinese privately-owned manufacturing firms, the plant is inspected by foreign-owned MNC clients before each contract is signed to supply products, but the company has never had problem in gaining approval from the inspectors.

Due to the labour intensive nature of the work, the vast majority of production workers are young males in their 20s or early 30s. Workers are mostly local residents or from nearby towns and villages. According to the owner-managers, workers are relatively well-paid by local labour market standards. The company also provides good welfare benefits such as uniforms, subsidised meals, entertainment, and so forth. There is no harsh discipline for workers when they violate company rules because the owner-CEO (in his late 50s) is benevolent. In his words:

> They are just kids. It is difficult to punish them when they make mistakes. I forgive them in order to give them another chance. But none of them understand my intention and good will. They misbehave again and again. Some of these kids were not well brought up. They are rude and rough. They

don't care about the property. They just vandalise the place. For example, I was making a surprise visit to the plant at 2:00am one night to see if everything was in order. I caught a young man hammering a tiny hole in a large glass window with a small hammer. I was furious and asked him why he did that. He replied, 'I wanted to have some breathing space'. [The worker was asked to write an apology letter and was fined 500 yuan but not dismissed. It cost over 2,000 yuan, equivalent to one month's wage of the worker, to replace the glass.]

The employee turnover rate is quite high even though the local labour market is slack. The owner-CEO disclosed that, despite being a large well-performing firm and paying good wages, it is difficult for the firm to attract good talent because young people want to work in state-owned enterprises or multinational firms. They are also disinterested in labour intensive jobs. As the HR manager revealed,

These young people belong to the post-80 generation. They are the only-child in the family. They grew up being spoilt by their families. So it is difficult for them to work in this environment.

Workplace conflicts exist amongst groups of workers who self-organise, often based on their origin-of-birth or residential area. Senior managers reveal that young men from certain towns tend to be aggressive and trouble seeking, the firm now avoids recruiting from these areas. In addition, the firm is careful when organising workers into shifts and allocating them into workshops to minimise opportunities for frictions, which are often hinged on their social identity rather than work-related issues.

A trade union was established in AutopartCo, headed by one of the family members of the owners. The function of the trade union is largely welfare-related rather than focusing on workers' rights and interests. Moral education is another responsibility of the trade union, similar to that found in the state-owned enterprises. According to the trade union chairperson:

The union's task is to 'educate' the workers when they make mistakes, when they have conflicts at work, or when they have personal problems. It is not about defending their rights, because the company is doing everything legally. There is no violation of labour rights.

Summary

The owner-/senior managers of AutopartCo have an ambitious internationalisation plan. The company has already developed a strong position in the domestic product market. However, the fulfilment of the strategic plan requires the commitment of managers at the lower level and the engagement of shopfloor employees. As the case study shows, neither management commitment nor employee engagement has been secured.

Like many family-owned businesses, AutopartCo is caught in a vicious circle of management deployment and is trapped by problems associated with the shortage of managerial talent in the labour market. On the one hand, rapid business development and expansion necessitates the firm to professionalise its management function. On the other hand, recruitment difficulties, unethical conduct of some managers, and kinship ties make the business owners favour family-member managers, thus creating significant barriers to the professionalisation of the management function and the development of the business.

Another challenge that AutopartCo is facing is how to align its business strategy with its HR strategy in order for the latter to support the former. While AutopartCo is doing well in the environmental aspect of the CSR, there remains much to be done to align employees' behaviour with the organisational goals.

Discussion questions

1) What should the CEO do to handle the corrupt behaviour of the sales managers? Provide two options to the CEO, highlighting the merits and drawbacks of each solution.

2) What do you think may be the reasons at a deeper level that account for the destructive behaviour of the shopfloor employees? What HRM interventions may be introduced to address shopfloor sabotage problems?

3) What advice would you give to AutopartCo on management development that would help prevent behavioural problems in both managerial and shopfloor employees as identified in this case study?

4) What implications do you think the managerial problems identified in this case study have for the globalisation/internationalisation of Chinese firms?

Suggested further reading

Wilkinson, B, Eberhardt, M, McLaren, J & Millington, A 2005, 'Human resource barriers to partnership sourcing in China', *International Journal of Human Resource Management*, vol. 16, no. 10, pp. 1886-900.

Chapter 35

Emiratization: Challenges of strategic and radical change in the United Arab Emirates

RACHID ZEFFANE AND LINZI KEMP

Introduction and background

A strategic geographical change took place in 1972 in the Persian Gulf when the United Arab Emirates (UAE) was formed from seven states. In the less than 37 years since its establishment, the UAE has incorporated substantial change in its business strategy, helping it to become one of the most modern developed countries in the world. Amidst this move for modernisation, the UAE government also embarked on an 'Emiratization' initiative in both the public and private sectors, which is aimed at enhancing the employment of its citizens in a meaningful and efficient manner (AME Info 2007). As a result, multiple government initiatives have been actively promoting Emiratization through training and institutionalised initiatives such as the establishment of: Tawteen UAE; the Abu Dhabi Tawteen Council; Emirates Foundation; and the Centre for Emiratization Research & Development (Emiratization Research Foundation 2009).

In essence, Emiratization is a strategy that seeks to use the country's human resources favourably through the transfer of skills and knowledge from expatriates to UAE nationals (citizens). Thus, Emiratization affects both public government agencies as well as private businesses (UAE-Change 2010). Expatriates in the UAE are currently the overwhelming majority in the working population, where non-nationals constitute 2.4 million (91%) of the working population (Al-Ali 2008). An argument is that this domination in expatriate numbers in the workforce has led to insufficient emphasis on education, English, employment skills, and even trust amongst the UAE nationals. It is believed that as a result, the UAE nationals suffer from poor career advancement in their own country (Al-Ali 2008). The strategic move for Emiratization thus presents a series of challenges and issues.

The employment of a high number of non-national workers has created economic and social problems in the UAE labour market. A significant imbalance between the numbers of UAE nationals and non-nationals in the UAE labour market, in both private and public sector organisations, is considered to be a major impediment to socio-economic progress. The issue of an unbalanced labour composition was also coupled with an unemployment rate among Emiratis that by 2009 had risen to 13.4% (Gulf News 2009). In addition, the majority of Emiratis are currently engaged in employment in the public sector. However, the private sector controls 52% of all jobs in the UAE, but the Emirati strength in this sector was just 1% in 2009, with the exception of the banking and insurance sectors (Gulf News 2009). As the private sector drives the engine of business growth, it was considered imperative that more Emiratis be encouraged to join private companies.

Emiratization: Females in the workforce

The Emiratization initiative also aimed to encourage national women into employment. The UAE Constitution states that,

> ...social justice should apply to all and that before the law, women are equal to men. They enjoy the same legal status, claim to titles and access to education. They have the right to practise the profession of their choice...[and] the family is the basis of society which shall be responsible for protecting childhood and motherhood. Laws shall be formulated in all fields to observe this protection and care in a way which safeguards the dignity of women... and suitable work [for them]. (Kemp 2008)

According to census data from 2005, 49.3% of the Emirati population is female, they contribute $3.4 billion to the UAE economy and represented 13.9% of the total workforce in 2008 (Shallal 2008). The literacy rate among women in the UAE rose to 88.7% in 1995, and by 1997, 72% of tertiary students were female (Kemp 2008). However, many UAE national women do not choose to take up employment after education; legal and societal forces in the culture contribute to this scenario. Although law in the UAE states that there is equal pay for males and females, there have been claims that 'at work women remain deprived of equal benefits such as housing and promotion' (Kemp 2008, p. 33). There are suggestions that a factor in the low numbers of women in the work force is company restrictions on the numbers of females employed (see for example Shallal 2008). A permit has to be issued by the husband before a wife can take up employment initially. There may be a personal preference to avoid the inconvenience of a career whilst running a household, and the family may raise objections to a wife, sister, or daughter working. Hence, Emirati women overwhelmingly prefer public sector employment, and generally remain unemployed if their employment conditions are not met. UAE female citizens employed in the Ministry of Education and the Ministry of Health outnumber national male employees, and account for 27% of the civil servants within the twenty-four government ministries (Kemp 2008).

Females have mainly taken up employment in the civil service, teaching, medicine, and in family businesses. In the rural and remote parts of the UAE, women's roles have been traditionally restricted to occupations where the genders do not mix, such as teaching. There are opportunities in nursing, but this is a career where national women are not involved, probably because of relatively low pay, long hours, and possibly cultural barriers of working in a mixed gender area in a rather intimate setting. In the health services, women (national and expatriate) account for 54.3% of the total number of employees, 'one out of every three doctors, pharmacists, technicians and administrators is a woman' (Kemp 2008, p. 34). Engineering is also a career field where Sheikha Lubna Al Qasimi, a prominent UAE female politician, notes women are already established and doing well. Recent research regarding the influences on job satisfaction amongst Emirati women reveals modern Emirati women are beginning to take up untraditional jobs that demand they work side by side with men (Shallal 2008). Older Emirati women are more satisfied with their jobs than younger females, and those females with education at a higher level than secondary schooling were also more satisfied than those with only high school education (Shallal 2008).

Emiratization: The driving force for change

The World Bank and the International Monetary Fund have long identified unemployment as a major hindrance to development in the Gulf countries. The Gulf countries are joined together in a confederation for economic purposes called the Gulf Cooperation Council (GCC). In response to the problem of unemployment, the GCC countries, and the UAE in particular, introduced economic policies to direct national labour markets and promote their citizens' employment. In the early 1990s, the UAE's council of ministers adopted Emiratization to apply to both public and private sectors, the former representing the vast majority of the work force. Emiratization, as a strategy, is the shared responsibility of the Ministry of Labor and Social Affairs for policy matters, and the National Human Resources Development and Employment Authority ('Tanmia'), which provides UAE nationals with employment, training and development opportunities (Al-Ali 2008).

In their endeavour, the UAE government put in place industry-based quotas for the employment of nationals. Other moves to encourage private sector Emiratization included wage subsidies and wage restraint for government employees, as well as quotas on expatriate labour in the private sector and employment targets for UAE nationals as a whole (TRA-Government News Services 2010). The big push for Emiratization seems to have been met with some success over the years. For instance, Du (a telecommunication provider) recently announced that 20% of its work force was now Emirati. Lloyds in the UAE also reported that just over one third of their employees are local. More recently, the National Bank of Abu Dhabi (NBAD) announced plans to recruit 300 UAE nationals in 2010, and increase Emiratization to 38% compared to 36% in 2009. NBAD also announced 50% Emiratization of its top management positions in 2009 (TRA-Government News Services 2010). These achievements in the workforce composition have been attributed largely to the significantly higher pay levels enjoyed by nationals by comparison to expatriates performing similar jobs (Maktoob 2009).

To further reinforce its drive and commitment towards Emiratization in the private sector, by June 2006 the UAE government declared that private companies must recruit nationals as human resource managers and secretarial staff (Dubai Memoir 2006), this move created over 21,000 jobs, including the opening up of close to 700 managerial positions for nationals (Gulf News 2009). Private businesses were given 18 months to replace their existing non-national Human Resource and Personnel Managers with UAE nationals. Also, no further work permits were to be available for non-national secretaries. It should be noted that foreign workers are only allowed to work in the UAE through the allocation of work permits. These permits are applied for by employers and issued by the UAE government. The employer is then a sponsor of the employee, and such sponsorship once withdrawn causes the employee to lose their right to be in the country. Foreign secretaries currently holding job contracts were allowed to remain in their jobs until the end of their limited period contracts. Furthermore, private companies were not allowed to transfer sponsorship of secretarial staff to another employer, and they would not be issued temporary or part-time work permits. Secretaries sponsored by their husbands or parents were no longer to be issued labour cards (work permits). Following this move, the UAE Labor Ministry announced that companies wishing to recruit UAE national secretaries would need to coordinate the changes through Tanmia, and other human resource development programs in the Emirates.

Barriers to Emiratization

Despite all the measures above, the private sector failed to meet the targets set for Emiratization. Although well-received in many quarters, and to some degree successful in the public sector, the Emiratization policy was met with some resistance from various perspectives.

One barrier to private sector employment, for a wider group of UAE underemployed, is a negative attitude towards physically demanding work. This type of work is usually performed by migrant workers, particularly in the building, roads and maintenance trades. Emiratization did not cater for the shift needed in attitude towards employment versus running one's own business affairs. Employability is not a prime consideration in the minds of many local Emiratis, especially amongst the youth. Even though many are willing to serve as business owners in their own economy, young Emiratis often prefer to work in the public sector (Gulf News 2009). The public sector is far more attractive for Emiratis as it provides superior employment conditions: remuneration, job security, hours of work, work content and generous vacations. The attractions also include an opportunity to work in the native language (Arabic), as well as an opportunity to practice 'wasta' (the use of networks and connections) to get a job.

Work days and working hours play a part in the resistance to work in the private sector. Nationals may find the private sector's working conditions of long and irregular hours unacceptable, coupled with the restrictions on time spent on cultural and religious observances, short periods of leave, and a relatively more stringent approach to employee performance. In the UAE, the official weekend is Thursday and Friday, however, many of the UAE's smaller private workplaces close only on Friday, and perhaps for a half day on Thursday. By contrast, government offices run on relatively shorter working hours (7.30 a.m. to 2.30 p.m.) from Saturday to Wednesday. Furthermore, private sector offices tend to keep longer hours (often 8 a.m. to 5 p.m.). These time considerations are important in a nation that culturally places commitments to family above obligations of work.

There is also the issue of retention or attrition of national employees. Due to the low numbers of available Emiratis in the population, demand is in excess to supply. Qualified Emiratis can easily move from job to job as they are sought by employers throughout the economy. It is claimed that over ten per cent of Emiratis resigned from the private sector in 2008 because of social and cultural factors (Al-Ali 2008). And a study conducted by Tanmia reported that three out of five Emiratis resigned from corporate positions due to a lack of career progression and the absence of a mentoring culture (Maktoob 2009a).

Overcoming resistance to Emiratization

In order to build Emirati nationals' leadership and management potential to manage the country's future development, the public service downplayed these from the expected full employment policy. This then forced new graduates to seek work in the seemingly less attractive/less financially beneficial private sector.

A preference for the public sector is overwhelming and has been demonstrated by several studies on attitudes and preferences of Emiratis towards employment (Al-Ali 2008). Most of these studies have shown that in addition to work style preferences, compensation was an important obstacle to private sector employment of Emiratis. To reinforce its commitment, the government allowed wage disparities, enabling Emirati citizens to earn more than expatriates who performed the same job role in private sector firms. This earnings differential was implemented by adding a substantial pay allowance to the earnings of citizens working in the private sector (Maktoob 2009). The head of Emiratization at Lloyds' claims Emiratis receive, on average, 35 per cent of their basic salary as a national allowance (Sakhri 2010). This is considered to be good practice for the purpose of increasing the number of UAE citizens working in the private sector, especially in jobs based in an office environment and in management positions. Several sectors (such as insurance) run a separate Emirati salary structure that affords higher pay to nationals in order to attract them. This strategy is controversial and there are various viewpoints. To some, adding a national allowance to the salary of citizens working in the private sector makes the jobs more lucrative and will help the UAE in the long run as the economy diversifies away from its reliance on oil/tourism/hydrocarbons. Others see a salary differential as a hindrance (or burden) to the principle of equity and fairness, which may trigger lower motivation of expatriates performing similar jobs, particularly at managerial levels. The views on this point vary greatly. While some are supportive of the policy, some express neutrality and others are reserved/critical of the policy. Below are sample excerpts of the viewpoints (Gulf News 2009a).

Viewpoints in support of the initiative

- *It makes sense when you recruit UAE national and pay them more. They add value, they are productive in the long run and they have a lot to contribute to the organisation.*

- *Hiring Emiratis in the private sector and paying them more makes great sense because they are better at navigating bureaucracy, have contacts in government and are more proficient at interpreting the country's changing labour laws.*

- *This is a good chance for UAE nationals. UAE is their country and they should be the ones to serve it to their best abilities – provided they have the drive and are really willing to work in all fields, and not choosy with regards to the time, pressure at work.*

- *As a UAE citizen, I salute the government for this decision. For all expatriates: You should be grateful this country took you on its peaceful grounds for so long and gave you jobs and packages you wouldn't get in your own country. We are not responsible for your future, your country is.*

- *What a great decision. I am a post graduate with 10 years' experience, currently working in the construction industry. All nationals are most welcome to take my job. Salary Dhs. 3500. Working Hours: 12 hrs/day and 6 days/week.*

Neutral viewpoints

- *Expatriates say that the move will leave them jobless, while others say it will help train UAE nationals to become competitive in various fields of work.*

- *Emiratization needs to be implemented on a broader horizon without causing loss to other people. At the end of the day it is the nationals who have to take care of their country.*

- *Well this is a great opportunity for all nationals to contribute their knowledge and abilities to their own country, but why only as HR managers or secretaries? The best thing we could do is to 'give and take' so that everyone can work for a living. Hiring manpower in general requires knowledgeable capacity to do the job and move the organisation on for individual growth.*

- *I'm in favour of Emiratization. It will be beneficial for the government but will have an adverse effect on the private sector. Salaries, days of work per week and training are likely to be affected. The government should give a gesture of goodwill to all affected expatriates and allow them to renew their visa for other available jobs that may suit them best.*

Viewpoints expressing reservations about the policy

- *The government has to challenge mentalities and change many wrong perceptions of the aspiring UAE nationals as well as that of the private sector. They should do this by engaging both and not imposing heavy-handed decisions.*

- *Emiratization at any cost might not pay off at the end. Qualification and experience should be looked at as well, not only nationality.*

- *This type of plan will never resolve the employment problem nor will the younger generation want to do anything creative with their lives. The current generation of nationals should be given opportunities but not things served on a plate, such that they don't improve or aspire or dream.*

- *The most qualified person should be the one who receives the job opportunity. All the effort exerted into selling Dubai as a world friendly place, has just been reduced to, 'Go home, we don't want you here'.*

- *As a HR professional, I would have had a more positive reaction to the announcement if the government had instead proclaimed their affiliation with colleges and universities in the Gulf to offer Human Resource Management courses and programs to properly train prospective managers in HR.*

- *I think it's unfair for the people who have been working for the development of the UAE for many years. They spend their life here. There should be opportunities for nationals to get a job but not if it means replacing people.*

- *I am not against the concept of prioritising UAE Nationals when it comes to hiring but replacing the people already working for a company by an Emirati is unjust.*

- *Employment should be given on the basis of qualification and capabilities irrespective of race and culture.*

Conclusion/summary

Recent statements reveal that despite the great efforts made, the situation remains that less than one per cent of private sector workers in the UAE are citizens (Maktoob 2009a). The reality is that most private companies in the Arabian Gulf still do not hire nationals and changing that attitude will take more time. Nationals continue to shy away from the private sector because of long working hours, lower pay, and relative insensitivity to their religious customs. When seeking employment, UAE nationals are often loathed to consider the private sector's working conditions and compensation levels. More recently, government officials complained that private firms were failing to live up to their Emiratization commitments and were unable to retain nationals. The complaints were that private companies often hired Emiratis as quota-fillers, thereby following the legal obligations but not their underlying intentions (Shaheen 2008).

It seems that employers faced complicated situations with the younger and inexperienced Emiratis who often assume that expatriates in general are more willing to work long hours at a substantially lower wage (AME Info 2006). Emiratization to some degree has failed in the task of instilling effective work habits in young Emiratis, particularly in some industries. UAE Companies may need to reconsider strategies currently in force internally to grow a more skill-based Emirati workforce.

Action, and more importantly preparation, needs to be taken by businesses now in order to achieve desirable success in Emiratization. While there is general agreement over the importance of Emiratization for social, economic and political reasons, there is also some contention as to the impact of localisation on organisational efficiency. It is yet unknown whether, and the extent to which, employment of nationals will generate corporate and economic returns. Clearly, Emiratization is not always seen as advantageous for the corporate sector as the take-up/follow through is insignificant. The effectiveness of an Emiratization strategy is not yet evident as its success depends largely on the array of contingent factors discussed above.

Discussion questions

1) What change management considerations arise for public and private sector managers as a result of the Emiratization policy?

2) If you were a private employer, what would be your internal strategies to retain nationals in your workforce?

3) Imagine yourself as an expatriate manager. How would Emiratization affect your role with your national managerial colleagues?

4) What are the steps needed to adopt an effective policy of Emiratization taking into account the barriers perceived by younger and female generational citizens?

References

Al-Ali, J 2008, 'Emiratization: Drawing UAE nationals into their surging economy', *International Journal of Sociology and Social Policy*, 28(9/10).

Al Awadhi, A 2010, 'Emiratisation of workforce 'pillar of growth'', viewed May 2010, http://www.uaeinteract.com/docs/Emiratisation_of_workforce_pillar_of_growth/41096.htm.

AME Info 2006, viewed May 2010, http://www.ameinfo.com/79535.html (March).

AME Info, 2007, viewed May 2010, http://www.ameinfo.com/133128.html (Sept).

Dubai Memoir 2006, viewed May 2010, *http://dubaimemoir.blogsome.com/2006/08/28/Emiratization-of-sec-hr-mgrs/trackback/.*

Emiratization Research Foundation 2009, viewed May 2010, http://www.jumeirah.com/en/Jumeirah-Group/The-Emirates-Academy/Emiratization-Research--Development/ (Newsletter).

Gulf News 2009, viewed May 2010,
http://gulfnews.com/news/gulf/uae/employment/new-Emiratization-drive-1.242285 .

Gulf News 2009a, viewed May 2010,
http://gulfnews.com/opinions/your-say/have-your-say-Emiratization-move-1.242277 .

Kemp, LJ, Oct 2008, Tejari – 'the Middle East Online Marketplace' under the leadership of Sheika Lubna Al Qasimi. International Journal of Leadership Studies, vol 4 no. 1, Accessed May, 2010 at http://www.regent.edu/acad/global/publications/ijls/new/previous_issues.htm.

Maktoob 2009, viewed May 2010,
http://business.maktoob.com/20090000463642/Pay_Gulf_nationals_more_than_expats_-experts/Article.htm, Maktoub Business letter.

Maktoob 2009a, viewed May 2010,
http://business.maktoob.com/20090000462598/Expat_cap_will_not_boost_locals_in_workforce/Article.htm.

Sakhri, R, April 28, 2010, 'Pay Gulf nationals more than expats-experts', *Gulf News*.

Shaheen, K 2008, 'Government attacks Emiratization laggards', *The National*, May 2010.

Shallal, M 2008, viewed May 2010,
http://emiratisation.org/index.php?option=com_content&view=article&id=275%3Awomen-shattering-job-barriers&catid=96%3Aaugus-2009&Itemid=67&lang=en.

TRA-Government News Services, 2010, viewed May 2010,
http://www.uaeinteract.com/docs/Mohammed_instructs_government_entities_to_open_door_for_national_job-seekers/40351.htm (30th-03-2010).

UAE-Change 2010, viewed May 2010,
http://internationalbusiness.wikia.com/wiki/U.A.E._Change.

Chapter 36

Survival and outsourcing in the South African clothing and textiles industry: The case of ClothTran

CHRISTINE BISCHOFF AND GEOFFREY WOOD

The context

South Africa is one of a number of emerging markets that have significantly expanded exports in the 2000s and have a considerable industrial presence – along with Brazil, India, Russia and China. However, as is the case with Brazil and India, South Africa's exports have not been at the same level as those of China. Indeed, whilst South Africa has been very successful in the exports of minerals, food products (notably deciduous fruit and wine) and motor cars and components, many other sectors have not fared nearly as well. Historically, South Africa had an extremely large clothing and textile industry; however, in recent years, many firms have been forced to close, and others to radically downsize in the face of low-cost Chinese imports.

Under apartheid, the government relied very heavily on gold exports, but when the gold price declined in the 1980s, serious economic problems resulted. This was exacerbated by successive waves of popular resistance, sanctions and the inefficiencies of the system. The apartheid government had pursued an active industrial policy, leading to a heavily protected and often inefficient manufacturing sector. The latter provided large-scale employment, low wages, racial discrimination and associated inequalities in skills and access to training led to relatively low productivity. As one South African HR manager remarked, firms used to solve problems, '*through throwing cheap labour at it*', rather than using labour intelligently (Wood & Els 2000). Domestically manufactured goods were often low quality, out-dated and expensive.

The rise of independent trade unions in the 1980s, and the increasing inefficiencies of the system, challenged the dominant production paradigm. This led to a shift from very low wage unskilled production centring on a racial division of labour to higher wage production, with the associated skilling of the black labour force. Hence, South Africa was shifting from a low-wage, low-skill economy to a more intermediate one. This process has been marked by large-scale job shedding, as employers reaped the rewards of very much higher productivity and as less competitive ones went under.

Democratisation in 1994 led to the principle liberation movement, the African National Congress (ANC), attaining power. Despite union backing, the economic policies adopted were largely neo-liberal. The ANC committed itself to the liberalisation of trade in line with WTO regulations, the phasing out of import tariffs and export subsidies. In some areas – such as motor car manufacturing – the process was carefully managed, leading to the sector becoming highly competitive; in others, such as clothing and textiles, this was not the case (Wood & Glaister 2008). The South African economy has enjoyed sustained growth for the last few years despite the global recession, yet some estimates place South African unemployment as high as 45 per cent.

The industry

The South African clothing and textile industry has faced major problems, not only as a result of reduced tariff barriers but also large-scale illegal imports. More specifically, the industry has had to contend with a flood of Chinese imports, in some instances at prices that appear difficult to comprehend, even in terms of the costs of raw material inputs only. One employer has claimed that at one stage, Chinese-made t-shirts were being landed in Cape Town for as little as GBP 1, and men's suits for GBP 10.

Moreover, certain constituent fabrics can be imported duty free by manufacturers. Such fabrics can constitute up to 40 per cent of the cost of the finished production item. Although in theory it is only constituent fabrics that are not produced in South Africa that may be imported duty free, this is very difficult to police. There are many small and medium-sized textile factories in the country, and officials lack the capacity to regularly inspect the usage of imported materials. This means that much of the value generated in production accrues abroad. In addition to wholesale smuggling, Chinese fabrics and finished garments are often under-invoiced to reduce the amount of import duties payable.

The South African clothing and textiles industry has historically been very heavily unionised. The dominant union in the industry, the South African Clothing and Textiles Workers Union (SACTWU) represents a merger of several unions from both the radical independent union tradition (notably from the Johannesburg region) and a large, bureaucratic, service-orientated and compliant union (with a strong base in Cape Town and to a lesser extent, Kwa-Zulu Natal). SACTWU has faced major challenges owing to an imploding membership base as a result of large-scale job losses in the sector. SACTWU is a member of the Congress of South

African Trade Unions (COSATU), which is in formal alliance with South Africa's ruling party, the African National Congress. Relations between unions and government have in recent years been somewhat variable. The unions played a central role in the ousting of President Mbeki, but relations with the current President Zuma have, at times, also been fraught; the ANC remains wedded to broadly neo-liberal macro-economic policies. Whatever political influence SACTWU enjoys does not appear to have been sufficient for the government to take concerted action against the dumping of textiles by Chinese producers into the South African market. SACTWU's membership includes large representation by members of ethnic minorities (coloured/mixed racial origin and Asian); the majority of the latter do not vote for the ANC, and this may have diminished SACTWU's political clout.

The case study organisation

The case study organisation historically was a medium-sized company that was heavily unionised. Over the period 2005–2006, the company was forced to undergo a major downsizing exercise, ending up as a small enterprise. The owner of the firm blames this forced downsizing on high labour costs, and what he claimed was a 'negative' attitude by the union. The company also moved most production away from the Gauteng Province (the greater Johannesburg/Pretoria region), South Africa's major industrial centre, where wages are relatively high. Some operations were outsourced to the Durban area of KwaZulu Natal, and others to Swaziland. The company retained its design operations in-house in Johannesburg.

Swaziland is a geographical neighbour of South Africa and is one of the last absolute monarchies in the world. The Swazi government has a very poor reputation when it comes to labour and general political rights. The country is significantly poorer than South Africa, and, with high unemployment and poor social protection, workers are in a very poor bargaining position. In order to circumnavigate the remaining protective tariffs, a number of Chinese clothing manufacturers have set up operations in Swaziland; many such operations have a reputation for extremely poor labour standards, which arguably have had the effect of driving labour standards down further in established locally-owned competitors (Similane 2008).

Issues in employment practices

ClothTran currently pays wages somewhat higher than the industry norms; in part this represents a historical legacy from when the organisation was very much larger and the union was in a stronger position. ClothTrans's owner claims that the current wage levels paid to his blue-collar, South African employees - amounting to some 700 Rands/week (that is approximately GBP 60 pounds or $100) are far too high. In addition, in South Africa, employers have to extend certain fringe benefits – for example paid public holiday leave and paid sick leave – that were again *far too high* in relation to that paid in competitor producing nations. ClothTran's owner further believes that, in response to this situation, most employers simply choose not to obey the law. Those who choose to play by the rules of the game reap few rewards and are simply penalised because enforcement mechanisms are weak.

Despite intense competition from China, South African textile employers lack unity. Indeed, a major employer association ceased operations in 2009. ClothTran's owner argues that the dominant union in the sector, the South African Clothing and Textiles Workers Union (SACTWU), lacks strategic vision and is primarily concerned with protecting jobs. This has resulted in SACTWU purchasing shares in a major employer in the clothing and textiles industry, Seardel; hence the union represents workers, yet has a vested interest in a major employer. By implication, this may affect union attitudes to other firms.

The owner of the case study organisation argues that SACTWU goes direct to government when confronted with a problem, rather than negotiating with employers; hence, the union appears unresponsive to the legitimate concerns of owners. On the other hand, it is clear that the union's position has been greatly weakened through downsizing across the industry, and it would perhaps have been surprising had it not sought all the assistance it could get from whatever quarter.

ClothTran's owner clams that employers are over-burdened with too many restrictions under the law. This includes restrictions on the ability to fire, union organising rights and leave entitlements. More specifically, he argues that the statutory dispute resolution mechanism, the Commission for Conciliation, Mediation and Arbitration (CCMA) *'goes too far'* in protecting the interests of workers. Little heed is taken of the interests of employers, and the difficulties firms face in surviving. Yet, whilst employers are restricted by what they can do under the law, little is done to control cut-throat competition from abroad.

Despite reservations towards both the union and the CCMA, ClothTran pays some 15 per cent above the legally binding minimum wage for the industry. In contrast, many other employers do not comply with the law in this regard; high unemployment means that there are many desperate job seekers who are prepared to conspire with employers in breaching the law. Moreover, whilst ClothTran does provide leave for statutory holidays, as well as vacation leave, this is often not the case for other employers. ClothTran's owner claims that many smaller employers in the industry work 234 days per year, including over weekends during busy periods, without necessarily granting over-time pay. In some respects he believes the latter is justified, in that firms face intense pressures, and regulatory authorities take little notice of the need for firms to remain cost-competitive during busy periods. As a result, *'the only compliant companies are big firms'*.

Collective bargaining within the clothing and textiles industry in South Africa is centralised and takes place within the statutory Bargaining Council. In practice, the Council is dominated by larger employers and the principle unions – smaller employers believe the body is unresponsive to their concerns, and indeed, lacks vision in promoting the viability of the industry or taking action when major firms close. In response, many smaller employers have partially disengaged from the process, giving up on hopes to impact on bargaining outcomes and return, ignoring aspects of agreements even if, formally speaking, this is illegal.

ClothTran's owner believes that the principle HR problem his firm faces is the sheer cost of labour. Whilst the union is seeking to narrow wage gaps across the industry, wages are already, he believes, far too high in South Africa. For example, in neighbouring Lesotho, wages are some GBP 20/week; similar wages rates are the norm in Swaziland, making relocation *very attractive for employers'*.

Key issues

A number of issues emerge from the case study. Firstly, both the firm and the industry have a historical legacy of high unionisation. Indeed, during the late apartheid years, the union was able to extract significant gains from employers. Whilst wholesale job losses have undermined the position of the union, it has been able to leverage its residual position to mount a rearguard action in defence of labour standards. From a management perspective, this is unrealistic given the grave competitive pressures facing the industry. Yet, from a union perspective, the central aim remains the defence of labour standards and jobs. And, if employers disengage from the collective bargaining system and are only hostile to unions, their chances of extracting concessions and promoting the industry at large may diminish even more. Nonetheless, it could be argued, that given both employers and the union are so occupied with survival, there is little time for long-term strategic planning at both industry and firm level.

The case study organisation's people management strategy can broadly be described as *contingent*, rather than benchmarked against an abstract set of *best practices*. It has two central dimensions. The first is to retain core knowledge in-house, with established HR policies and procedures, including paying more than industry norms. The latter reflects firstly a desire to retain specific sets of core competencies and, secondly, owing to a historical legacy of adversarial employment relations, a desire to avoid sustained confrontations with the union. The second central dimension – given perceived difficulties in dealing with the union, apparent over-regulation, wage costs, and the unresponsiveness of the Bargaining Council system – has been to outsource as much of production as possible. In other words, to resolve HR problems through 'getting rid of them'. In the end, it is design and ideas that remained firmly in house, with as much as possible of the process of production being outsourced to low cost more peripheral producers.

This model has become increasingly common in a wide range of industries. It has led some commentators to argue that there has been a rise of 'virtual firms', who have increasingly little involvement with products that bear their name and incorporate their ideas. Outsourcing does, of course, impose a range of costs: a potential loss of skills and expertise, less direct control over quality, a less close integration between design and production and low morale among remaining employees as a result of redundancies. However, in a context of intense competition from abroad, and apparent regulatory failures, the range of policy alternatives appears limited.

Discussion questions

1) To what extent are the problems experienced by ClothTran really the fault of unions? Why do you think the employer blames unions for the problems experienced?

2) Critically discuss the risks associated with outsourcing production to Swaziland and Durban? What alternatives could there be?

3) Are there any alternative HR strategies that the firm could have employed to the ones presently utilised? What would these be?

4) 'Governments should have no role in protecting industries that cannot compete on global markets'. Critically discuss this statement.

References

Similane, X 2008, 'Textiles and Employee Relations in Swaziland', *Employee Relations*, 30, 4: 452-465.

Wood, G & Glaister, K 2008, 'Union Power and New Managerial Strategies', Employee Relations, 30, 4: 436-451.

Wood, G & Els, C 2000, 'The Making and Remaking of HRM: The Practice of Managing People in the Eastern Cape Province, South Africa', *International Journal of Human Resource Management*, 11, 1:112-125.

Index